# OUT OF THE CRUCIBLE:

*Black Steelworkers
in Western Pennsylvania,
1875–1980*

## Dennis C. Dickerson

D1522781

*State University of New York Press*

The author wishes to thank the following persons and institutions for making available photographs and granting permission to use them: Mrs. Dorothea Austin Brown and Reverend J. C. Austin, Jr., Chicago, Illinois; Mr. and Mrs. Carl O. Dickerson, Philadelphia, Pennsylvania; Mr. Russell Gibbons, United Steelworkers of America, Pittsburgh, Pennsylvania; the late Mr. William Henry Harrison, Duquesne, Pennsylvania; Mrs. Colesta Long, Philadelphia, Pennsylvania; Mr. Stefan Lorant and Authors Edition, Lenox, Massachusetts; Mrs. Mildred Trent, Philadelphia, Pennsylvania; Mr. Bartow Tipper, Aliquippa, Pennsylvania; The Carnegie Library of Pittsburgh, and The Russell Sage Foundation, New York, New York.

Published by
State University of New York Press, Albany

© 1986 State University of New York

For information, address State University of New York Press, State University Plaza, Albany, N.Y., 12246

**Library of Congress Cataloging-in-Publication Data**

Dickerson, Dennis C., 1949–
    Out of the crucible.

    (SUNY series in Afro-American studies)
    Bibliography: p. 307
    Includes index.
    1. Afro-American iron and steel workers — Pennsylvania — History.
2. Afro-Americans — Employment — Pennsylvania — History.   3. Discrimination in employment — Pennsylvania — History.   I. Title   II. Series.
HD8039.I52U535   1986      331.6'3'960730748      85-30450
ISBN 0-88706-305-5
ISBN 0-88706-306-3 (pbk.)

10 9 8 7 6 5 4 3 2 1

# Contents

# Figures

and their families attended here. (Courtesy of Mr. and Mrs. Carl O. Dickerson, Philadelphia, PA.)

# Tables

# Preface

I will not claim complete impartiality in writing this book since my father, both grandfathers, and a great grandfather over a span of fifty years labored in the Pittsburgh vicinity at the Homestead and Duquesne plants of the United States Steel Corporation. Nonetheless, exhaustive research in several libraries and archives have yielded valuable information which I believe accurately describe and explain the century long experience of Blacks in the steel industry in Western Pennsylvania. I owe many thanks to the staffs at the Western Pennsylvania Historical Society, the Historical Society of Pennsylvania, the Library of Congress, Manuscript Division, the National Archives, the B. F. Jones Public Library, Aliquippa, Pennsylvania, the Carnegie Public Library, Munhall, Pennsylvania, the New York Public Library, Schomburg Center for Research in Black Culture, the University of Pittsburgh Libraries, and the Williams College Library. I express special gratitude to Frank Zabrosky of the Archives of Industrial Society at the University of Pittsburgh, John E. Bodnar and Carl Oblinger, formerly of the Ethnic Studies Program at the Pennsylvania Historical and Museum Commission in Harrisburg, and Ronald Fillippelli, formerly of the Labor Archives, Pennsylvania State University, University Park. Arthur Edmonds, executive director of the Pittsburgh Urban League and Richard S. Dowdy of Hamden, Connecticut permitted me to examine their files of the Pittsburgh Urban League. Also, I thank Henry W. Berger of Washington University and Peter Rachleff who shared with me important documents and references from their own research. Numerous persons kindly and cheerfully submitted themselves to taped interviews with me. Without their testimonies much of this book could not have been written. Additionally, the Labor Archives at Pennsylvania State University and the Ethnic Studies Program at the Pennsylvania Historical and Museum Commission collected numerous interviews with Pittsburgh area steelworkers and placed them at my disposal. They too proved important to my research.

While in the dissertation stage in the Department of History at Washington University, this work profited from critical comments from my advisors, Henry W. Berger and Glen E. Holt. As I developed my work into a book, Milton Cantor of the University of Massachusetts-Amherst, Richard S. Dowdy and two colleagues at Williams College, Charles B. Dew in History and Lee Alston in Economics, read in whole or in part the manuscript and offered helpful suggestions. The editor at SUNY Press, Michelle Martin was patient and encouraging, and she along with others at the Press made useful comments which strengthened the book.

Williams College supported an Assistant Professor leave during the spring semester of 1980 and the American Philosophical Society provided travel funds which enabled me to do further research and transform the dissertation into this book. Mrs. Georgia Swift, secretary of the Williams History Department, typed several drafts of the manuscript. Dean Gerald Duff of Rhodes College made funds available for typing of the final draft. President James H. Daughdrill, Jr. and Professor James C. Lanier, Chairman of the History Department of Rhodes College helped in other ways to facilitate the completion of the book.

My wife, Mary, and my four children, Nicole, Valerie, Christina, and Dennis, Jr., offered inspiration and relief which helped me greatly. My parents, Carl and Oswanna Dickerson, to whom this book is dedicated, sustained me morally and financially for what seemed an indefinite period of time. I alone bear responsibility for whatever shortcomings remain in the book.

# Acknowledgments

I wish to acknowledge Professor Henry W. Berger of Washington University for sharing the following documents with me:

Roy Wilkins, Assistant Secretary, N.A.A.C.P. to John Frey, Labor Advisory Board, National Recovery Administration, August 3 and 10, 1933, *John Frey Papers*, Library of Congress, Washington, D.C.

John P. Davis to All Local Councils (of the National Negro Congress) July 10, 1936, Memorandum, *Adolph Germer Papers*. Box 3, State Historical Society of Wisconsin, Madison, Wisconsin.

"Statement by Philip Murray to C.I.O. meeting, November 8, 1936," *Katherine Pollack Ellickson Papers*, microfilm edition, Reel #1, Pennsylvania State University, University Park, Pennsylvania.

John P. Davis to John L. Lewis, August 13, 1937; Ralph Hetzel to John P. Davis, August 27, 1937; John P. Davis to Ralph Hetzel, July 20, 1940; Ralph Hetzel to John P. Davis, July 29, 1940. *C.I.O. Central Office Correspondence*, Alpha File, Box 16, Catholic University, Washington, D.C.

I also wish to thank Dr. Peter Rachleff for providing the following references to me:

*Proceedings of the Seventh Annual Convention of the National Lodge of the Amalgamated Association of Iron and Steelworkers* (Pittsburgh, 1882)

*National Labor Tribune*, October 1, 1881; February 18, 1882.

# Introduction

Race, not class, has fixed the status of contemporary Black workers and has created the poverty and unemployment which perennially afflicts them. The experiences of Black laborers in such important industries as steel, auto, coal, and rubber help to illustrate this unpleasant reality. Persistent racial discrimination in hiring, promotion, and job assignments restricted Black occupational advancement and kept Blacks behind most White workers in the attainment of better wages and working conditions. Labor unions sometimes aided Blacks, but only when strikes occurred and Black support was needed. Throughout most of their history, unions either barred Blacks from membership or refused to fight vigorously for their economic interests.

At different times, Blacks suffered discriminatory treatment from management's refusal to hire them, union indifference to their occupational interests, failure of foremen to promote them, and from White employees who would not work with them. Although important and powerful allies came to the assistance of aggrieved Black workers, their efforts usually proved to be either short-lived or ineffective. During the 1940s and again in the 1960s, for example, the federal government, first through the Fair Employment Practices Committee (FEPC) and later through the Equal Employment Opportunity Commission (EEOC), strong executive action and helpful legislative and judicial support pushed management and unions toward more effective efforts to improve the occupational status of

1

Blacks. However, the end of World War II killed FEPC and decline in such important industries as steel, auto, rubber and coal slowed and, in some instances, wiped out Black employment gains.

Often Whites shared with Blacks the vicissitudes and harsh realities of employment in heavy industry. Labor exploitation kept wages down for both groups. The agonies of layoffs and unemployment harmed Whites as well as Blacks. When unions became strong, basic benefits of union membership such as seniority, wage increases, and paid vacations accrued to eligible Blacks and Whites alike. As heavy industry declined in the 1970s, both groups suffered. These factors seemingly argue for an emphasis upon the similarity of industrial experiences encountered by Blacks and Whites. This stress upon class, however, would obscure and distort the unique and more painful circumstances confronted by Black workers in industrial America.

White employers often favored White workers for jobs. White foremen gave promotions more readily to fellow Whites. White unionists usually advanced Black grievances with less vigor than those of Whites. When layoffs occurred, favoritism for Whites produced disproportionate unemployment for Blacks. Even when the misfortune of industrial decline in the 1970s doomed Black and White workers alike, Blacks lost their jobs first and in disproportionate numbers.

What follows is a study of a century of Black workers' experiences in the iron and steel industry of Western Pennsylvania from 1875 to 1980. It documents how racial discrimination limited the occupational advancement of Black laborers and kept most of them in the industry's less desirable positions. An important industry which employed Blacks in large numbers during most of the twentieth century, iron and steel firms provide an excellent case study of what happened to Black workers in a major industry over a period of several decades.

Employment opportunities created by numerous strikes in the Pittsburgh area between 1875 and 1909 brought the first black iron and steelworkers to Western Pennsylvania. Their numbers were expanded further by a small, but steady stream of Black migrants mostly from Border and Upper South States, and by Black workers recruited into the region by major employers. In 1910 they numbered 789 persons and comprised about 3 percent of all steel employees.[1] The Black migration of the World War I era, however, increased their numbers to 7,000 steel employees or 13 percent of all employees in 1918,[2] and to 16,900 or twenty-one percent of all steelworkers in 1923.[3]

Despite some success in attaining skilled positions between 1875 and 1916, Blacks during the following five decades failed to achieve occupational parity with fellow White employees. Foremen and other supervisors blocked their efforts to transfer into departments where they could earn better pay and benefit from improved working conditions. White workers in racially exclusive departments persuaded mill officials that to assign Black employees to these units would create disharmony and negatively affect production.

Black steelworkers found occasional assistance from steel unions. The Amalgamated Association of Iron and Steelworkers remained hostile to Black steelworkers until the 1930s. When New Deal legislation in 1933 and 1935 helped to revive and strengthen organized labor and create the CIO, steel unionists realized that labor solidarity required the inclusion of Black workers. The Amalgamated Association and its successors, the Steelworkers Organizing Committee and the United Steelworkers of America, encouraged Black membership and attempted to deal with its grievances. During the 1940s and 1950s, however, Black unionists had great difficulty in persuading White steel union officials and members to resolve such crucial issues as departmental seniority, poor promotional opportunities, and the lack of effective Black representation in the union hierarchy.

Black steelworkers discovered during the 1940s and again in the 1960s and early 1970s that federal intervention in Black labor affairs yielded greater gains than either union or company action. The Fair Employment Practices Committee (FEPC) during World War II received numerous appeals for assistance in hiring and promotions. When union and company officials ignored Black complaints, the FEPC intervened to adjudicate these grievances. The civil rights movement of the 1960s and early 1970s produced important legislation and court decisions which required steel companies and the United Steelworkers of America to insure equal employment opportunity to Black steel employees. The consent decree of 1974, in which nine steel firms and the United Steelworkers in a federal district court, acknowledged racial discrimination against Black steelworkers, and ordered these firms to take concrete steps to improve the occupational status of Blacks in the steel industry.

This book differs from most studies on Black workers. Philip S. Foner's useful study, *Organized Labor and the Black Worker, 1619–1973*, and William H. Harris's *The Harder We Run: Black Workers Since the Civil War*[4] synthesize existing literature, focus mainly upon the relationship of Blacks and labor unions, and survey Black laborers in several industries. Most historians, however, have tried to explain the social and economic condition of twentieth century urban Blacks by choosing to write community studies on ghettoization. In such works as Gilbert Osofsky, *Harlem: The Making of a Ghetto, 1890–1930*,[5] Allan H. Spear, *Black Chicago: The Making of a Negro Ghetto, 1890–1920*, and Kenneth Kusmer, *A Ghetto Takes Shape: Black Cleveland, 1870–1930*, emphasis is placed upon the creation of physically and institutionally separate Black communities of major Northern cities. Employment discrimination is viewed as one of several manifestations of ghettoization. Although these community studies examine Black workers in a local context, they fail to explore their experiences as Black laborers in a specific industry over time. The late Herbert G. Gutman, the distinguished labor historian, has written that:

> . . . much concerning the Negro worker in the early decades of the twentieth century (just before and after the great migration) awaits its historians . . . Labor historians and others have spent much time disputing the intent of the national leaders of the American Federation of Labor vis-a-vis the Negro, a dispute that has generated much heat, shed less and less light, and used up unnecessary energy. Much of this talent could have been used more fruitfully to explore in detail the confrontation of the Black worker and industrial America in particular settings. Here a great gap still exists. Even the recent superior studies of Gilbert Osofsky and Allan H. Spear are disappointing in their treatment of the Negro worker . . . .[6]

August Meier and Elliott Rudwick in *Black Detroit and the Rise of the UAW* seemingly heeded Gutman's message. By combining the Osofsky model of the ghetto study and the Foner model of focusing upon Blacks and organized labor, Meier and Rudwick explored the experiences of Blacks in a specific industry in a particular geographical area between 1917 and 1945. A landmark study, Meier and Rudwick's book suffers from a limited chronological perspective. The efforts of Joe William Trotter, Jr. in *Black Milwaukee: The Making of an Industrial Proletariat 1915-1945*,[8] are especially welcome. He goes beyond the ghettoization model and discusses Black northern urban dwellers as industrial laborers. He argues that their experiences as workers were shaped by the city's industrial and racial realities and that Black laborers used Black institutions and various social and economic networks within the ghetto to resist second class citizenship.

This study on Black steelworkers focuses upon Black laborers in a single industry over a broader geographical area and for a longer period of time. It explains how over several decades Blacks in an important industry suffered employment discrimination and how it shaped their social and economic condition more than did ghettoization. I argue that a complex array of factors kept Blacks in low-paying, dead-end jobs. Since Blacks in the iron and steel industry worked in Pittsburgh and numerous other industrial communities, the historian must focus upon the industry rather than the ghetto community as the principal determinant of the Black worker's economic status.

The book argues that for more than a century Blacks persistently encountered discriminatory treatment from companies and unions. At times, these institutional barriers became penetrable when militant Black protests and federal intervention persuaded union and company officials to treat Black steelworkers with greater equity. Despite the perennial presence of Blacks in the iron and steel industry of Western Pennsylvania, they failed to achieve occupational parity with White workers. When the Consent Decree of 1974 made equal opportunity appear attainable, the steel industry, because of intense foreign competition and outmoded plants and facilities, faced decline and obsolescence. To understand the contemporary condition of Black steelworkers in Western Pennsylvania, one must grasp the significance of their century-long struggle to gain employment opportunity and equality in this important industry. The dismal fate of these Black laborers in the 1970s is relevant to understanding the contemporary predicament of the Black working class and the development of a chronically unemployed underclass in declining industrial centers like Pittsburgh, Gary, Youngstown, Detroit, Chicago and numerous other places where heavy industry once flourished.

# 1
# Black Sons of Vulcan, 1875–1916

During the late nineteenth and early twentieth centuries, Blacks in the iron and steel industry in Western Pennsylvania encountered discriminatory treatment from employers and enmity from White workers. For Black laborers, however, in a few important mills in the Pittsburgh vicinity, racial discrimination failed to restrict their occupational mobility or permanently relegate them to lower echelon jobs. Black workers, mostly from Virginia, Tennessee, and other Upper South and border states, entered local mills and foundries between 1875 and 1916, and gained a foothold in the iron and steel industry. Within a short time the excellent reputation they earned as iron and steel laborers as well as their aversion to unionism induced employers to hire additional Black workers. Many of these new Black employees rose to responsible positions, and earned wages which frequently equalled those of Whites. Although company recruitment and Black migration to Western Pennsylvania enlarged the ranks of Black iron and steelworkers, they remained a tiny portion of all industry laborers. Since Black millworkers were vastly outnumbered by native Whites and foreign-born laborers, they were prevented from conferring major occupational advantages upon future groups of Black employees.

Blacks initially entered the iron and steel mills of Western Pennsylvania a decade after the Civil War. At that time, puddlers in Pittsburgh defied their employers by refusing to accept a wage reduction. In January 1875, they went on strike. During the dispute, mill officials at the Pittsburgh Bolt Company surprised their employees, and brought Black puddlers from Richmond, Virginia to operate four of its twenty-four furnaces. A few weeks later, another group of Black puddlers arrived from Chattanooga, Tennessee to put "the bolt works (into) full blast again." Since White heaters and rollers remained on their jobs, and cooperated with Black puddlers, the conflict ended in victory for the company.[1] Black workers also gained new positions at the steel facility of another Pittsburgh manufacturer, Parke, Brother and Company. When puddlers at the firm's Black Diamond Steel Works went on strike in 1875, the proprietor hired Blacks to fill these positions, and then retained them as permanent employees.[2]

The previous use of Black ironworkers in Southern mills and foundries persuaded employers in Western Pennsylvania to introduce Black labor into their facilities. Since 1842, Joseph R. Anderson successfully employed slave ironworkers as puddlers, heaters, and rollers at the Tredegar Iron Works, a foundry and rolling mill complex in Richmond, Virginia. During the 1860s, his slaves played a key role in producing ordinance and munitions for the Confederate Army and Navy. In 1870, Blacks constituted almost half of Anderson's 650 employees.[3] Shortly before the Civil War, over 2,000 slaves labored in numerous iron mills in Tennessee's Cumberland River Valley. They also worked in other foundries in South Carolina, Kentucky, Alabama, Georgia, and Missouri.[4] Consequently, in 1875, when the puddler's strike crippled the iron industry in Pittsburgh, local mill officials sought experienced Black Southerners to replace their striking employees.

In succeeding decades, iron and steel officials in Western Pennsylvania tried repeatedly to use Blacks to defeat White unionists. A labor dispute between the Solar Iron Works in Pittsburgh and the Amalgamated Association of Iron and Steelworkers resulted in a plant shutdown in December, 1887. When officials resumed operations in early 1888, they demanded that their employees return to the mill, and renounce their union memberships. Since workers who belonged to the Amalgamated Association ignored the ultimatum, they were replaced by nonunion laborers, most of whom were Black. Again, as in 1875, Black workers brought defeat to White unionists.[5] Another strike occurred at the Solar Iron mills in 1889. The firm's eighty-nine Black puddlers continued at work while their employers made plans to recruit Black Southerners to operate the plant's other idled sections.[6] During the infamous strike of 1892, non-union Blacks, in spite of their minor role, labored in the Homestead Works of Carnegie Steel.[7] In 1909, the Pressed Steel Car Company in McKees Rocks used Blacks both as laborers in the mills and as cooks in the plant commissary.[8]

Although Black workers did not participate in some labor disputes, rumors and admonitions about their imminent presence still persisted. During the 1901 strike against the United States Steel Corporation, an Amalgamated official from Birmingham, Alabama arrived in Pittsburgh, and discounted "published reports that steel companies proposed to bring colored men from the South" to replace the strikers. "That's all bosh," said the Alabama unionist, "the Amalgamated people have nothing to fear from the Negroes of the South."[9] In 1913, officials at the Fort Pitt Steel Foundry in McKeesport warned striking employees who belonged to the Industrial Workers of the World that New York "negroes" might be hired to fill their positions.[10]

The presence of nonunion Blacks convinced White employees that mill owners deliberately tried to use Blacks "to pull down White labor."[11] In some instances, these sentiments led them to retaliate violently against Blacks who ignored the strikes and remained loyal to local iron and steel officials. During the 1888 strike at the Solar Iron Works in Pittsburgh, White workers initially threatened and then assaulted Black strikebreakers.[12] In Connellsville, in 1907, a strike occurred at the Sligo Iron and Steel Mills. The plant superintendent brought in "several carloads of negroes from Pittsburgh and other towns" to end the stalemate between Sligo officials and the Sons of Vulcan. After the trains arrived, White workers and Blacks clashed and violence resulted. A Black laborer was stabbed in the back, and two other Blacks were arrested and held for court for carrying revolvers.[13] The Pressed Steel Car Company in

McKees Rocks brought in two groups of strikebreakers during a 1909 labor dispute. The first trainload consisted of a racially mixed group of two hundred Blacks and foreigners. The other group which arrived a day later was an all-Black contingent of fifty men. When the final trainload of nonunion laborers came, the strikers tried to stop them from entering the plant. As a result, a few gunshots were fired, and a striker was killed. Authorities charged Major Smith, a Black man, with the shooting. Within a short time, however, a sympathetic iron mill official, C. W. Friend of the Pennsylvania Malleable Works, put up bail money to win Smith's release.[14]

Black exclusion from organized labor provided industrial employers with opportunities to use Black workers to defeat striking White unionists. Uncertainty on the issue of biracial unionism characterized the positions of most labor federations in the late nineteenth century. Within individual unions, however, forthright statements and practices which barred Black membership usually prevailed. The National Labor Union, founded in 1866 and the Knights of Labor, established in 1869, discouraged Black exclusion, but allowed separate Black groups to function within each organization. When the American Federation of Labor (AFL) started in 1886, Samuel Gompers, its perennial president, encouraged affiliate unions to admit Black members. To punish recalcitrant unions, Gompers granted charters to dissident groups which agreed to accept Blacks. Since the Brotherhood of Locomotive Firemen, the Order of Railroad Telegraphers, the International Association of Machinists, the Brotherhood of Railway Trackmen and other groups steadfastly refused to admit Black members, Gompers abandoned this tactic. By the turn of the twentieth century, he was convinced that Blacks interested in joining the AFL should found their own separate organizations. Although some Black unions received AFL charters, the Federation remained overwhelmingly White. Since the majority of affiliate unions enforced racial restrictions through constitutional and ritualistic bans and through informal exclusionary practices, Black members in the AFL remained pitifully few.[15]

This same pattern of racial exclusion and separation prevailed in Western Pennsylvania. Most AFL-affiliated unions in the region either barred Black members or ostracized them once they joined the organization. In 1909, two Black ministers on Pittsburgh's North Side, Reverend J. H. Holder of Metropolitan Baptist Church and Reverend Carlton M. Tanner of Brown Chapel African Methodist Episcopal Church, condemned such racially discriminatory unions for denying work to Black laborers.[16] Richard R. Wright, Jr., a Black sociologist, surveyed Black workers in Pittsburgh in 1912 and early 1913, and inquired about their experiences with organized labor. A Black bricklayer who migrated from Virginia abandoned his trade to work as a porter because the union refused to admit him. Similarly, a Black janitor who came to Pittsburgh from North Carolina in 1907 relinquished the carpenter's trade because of union discrimination. A Black printer from Baltimore, Maryland succeeded in joining a Pittsburgh local, but the White members refused to work with him.[17]

A few predominantly White unions which admitted Blacks along with a few separate Black unions in the Pittsburgh vicinity advanced the interests of Black workers. During the 1880s, Jeremiah Grandison belonged to a Pittsburgh Knights of Labor assembly and represented the group at the founding convention of the AFL. In 1882, mainly in response to Black strikebreaking activities, Whites in the miners' union promoted the organization of a Knights of Labor assembly in McDonald among Black coal miners.[18] In the early 1900s, the United Mine Workers of America had numerous Black members in other coal fields in Western Pennsylvania.[19] Hod-carrier locals in Pittsburgh, McKeesport, and Braddock were dominated by Blacks since few Whites labored in these jobs. In 1903, James M. Davis, a practical engineer at the Nixon Theater in Pittsburgh, organized the National Association of Afro-American Steam and Gas Engineers and Skilled Workmen of America. The group which had two locals in Pittsburgh consisted partially of Black stationary engineers and firemen.[20] In spite of these efforts, the lily-White policy of most Pittsburgh area trade unions continued to inhibit Black participation in the labor movement.

This legacy of racial exclusion and segregation also retarded the development of steel unionism among Blacks in Western Pennsylvania. The Sons of Vulcan, whose 1875 strike was broken by Southern Blacks, allowed only Whites to join. Likewise, the Associated Brotherhood of Iron and Steel Heaters and the Iron and Steel Roll Hands Union extended membership only to Whites. When the groups merged in 1876 to form the Amalgamated Association of Iron and Steelworkers, they tried to discourage strikebreaking activities by permitting Blacks to belong.[21] Within a few years, the organization made substantial moves to implement its new racial policy.

In 1881, *The Iron Age*, an influential magazine, made favorable comments about the skilled performance of Black workers in various mills and foundries throughout the country. Moreover, it predicted that "negroes" would not allow the employment opportunities in the iron and steel industry "to pass." The wages they would earn as boilers, heaters, and rollers, argued the industry journal, "will seem fabulous to men who have been working for 50 to 75 cents a day." Since *The Iron Age* hinted that wider use of "negro labor" would benefit employers, the *National Labor Tribune* responded by warning White unionists to organize Black workers. If they continued to ignore Blacks, contended the newspaper, decreased wages would "drive Whites out of the" industry. At its 1881 annual convention, the Amalgamated Association took up the challenge and voted to admit "colored lodges" to full membership in the organization. The *National Labor Tribune* quickly congratulated the union for a "move wisely made."[22]

Black workers responded to these changes by establishing Amalgamated lodges in Pittsburgh and Richmond. Black boilers at the Black Diamond steel works founded Garfield Lodge No. 92 on October 1, 1881 with twenty members.[23] On February 11, 1882, Sumner Lodge No. 3 started in Richmond with 125 members. It had the endorsement of John Jarrett, national president of the Amalgamated Association, who had instructed a Richmond subordinate to organize the Sumner group.[24]

For a short time, Blacks in the Amalgamated lodges in Pittsburgh and Richmond committed themselves to trade unionism and supported solidarity with White workers. In October 1881, the newly organized members of Garfield Lodge in Pittsburgh went on strike for higher wages at the Black Diamond steel works. In February 1882, while maintaining their strike, these union Blacks went to a Beaver Falls mill to work. When they arrived, "several of the White workmen . . . waxed indignant . . . and vowed that they would not work with the colored men." Local union officials and the national secretary of the Amalgamated Association called a meeting of Beaver Lodge No. 31, and "championed the cause of the colored" workers. As a result of this firm defense, the Black Diamond strikers were allowed to work at the Beaver Falls mill.[25]

Cooperation from Black unionists in Richmond and solidarity between Black and White Amalgamated members enabled Black Diamond strikers to survive management attempts to defeat them. In March 1882, mill officials sent a recruiter to Richmond to hire Black replacements for their striking employees. Since most Black ironworkers in the city belonged to Sumner Lodge No. 3, the visit of the Black Diamond representative proved fruitless. "A colored ironworker" in Richmond informed the *National Labor Tribune* that the recruiter succeeded in convincing only one Black to come to Pittsburgh. He reported that the strikebreaker was "a professional drunkard" who had been dismissed from a Knoxville, Tennessee mill for intoxification. The newspaper also told its readers that managers at the Black Diamond facility had tried "every device" to persuade "the colored puddlers" to abandon their strike and disband Garfield Lodge. Since it was difficult to get Black replacements in Richmond and because the striking Black workers found jobs in Beaver Falls "with their White brethren," Black Diamond efforts to defeat Black unionists ultimately failed.[26]

The presence of Black Amalgamated members in both Pittsburgh and Richmond, however, did not reflect the larger reality of racial antagonism between workers in the iron and steel industry. Most White unionists disliked Blacks and did not want them in the Amalgamated Association. Many Blacks, mindful of these racial antipathies, took advantage of employment opportunities which strikes provided, and expressed little sympathy with Amalgamated union struggles. In 1882, before a crowd of Cleveland millworkers, a disgruntled John Jarrett, national president of the Amalgamated Association, condemned Black laborers for not cooperating with union efforts. He reminded his listeners that while men fought in the Civil War to free Blacks "from a terrible slavery." Now, "those same negroes . . . turn and aid in forging a worse slavery on you." In February 1888, employers stirred racial animosities between Black and White laborers in Pittsburgh. The *National Labor Tribune* blamed management and "negro nonunion employees" for defeating Amalgamated workers in a lockout at the Solar Iron Mill. Some members of the Amalgamated Association wanted to punish "the colored puddlers" for opposing the union. At the group's 1888 convention, an attempt was made "to insert the word 'white' in the constitution" in order to exclude "colored men". Although the motion did not succeed, ill feeling toward Blacks remained.[27] In 1889, another strike occurred at the Solar Iron Works. Black puddlers wanted to join union efforts to secure higher wages, but their offer of cooperation was refused.[28] In 1890, an Amalgamated local at another Pittsburgh mill ordered 400 of its 500 members off their jobs to protest the presence of Black employees.[29]

Iron and steel unionists entered the twentieth century without abandoning their ambivalent attitudes toward Blacks. In 1902, W. E. B. DuBois, a Black sociologist at Atlanta University, reported in *The Negro Artisan* that very few Blacks belonged to the 8,000-member Amalgamated Association.[30] In 1902, at the group's national meeting, delegates approved a resolution which opposed the organization of Black workers, and discouraged their entrance into skilled occupations. They feared that Blacks might leave the South to compete with Whites for jobs in Northern industry. In 1907, however, the Amalgamated Association ambivalently reversed its stand and promised to organize Blacks "wherever possible."[31] In 1913, Amalgamated president, John Williams of Pittsburgh, declared that any iron and steel employee was eligible to join the organization. He noted that "Negroes, if given the opportunity, make good union men," but he cautioned that they "should be educated in the principles and ideals for which the labor . . . movement stands."[32]

Although significant changes in the racial composition of the Amalgamated Association did not occur, White puddlers believed that the union had gone too far in trying to attract Black workers. They also held Amalgamated leaders responsible for a deterioration in the economic position of puddlers and for failure in recruiting additional White members. In 1907, they broke away and reactivated the Sons of Vulcan, one of the lily-White predecessors of the Amalgamated Association. These puddlers revived Vulcan locals in Indiana, Illinois, Alabama,

Ohio, and Pennsylvania, particularly in the Pittsburgh vicinity. Puddlers restored lodges in McKees Rocks, Connellsville, Kitanning, Monaca, and at several foundries in Pittsburgh.[33] A Vulcan supporter in the Smoky City blamed the Amalgamated Association for admitting "colored puddlers into full membership" and compelling "white men to work side by side with them." He believed that this action "was in itself cause sufficient to drive the puddlers into open rebellion."[34]

The vacillating racial policies of the Amalgamated Association and the racial enmity of the Sons of Vulcan engendered cynicism among Blacks and encouraged them to eschew union membership. Several Black workers at the Clark Mills in Pittsburgh had been Amalgamated members. One had served as a local president in the South and as a delegate to the association's national convention. Others had assisted White strikers in their quest for better working conditions. Yet, in spite of their previous participation in Amalgamated activities, they viewed unions as "a hindrance rather than a help to them." In 1907, they told Richard R. Wright, Jr., that their distrust of the Amalgamated Association was based on its history of race prejudice and its failure to advance the interests of Black workers. Blacks, they asserted, secured jobs in the iron and steel industry without union cooperation, and they claimed that membership was offered to them only after they gained employment at such plants as the Clark mills in Pittsburgh and the Carnegie steel facility in Homestead. After interviewing scores of Black steelworkers in Pittsburgh, Wright concluded that they "believed most fervently in the ideas of labor unions," but "were obliged to oppose them because of their [racial] practice[s]." He blamed White workers for "letting prejudice and undemocratic ideas" alienate Blacks from the labor movement, and he chided them for giving union opponents "a weapon to . . . defeat plans for the betterment of every laboring man, regardless of race or color."[35] As a result, conflicts between White laborers and management became opportunities for Blacks to enter the iron and steel industry. The indifference and hostility of the Sons of Vulcan, the Amalgamated Association, and other iron and steel unions freed Blacks to cross their picket lines at the Pittsburgh Bolt Company in 1875, the Solar Iron Works in 1888 and 1889, the Carnegie Steel plant in Homestead in 1892, and in other

Figure 1. Black steelworkers at the Clark mills in Pittsburgh, 1907. (From *Wage Earning Pittsburgh*, Russell Sage Foundation, New York, The Pittsburgh Survey, 1914.)

instances when White unionists battled employers for higher wages and better working conditions.

Employer opposition to organized labor also discouraged Black participation in union activities. In 1905, for example, the Spang-Chalfant Company in Etna evicted the families of about twelve Black puddlers from company-owned houses. These Black employees had gone on strike, and Spang-Chalfant officials "immediately" dismissed them, and hired others to take their places.[36] Blacks discovered that union membership was an anathema to most employers, and that it did little to improve their economic condition. Consequently, these experiences reinforced Black anti-unionism and further alienated them from organized labor.

Since most Blacks avoided labor unions, iron and steel officials were anxious to hire them. The positive reputation they had gained as workmen also increased their attractiveness to employers. In 1889, *The Iron Age* declared that "wherever the negro has had a chance to acquire the necessary skill . . . he has shown himself capable."[37] These factors motivated industry officials in Western Pennsylvania to recruit regularly Blacks to work in their mills. In 1900, the Carnegie steel works in Pittsburgh offered jobs to a large force of Black ironworkers in Knoxville, Tennessee.[38] In 1902, managers at the Pittsburgh Steel Company in Monessen brought in thirty-two Black wire drawers from Joliet, Illinois.[39] In 1911, officials at Carnegie Steel in Clairton, brought in Black Southerners to work in their facilities.[40]

Despite strikebreaking opportunities and the active recruitment of industrial employers, Blacks usually entered the iron and steel industry in Western Pennsylvania as a result of the Black migration. A total of 220,903 Southern Blacks settled in the North between 1880 and 1910. Some of them moved to Pittsburgh and other industrial communities along the Allegheny, Monongahela, and Ohio Rivers. Because of the migration, Pittsburgh's Black population quadrupled from 6,136 in 1880 to 25,623 in 1910.[41] Similar increases also occurred in such outlying towns as Homestead, Braddock, Duquesne, and McKeesport. Most Black newcomers came from Virginia while others migrated from Maryland, Tennessee, North Carolina, and a few other Upper South and border states.

According to Richard R. Wright, Jr., most Blacks migrated to the North to improve their economic condition. In the early 1900s, he questioned 500 migrant Blacks, and found that the majority viewed the North as an economic Eden where better jobs were widely available. Wright discovered tht the wages of Black men in the South averaged $2 to $3.50 per week in small towns and farms and between $5 and $9 in Southern cities. When they arrived in the North, the majority earned between $6 and $14 per week.[42] Clyde V. Kiser, who studied the Black migration from St. Helena, South Carolina to New York City, arrived at similar conclusions about the economic motives of Southern Blacks. One Black man who left St. Helena in 1909 declared that there "wasn't any means of making any money . . ." He worked for a while in Savannah, Georgia and Jacksonville, Florida, but he "began to see that wages were better up North." Some of the migrants whom Kiser studied went to nearby cities, but eventually left for more lucrative jobs in the North.[43]

Employment opportunities also flourished in Western Pennsylvania where iron and steel entrepreneurs spearheaded the development of mill communities along the Ohio, Monongahela, and Allegheny Rivers. The Duquesne Steel Company constructed a foundry in Duquesne in 1885. Production did not begin, however, until February 1889 when the new owner, the Allegheny Bessemer Steel Company, opened a blooming mill. That same year, labor troubles caused the firm to sell the facility to the rapidly expanding Carnegie Steel Company. Duquesne's burgeoning steel industry drew Jefferson Jackson from King George County, Virginia in 1885 and James Claggett from Mt. Zion, Maryland in 1888. In the early 1890s they became employees at the Carnegie steel plant. During this period, John Mitchell of Frederick County, Maryland, joined them in the Duquesne steel works. In the early 1900s, other blacks became laborers in the Carnegie mills. They included William Alexander who came from Beilton, West Virginia, and Henry Marbley who arrived in 1906 from the Old Dominion. The Black migration to this developing steel community compelled a presiding elder in the Pittsburgh Annual Conference of the African Methodist Episcopal Church, to observe optimistically in 1899 that "Duquesne is a new and growing town . . . (where) our people will settle . . ."[44]

Clairton was another burgeoning steel center along the Monongahela River. The original settlement, North Clairton, began during the early 1900s when the Pittsburgh, Virginia and Charleston railroad was completed. Large brickmaking enterprises also were located in the area. Blacks found jobs both on the railroad and in the brickmaking installations. Moreover, the Crucible Steel Company organized St. Clair Steel and the St. Clair Furnace Company during this period. The two subsidiaries later merged and formed the Clairton Steel Company. In 1904, Clairton Steel became a part of the United States Steel Corporation. These industries attracted Black migrants to Clairton to share in the economic prosperity. In the early 1900s, Henry Carter arrived from Martinsburg, West Virginia to labor on the grading works of the Clairton steel plant. Jasper Jones, a Georgia sharecropper, came in 1903, after working for three years in Ensley, Alabama in the iron mines of the Tennessee Coal, Iron and Steel Company.[45]

Although economic factors prompted most migrants to settle in Western Pennsylvania, some Blacks sought an escape from second-class citizenship and southern racial oppression. The case of Cager Cardwell, a Black steelworker in Homestead, and his two brothers, was typical. The Cardwells lived in Madison, North Carolina, and owned land in the town. Because of a race riot durint the 1890s, a sympathetic White physician encouraged Cager and his brothers to leave the South, and settle in Western Pennsylvania where the racial atmosphere was seemingly more congenial. Since the doctor knew an official of Harbison-Walker, a brickmaking firm in West Homestead, James and Henry Cardwell moved to the area, and became employees of the company. Cager migrated to Homestead around 1900 and secured a job in the steel industry.[46]

Black iron and steel employees worked in a range of occupations extending from custodial jobs to white collar positions. These occupational extremes demonstrated that race was not yet an insuperable barrier to Black employment mobility. Those Blacks who held mill positions unrelated to iron and steel production usually worked as janitors. Beginning in 1897, Philip Cochran, a native of Monongahela, Pennsylvania, labored as a custodian at the Duquesne steel works. William P. Matthews, who came from North Carolina in 1903, worked both as a janitor and driver at the Pittsburgh Steel Company in Monessen. At the other end of the spectrum was William Nelson Page, private secretary to W. G. Clyde, the general manager of sales for Carnegie Steel. In 1911, John Harley, a Black graduate of the University of Pittsburgh, became a draftsman at the Crucible Steel Company. William Demon, another Black alumnus of the University of Pittsburgh, joined the engineering department at the Farrell plant of the United States Steel Corporation in 1916.[47]

Some employment mobility also existed for Black production workers. In 1898, a writer for *Atlantic Monthly* noted that the Black Diamond Steel Works in Pittsburgh drew no color line. One Black employee worked in the exclusive crucible melting department while others held such important positions as plumber, engineer, die grinder, and puddler. In 1907, Richard R. Wright, Jr. wrote about the remarkable achievements of Black employees at the Clark mills in Pittsburgh. At least 39 workers or about one-third of the plant's 110 Black employees labored in such skilled jobs as roller, rougher, finisher, puddler, millwright, and heater. Moreover, these skilled Blacks frequently had White subordinates. Wright observed that " on one mill . . . where the two chief rollers were Negroes . . . several White men (worked) under them." Black chief rollers also worked at two of the furnaces, and they too had White helpers. Margaret Byington, an expert on Homestead steelworkers, noted that Blacks who entered the mills in 1892 had "advanced to well-paid positions" by the early 1900s. One Black employee who started as a laborer rose dramatically to a job as roller.[48]

In several instances, Blacks ascended the occupational ladder as rapidly as some Whites. In 1907, skilled workmen made up 17 percent of all Black employees at the Homestead Steel Works. In 1910, they comprised 27 percent of Pittsburgh's Black iron and steelworkers. Native-born Whites and immigrants from northern and western Europe preceded Blacks in the mills, however, and outdistanced them within skilled occupations. Although newcomers from southern and eastern Europe entered the iron and steel industry during the same period as Blacks, they were handicapped by an unfamiliarity with English and more limited industrial experience. Consequently, they temporarily trailed Blacks in the industry's skilled occupations.

At the Homestead Steel Works, for example, where skilled Blacks constituted 17 percent of all Black employees, skilled American Whites and English born workers made up more than 40 percent of all laborers within their respective groups. At the other end of the spectrum, a tiny 2 percent of all Slovak workers and 5 percent of all Polish employees held skilled positions (see Table 1.) Blacks also competed successfully with Whites in average weekly earnings. A survey of iron and steelworkers in Pittsburgh in 1910 revealed that Black laborers received an average weekly wage of $14.98. While the income of most native Whites and immigrants from northern and western Europe exceeded this figure, the wages of workers from southern and eastern Europe were usually less. Slovak employees, for example, received a weekly average of $12.39 while Polish workers earned $12.21.[49] (See Table 2.)

Athough Black migrants regularly responded to employment opportunities in the iron and steel industry of Western Pennsylvania, the number of Black employees remained small. Pittsburgh, Homestead, and Monessen possessed the largest groups of Black iron and steel laborers. In 1890, 213 Black employees resided in the adjoining cities of Pittsburgh and Allegheny. Their numbers rose to 396 in 1900, and to 789 in 1910. Homestead had 104 Black steelworkers in 1900, and 121 in 1907. Also during this period, the Pittsburgh Steel Company in Monessen employed 150 Black laborers. At the beginning of the twentieth century a group of 90 Black iron and steel workers lived in the adjacent cities of Rankin, Braddock, and North Braddock. Although McKeesport had 32 Black mill laborers, most other industrial communities had fewer than a dozen Black iron and steel employees.[50]

Since native Whites and European immigrants held most of the jobs in the iron and steel industry, Blacks comprised a tiny percentage of all mill employees. In 1907, for example, the 121 Black employees at the Homestead steel works made up 2 percent of its 6,772 laborers. The 1,925 native Whites and 4,726 foreign-born Whites comprised 28 percent and 70 percent, respectively, of all Homestead steelworkers. Similarly, in 1910, almost 30,000 employees worked in various Pittsburgh iron and steel mills. Blacks numbered merely 789 persons, and comprised barely 3 percent of the total work force. Native Whites

TABLE 1. Nationality Composition of Workers in U.S. Steel's Homestead Plant, 1907

| Nationality | Skilled | Percent | Semi-Skilled | Percent | Unskilled | Percent | Total |
|---|---|---|---|---|---|---|---|
| Native White | 767 | 40 | 707 | 37 | 451 | 23 | 1,925 |
| Black | 21 | 17 | 32 | 26 | 68 | 56 | 121 |
| English | 182 | 46 | 149 | 37 | 55 | 17 | 397 |
| Irish | 62 | 24 | 81 | 35 | 20 | 16 | 129 |
| Scotch | 66 | 51 | 43 | 33 | 20 | 16 | 129 |
| German | 56 | 32 | 48 | 27 | 72 | 41 | 176 |
| Italian | 1 | 1 | 2 | 3 | 72 | 96 | 75 |
| Other Europeans except Slavs | 31 | 35 | 25 | 28 | 33 | 37 | 89 |
| Slovak | 45 | 2 | 275 | 15 | 1,542 | 83 | 1862 |
| Magyar | 12 | 2 | 37 | 7 | 483 | 91 | 532 |
| Polish | 10 | 5 | 39 | 18 | 166 | 77 | 215 |
| Russian | 3 | 1 | 71 | 20 | 271 | 79 | 345 |
| Lithuanian | 7 | 5 | 26 | 20 | 97 | 75 | 130 |
| Rumanian | 1 | 1 | 7 | 1 | 361 | 98 | 369 |
| Other Slavs | 2 | 2 | 4 | 2 | 142 | 96 | 148 |

**TABLE 2. Average Weekly Earnings of Iron and Steelworkers in Pittsburgh, 1910**

| Nativity | Number reporting complete data | Average earnings per week |
|---|---|---|
| Native-born of native father | | |
| White | 10,941 | $17.81 |
| Black | 493 | 14.98 |
| Native-born of foreign father — country of birth of father | | |
| Austria-Hungary | 216 | 12.77 |
| England | 1,077 | 17.40 |
| France | 106 | 20.79 |
| Germany | 2,350 | 17.13 |
| Ireland | 1,850 | 17.07 |
| Scotland | 353 | 17.78 |
| Wales | 611 | 17.47 |
| Foreign-born | | |
| Bohemia and Moravian | 175 | 12.75 |
| Croatian | 2,311 | 11.46 |
| English | 1,658 | 18.80 |
| French | 94 | 17.26 |
| German | 2,378 | 14.55 |
| Greek | 306 | 11.85 |
| Irish | 1,670 | 15.85 |
| Italian, North | 749 | 12.01 |
| Italian, South | 962 | 11.83 |
| Lithuanian | 737 | 13.06 |
| Magyar | 2,566 | 12.44 |
| Polish | 3,770 | 12.21 |
| Rumanian | 688 | 11.24 |
| Russian | 878 | 12.47 |
| Scotch | 471 | 19.01 |
| Servian | 541 | 11.66 |
| Slovak | 7,633 | 12.39 |
| Slovenian | 521 | 11.89 |
| Swedish | 410 | 19.92 |
| Welsh | 954 | 22.15 |
| Totals | 47,469 | $15.10 |

Source: U. S. Congress. Senate. Reports of the Immigration Commission, *Immigrants in Industry*, Part 2: Iron and Steel Manufacturing, Vol. I, 61st Congress, 2nd Session, 1910, p. 259.

and foreign-born made up 8,630 and 20,574 employees, respectively, and constituted 29 percent and 68 percent of all Pittsburgh iron and steelworkers.[51] (See Table 3.)

It is likely that the number of Black laborers in the iron and steel mills in Western Pennsylvania ranged between 1,000 to 1,200 employees in 1910, and their percentage probably reached about 3 percent of all industry laborers.

When World War I accelerated the Black migration to Western Pennsylvania beginning in 1916, several Pittsburgh area mills already employed Blacks in a variety of important occupations. Since the 1890s, W. A. Clay worked as a molder and boss rougher at the Carnegie steel mills in Pittsburgh. David C. Turner, who started at work at the American Sheet and Tin Plate Company in Sharon in 1909, labored as a doubler, a job which required "much skill and adaptability." The number of Blacks who held key skilled and semi-skilled positions in area mills was small compared to the growing representation of native Whites and foreign-born laborers. Moreover, Blacks who worked as puddlers, an occupation in which they had made significant inroads, became increasingly obsolete between 1890 and 1910. Mechanization, which was causing a general decline in several other skilled occupations, provided new job opportunities for the larger groups of native and foreign-born Whites. Consequently, White employees clustered in crucial departments in area mills where they moved up to choice positions as foremen and production workers. By World War I, these White iron and steelworkers, because of their large numbers and their ethnic and kinship networks, dominated various departments and the important occupations within them. At the Jones and Laughlin Steel Plant in Pittsburgh, for example, the Germans gained ascendancy in the carpentry division, while the Poles claimed the hammer shop and the Serbs dominated the blooming mill. None of the company's few hundred Blacks predominated in any department or worked in any crucial occupations.[52]

Although some Blacks enjoyed these opportunities, their limited numbers restricted their participation in important mill occupations and prevented them from dominating some aspects of iron and steel production. Moreover, the region's 1,000 to 1,200 Black iron and steel employees were scattered widely in several mills and foundries throughout the Pittsburgh area where they usually appeared in small numbers. Consequently,

**TABLE 3. Steel Employees in Pittsburgh and Allegheny City**

| Race | 1890 | | 1900 | | 1910 | |
|---|---|---|---|---|---|---|
| | Number | Percentage | Number | Percentage | Number | Percentage |
| Native Whites | 5,569 | 45 | 6,570 | 48 | 8,630 | 29 |
| Foreign-born | | | | | | |
| Whites | 6,597 | 53 | 6,756 | 49 | 20,574 | 68 |
| Blacks | 213 | 2 | 396 | 3 | 789 | 3 |
| TOTAL | 12,379 | 100% | 13,722 | 100% | 29,993 | 100% |

Compiled from U.S. Congress, Senate, Reports of the Immigration Commission, *Immigrants in Industry, Part 2: Iron and Steel Manufacturing,* Vol. I, 61st Congress, 2nd Session, 1910, p. 234; U. S. Department of Commerce, Bureau of the Census, *Thirteenth Census of the United States: Population: 1910,* Volume IV, occupation statistics, pp. 590–591.

they could not confer major occupational advantages upon succeeding groups of Black workers. When Black migrants arrived in Western Pennsylvania, chiefly from the Deep South, between 1916 and 1930, they entered lower echelon jobs with few opportunities to advance. Moreover, numerous skilled Blacks tended to hold positions in the iron industry which became increasingly obsolete. Moreover, such jobs as puddling were unrelated to new technologies in steel manufacturing. Consequently, the presence of this preceding generation of Black iron and steelworkers did not benefit the new group of Black workers who beginning in 1916 migrated in large numbers to Pittsburgh and other industrial communities throughout Western Pennsylvania.

# 2
# World War I and the Black Migration to Western Pennsylvania: 1916–1930

As World War I and unfavorable economic conditions in the South combined to stimulate a massive Black migration to Northern industrial areas between 1916 and 1930, few veteran Black iron and steelworkers remained in Pittsburgh area mills to interact with these new groups of Black employees. Death was the principal reason. It removed Joseph Walker from the Ninth Street Wire Mill in Braddock in 1916. A year later, it took Edward Crippen, a former Tennessee slave who had worked as a puddler at the Mohand Mills in Sharpsburg since 1897. It also claimed Myls Wains, one of the oldest Dinkey engineers at the Homestead steel works in 1924.[1]

Although employers anxiously recruited and hired Blacks during World War I and the 1920s, the workers enjoyed fewer opportunities than their Black predecessors. The previous generation of Black iron and steel employees held an impressive array of skilled positions and experienced a remarkable degree of upward mobility. Their numbers, however, were too small to confer significant occupational advantages upon succeeding groups of Black workers. Moreover, thousands of European immigrants flocked to the iron and steel industry between 1880 and 1910, and vastly outnumbered Blacks. When an increasing number of Black migrants finally came to Western Pennsylvania during and after the war, both native Whites and foreign-born laborers had already gained ascendancy in important skilled positions throughout the industry. The late arrival of large numbers of Black employees restricted their ability to ascend the occupational ladder and made them more vulnerable to discriminatory treatment from foremen and hostility from White workers.

The outbreak of World War I inaugurated the massive movement of Black workers away from unprofitable toil in Southern farming to more lucrative work in Northern mills and factories. Immigration to America, mostly from southern and eastern Europe, had normally provided Northern industrial establishments with large reservoirs of unskilled labor. Hostilities, however, caused a precipitous decline in the annual rate of European immigration. Prior to the conflict, during the years between 1910 and 1914, about one million foreigners were settling in the United States every year while between 1915 and 1919, less than 350,000 Europeans annually crossed the Atlantic bound for America. In 1915, 326,700 immigrants came to the United States. In 1917, the year the United States entered the War, the number dropped to 295,403. Two years later in 1919, only 141,132 foreigners arrived in America.[2] In the meantime, America's material assistance to its European Allies and its own involvement in the war put large demands upon the nation's heavy industries. As a result, new plants were constructed and existing facilities in steel, shipbuilding, munitions manufacturing, and other war-related industries were expanded. Increased production resulting largely from war orders also required an expanded labor force. Factory owners and managers recognized the need for a group of workers to replace the dwindling supply of immigrant laborers and decided to recruit Southern Blacks to alleviate their manpower shortages.

Black tenants and sharecroppers responded quickly and eagerly to these new employment opportunities. Just prior to America's entry into World War I, a series of economic hardships and natural disasters struck much of the South's cotton-growing region, adversely affecting the Black population living there.[3] Because they worked primarily as farm laborers, Southern Blacks were particularly vulnerable to the fluctuations of the market and the uncertainties of nature. In Alabama, for example, between 1913 and 1914, low cotton prices caused many to attempt to borrow money at a time when banks were reluctant to give loans because they saw no quick end to the glut on the market. In July of 1916, floods wiped away crops throughout the Black Belt counties of Georgia, Florida, Alabama, Mississippi and Louisiana.[4] Their crops destroyed, many Black sharecroppers had no way of repaying their debts for food and provisions advanced to them during the previous winter. Consequently, mules and other items of personal property were claimed for rents and debts at local stores, and many Blacks were evicted from their land.[5] Moreover, the boll weevil, which initially crossed the Mexican border into the United States in 1892, infested the Black Belt beginning in 1914, ravaging cotton crops and causing even more Black workers to move away from the soil.[6]

Because of these difficulties in Southern cotton production the number of Black farmworkers, the vast majority of whom lived in the South, declined from 2,881,454 on the eve of World War I, to 2,178,888 in 1920, a decrease of 24.3 percent. The amount of farm land tilled by Blacks, which increased by 11.7 percent between 1900 and 1910, declined by 1,687,784 acres, a decrease of 3.6 percent, between 1910 and 1920. Weevil infestation lasted into the 1920s. Much of the Black rural population began to leave the cotton-producing states. Between 1910 and 1930, the number of Black farmworkers in Georgia, for example, fell from 122,554 to 86,787, a decrease of 29.2 percent. A 20.1 percent decline in South Carolina yielded a decrease in the number of Black farmworkers from 96,772 to 77,331.[7] Consequently, the percentage of Blacks in the total population of these cotton states declined. In 1910, Blacks in Georgia comprised 45.1 percent of the populace. Their proportion dropped to 41.7 percent in 1920 and to 36.8 percent in 1930. A slide from 55.2 percent of the total population to 41.4 percent occurred in South Carolina between 1910 and 1920. By 1930, Blacks comprised 45.6 percent of the state population. Blacks made up 42.5 percent of Alabama's populace in 1910. In 1920 and 1930, they respectively comprised 38.4 percent and 25.7 percent of the state population.[8] At the same time, downward fluctuations in national cotton production occurred between 1914 and 1920. Between 1914 and 1915, the first year of the boll weevil's Black Belt invasion, annual cotton production dropped from 16,112,000 bales to 11,172,000 bales per year.[9] The price of cotton declined from 12.4 cents in June, July, and August, 1914 to 6.3 cents in November 1914. It remained low in 1915 and did not rise to 12 cents until June 1916. Cotton prices continued to increase through the war years until they reached 37.7 cents in May 1920.[10] In each successive year between 1915 and 1920, however, annual cotton production averaged only 11,826,000 bales.[11]

The sharp decline in cotton production and natural catastrophes afflicting Southern agriculture loosened the ties of tradition that had bound Black Southerners to the soil and stimulated their migration to the industrial North. As economic hardships increased, Black Southerners became more willing to permanently escape Jim Crow laws which relegated them to a status of political and social inferiority. The trend toward institutionalizing Jim Crow had begun only a few decades before the World War I migration of Blacks northward. Beginning with the Mississippi Plan to disfranchise Black voters in 1890, other Southern states soon followed their own statutes restricting Black political activity: South Carolina in 1895, Louisiana in 1898, North Carolina in 1900, Alabama in 1901 and Virginia in 1902.[12] Affirming the "separate but equal" doctrine of the *Plessy vs. Ferguson* decision in 1896, the Supreme Court gave federal sanction to a whole series of racially discriminatory laws and segregation practices. Thereafter, the treatment of Blacks as second-class citizens in schooling, transportation, public accommodations, and every other facet of Southern life gained full support of the law, both on the state and federal level. An increase in lynchings was a cruel result of legalized segregation. Everything from a criminal act to an inadvertent breach of racial etiquette and custom could invite the wrath of a howling White mob upon any hapless member of the Black community. Under these circumstances, industrial opportunity in the urban North beckoned to Black Southerners, who sought to escape from deteriorating economic conditions, social degradation, and second-class citizenship imposed by Jim Crow laws, and increasing violence against them by Southern Whites.

Although some Blacks actively resisted racial oppression, the vast majority expressed their opposition by leaving the South.[13]

The wartime migration thus suddenly shifted Black workers in large numbers from the rural and urban South to Northern industrial centers. Because an average of 83.7 percent of the Black population and only 43.6 percent of the White population in the heaviest Black populated states worked as sharecroppers and tenants, the numbers of Blacks migrating North exceeded those of Whites.[14] Close to 500,000 Blacks and 822,000 Whites migrated out of the South as a whole between 1910 and 1920. But approximatly 349,600 Blacks and only 151,000 Whites left the cotton-producing and weevil-infested states of Mississippi, Alabama, Georgia, and South Carolina.[15] As a result, an unprecedented increase occurred in the Northern Black population. The number of Blacks in Chicago increased by 148.2 percent between 1910 and 1920. During that decade, due largely to wartime demand the Black population rose from 44,103 to 109,408. In the same period, migrants to Detroit caused the Black population there to expand dramatically from 5,741 to 40,838, a 611.3 percent increase.[16] Blacks in Cleveland totalled 8,448 in 1910; a 307.8 percent increase brought their numbers to 34,451 in 1910.[17]

Labor shortages during World War I motivated most, but not all Blacks to settle in the North between 1916 and 1930. Migratory patterns established prior to World War I drew thousands of Black settlers to Northern industrial areas during the late nineteenth and early twentieth centuries. Between 1880 and 1910, Black Southerners who encountered economic difficulties or experienced gross dissatisfaction with their area's racial atmosphere left home, and frequently went to a nearby Southern city. This was an example of chain migration. Some remained only temporarily, but their exposure to the outside world alerted them to better opportunities beyond their immediate surroundings. Once these patterns were established, an awareness of employment prospects in Northern cities resulted and prompted these migrants to move again. After they found lodging and employment, they wrote letters to relatives and friends still in the South about their experiences. These persons usually responded by initiating a secondary migration which brought them to the North to join the original migrants.[18]

The migratory patterns of Blacks in Promise Land, South
Carolina were typical. Approximately 43 percent of the families
in this community migrated to the North between 1897 and
1915. Economic problems related to the unstable cotton market,
unsuitable credit arrangments, and deteriorating soil convinced
several residents of Promise Land to seek opportunities somewhere else. Initially, these migrants went to Atlanta, but eventually they trickled northward to Philadelphia, New York and
Chicago. Martha Letman Reynolds, for example, settled in the
Windy City in about 1910 with her husband. Soon she wrote
her sharecropper brothers, and convinced them to abandon
farming and come North. Tim, who was blind, came first. Allen
came next, and Martha's husband helped him find work in a
foundry. Allen, in turn, encouraged another sister and her husband to quit the land and come to Chicago in 1920.[19]

Agents from railroads, steel companies, munitions factories,
and other defense industries facilitated the migration North.
Initially, the shortage of labor made it difficult for some railroad
companies to keep their equipment in repair. Consequently, in
the summer of 1916, the Pennsylvania and Erie Line (P and E)
began to employ Black workers from Jacksonville, St. Augustine
and Pensacola, Florida and brought them North to work in its
various railroad yards. During the war, this railway company
imported into Pennsylvania 12,000 Blacks, mostly former tenants and sharecroppers willing to try industrial labor. Needing
additional labor themselves, the Baltimore and Ohio, Philadelphia and Reading, the New York Central and the Pennsylvania
railways followed the lead of the P and E Railroad and brought
in their own Black workers from the South. One midwestern
railroad, the Illinois Central, offered free transportation to any
Black Southerner willing to work for the company.[20] Aggressive
recruitment as well as the offer of free passes and promises of
high wages enticed Blacks northward to meet the expanded
needs of the railroads.

The railroads were another important factor in helping to
bring Southern Blacks to other Northern industries. They were
able to supply Black laborers to others as well as themselves.
The railroads and many Northern industrial firms frequently
made mutually beneficial arrangements for transporting Blacks
from the South. In most cases, a company would persuade a

railroad to provide free transportation to prospective Black laborers. Upon reaching their destination, these workers authorized their new employers to deduct travel expenses from their paychecks in order to compensate the railway company.[21] This kind of cooperation provided large numbers of Black workers to Northern industries. Even those companies with no binding agreements with a railroad received their share of Black laborers. The fact that these migrants often drifted from firm to firm in search of better jobs allowed several companies to draw from the available pool of unskilled laborers. Hence, the railroads, both directly and indirectly, were instrumental in easing the manpower shortage affecting industries throughout the North.

Once railway transportation became readily available, Northern industrialists used the services of labor agents to stimulate the Black migration further. They hired men, both Black and White, to go South to recruit Black workers.[22] In many cases, these agents were already company employees. For example, Negro welfare officers working for Jones and Laughlin (J and L) and Carnegie Steel frequently went South to secure Black laborers for mills in Western Pennsylvania.[23] Normally, these agents did most of their recruiting in Southern cities and towns to which Black farm workers had migrated. There they found clusters of Black men, many of them without work, on street corners, in barbershops and at confectionaries. These labor agents told Blacks about job opportunities in the North, and they persuaded many Blacks in Nashville, Memphis, Chattanooga, Birmingham, Augusta, and other cities to try their luck above the Mason-Dixon line. In no time, the news about employment opportunity in the North spread by word of mouth to innumerable small towns and throughout rural areas. However, in practically every place in the South from which substantial migration took place, a labor agent had been nearby, luring away Black workers.[24] The work of labor agents in Augusta, Georgia was so effective that in 1917 an official of the Southern States Phosphate and Fertilizer Company complained to the U.S. Secretary of Commerce, saying:

> Within the last few days over 1,000 negroes have been carried out of Augusta as a result of the work of these emigrant agents, and we wish to enter our protest . . . a very serious

condition will ensue unless some steps are promptly taken to arrest this migration . . . Can't you do something to give us relief?[25]

Officials in the Department of Commerce immediately referred complaints of this kind to Louis Post, the Assistant Secretary of Labor.[26] The Department of Labor had been cooperating in the effort to attract workers to defense industries located in the North. But in January 1918, in response to growing labor shortages especially in Southern agricultural areas, the Department of Labor stopped encouraging Black migration to the North. The department, however, continued to find employment "for individuals regardless of race."[27]

Alabama, Arkansas and Mississippi enacted laws restricting the activity of labor agents, including the imposition of heavy fines for violations, and many communities charged exorbitant fees for licenses. A Jacksonville, Florida ordinance compelled agents to pay $1,000 license fees. Failure to purchase the permit resulted in imprisonment for sixty days or a fine of $600. In addition, labor agents were harassed and arrested on flimsy charges. Mounting opposition of Southern employers and landowners fearful of losing their Black laborers compelled labor agents to resort to the mails. Migrants already settled in the North gave the agents names of relatives and friends still in the South. Using these names in postal solicitations enabled labor agents to circumvent restrictions and to persuade migrants to come North.[28] Thus, the counter efforts of Southerners to stem the flow of migration northward were only partially successful.

Employment ads in Black newspapers were as effective as the work of labor agents in encouraging Blacks to move northward. The widely circulated *Chicago Defender,* for example, extolled promising economic conditions in the North and urged many Blacks to abandon farm work for industrial labor. Seeing actual notices in Black newspapers specifically requesting Black workers was ample proof to prospective migrants that Northern industry needed and wanted their labor. A typical advertisement read:

3,000 laborers to work on railroad. Factory hires all race help. More positions open than men for them.

and

Men wanted at once. Good steady employment for colored
. . . For out of town parties of ten or more, cheap transportation will be arranged.[29]

Industries clearly indicated their preferences for Black workers,
and this alone gave great stimulus to the migration.

Once in the North, Black migrants entered a variety of
industrial occupations, primarily in iron and steel, auto
manufacturing, shipbuilding, and railroad labor. Employable
males among the 25,000 to 30,000 Black migrants settling in
Detroit between 1916 and 1917 found jobs in automobile plants
and with firms manufacturing auto parts and accessories. In
1914, less than 1,000 Black auto workers were employed in area
plants. As a result of the migration, however, 12,000 to 18,000
Blacks gained employment in the Detroit auto industry between
1916 and 1918.[30] Similarly, the stockyards, packing houses, and
iron and steel mills of Chicago provided wide employment
opportunities for the city's 50,000 Black newcomers.[31] During
the same period, the Pennsylvania, the Reading, and the Baltimore and Ohio Railroads, as well as Midvale Steel and several
munitions and shipbuilding firms in Philadelphia, hired the
majority of their 40,000 employable Black migrants.[32] Between
1910 and 1920, largely because of the wartime migration in the
second half of the decade, the number of Blacks performing
industrial labor in various manufacturing and transportation
pursuits rose from 834,422 to 1,152,164. In 1910, they
represented about 18 percent of all gainfully employed Blacks.
In 1920, they comprised 31.2 percent of all Black laborers.[33]

The influence of a labor agent, a newspaper ad, or a relative
already settled in the Pittsburgh area were responsible for
attracting Blacks to Western Pennsylvania, the location of this
particular study. As in other Northern industrial centers, the
wartime lull in European immigration caused mill owners and
managers in and around Pittsburgh to begin their own recruitment of Black Southerners to ease manpower deficiencies in
local plants and foundries. In 1916, Allegheny County, the principal steel producing region in Western Pennsylvania, had 2,456
industrial plants. However, immediate wartime obligations

required the construction of 124 additional facilities, bringing the number of area manufactories to 2,580 in 1919. Although the total number of workers varied very little during the war period,[34] the composition of the labor force did change quite significantly. The number of native White laborers did rise from 115,495 in 1916 to 121,381 in 1919. However, the supply of unskilled immigrant workers in the Pittsburgh area dropped sharply during the war. Many had returned to war-torn Europe to rejoin family and friends, while others went back to take up arms in defense of their homelands. In any case, between 1910 and 1920, because of this wartime emigration to Europe, the number of foreign-born residents in Allegheny County declined from 271,350 to 248,581. A similar decrease also occurred in Pittsburgh, where the immigrant population dropped from 140,436 to 120,266. More important, the number of foreign-born laborers in Allegheny County decreased from 96,668 in 1916 to 85,630 in 1919. Black Southerners, primarily from the weevil-infested Black Belt, were then imported to replenish the dwindling ranks of immigrant workers. Immediately before the war, Black industrial laborers in the Pittsburgh district numbered 2,550. However, reductions in European immigration and general employment demands brought on by the war swelled their numbers to 7,897 in 1916 and to 14,610 in 1919, a nearly six-fold increase in just four and a half years.[35]

The greatest increase in Black employment in the area came in the steel industry. Blacks first entered the Pittsburgh mills during a puddler's strike in 1875. In 1910, they numbered only 789 workers and comprised only 3 percent of all steelworkers. Carnegie Steel plants in Pittsburgh, Homestead, Braddock and other mill towns along the Monongahela, Allegheny and Ohio Rivers employed the majority of these workers.[36] By 1918, the wartime migration had brought the total number of Black steelworkers in the region to about 7,000 or 13 percent of all steelworkers. The 4,000 Blacks working at various Carnegie steel plants throughout Allegheny County and the 1,500 Black steelworkers employed at Jones and Laughlin in Pittsburgh comprised well over half of the total.[37] Prior to 1916, the Carnegie steel works in Duquesne employed no more than a dozen Black workers. In the spring of that year, however, plant managers imported their first group of Black Southerners from

Virginia and assigned them to the merchant bar mill, a new facility built for the company's expanded wartime production.[38] Between 1916 and 1918, an additional 305 Blacks settled in Duquesne and became mill employees, bringing the total number of Black steelworkers to 344.[39] Similarly, in 1916, the small group of Black steelworkers at the Carnegie Works in Clairton was greatly expanded by the arrival of 150 to 200 Blacks from Charlottesville, Virginia. During the war, other Black migrants entered the Clairton mills, and by 1919, they had brought the total number of Black employees to 300.[40] As early as 1907, 121 Blacks comprised nearly 2 percent of the work force at the Carnegie mills in Homestead, but the wartime migration increased their numbers to 1,737 in 1919, at which time they made up 11 percent of all plant employees.[41]

As Black migrants flocked into Western Pennsylvania during the war, they swelled the Black population of cities and milltowns throughout the region. *The Iron Age*, a major journal in the steel industry, took notice of trains "filled with negroes bound from the South to Pittsburgh . . . "[42] According to one contemporary observer, over 18,000 Blacks arrived in the city between 1915 and 1917.[43] These wartime migrants increased the number of Black settlers in Pittsburgh from 25,623 in 1910, or 4.8 percent of the total population, to 37,725 in 1920, or 6.4 percent of the total population. In the same manner, hundreds of migrating Blacks settling in the outlying steel milltowns caused the Black population to expand. The migration increased Homestead's Black population from 867 in 1910 to 1,814 in 1920. Their percentage in the total population rose from 4.6 percent to 8.8 percent. In Rankin, the Black population more than doubled from 443 in 1910 to 873. Their percentage in the total population increased from 7.3 percent to 11.9 percent. Similarly, in Duquesne, the Black population rose from 246 in 1910 to 817 in 1920, an increase from 1.5 percent to 4.2 percent of the total population. (See Figure 2 for location of places of Black settlement and Table 4 for population figures.)

Most Black Southerners settling in Western Pennsylvania during the war had come to the area to improve their economic and social status. A student at the University of Pittsburgh conducting a survey in 1918 among 400 migrant Blacks in Pittsburgh found that 325 of them had left the South primarily for

Figure 2. Map of western Pennsylvania.

the higher wages and broader employment opportunities available in local mills and foundries.[45] Newspaper advertisements, mainly in the Black press, stressed the economic opportunities which the iron and steel industry offered to prospective Black

**TABLE 4. Black Population Increases in Selected Milltowns in Western Pennsylvania 1910–1930**

| | 1910 | | | 1920 | | | 1930 | | |
|---|---|---|---|---|---|---|---|---|---|
| | Total | Black Population | % of Tot. Pop. | Total | Black Population | % of Tot. Pop. | Total | Black Population | % of Tot. Pop. |
| Pittsburgh | 533,905 | 24,623 | 4.8 | 588,343 | 37,725 | 6.4 | 669,817 | 54,983 | 8.2 |
| Homestead | 18,713 | 867 | 4.6 | 20,452 | 1,814 | 8.8 | 20,141 | 3,367 | 16.2 |
| Rankin | 6,042 | 443 | 7.3 | 7,301 | 873 | 11.9 | 7,956 | 1,556 | 19.5 |
| Braddock | 19,357 | 421 | 2.1 | 20,879 | 735 | 3.5 | 19,329 | 2,224 | 11.5 |
| No. Braddock | 11,824 | 287 | 2.4 | 14,928 | 393 | 2.6 | 16,782 | 488 | 2.9 |
| Duquesne | 15,727 | 246 | 1.5 | 19,011 | 817 | 4.2 | 21,396 | 1,817 | 8.4 |
| McKeesport | 42,694 | 799 | 1.8 | 46,781 | 928 | 1.9 | 54,632 | 1,893 | 3.4 |
| Clairton | — | — | — | 6,264 | 621 | 9.9 | 15,291 | 2,070 | 13.6 |
| Donora | 8,174 | 359 | 4.4 | 14,131 | 855 | 6 | 13,905 | 986 | 7 |
| Monessen | 11,775 | 232 | 1.9 | 18,179 | 588 | 3.2 | 20,268 | 1,201 | 5.9 |
| Farrell | — | — | — | 15,586 | 1,349 | 8.4 | 14,359 | 1,606 | 11.1 |
| Sharon | 15,270 | 194 | 1.2 | 21,747 | 701 | 3.2 | 25,908 | 506 | 1.9 |
| Aliquippa | — | — | — | 2,931 | 5 | 0.01 | 27,116 | 2,592 | 9.5 |
| New Castle | 36,280 | 529 | 1.4 | 44,938 | 867 | 1.9 | 48,674 | 1,572 | 3.2 |
| Johnstown | 55,482 | 442 | .07 | 67,327 | 1,650 | 2.4 | 66,993 | 1,444 | 2.1 |
| Vandergrift | 3,876 | 28 | .06 | 9,351 | 65 | .06 | 11,479 | 160 | .01 |
| TOTALS | 779,119 | 29,470 | 3% | 940,149 | 49,986 | 5% | 1,053,946 | 78,465 | 7% |

Source: U.S. Department of Commerce, Bureau of the Census, *Negro Population in the United States, 1790–1915*, pp. 102–103; U.S., Department of Commerce, Bureau of the Census, *Negroes in the United States, 1920–1932*, pp. 63–64; U.S., Department of Commerce, Bureau of the Census, *Fourteenth Census of the United States, 1920: Population*, 1:285, 292, 294–295, 586–587.

migrants. In 1917, the *New York Age*, a Black newspaper with national circulation, featured special articles on job opportunities in the milltowns of Sharon and Farrell, Pennsylvania. It said that the American Sheet and Tin Plate Company "sorely . . . need . . . good colored men" who can replace more than five hundred Slavic workers who plan to return to Europe. "Unless colored men can be had in" sufficient numbers, the article declared, "open hearths will be crippled for some months." In another section of the newspaper, biographical sketches of some prominent Blacks in Sharon and Farrell were presented. Included were Blacks who had worked in the mills, and eventually became property owners and leading citizens in the Shenango Valley. One was Charles Wayne, a Farrell resident since 1910 as well as an employee of the Carnegie steel works. Since he earned from $6 to $10 per day, "These flattering sums" allowed him to purchase several pieces of real estate and to build "two splendid houses." Another success story concerned Thomas H. Robinson, a migrant from Millwood, Virginia, who operated a Drill Machine in the Driggs Seabury Gun Works in Sharon. Like Charles Wayne, the "flattering sums" of money which he earned marked him as another prosperous member of the Black community of Sharon and Farrell.[46]

Networks of relatives and friends also attracted scores of Black Southerners to Western Pennsylvania. Sometimes migrants explored job opportunities in other areas of the North and South before settling in the Pittsburgh vicinity, but in most instances, the experience of a parent or sibling or friend drew them to the iron and steel industry. William Henry Harrison left his native North Carolina in 1916 in search of a better job in Northern industry. After working for a brief time in Norfolk, Virginia, young Harrison migrated to New Haven, Connecticut. Shortly thereafter, his brother Charles, a newly hired steelworker in Duquesne, Pennsylvania, told him of even better opportunities in the steel region around Pittsburgh. Before the year had ended, Harrison had settled in Western Pennsylvania, and was working as a bricklayer helper at Carnegie's Duquesne steel works.[47] Julius Clawley heard about various railroads which brought Blacks from Prince George County, Virginia to take jobs in Pittsburgh area steel mills. Clawley left on one of

Figure 3. William Henry Harrison who migrated to Duquesne, PA in 1916 and became an employee in the local steel mill is pictured in France in 1918 with fellow Black soldiers from Pittsburgh. Harris is standing in the center. (Courtesy of Mrs. Cora Harrison of Duquesne, PA.)

those trains in 1915. After he secured employment at the Duquesne steel plant, his brother-in-law, Edward Lipscomb, decided to follow him. In 1917, young Lipscomb arrived in Duquesne and began working as a common laborer in the mill masonry department.[48] Another Black, Reuben Montgomery, had been a sharecropper in Troy, Alabama before he migrated to Vandergrift to work for the American Sheet and Tin Plate Company in 1917. He followed his parents, who had come

Figure 4. Reuben and Bessie Montgomery of Vandergrift, PA in a picture taken in the 1930s. The Montgomeries migrated from Alabama to Vandergrift, in 1917. Reuben Montgomery was a steelworker at American Sheet and Tin Plate Company in Vandergrift. (Courtesy of Mrs. Mildred Trent, Philadelphia, PA.)

there a short time before. Other Blacks followed Montgomery, migrating from Troy and other rural communities in Alabama to Vandergrift in search of higher wages.⁴⁹

The end of the First World War in no way diminished the desire of Black Southerners to come North. The economic difficulties afflicting Southern agriculture, exacerbated by the end of the war, continued to drive Black workers away from the land and into Northern industry. As was true during the war, Black Southerners responded to industrial opportunities in cities like Chicago, Detroit, Cleveland, and in Pittsburgh and other mill communities in Western Pennsylvania. Willie Smith, a sharecropper's son, left Georgia in 1921 to improve his economic situation. He arrived in Chattanooga, Tennessee, and worked in a pipe foundry until 1922. At the urging of some Georgia acquaintances living in Pittsburgh, Smith quit his job and migrated to Western Pennsylvania, where he secured a better position at the Crucible steel mills in McKees Rocks.⁵⁰ Ashton Allen of Broadnax, Virginia raised cotton and tobacco on 100 acres of land given to him by his father, a Black who had managed to own his own farm. Because market prices for both of his cash crops plunged downward continuously between 1918 and 1922, Allen found it increasingly difficult to earn a living. In December 1922, when he was on the verge of bankruptcy, Allen saw a notice in the *Richmond Planet* advertising jobs in the Pittsburgh steel district. At that point, he decided to abandon farming and migrate to Western Pennsylvania. For the remainder of the winter, he worked in a box factory in South Hills, Virginia, earning his fare to Pittsburgh. Upon reaching the city in April 1923, Allen secured employment at the Jones and Laughlin Steel plant.⁵¹ Albert Corley, who, as a sharecropper, was more typical of migrants, took "transportation" out of Georgia in 1921 and found a better job at the Monessen plant of the Pittsburgh Steel Company⁵² and James Wilson left South Carolina in 1923 in search of a "better living" at the Duquesne Works of Carnegie Steel.⁵³.

Smith, Allen, Corley, and Wilson were responding to new postwar job opportunities in several steel plants in the Pittsburgh vicinity. They became a part of a larger migration of Blacks into Western Pennsylvania beginning in late 1922. After new construction activity and emerging demand brought the steel mills out of this brief 1921 to 1922 recession, regional firms required even larger numbers of laborers to work their mills and furnaces. As during World War I, they placed ads in Black newspapers, primarily in the South, in hopes of stimulating a second wave of Black migration into Western Pennsylvania. The Pittsburgh Urban League, acting as a liaison for Jones and Laughlin, Carnegie Steel, and other area firms, received immediate responses from 200 interested Blacks during November and December, 1922. Within another 60 days, 1,500 additional inquiries came through the mail.[54] Shortly thereafter, trainloads of Black migrants began arriving at Pittsburgh's five railroad stations. One steel firm received an average of 1,000 Black laborers per month from January to March, 1923; six other companies were importing a weekly "shipment" of 35 to 360 prospective Black steelworkers. For twenty consecutive days in May 1923, a "colored" Traveler's Aid worker at Pittsburgh's Union Station reported a total influx of 1,165 Black men, women, and children. Hundreds of other migrating Blacks from the South Atlantic states journeyed to Washington, D.C. and Baltimore, and boarded "motor trucks" bound for Pittsburgh. John T. Clark, the executive director of the local Urban League, estimated that 25,000 Blacks had come into Pittsburgh during this second wave of migration in 1922 and 1923.[55]

Renewed employment demands in the steel plants of Western Pennsylvania caused a resumption of this migration. Additional increases in the Black population of area milltowns naturally resulted. Between 1920 and 1930, the number of Blacks in Pittsburgh rose from 37,725 to 54,983; their percentage of the total population increased from 6.4 percent to 8.2 percent. Homestead's Black populace expanded from 1,814 to 3,367, a rise from 8.8 percent to 16.2 percent of the total population. In Duquesne, the Black population more than doubled, from 817 in 1920 to 1,817 in 1930. Their increase in the total population rose from 4.2 percent to 8.4 percent. The number of Blacks in Baddock during this period rose from 735 to 2,224, an increase from 3.5 percent to 11.5 percent of the total population. In Monessen, it grew from 588 in 1920 to 1,201 in 1930, an increase from 3.2 percent to 5.9 percent of the total population.[56] (See Table 4.)

**TABLE 5. Black Employment at Selected Steel Mills in the Pittsburgh Area During World War I, 1918**

| Plant | Highest Number During World War I |
|---|---|
| Carnegie Steel (11 plants) | 4,000 |
| Jones and Laughlin Steel (4 plants) | 1,500 |
| National Tube Company (3 plants) | 250 |
| Pressed Steel Car Company | 25 |
| Pittsburgh Forge and Iron | 75 |
| American Steel and Wire (5 plants) | 25 |
| Oliver Iron and Steel | 50 |
| Crucible Steel (4 plants) | 400 |
| A. M. Byers Company | 200 |
| Lockhart Iron and Steel | 160 |
| TOTAL | 6,685 |

Source: Data compiled from Abram L. Harris, Jr., ''The New Negro Workers in Pittsburgh'' (M.A. thesis, University of Pittsburgh, 1924), pp. 45–46.

The wartime migration increased the total number of Black steelworkers in the Pittsburgh area from 789 in 1910 to about 7,000 during the peak of the war, making them 13 percent of the industry's local work force. (See Table 5). The postwar influx of Blacks into Western Pennsylvania pushed their numbers up further, to 16,900 by September 1923. At that time, Black steelworkers comprised 21 percent of all employees in the area's major steel plants.[57] The Carnegie mills in Pittsburgh, Homestead, Braddock, Duquesne, and Clairton collectively employed 6,758 Black laborers in 1923. Another 2,900 Blacks worked in the four Jones and Laughlin steel plants. In McKees Rocks, there were 1,700 Blacks at the Pressed Steel Car Company, and 350 in the employ of Lockhart Iron Steel. Other steel companies, both in Pittsburgh and the outlying milltowns, also resumed their hiring of Black Southerners in the postwar period.[58]

Like their World War I predecessors, the vast majority of Black workers responding to the newly advertised positions in the Pittsburgh steel mills had economic reasons for wanting to come forth. Writing to the Pittsburgh Urban League for himself and seven other Black men in Thomasville, Georgia in May 1923, Barnie Smith made clear their desire to migrate to Western Pennsylvania for higher wages:

> We Southern negroes want to come to the north . . . they ain't giving a man nothing for what he do. Time he pay for groceries he don't have a dollar . . . you know just how it is with the poor race here. They is down, and they [white southerners] is trying to keep us down . . . Just as soon as we get a answer we will be ready to come . . .[59]

Rush Gaylord of Savannah had similar difficulties in earning a living:

> I don't hardly know how too [sic] explain myself as I am so awful . . . I want to find a good job where I can make a living as I cannot do it here. I would be only too glad to get a hearing from you stating that you would be glad too have me . . . let me know if you wants me or not . . .[60]

Another Georgia resident, John D. Maxwell, wrote to the League as a representative of "200 laboring men" who were trying to escape the boll weevil and the "strengious" [sic] time it created around Savannah.[61] W. B. Mitchell of Shreveport, Louisiana wrote that he had been working on a plantation for the last few years. He blamed the boll weevil and the "high cost of living" for placing him into "debt on the share crop system." Since "conditions don't look any better yet," Mitchell inquired about employment in the Pittsburgh steel mills for himself and his three sons. He concluded his letter by describing himself as a man "with plenty (of) ambition an no money."[62] This persistent migration of Black Southerners to Western Pennsylvania during the 1920s was best explained by Lillie Smith of Mt. Zion, South Carolina, who, in writing the Pittsburgh Urban League for her "two grown son[s]," said, "we want to settle down somewhere north . . . wages are so cheap down here we can hardly live . . . "[63]

Black Southerners also hoped to improve their social conditions by coming to Pittsburgh. W. S. Hurt, a prospective Black steelworker from Georgia, was "anxious to get somewhere that I can make a livelihood, and . . . educate my children."[64] S. M. Jenkins of Houston, Texas, was " . . . glad to know that a colored man could get in a country where he could work and live at ease."[65] And G. P. Washington of Savannah, Georgia, in a letter to the Pittsburgh Urban League, thought he could "do a great good of getting the negro away from" the South.[66] Another Black Southerner, who lived briefly in St. Louis, also made plans to settle in Pittsburgh. He had worked as a railway fireman in the South, but lost a job he had held for seventeen years. He made no attempt to regain his former position because discrimination had gotten "so hard against colored fireman down South." Instead he wanted to take his wife and two daughters and migrate to Western Pennsylvania to get "a steady position."[67] Both during and after World War I, Black workers steadily abandoned Southern agriculture for the attractions of Northern industry. By settling in Western Pennsylvania, Black Southerners affirmed their desire for better wages and for a life free of the indignities of Jim Crow.

Black migrants in search of the best employment opportunities also settled in the Pittsburgh area. Some migrated within the South to find better jobs, and then moved to Western Pennsylvania hoping to take advantage of even greater economic opportunities. John McKinley Worthey moved from his birthplace, Troy, Alabama to Birmingham. For several years, he worked in the quarry of the Tennessee Coal, Iron, and Steel Company. In 1923, he migrated to Homestead, Pennsylvania, and secured a job at the nearby Edgar Thomson steel works in Braddock. E. A. Brown, a native of Spartansburg, South Carolina, migrated to Dante, Virginia to labor in a coal mine. During the early 1920s, he, like scores of other Black Southerners, wished to find more lucrative employment in the steel mills of Pittsburgh.[68]

By the beginning of the 1920s, scores of Black migrants had already experienced mill and factory labor in Northern industry. Many became disillusioned with industrial labor, however, and left their jobs. Some disliked their job assignments and complained about unsafe and unsanitary working conditions. Others were drawn back to the South because of family concerns while hundreds of others left because of better job opportunities either in another plant or another city. At the A. M. Byers Company in Pittsburgh, for example, most Black employees of this wrought iron facility stayed on the job for three months or less during the period between 1916 and 1930.[69] Henry Pearson, an Alabama native, labored at the Byers mill between October and November 1920. He quit because his work was too heavy. Frank Arnold, a migrant from Georgia, became a laborer in the Bar Mill at Byers in 1922. After working for one day, he quit to take a better job at another plant. In 1923, Howard Holliday, another Georgian, relinquished his job in the No. 14 Bending Department to return South because of a death in his family.[70]

A similar pattern prevailed in other mills in Pittsburgh and elsewhere in the industrial North. When the second wave of Black migration to Western Pennsylvania began in 1922 and 1923, hundreds of Black migrants who had left Northern industry, found the economic conditions in the South no more promising than before World War I. As soon as job opportunities became available in the Pittsburgh mills, they returned to the North to try industrial labor once again. Alex Brown of Sumter, South Carolina once worked for Jones and Laughlin Steel for nearly two years. In December 1922, he told an official of the Pittsburgh Urban League that he and several other Blacks "would like to come back."[71] Robert Tippins of Savannah, Georgia was a former employee of the Pratt and Cady Foundry in Hartford, Connecticut. In 1923, after his return to Savannah, he expressed an interest in the Carnegie steel mills because "I needs the work."[72] Another Black Savannah resident had labored as a fireman at the American Steel Works and as charger at the Pin Steel Works both in Chester, Pennsylvania. In 1923, he, like Brown and Tippins, wanted a job in the Pittsburgh steel mills.[73]

Southern Whites, particularly large landowners who feared the loss of cheap Black labor, opposed the Black migration to the North. In 1917, an employment agent for the Pennsylvania Railroad tried to bring 200 Blacks from Shreveport, Louisiana to Pittsburgh. Two local officials, a sheriff and a police chief, at the prompting of some area planters, warned him that Louisiana law prohibited him from enticing labor away from the state. The threat of arrest caused him to abandon his plans.[74] In 1923, the Mayor of Selma, Alabama, in an effort to stop the Black migration falsely stated that Pittsburgh was infested with smallpox. He suggested that Blacks already in the Smoky City return to Alabama and Mississippi farms where they were needed.[75] Despite these efforts, the Black migration continued unabated to the Pittsburgh vicinity and to other areas of the industrial North.

When Black migrants arrived in Western Pennsylvania, steel owners and managers hired them primarily as unskilled laborers. In 1918, nearly all Black steelworkers in the Pittsburgh area labored as unskilled workers.[76] Although these jobs frequently required nothing more than physical strength and endurance, such employment permitted Black migrants to improve their economic condition significantly. In 1918, a University of Pittsburgh survey among 453 Black newcomers in Pittsburgh revealed that 56 percent of the group earned wages under $2.00 per day while living in the South. Only 5 percent of those who migrated to Western Pennsylvania were paid such low wages. Approximately 62 percent of the Black migrants received between $2.00 and $3.00 per day in the steel mills of Pittsburgh. Only 25 percent of them earned a comparable daily wage while working in the South.[77] In 1925, a sample of 500 Black families in Homestead reported they had earned an average of $15.30 per week before moving North. In Pittsburgh, household income had nearly doubled to $30.21 per week, while Black residents in Homestead and other steel milltowns received only 65 cents less. The average weekly wage of Black steelworkers in the whole Pittsburgh area was $29.24.[78].

Offsetting some of these gains were higher living costs. In Western Pennsylvania in the early 1920s, recent Black migrant families paid nearly $6.50 per week more for rent, food and other basic living costs than before moving. Even with these higher costs, however, net family earnings were an average 70 percent higher than they had been in the South.[79] This difference was clearly understood by Blacks. It was a major stimulus for their continuing migration to the Pittsburgh area.

Since plant officials in Western Pennsylvania more generally assigned Black employees to unskilled laboring positions, their wages were usually lower than native Whites and foreign-born steelworkers. In 1920, in Pittsburgh, various manufacturing and mechanical industries, particularly iron and steel, employed a total of 92,063 workers. Approximately 48,637 were native Whites, 35,446 were foreign-born, and 7,971 were Black. Among native White workers, only 6,635 or 13.6 percent, held unskilled laboring positions. A total of 11,245, or 31.7 percent of the foreign-born were unskilled workers. But 4,350, or 54.4 percent of all Black mill employees worked in unskilled positions[80] and earned an average of 40 to 50 cents per hour in the basic steel and manufacturing industries of Pittsburgh. Although these Black employees improved their economic condition by securing jobs in area mills and received wages which enabled them to meet living costs in Western Pennsylvania, they, nonetheless, earned a rate of pay below that of most Whites.[81]

On many skilled and semi-skilled jobs, steel employees could earn between 60 and 90 cents per hour. Boilermakers, for example, made between 70 and 90 cents per hour. The few Blacks who acquired such positions sometimes earned the same wage as their White or foreign-born colleagues. However, on many occasions, Blacks suffered wage differentials based on race. Between 1920 and 1925, for instance, about 5,986 machinists worked in various steel mills and other industrial plants in Pittsburgh. Approximately 4,126 machinists, or 68.9 percent, were native White, 1,759 or 29.3 percent were foreign-born, and 101, or 1.6 percent were Black. White and foreign-born machinists earned an average of 70 to 90 cents per hour, while Blacks earned an average of 60 cents per hour.[82] Although Blacks recognized that they often earned less for the same jobs than did Whites and the foreign-born, their pay still exceeded their earnings in the South. Most Black steelworkers used this yardstick, not a comparison with White steelworkers in similar positions, to judge the benefits they gained in Western Pennsylvania.

In some instances, a few Pittsburgh area steel companies hired Blacks in skilled positions and in important semi-skilled occupations. The Standard Steel Car Company employed "a large number" of Black riveters from Norfolk, Virginia. The Reliance Steel Casting Company had fifty-one Black employees in 1925, and of this number, thirty worked either in skilled or in crucial semi-skilled positions, mainly as chippers and grinders.[83] The American Sheet and Tin Plate Company employed "187 skilled and semi-skilled colored workers" in its Sharon Plant.[84] These facilities, however, tended to be the exception rather than the rule.

Most mills employed large groups of unskilled Blacks. Carnegie Steel and Jones and Laughlin Steel hired the vast majority of Black migrants in their several plants along the Three Rivers. Most of Carnegie's 4,000 Black employees held unskilled positions in 1917, and practically all of J and L's 1,500 Blacks were similarly situated. The same pattern prevailed at other smaller plants like Lockhart Iron and Steel in McKees Rocks, Pittsburgh Forge and Iron, Crucible Steel, and American Steel and Wire.[85] (See Table 6.) A White employee at National Tube in McKeesport remembered in later years that Blacks had "the rottenest jobs" in the mill.[86]

Discrimination by White foremen and other mill officials and hostility from White workers locked Blacks in undesirable, unskilled positions. At most mills, foremen exercised control over workers in their respective departments. They hired their own men, paid them, and discharged those whom they disliked. Those who harbored racial prejudice became major obstacles to Black occupational advancement. The By-Products plant of Jones and Laughlin Steel in Pittsburgh employed several White foremen from Alabama and Mississippi. They arbitrarily fired Black workers and replaced them with foreigners. In many instances, Blacks labored under foreign-born foremen who "too often fire men" on petty charges. One French Canadian boss at National Tube in McKeesport gave most of his workers a difficult time, but "if one of these colored men would just look at him crossways, he'd just cuss him up and down and fire him." A contemporary sociologist concluded that "the foreman is the crux of the problem of unskilled labor in industry." He added that when foremen "have the power to hire and fire their men . . . the Negro often suffers."[87]

**TABLE 6. Percentage of Unskilled Blacks at Selected Iron and Steel Plants in Western Pennsylvania, 1917**

| Company | Number of Blacks in July 1917 | Percentage Doing Unskilled Labor |
| --- | --- | --- |
| Carnegie Steel (all plants) | 4,000 | 95 |
| Jones and Laughlin (all plants) | 1,500 | 100 |
| National Tube (all plants) | 250 | 100 |
| Pressed Steel Car | 25 | 50 |
| Pittsburgh Forge and Iron | 75 | 100 |
| American Steel and Wire | 25 | 100 |
| Clinton Iron and Steel | 25 | 75 |
| Oliver Iron and Steel | 50 | 100 |
| Carbon Steel | 200 | 75 |
| Crucible Steel | 400 | 90 |
| A. M. Byers | 200 | 60 |
| Lockhart Iron and Steel | 160 | 95 |

Compiled from: Abraham Epstein, *The Negro Migrant in Pittsburgh* (Pittsburgh, The University of Pittsburgh, 1918), p. 31.

The occupational advancement of Black workers was seriously hampered by racial prejudice of foremen and other supervisors. The general superintendent of the seamless tube mill at the Aliquippa plant of Jones and Laughlin Steel, for example, refused to allow Blacks to work in his department. Similar attitudes kept Blacks out of the plant's North mill boiler house, the blacksmith shop, the central pump station, and other departments.[88] In other instances, management tolerated the racial hostilities of White workers. At MacIntosh Hemphill in Pittsburgh, White mechanics refused to train Black apprentices, so the company hired only Whites. White bargemen at another

Pittsburgh mill declined to work with Blacks, but were "appeased" when the company provided the migrants with segregated "quarters."[89] In many instances, particular immigrant groups held ascendancy in important parts of the mills, and were unwilling to work with Blacks. The tin plate mills in New Castle were one example. They were largely dominated by Welsh workers and those from a few other immigrant groups. They influenced management to bar Blacks from the hot mills, the tin house and the sorting room, and hire them mainly in unskilled occupations.[90]

To alleviate the problem of prejudiced White foremen, several steel managers hired Black foremen or straw bosses to head predominantly Black labor gangs and track crews. Some of these groups included foreign-born Whites.[91] Nonetheless, these straw bosses worked under White superiors, so they could not entirely shield Blacks from discriminatory employment practices.

Discriminatory treatment from foremen and other mill officials and hostility from White workers relegated Blacks to hard, hot, and dirty jobs throughout the iron and steel industry of Western Pennsylvania. At the Jones and Laughlin Steel plant in Aliquippa, for example, the majority of undesirable jobs were in the South coke works, the by-product coke works, and the 14-inch rolling mill where Blacks outnumbered all other workers. In the South coke works, where Blacks took coke out of the hot ovens, they "had to constantly chew tobacco . . . to clean their mouths of coke fumes and residues."[92]

Nonetheless, their improved economic condition convinced them that employment opportunities were better in the Pittsburgh steel district than in the South. The "push" of discontent and the "pull" of economic opportunity in the North, facilitated by the persuasion of a labor agent, a newspaper ad, or a letter from a migrant relative or friend were enough to lure Southern laborers and sharecroppers to steel mills in Pittsburgh, Homestead, Aliquippa, Clairton, Monessen and other industrial towns in Western Pennsylvania. How they lived and worked in their new surroundings is the subject of the next chapter.

# 3

# Black Steelworkers Confront Their New Environment

For migrating Black Southerners, the prospects of better pay and improved social conditions made Western Pennsylvania an attractive place in which to settle. The absence of statewide Jim Crow laws in Pennsylvania seemed to make such a move even more appealing. Miserable working conditions in the mills and inferior housing accommodations in Pittsburgh and the surrounding milltowns, however, dashed the hopes of many migrants who though of the North as a "promised land." Moreover, local racial discrimination was widespread in all aspects of living throughout the region. In short, the utopia that some Black Southerners expected to find in Pittsburgh and its environs simply did not exist.

The physical environment in Western Pennsylvania was grim. On many cobblestoned alleys stood dirty and dilapidated buildings. Great quantities of industrial waste emptied into the Monongahela, Allegheny, and Ohio Rivers from the steel plants lining their banks. Smoke from the mills polluted the air. Frequently, street lamps glowed in midafternoon to chase away the darkness created by the smoke-filled skies.[1] For many, the region looked like "hell with the lid off".[2] To one Black Georgian, Pittsburgh was the "ugliest, deadest town" he had ever seen![3]

Black migrants settling in Western Pennsylvania were most immediately affected by poor housing conditions. Because of inadequate preparations by the steel companies and the towns in which they were located, living space for these newcomers was sharply limited. Customarily, the steel companies purchased housing facilities to rent to their incoming Black employees. In some cases newly arrived Southern Blacks rented facilities especially constructed for them by their employers. In most instances, however, migrants were forced to overcrowd in housing units too small to meet their needs. The Carnegie steel works in Clairton planned to build only fifty houses for its rapidly growing force of Black laborers.[4] Those newcomers unable to locate company housing competed for equally limited space in privately owned facilities. Steel plants in Duquesne, Braddock, Homestead, Johnstown, and other mill communities crowded their Black employees into unsanitary bunkhouses and tenements. Their numbers were frequently so large that men would double up and use the same bunk according to their respective work shifts in the mill. At boarding houses in Pittsburgh, both privately and company owned, one could find as many as sixteen people occupying a four-room dwelling.[5]

These crowded conditions were especially hard on Black migrant families. Moreover, the availability of housing was more sharply limited for them than for Whites. In Pittsburgh, for example, in 1920, 42 percent of the city's 37,725 Blacks crowded into only two of its twenty-seven wards.[6] A similar situation existed in 1930 when 44.6 percent of Pittsburgh's 54,983 Blacks lived in Ward 3 and Ward 5. Also in 1930 45 percent of McKeesport's 1,893 Blacks were clustered in just one of its eleven wards.[7] In most cases, they lived in generally dirtier surroundings than Whites, and their substandard dwellings usually had improper ventilation and inadequate toilet and sewage facilities. One Black family rented an old brick house in the Hill District of Pittsburgh, a section of the city where most Blacks resided. Seven people jammed into this three-room dwelling. The first floor, where the kitchen was located, was sunk three feet below street level. The absence of water connections to the house left the family without sewage and required them to use an outside toilet. Also in the area was "an old frame house on a hill too steep for vehicular traffic." One ascended the hill by climbing a wooden stairway stretching three blocks. The house had a total of five rooms in addition to a shed in the back. In two of the rooms lived a family of five. Another family of three occupied the shed.[8]

Blacks already settled in Pittsburgh and other towns in the area tried to ameliorate the situation by searching for more and better housing for the newly arrived migrants. The Reverend J. C. Austin, the pastor of the huge Ebenezer Baptist Church in the Hill District of Pittsburgh, organized a Home Finder's League in the early 1920s to pursue this objective.[9] Reverend H. G. Payne, the pastor of Park Place AME Church in Homestead made a similar attempt. In 1923 he led his congregation in establishing a real estate agency to secure homes to sell or rent to "colored people . . . on low monthly installments."[10] Often an incoming migrant secured lodging with a relative in the area or with friends who had come from his native state or county. In spite of these individual efforts, however, most Black newcomers in Western Pennsylvania continued to live in congested and substandard dwellings because little else was available.

Residential segregation in Pittsburgh and the surrounding milltowns also gave Black migrants a limited choice in housing. Lodging was available primarily in designated "colored areas": Port Perry in Braddock, Castle Garden in Duquesne, Rosedale in Johnstown, and the Hill District in Pittsburgh. Steel company officials, realtors, and landlords seldom directed incoming migrants to any place beyond these segregated enclaves. Custom, not statute, allowed these housing agents to enhance the growth of segregated neighborhoods by restricting Black workers to these racially exclusive areas. In Aliquippa during the 1920s, for example, the Woodlawn Land Company, a real estate subsidiary of Jones and Laughlin Steel, deliberately segregated Blacks into an area called Plan Eleven Extension. It was a part of a larger policy to separate geographically workers of different racial and ethnic groups.[11] Moreover, as the migration filled Negro sections in Pittsburgh and the outlying milltowns, the excess Black population settled and developed other segregated enclaves which were usually in "declining neighborhoods" being vacated by Whites.[12]

The vast majority of Black residents in Western Pennsylvania lived on rental property within these segregated enclaves. A total of 18,682 Black families resided in Allegheny County in 1930. Approximately 15,398 households, or 82.4 percent of all Black families, rented their dwellings. Conversely, only 56 percent of all native Whites and only 44.9 percent of all foreign-born residents were classified as non-homeowners. In Pittsburgh and the surrounding milltowns, the proportion of tenants in the total Black population was even higher. In the Smoky City, 82.9 percent of 12,479 Black families were non-homeowners. Among native Whites and the foreign-born, the proportions were significantly lower, at 61 percent and 47.7 percent, respectively. In Braddock, the rate of home ownership was low for all. For Blacks, however, it was virtually nonexistent. Nearly 95 percent of the 520 Black families living there rented their dwellings. Tenancy existed for 76 percent of all native Whites and 56 percent of all foreign-born residents in Braddock. A similar situation prevailed in Clairton, where 91.7 percent of 453 Black families rented their housing. For native Whites and foreign-born residents, the rate of tenancy was 70 percent and 39.4 percent, respectively. Likewise, in Duquesne 90.7 percent of 394 Black families rented housing, while the rate for native Whites and the foreign-born was 80 percent. and 44 percent, respectively.[13]

Although tenancy existed among Whites as well as Blacks, Blacks were more often victimized by high rents in badly maintained neighborhoods. In Pittsburgh during the 1920s, Black steelworkers paid an average of $6.77 per unfurnished room per week, while their White counterparts weekly disbursed $6.38 per unfurnished room, usually in a considerably better dwelling. In 1930, Blacks in Pittsburgh continued to pay rents generally higher than any other segment of the population. Approximately 20.8 percent of all city residents paid between $20.00 and $29.00 per month in rent. The proportion of Blacks was 31.9 percent. Only 25 percent of all foreign-born Whites and 18.7 of all native Whites fitted this rental category. Another 33 percent of the total population disbursed between $30.00 and $49.00 per month for rent. The proportion of Blacks paying such amounts was 39 percent. The percentages of native Whites and the foreign-born were slightly lower at 37.4 percent and 30.1 percent respectively.[14]

Overcrowded housing and the unsanitary and polluted atmosphere of Pittsburgh and the milltowns made Black migrants extremely susceptible to serious, and sometimes fatal, illness. Between 1915 and 1930, the rate of death per 1,000 people for Blacks in Pittsburgh ranged between 19.1 and 33.8. For Whites in the city, it was substantially lower, 12.0 to 26.3. In the 1920s, most Whites in Pittsburgh who survived their first year did not die until they reached ages 70 through 79. For Blacks, the comparable figures were 35 through 39 years of age. Over half of the deaths among Blacks occurred at age 40 or younger. Only 34.1 percent of all White deaths occurred within this age category. The infant mortality rate which declined for both Blacks and Whites in the 1920s remained substantially higher for Blacks. Between 1918 and 1928 Black infant mortality declined from 215 per 1,000 births to 113.1 per 1,000 births while the White rate dropped from 136 to 74.7. The Pittsburgh Chamber of Commerce in 1926 found that most deaths among the city's Black population were attributable to contagious diseases such as influenza, infantile paralysis, and tuberculosis. Although Blacks made up 8.9 percent of the total population in Pittsburgh in 1928, they accounted for 13.9 percent of all deaths from tuberculosis, 14 percent of all deaths from pneumonia, and 19.9 percent of all deaths from syphilis and gonorrhea.[15]

Upon arriving in Western Pennsylvania, Black Southerners found themselves the immediate victims of several communicable diseases. In 1918, an influenza epidemic killed Black and Whites alike. The percentage of Blacks in Pittsburgh dying from influenza in 1918 was roughly equivalent to their proportion in the total population. During that year, 100 Blacks succumbed to influenza, and they comprised 5.1 percent of all persons dying from the disease. However, it was pneumonia that surpassed all other illnesses as a major cause of death among Black migrants during this period. Some Black newcomers in the Pittsburgh area developed pneumonia after contracting influenza. Often they lay unattended in mill bunkhouses and later died from these ailments unnoticed. For Blacks in Pennsylvania in 1924, the rate of death from this disease was 268.89 per 100,000. A substantially lower rate, 140.31 per 100,000 however, prevailed for Whites. Poorly heated apartments and bunkhouses and very cold winters caused Black migrants in Western Pennsylvania to contract the disease more often than Whites. Similarly, Black steelworkers in the surrounding milltowns inhabited drafty boarding houses and were frequently given job assignments outside during the winter. They, too, died more often from pneumonia than their White counterparts.[16] Homer Daniel, a twenty-year old migrant from Centreville, Georgia came to work in the Duquesne steel mills in late 1917. In January 1918, he died from pneumonia at a company boarding house.[17] In

May 1919, the remains of Luther C. Burney were shipped to Wetumpka, Alabama after his fatal encounter with the dread disease. He, too, had come to Duquesne in 1918 to work in the mills during the wartime labor shortage.[18] Another boarding house resident and mill employee, James Swindell of Clarkson, North Carolina, died of pneumonia in February, 1920.[19] During late December 1919, so many Black steelworkers in the Monessen and Clairton vicinity contracted pneumonia that they comprised over half the patients in the Memorial Hospital in nearby Monogahela City.[20]

The environmental setting and working conditions inside the mills closely paralleled the dismal appearance of Pittsburgh and the steel towns. For everyone, White and Black, work in the steel mills was hot, dirty, and frequently dangerous. The ten-hour days, six days a week, were long, and labor was hard. Even within this context, Black steelworkers usually fared worse than their White counterparts. They received the least desirable jobs. A disproportionate number of them toiled as unskilled workers in labor gangs in the open hearth, blast furnace, and bar mill departments. In these particular areas of the mills, they were directly and consistently exposed to hot molten metal coming forth from the furnaces or rolling through the bar mills. Even when Black steelworkers began working in plants which fabricated red hot billets, these semi-skilled positions in no way exempted them from hot, exhausting labor.[21]

In most mills, Black employees were usually clustered in particular departments where the work was hardest and the conditions least tolerable. At the Jones and Laughlin Steel facility in Pittsburgh, the entire boiler room consisted of Black workers. At the McKeesport Tin Plate Company plant in Port Vue, no Blacks worked in the "hot" mill, "where all the money could be made" and the work was a little easier. Instead, they predominated in the cold roll department, where laborers normally toiled for eleven to twelve hours per shift.[22] Both during and after World War I, the A. M. Byers Company hired a steady stream of Black migrants from the South. Company officials assigned a large number of them to the galvanizing, the bar mill, bell weld, and several finishing departments. In the galvanizing department, for example, zinc was used to coat the wrought iron pipes to prevent corrosion, a process damaging to the health of those who engaged in it. The acid fumes were usually so intense that many Black workers simply quit their jobs. In other departments, the work was either "too hard" or "too heavy." Sid Dickson was hired by A. M. Byers on August 28, 1918, as a laborer in the bar mill department. He quit a day later, because the work was "too hard." Thomas Dicks had come to Pittsburgh in 1918 from Alabama. He became an employee of A. M. Byers on October 18, 1920. After working for a day as a laborer in the No. 3 finishing department, he quit his job, because the work was "too heavy." He was rehired on May 16, 1922, as a laborer in the galvanizing department. On September 14, 1922, he walked off the job because acrid gas from the galvanizing acid became too much to bear. Arthur Hicks, a Black migrant from North Carolina, was hired by Byers on January 13, 1927. He too quit his job in the bell weld department on February 1, 1927 because it exposed him to too much heat.[23]

The hazardous jobs held by Black steelworkers in the mills made them particularly vulnerable to industrial accidents. Moreover, the relative absence of safety enforcement by steel companies aggravated an already dangerous situation. Workers frequently labored close to furnaces and near mill machinery without proper safety precautions and instructions. In 1919, for example, a total of 40,558 industrial accidents occurred among workers in metal products factories in Pennsylvania. Although Blacks comprised 4.6 percent of all workers in iron, steel, and manufacturing pursuits, 8.5 percent of all industrial mishaps victimized them. Similarly, immigrant workers who made up 28 percent of the work force in these heavy industries were affected by 35 percent of the accidents. Native Whites fared best. They composed 64 percent of the work force in Pennsylvania mills and factories, and they experienced 51 percent of all industrial accidents in 1919. Also, a slightly higher percentage of Black workers were the victims of serious and fatal mishaps. Approximately 26 percent of all Blacks in metal products industries suffered severe injuries or death. The percentages for immigrants and native Whites were 24 percent and 22 percent, respectively.

Industrial accidents among Black steelworkers in Western Pennsylvania fitted this statewide pattern. The Jones and Laughlin steel plant in Pittsburgh gained a reputation among recent migrants as a dangerous mill where Black men were frequently hurt or killed.[25] Local newspapers such as the *Duquesne Times* and the *Pittsburgh Courier* made constant references to injuries incurred by Black steelworkers in the local mills. In June 1919, John Jordan, for example, sustained an injury to his side while working in the merchant mill of the Duquesne steel works.[26] John McKeever lost one of his toes while at work in the Duquesne mills later that year.[27]

Other Black steelworkers, however, were not so lucky. One nineteen-year-old migrant from Wilmington, North Carolina, died in June 1923, from burns he received while at work at the Duquesne Steel Works.[28] Another young laborer living in Farrell, met a similar fate. He was an employee at the open hearth department in the Carnegie steel plant in Sharon and was instantly "roasted into a crisp" when a seventy-ton ladle of molten steel poured upon him and five other workers. A cable holding the ladle of steel broke, causing it to upset onto these unfortunate victims.[29] In 1923, three Black steelworkers at the Clairton mill burned when a stream of molten metal flowed onto them in the plant's ladle pit.[30] Another Black steelworker at the MacIntosh-Hemphill foundry in Midland was killed when a steel roll crushed him to death in September 1925. The bar apparently rolled off the giant table, quickly crushing him between it and the opposite wall.[31]

Racial discrimination against Blacks was not limited to places where they worked and lived. Throughout the period under study, public facilities in Pittsburgh and elsewhere would neither admit nor serve Black patrons. In the entire downtown area, only a basement concessionaire in Rosenbaum's Department Store would serve food to a Black customer. No Black could enter a theatre unless he sat in the balcony.[32] Police in Duquesne and other area milltowns frequently arrested Blacks without legitimate cause and treated them with total disrespect. Judges would often use "indecent language" and make "disparaging remarks" to Black defendants.[33]

The influx of Black Southerners into the mill communities of Western Pennsylvania intensified the prejudices of many Whites. The initial presence of Black newcomers in Homestead during the war pushed White residents, particularly steelworkers, to the verge of race riots.[34] Whites in Duquesne reacted very negatively to an expanding Black presence after 1916. Upon their arrival there, these Black newcomers were segregated into company boarding houses very close to the mill-yards. In response to community concerns about the alleged character of these recent Black arrivals, the Duquesne police, on at least three occasions between June and October 1916, arrested Black migrants at their boarding houses for shooting "crap." In each case, groups of seven or eight Black steelworkers were arraigned before the town magistrate and fined. Also during this period of time, John Clark, another Black Southerner imported to the Duquesne mills, was unfairly accused of insulting White women as they passed each other on the street. He was jailed, found guilty, and fined despite questionable evidence and unfair procedures.[35] The editor of the *Duquesne Times-Observer* responded to these "colored visitors and their offensive acts" by suggesting that White townsmen perform "a physical drubbing" of these Black newcomers if their conduct continued to go "beyond the bounds of reason."[36]

By 1923, the growth of the Black population in Johnstown had created a tense racial atmosphere which culminated in a "police riot" against the city's recent Black migrants.[37] Both during and immediately following World War I, the Cambria Steel Company (later renamed Bethlehem Steel), like other manufacturers in Western Pennsylvania, recruited Black Southerners for its mills. The migration caused the town's Black population to increase 262 percent between 1910 and 1920 from 462 to 1,650. In 1923, Johnstown had an estimated 3,000 Blacks living within its borders. Most of them were crowded into Rosedale, a segregated section of town where the majority of the Black population resided in grossly inadequate housing owned primarily by Bethlehem Steel.[38]

The dramatic increase in the number of Johnstown Blacks created anxiety among the town's White residents. As in Duquesne, Blacks suspected even of the slightest misdemeanor were thought to be menaces to the community. These sentiments prompted some Johnstown Whites to organize a chapter of the Ku Klux Klan (KKK) in 1921. White fears about losing jobs to Black migrants and nervousness about "negro invasion" into previously all-White neighborhoods contributed to the growing racial polarization of the Johnstown community.[39]

In 1923, a shooting incident involving a recent Black migrant and the Johnstown police prompted the indiscriminate arrests of Black residents. The mayor, who blamed all the trouble on the Blacks, responded by ordering all of Johnstown's Black newcomers "to pack up" and "go back from where they came." Echoing the mayor's sentiments, local magistrates directed Black defendants appearing before them to leave the city. This unwelcome atmosphere created by the mayor, the police and other town officials, along with heightening racial tensions and increased Klan activity, prompted an estimated five hundred Black steelworkers and their famillies to migrate out of the area.[40]

The rise of the Ku Klux Klan in Johnstown was part of a national revival of this White supremacist organization. Originally founded in 1866 in Tennessee, the KKK intimated and frequently murdered Blacks and their sympathizers during the post–Civil War period for participating in Southern politics and attempting to improve the freedmen's general socioeconomic condition. The revival of the Klan in 1915, and its dramatic growth during the 1920s was due mainly to nativist sentiments and hostility toward Catholics and Jews. The organization, however, did not abandon its traditional antipathy toward Blacks.[41]

During the 1910s and 1920s, the Klan spread throughout the country, and claimed members in scores of cities and towns affected by the Black migration. Johnstown was not the only industrial community in Western Pennsylvania in which the group flourished. Klan organizers initially entered the state in 1921, and chapters soon started in Pittsburgh, Homestead, New Kensington, Connellsville, and Altoona. Other groups were eventually founded in Duquesne, Jeannette, Latrobe, and Vandergrift. By 1924, the Klan boasted a membership of 125,000 in Western Pennsylvania.[42] As in Johnstown, the Klan became active in the steel town of Monessen where scores of Southern Blacks came to work at the Pittsburgh Steel Company. Crosses were frequently burned. This activity lasted into the1930s when at least once a month Klansmen ignited their blazing symbol of White supremacy.[43]

Such separate Black institutions as the church and fraternal organizations served as a refuge from Klan hostility and from racial prejudice in the workplace and in the cities and towns where Black migrants settled. These organizations provided Black workers with familiar religious and social surroundings, and helped them to adjust to their new industrial environment. Several of these institutions in Western Pennsylvania, especially the church, owed their existence to an earlier generation of Black iron and steelworkers who migrated to the area during the late nineteenth and early twentieth centuries. James Claggett, a native of Mt. Zion, Maryland, for example, became an employee at the Duquesne steel works in 1888 and a charter member of the Payne Chapel African Methodist Episcopal Church in 1891. Another early migrant, Samuel Marshall of Halifax, Virginia, was an organizer of Bethlehem Baptist Church in McKeesport in 1889, and an employee at National Tube since 1892.[44]

When World War I started the massive Black migration to Western Pennsylvania during the 1910s and 1920s, a succeeding generation of Black iron and steelworkers joined these existing congregations, and caused their dramatic growth, particularly in Pittsburgh. During this period, the already large membership of Ebenezer Baptist Church rose sharply from 1,500 to 3,000. Central Baptist Church attracted 544 new members during 1917 and early 1918, bringing its total membership to 1,752. Between 1920 and 1926, John Wesley African Methodist Episcopal Zion Church drew 1,200 new members to its congregation.[45]

Black churches in nearby mill communities experienced similar, but less dramatic increases. Jerusalem Baptist Church in Duquesne grew from 40 members in 1915 to 200 members in 1919. Park Place African Methodist Episcopal Church in Homestead increased its membership from 90 in 1916 to over 400 in 1924. Tried Stone Baptist Church in Aliquippa nearly tripled its membership from 136 in 1921 to 382 in 1926.[46]

Black migrants found, however, that some Black churches in the Pittsburgh areas were inhospitable. A few of them, such as Bethel African Methodist Episcopal Church, Grace Memorial Presbyterian Church, and Holy Cross Episcopal Church, all in Pittsburgh, were elitist and drew a color line which disfavored darker-skinned blacks. They also discovered that the style of worship in some existing congregations differed from traditional Southern Black religion, and in some instances they could not exercise their denominational preferences.[47] However, Black migrants pursued a range of alternatives to meet their religious needs.

Figure 5. Reverend Junius Caesar Austin, pastor of Ebenezer Baptist Church in Pittsburgh, whose congregation had a large number of Black steelworkers. Austin led efforts to improve the social and economic condition of Black steelworkers. (Courtesy of Randall K. Burkett, Harvard University.)

Scores of Black newcomers banded together with people from the same areas of the South to found new churches. Between 1916 and 1926, Black migrants in Pittsburgh organized twelve new Baptist congregations. Prior to World War I, Johnstown's small Black population worshipped at Cambria Chapel AME Zion Church and Mt. Olive Baptist Church. The city's Black newcomers preferred to start churches of their own. They established five Baptist churches, three Methodist congregations, and at least three Pentecostal groups between 1917 and 1930. Black migrants to Coraopolis organized two new congregations, a Church of God in Christ and St. James AME Church, in 1925 and 1928, respectively. Blacks who came to the Homestead vicinity organized twenty-three new congregations between 1915 and 1939. Although only ten churches, including four Baptist, three Spiritualist, a Church of God in Christ, and an African Orthodox Science Church survived beyond 1940. They all expressed the desire of migrants to establish their own institutional autonomy in the raciallly segregated environment of Western Pennsylvania.[48]

Other migrants responded to overtures made to them by denominational officials who wished to establish new congregations in the Pittsburgh vicinity. In 1917, the Colored Methodist Episcopal Church gave Bishop Robert A. Carter $2,000 to found the denomination's first congregation in the Smoky City. As a result of these efforts, three CME churches, Carter Chapel, Cleaves Temple, and Beebe, were organized in Pittsburgh by 1926. The denomination also spread to several steel mill communities including Vandergrift, Johnstown, Washington, Monessen and Donora.[49] In 1921, officials of the Black Washington Annual Conference of the Methodist Episcopal Church, North created a Pittsburgh district "to aid in meeting the increasing needs of the colored people coming into the Northern industrial centers." Although Warren Methodist Episcopal Church already existed in Pittsburgh, denominational funds enabled Black preachers to organize three additional congregations in the Smoky City. These ministers also attracted Black migrants to new ME churches in Aliquippa, McKeesport, Beaver Falls and Johnstown. Also during that period, a group of North Carolina migrants, former members of the AME Zion denomination, became dissatisfied with worshipping at Corey Avenue AME

Church in Braddock. With the help of a denominational official, they organized Holliday Memorial AME Zion Church.[50]

The presence of a growing number of dues-paying members allowed several congregations to build or purchase new and expanded facilities. Jerusalem Baptist Church in Duquesne, whose membership had quintupled because of the migration, erected in 1919 a new edifice which seated three hundred people. In the early 1920s, members of Macedonia Baptist Church, also in Duquesne, worshipped in an old dilapidated building, but by 1926, they too had built a new edifice.[51] During this period, Reverend A. W. Watts became the pastor of New Hope Baptist Church in Coraopolis, and his congregation of mostly millworkers demanded "a better place to worship." Consequently, they purchased in 1929 from a White congregation, a building which ranked "among the foremost religious edifices in Allegheny County."[52]

Black steelworkers gained considerable pride from these new church buildings, since they owed their existence to their earnings in Western Pennsylvania mills. Denied integration, recognition, and achievement in area steel plants, migrants

Figure 6. Payne Chapel A.M.E. Church in Duquesne, PA in the early 1930s; many of the town's Black steelworkers and their families attended here. (Courtesy of Mr. and Mrs. Carl O. Dickerson, Philadelphia, PA.)

attained status within Black churches as members, officers, and preachers. Warren White, who migrated to Duquesne from Alabama in 1917, belonged to the Church of the Living God. He served his congregation both as treasurer and deacon. Galloway Robinson, a North Carolina native, came to Duquesne in 1923 and joined Payne Chapel African Methodist Episcopal Church. He held a succession of key positions including Sunday School superintendent, Steward, and class leader. An Alabama migrant, Fred Douglas Hayes, settled in Clairton in 1928. After getting a job with Carnegie Steel, he joined Morning Star Baptist Church, and served on its usher board and as treasurer of the Sunday School.[53]

Occasionally, Black steelworkers pursued preaching while still working in the mills; usually, they ministered to small congregations in outlying steel communities where hundreds of Black migrants settled. Like their parishoners, these steelworker-preachers came to Western Pennsylvania during World War I and the 1920s to improve their economic condition. Two migrants, Reverends J. H. Flagg and Isaac S. Freeman, had belonged to the African Methodist Episcopal Church in their respective Southern states. Flagg, a blacksmith in Enterprise, Alabama, migrated to Johnstown in 1916 to work in the Cambria steel mills. Freeman, a migrant from Blakely, Georgia, came from Philadelphia, to Aliquippa in 1924. Like scores of other Black migrants, he secured a job in the nail mill at Jones and Laughlin Steel. In 1917, Flagg organized Bethel AME Church in Johnstown, and later Freeman founded Ebenezer AME Church in Aliquippa.[54] Similarly, Warren A. Mason, came to Apollo in 1920 from Alexandria, Virginia. After completing his schooling, he held jobs in both the Apollo and Vandergrift mills. The year he arrived in the area, Mason assumed the pastorate of the First Baptist Church of North Vandergrift, a small congregation established in 1918 by Alabama migrants.[55] J. L. Simons migrated from Georgia to McKees Rocks in 1924 to work as a trackman at Lockhart Iron and Steel. In the 1930s, he became the pastor of Baptist Churches in Pittsburgh's West End and in Carnegie.[56]

Perhaps the most prominent of steelworker-preachers was Charles W. Torrey. Born in Carnegie County, Alabama, Torrey migrated in 1917 to Braddock to work at the Edgar Thomson steel works. His call to the ministry drew him to the Keystone

School of the Bible in Pittsburgh. He became pastor of Macedonia Baptist Church in Duquesne in 1937. After bringing dissident members who had formed another church back into Macedonia, he developed it into the town's largest congregation.[57] Some migrants with ministerial aspirations, however, served area congregations as assistant pastors. In Duquesne, for example, William Hall, a Virginian, and William Thomas, a South Carolinian, migrated to Western Pennsylvania in 1921 and 1923, respectively. Both men labored at the Duquesne Steel Works. Hall was assistant pastor at Jerusalem Baptist Church while Thomas held the same position at Payne Chapel African Methodist Episcopal Church. In Braddock, a Black employee at the Edgar Thomson steel works served on the ministerial staff of New Hope Baptist Church.[58]

Whether Black steelworkers were clergy, church officers or ordinary members, many of them looked forward to revivals. As opportunities for social fellowship, diversion, and in some respects entertainment, revivals aided in making life in Northern industrial towns more familiar and comfortable for Southern Black migrants. They were thrilled to see gifted preachers deliver soul-stirring sermons and hear uplifting gospels and spirituals. In 1919, several Black churches held revivals to attract new members and to preserve the distinctive styles of worship and preaching which were characteristic of Southern Black religion. Payne Chapel AME Church in Duquesne planned a series of services "along the line of Methodist revivals."[59] Jerusalem Baptist Church presented a guest preacher to deliver four revival sermons to its parishoners. A total of 215 people heard him and witnessed 49 persons accept membership in the Jerusalem congregation.[60] A few months later, the church brought in another revivalist who preached another series of sermons on five consecutive nights.[61] Park Place AME Church in Homestead planned a three-week revival campaign, with Dr. H. Franklin Bray, "the Rocky Mountain evangelist," and Professor George E. Wright, "the sweet Gospel singer of Chicago," as its guests. Bray preached on several themes, including "The Withered Hand" and "Three Old Wells."[62]

Black churches functioned in a similar way for Black women. Mostly, the wives of Black steelworkers, women in the milltowns of Western Pennsylvania, depended upon churches

Figure 7. Payne Chapel A.M.E. Church in Duquesne, PA, circa 1940. Steelworkers and their families worship at the newly renovated Payne Chapel congregation. (Courtesy of Mr. and Mrs. Carl O. Dickerson of Philadelphia, PA.)

to provide outlets for talent and leadership and as a forum for social fellowship. They joined men in founding Black churches throughout the Pittsburgh area between 1890 and 1930, and they served as officers in important church auxiliaries. Rue Jennings, for example, born in Patrick County, Virginia in 1865, migrated to Duquesne in 1908. She became an organizer and charter member of Macedonia Baptist Church. In later years, she assumed the title of "church mother." Occasionally, Black women, while spouses to millworkers, ministered to them and other laborers as pastors. In Coraopolis, St. Paul AME Zion Church which had been established in 1900 had the Reverend Mrs. U. L. Stout as one of its early pastors. The Reverend Mrs. Carrie Smith served as the minister of the Church of the Living God, Pillar and Ground of Truth in Duquesne. Her death in 1928, however, cut short her ministerial career.[63]

Like Black churches, fraternal organizations provided Black steelworkers with opportunities to participate in their own institutions and to find status and recognition within them. With the exception of the Masons, which Prince Hall started in 1787 in Boston, these fraternal societies began during the nineteenth century, mainly in the post-bellum period. The Improved, Benevolent and Protective Order of Elks of the World (IBPOEW) organized by a Cincinnati Pullman porter in 1898, was the youngest of the groups.[64] These organizations spread to Western Pennsylvania before World War I and included the region's first Black steelworkers among their members. Grafton Miller who had worked at Carnegie steel since 1891 and Wainwright Beckett, a Washington, D.C. native who had labored at Oliver Iron and Steel since 1906, were important members in Pittsburgh's Eureka Lodge of Oddfellows. W. A. "Daddy" Clay, another employee at the Carnegie mills since the 1890s, was a well-known Elk in the Smoky City.[65]

Black lodges proliferated as a result of the migration. During the World War I period, Bluford Cooper, a Duquesne steelworker and a migrant from South Carolina, was an organizer of Enterprise Lodge No. 15, Ancient Free and Accepted Masons. Another wartime migrant, Lewis Green, a native of Georgia, became a steel employee in Duquesne and a member of "the colored Masons" before his death in 1918. Similarly, in 1930, Blacks in Johnstown founded Cambria Lodge No. 54, A. F. and A. M.[66]

Elks' lodges also began in numerous mill communities in Western Pennsylvania. In 1916, 175 initiates formed Monongahela Lodge in Donora. Members who lived in Monessen withdrew a few years later and established Oaky Lodge. Allen Griffey, an employee at the American Chain and Cable Company in Donora, served as an officer.[67] Between 1923 and 1943, at least eight Elks' lodges began in several steel towns including Johnstown, Aliquippa, Midland, Braddock, and others.[68] Paul L. (Red) Payne, a migrant from West Virginia and an employee at the Clairton steel works, started the City of Progress Lodge. Although Payne had worked in the steel mills since 1922, he had secured several leaves of absence during the summer months to play baseball on several Black teams, including the Homestead Grays, two Baltimore clubs, and the Havana (Cuba) Red Sox. As Payne traveled the country, he discovered that racial discrimination restricted the range of establishments willing to provide him and his fellow Black players with food and lodging. Usually they stayed at Black Elks lodges, where meals and bathing facilities were almost always offered to them. This positive exposure to the IBPOEW motivated Payne to found in 1939 an Elks lodge in Clairton. He and other Black steelworkers formed the "If Club." When another group of forty-four men agreed to join, they invited the Elks district deputy, a retired Black Donora steelworker, to organize formally the City of Progress Lodge. Payne became its first exalted ruler.[69] Also in 1939, Black steelworkers in Duquesne, Charlie Lee Dickerson, Thomas Jeffries, and James Griggs, formed an "Elks-to-be Club." Two other steelworkers served respectively as president and secretary. In 1940, an Elks district deputy from Beaver Valley came with an invitation team from the Greater Pittsburgh Lodge to establish Duquesne's J. T. Brandy Lodge.[70]

Both the Masons and the Elks had female auxiliaries although each functioned as autonomous organizations. Both the Order of the Eastern Star of the Masons and the Daughter Elks shared buildings with their male counterparts. Some female secret societies functioned even after the male groups had disbanded. In Duquesne, for example, the wife of a Black steelworker found Unity Court No. 79, Court of Calanthe, the female auxiliary to the Knights of Pythias. Although the Knights apparently lost members in Western Pennsylvania to the Masons and Elks, the Court of Calanthe held their own in competition with the

Eastern Star and Daughter Elks. The ties between the male and female organizations were especially close since spouses and siblings frequently and simultaneously held office. Janie White, for example, was the wife of a Duquesne steelworker. When the Mattie Virginia Prillerman Temple No. 715 of the Improved, Benevolent and Protective Order of Elks of the World was organized in Duquesne in 1940, Mrs. White became the first Daughter Ruler. The temple received its charter the same year as J. T. Brandy Lodge No. 1047 in Duquesne. Her brother, William Patterson, a steelworker whom she reared from childhood, became the first exalted ruler. Temples, some with similar familial patterns, were established between 1920 and 1940 in New Castle, Johnstown, Coraopolis, McKeesport, Rankin, and numerous other mill communities.[71]

Black veterans who could not or preferred not to affiliate with White posts of the American Legion formed their own units after World War I. Like the Masons, Elks, and other fraternal societies, Black veterans' organizations gave steelworkers the chance to operate their own autonomous groups. Plans for a Black post of the American Legion in Monessen began less than a year after the armistice. Black steelworkers in Duquesne who had served in the Armed Forces established the Charles W. Stewart Post No. 532 and attracted a number of local employees. Frank Coleman came to Duquesne in 1915 from Spartansburg, South Carolina to work in the steel mills. After returning from military service, he became a member of the Stewart Legion group. Two other Black migrants to Duquesne from Cornacre, South Carolina and Waverly, Virginia, respectively, had served in the war and joined Coleman as members of the Stewart unit.[72] Two Black legion posts also served Black veterans in the adjacent towns of Braddock, North Braddock, and Rankin. Each of them, the Richard L. Ferguson Post No. 527 and the Robert Smalls Post No. 511, were named for Black soldiers from the triborough vicinity who had been killed in World War I. The two units, which eventually merged, had in 1947, a total of 120 members. [73]

Athletics provided another recreational outlet for Black steelworkers. Steel companies sponsored baseball teams for their Black employees and local Black entrepreneurs established athletic clubs in which Black laborers participated both as players and spectators. Lockhart Iron and Steel in McKees Rocks sponsored senior and junior baseball clubs called the Lockhart Giants. The Homestead Steel Works and Pittsburgh Steel in Monessen also established Black baseball teams.[74]

Although the financial support of the steel companies played an important role in the development of Black athletics in the Pittsburgh area, their efforts paled in comparison to those of Cumberland W. Posey, Jr. and W. A. (Gus) Greenlee. Cum Posey was born in Homestead in 1891. His father, Cumberland Willis Posey, Sr., a Maryland native, who owned both a steamboat and a coal company, apparently left some money to his son. Young Posey became interested in athletics as a basketball player at Duquesne University and Pennsylvania State. He joined in 1911 the Murdock Grays, a baseball team organized in 1900 by Black Homestead steelworkers. In 1912, the team became known as the Homestead Grays. He played as an outfielder and eventually became the manager and over time, the team's part owner. Many of the star players were steelworkers. Some like Paul L. (Red) Payne, an employee at the Clairton steel works, received regular furloughs from the mill to play for the Grays. The team also gave other Black steelworkers a chance to develop into professional full-time players. Take Josh Gibson, for example. Born in 1911 in Buena Vista, Georgia, Gibson came to Pittsburgh in 1923, when his father took a job with U.S. Steel. Gibson, who worked for a brief time in a mill, played for an amateur Black baseball club, the *Gimbels Athletic Club*. He eventually became a catcher for Gus Greenlee's Crawford Colored Giants of Pittsburgh. In 1930, Cum Posey and manager Judy Johnson persuaded him to join the Grays as a star slugger.[75]

Due in part to Posey's business acumen, the Homestead Grays Athletic Club grew to include a basketball team and a retinue of boxers. Additionally, he became secretary-treasurer of the Negro National Baseball League and national commissioner of athletics for the Improved, Benevolent and Protective Order of Elks of the World. Between 1939 and 1942, he organized twenty-eight lodges and temples in the Pittsburgh vicinity into the IBPOEW Athletic Committee of Western Pennsylvania. In 1942, Posey sponsored a National Basketball Tournament in New York. Twin City Lodge in the milltown of Farrell became the contest winner. Furthermore, teams from Beaver Falls, Ali-

quippa, Rankin, New Kensington, and Pittsburgh lodges participated in area elimination games prior to the New York finals.[76]

W. A. (Gus) Greenlee made his money as Pittsburgh's leading Black numbers "king." In 1930, Greenlee bought the Crawford Colored Giants, a baseball team organized by a Black social
worker in the Hill District. He also, in 1932, built his own baseball stadium with $100,000 of his own money. He built his team
by raiding top players from other Black teams including Cum
Posey's Homestead Grays. He stole back Josh Gibson and
acquired other greats like the legendary Satchel Paige.[77] With
such intense athletic competition in their midst, Black steelworkers had much to cheer about.

These various athletic groups played each other regularly,
and drew crowds of area Black residents to games and boxing
matches. On some occasions, they even challenged White baseball and basketball teams. Two Black baseball groups, the
Homestead Steel Club and the Homestead Grays, played a
double-header on Memorial Day in 1919 with each winning a
game. The same year, the Homestead Grays Athletic Club held
a ten-round boxing match between Eddie Carver of Pittsburgh
and Bud Brown of Homestead. Carver won a decision. However, Bill Armistead knocked out a fellow Black Pittsburgher,
Billy Johnson, in the third round of their boxing bout. "A fair
sized crowd" came to Homestead to watch both matches. A
White team, Ray Pryel All Stars of Homestead, played basketball with the Loendi Club, "Pittsburgh's fast colored team."
Similarly, the Black Pittsburgh Steel team played the all-White
Scholastics in baseball in an elimination tournament for the
Monessen city championship. Of course, the rivalries between
the Homestead Grays and the Pittsburgh Crawfords became
classic contests which filled the leisure hours of numerous Black
steelworkers.[78]

Despite the importance of religious, fraternal, and athletic
organizations among Black mill laborers, these groups played a
minor role in the fight for racial equality in the industrial areas
of Western Pennsylvania. Efforts to protect the rights of Black
steelworkers and other Black residents in Pittsburgh and the
surrounding mill communities became a task for the National
Association for the Advancement of Colored People (NAACP)
Founded in 1909, and officially established in 1910, the NAACP

Figure 8. The Duquesne Community Baseball Team sponsored by the Duquesne Steel Works, United States Steel. Black steelworkers on the baseball team are shown with Charles Broadfield, the Black welfare worker at the Duquesne Steel Works (standing third from the right). (Courtesy of Mrs. Colesta Long of Philadelphia, PA.)

was an interracial organzation which sought to protect the legal rights of Black Americans mainly through the courts. During the first several years of its existence, branches were organized in such large cities as New York, Boston, Chicago, Philadelphia, Washington, D.C., and Baltimore. In 1918, the NAACP had 165 branches in thirty-eight states, and a membership of 43,994.[79]

Efforts to start a Pittsburgh branch began in 1915 when a national official came to the city to speak. His listeners responded, and soon the chapter had 285 members. Plans were made to protest the movie, "Birth of a Nation," to work for a national antilynching law, and to achieve the hiring of Black teachers in the public schools. Despite this promising start, however, the Pittsburgh branch made little progress toward becoming a viable chapter.[80] In 1921, the popular Reverend J. C. Austin of Ebenezer Baptist Church, Pittsburgh's largest Black congregation and founder of the Steel City Bank, became the branch president. Austin already had involved his church in meeting the housing, financial, and recreational needs of Black migrants, and he wished to orient the local NAACP toward similar goals. He wanted to stop labor unions, for example, from encouraging the police to arrest migrants for vagrancy with the aim of driving them "back to the flames of the torturing South." He also tried to get Black teachers hired, to place Black students into mixed schools, and to secure the passage of a state civil rights law.[81]

Austin's concern for Black workers also affected Sara Writt, the membership chairman of the Pittsburgh branch. In 1924, scores of Black laborers, particularly steel employees, encountered periodic unemployment. Unemployed Whites usually went to an industrial hotel operated by the Pittsburgh Association for the Improvement of the Poor. Writt wanted the group to extend the same service to Blacks laid off from their jobs. Her efforts, however, failed to attract unanimous support from the Pittsburgh NAACP. There were branch members who thought the organization should avoid "social problems," but focus narrowly upon the legal status of Blacks.[82] As late as 1934, one member complained to Walter White, the national executive director of the NAACP, that the Pittsburgh branch was cliquish and excluded some members from events "which have assumed a social aspect." She declared that "this thing cannot go on in an industrial center such as Pittsburgh" because the branch must reach out "to cover all classes."[83]

Unlike the Pittsburgh Branch, NAACP chapters in the outlying mill communities of Western Pennsylvania tended to have a greater representation of Black laborers. Black professionals, despite their small numbers, sometimes headed these branches, but they espoused issues which were relevant to their working-class constituency. The Donora Branch, founded in 1921 with fifty members, was composed primarily of steel employees.[84] Similarly, the Westmoreland County Branch, based in nearby Monessen and established in 1929, included an overwhelming number of mill workers among its seventy-one members.[85] Led by a local Black dentist, the branch became concerned primarily with police brutality toward Monessen Blacks. They also notified the national office about attempts by town and mill officials to harass Blacks who opposed the local Republican organization. Blacks who backed the independent candidate for the city council "were called before the Superintendent of the Mill and told flatly that they would lose their jobs if they voted against the G.O.P." Though the branch, like most in the Pittsburgh area, was largely ineffective in improving the Black social, economic, and political conditions, Black workers like Sam Spurlock of Monessen still wanted "the support of the NAACP in fighting" for their rights.[86]

The Universal Negro Improvement Association (UNIA) clearly had greater mass appeal among Black steelworkers in the Pittsburgh area than the NAACP. Started in 1914 by Marcus Garvey, a colorful and articulate Jamaican immigrant, the UNIA stressed Black nationalism and Black pride, the redemption of Africa, and the need for unity among Negro people throughout the world. Beginning with a strong base in New York's Harlem, the organization rapidly spread across the United States and other parts of the Western Hemisphere and Africa. During the 1920s, Garvey claimed to have a following between six and eleven million persons in 3,000 branches worldwide. Although these figures were probably exaggerations, several thousand Black Americans did either belong to the UNIA or supported its various self-help enterprises including *The Negro World*, an influential newspaper, and the Black Star Line, an ambitious shipping concern.[87]

The UNIA expanded to almost twenty industrial communities in the Pittsburgh area including such steel towns as Homestead, Duquesne, Clairton, McKeesport, New Castle, and Farrell.[88] In several of these municipalities, Marcus Garvey attracted financial support for many of his UNIA ventures such as the Black Cross Navigation and Trading Company, the Colonization Fund, and the Black Star Line.[89] He gave particular attention to UNIA divisions in Western Pennsylvania, and to problems faced by members and other Black residents in the region. He sent Reverend George Weston, an immigrant from Antigua and a Methodist Episcopal minister, to Pittsburgh in 1921 to settle disagreements between two factions in a UNIA division. In 1923 Garvey denounced the mayor, police, and White workers in Johnstown for driving Black steel employees out of town in the aftermath of racial troubles. He contended that "unemployed Whites were waiting for an opportunity to run" Negroes away from Johnstown "so as to brighten their prospects for employment."[90]

The UNIA also gained some limited support from Black clergymen in the Pittsburgh vicinity who responded to Garvey's emphasis upon racial pride and to his appeals for racial solidarity. The versatile Reverend J. C. Austin of Ebenezer Baptist Church and president of the Pittsburgh NAACP was the best-known backer of Marcus Garvey. He gave an address at the organization's 1922 International Convention, he allowed discussions of Garveyism at his church, and invited UNIA speakers to his pulpit. Reverend John Gibbs St. Clair Drake, a Barbados native and pastor of Bethany Baptist Church in Pittsburgh, served the UNIA as International Organizer. Reverend E. R. Bryant of Braddock Park African Methodist Episcopal Zion Church supported the Braddock Division of the UNIA, and permitted the members to meet in his church.[91]

These clergymen, however, tended to be the exception rather than the rule. The pastor of John Wesley African Methodist Episcopal Zion Church permitted Marcus Garvey and his UNIA followers to meet in his church. The cleric noted "that he had been advised by certain other colored ministers . . . not to allow Garvey to speak, claiming that he was too radical." The Zion pastor retorted that "if radicalism meant telling the truth, he was glad to have Garvey with him." Unlike numerous other

Pittsburgh pastors who owed their membership increases to the Black migration, the minister of John Wesley identified his church with the UNIA, an organization that his parishoners deemed relevant to their quest for social and economic equality.[92]

Black steelworkers believed that the UNIA, unlike the church, could help to protect them from racial hostility and the racist acts of such groups as the Ku Klux Klan. The KKK in Aliquippa boldly burned crosses, held marches, and made speeches against Blacks and the foreign-born. In response to the rise of the Klan, Matthew Dempsey, a recently fired steelworker who had migrated to the area in 1917 from Georgia, organized a local division of the UNIA. Dempsey had heard Garvey deliver speeches in Pittsburgh, and he came away impressed with the organization. He wanted the UNIA to guard Blacks against the Klan, and from racist employment practices at J and L Steel. About fifty persons, mostly Black steelworkers, came regularly to the meetings. When J and L officials uncovered the identity of UNIA members, however, they immediately lost their jobs.[93]

The harassment of Matthew Dempsey, Joe Williams, and other Black steelworkers who belonged to the UNIA in Aliquippa was a part of a larger effort of steel officials and FBI agents to undermine and discredit Garveyism in Western Pennsylvania. Two friends, R. B. Spencer, an FBI official assigned to the Pittsburgh vicinity, and Harry Mauk, Superintendent of the Police Department of Jones and Laughlin's Aliquippa Steel Works, collaborated in checking the spread of the UNIA. Mauk was instrumental in having both Dempsey and Joe Williams relinquish their jobs at J and L Steel for their membership in Garvey's group. Spencer reported that Mauk "is very anxious to see Garvey tried and convicted in order that his influence among the negroes at the Jones and Laughlin Steel plant will disappear."[94]

Mauk and Spencer attended a meeting of the Pittsburgh UNIA held at Gospel Tabernacle, an auditorium owned by J. C. Austin's Ebenezer Baptist Church. At the gathering, Marcus Garvey spoke about "the fundamentals and principles of the UNIA." The two Whites expected him to say something about the United States government, but Garvey wisely "confined his talk to the social equality rights of the negro." In 1922, Mauk reported to H. L. Morgan, another FBI agent about an upcoming UNIA meeting in Aliquippa. Mauk and Morgan were present to hear George Weston deliver a talk in place of Garvey who was delayed in New York City. They were probably surprised that Weston's speech was not "offensive," but "lauded the United States and stated that the hopes of the Universal Negro Improvement Association were centered in the American flag."[95]

Although Weston said nothing treasonous about the United States government, he criticized the opposition of some "colored preachers" to the UNIA. He was probably referring to Reverend W. W. Johnson, the pastor of Emmanuel African Methodist Episcopal Zion Church. Johnson went to Pittsburgh's FBI office to complain to R. B. Spencer about the UNIA. He claimed that many of Aliquippa's 1,500 Blacks, most of them J and L employees, belonged to his congregation, but "now, owing to the teachings of Marcus Garvey, only about one hundred of them attend." He added that "Garvey's representatives have taught and are still teaching them that the bible is simply a White man's bible and is not fit for the negro to read and the hand of the White man is against them." Johnson held that Garvey had so excited local Blacks that a race riot could possibly occur. However, by 1923, when J and L fired some Black employees involved in the UNIA, the group disbanded. The efforts of Mauk and the FBI ultimately succeeded in ridding Aliquippa of Garveyism.[96]

The scourge of racial animosity was thus not absent above the Mason-Dixon line. To be sure, salient differences between the North and South did exist. In Western Pennsylvania, Blacks were free to vote, and since 1866, they could board public conveyances on a nonracial basis. Moreover, Black steelworkers generally earned higher wages than Black laborers in the South. But for many Black Southerners coming to Western Pennsylvania during the war period and the 1920s, there was much to remind them of life in the South. Although statewide Jim Crow laws did not exist in Pennsylvania, local custom and tradition legitimized segregation practices, especially in housing and employment. Public facilities frequently refused to serve Blacks, and almost everywhere they lived in segregated, substandard dwellings with few options to reside elsewhere. To shield themselves from the hostility of Whites, Black migrants relied upon such social institutions as churches and fraternal organizations for status and recognition. They also participated in a variety of racial betterment organizations such as the NAACP and the UNIA to fight against the Klan and other groups wishing to check their social and economic advancement. However, rampant racial discrimination in area mills and foundries placed limits upon the occupational advancement of Black steelworkers in the Pittsburgh vicinity. These factors intensified the problems of adjustment. Labor strikes and periodic unemployment were additional challenges Black migrants had to confront, particularly after World War I.

# 4
# The Steel Strike of 1919 and its Aftermath

The migration of Black Southerners into Western Pennsylvania during and after the First World War gave steel managers a weapon to break the great steel strike of 1919. They knew that employment opportunity in Northern steel mills was important to agrarian Blacks, and that few would deny themselves a chance to improve their economic situation. Consequently, those Blacks who had become employees in the mills during the war, as well as those specifically imported to replace striking steelworkers, remained loyal to their new employers. Like the wartime labor shortage, the steel strike of 1919 represented another rare opportunity for Black workers to secure gainful employment at a decent wage and to escape the less desirable conditions of the South.

By using Black Southerners to end the strike of 1919, steel managers in Western Pennsylvania were following well-established precedents. At various times in the late nineteenth and early twentieth centuries, labor troubles in area iron and steel mills resulted in the importation of Blacks to replace White workers. A puddlers' strike in 1875, for example, was broken when Pittsburgh millowners imported Southern Black iron-workers to keep their furnaces running. In 1888 and 1889 during labor disturbances at the Solar Iron Works in Pittsburgh, Black puddlers remained on their jobs while newly recruited Black Southerners helped them maintain production. In 1907 at

85

Sligo Iron and Steel in Connellsville and in 1909 at the Pressed Steel Car Company in McKees Rocks, mill officials used Blacks to oppose the labor demands of White unionists.[1] In most instances Blacks were unwittingly pitted against striking White workers. The majority of Black laborers in Western Pennsylvania had a deep distrust of labor unions. The American Federation of Labor continued a policy of Black exclusion or separatism. Although resolutions were passed at the 1917 and 1918 national conventions, little was done to organize Black workers.[2] In Pittsburgh, several unions, mostly AFL affiliates, continued to promote either racial exclusion or separatism. The painter's union barred Blacks from joining. The plasterers refused to allow the chartering of a separate local of Blacks. White waiters would not work with Blacks and preferred that they establish a segregated union. A few unions, like the hod carriers and the hoisting engineers admitted Blacks, but these groups proved to be the exception rather than the rule.[3] Consequently, by 1925, only 518 Pittsburgh Blacks were union members. Those who were electrical workers, plumbers, sheet metal workers, and elevator constructors were completely barred from local labor organizations. Other unions such as the bricklayers and carpenters had a few Black members, but discouraged Blacks from joining. The all Black Brotherhood of Sleeping Car Porters had an affiliate in Pittsburgh in 1925, but its 50 members did not significantly increase Black union participation in Western Pennsylvania.[4]

The Amalgamated Association of Iron, Steel and Tin Workers, the organization initiating the 1919 strike, was also responsible for the heritage of anti-unionism prevalent among Blacks in the Pittsburgh vicinity. During World War I the union made a minimal effort to extend membership to Blacks. Most local lodges like the one in New Castle restricted the group to Whites. An exceptional few made a feeble attempt to enlist Black members. In early 1919, primarily because of the upcoming strike, the Amalgamated Association pressured some Blacks to join the Monessen lodge. One of these Black Amalgamated members was Ernest Branch, a local steel employee since 1913. In Johnstown, Walter Hardin, a migrant from Tennessee and a former member of the Industrial Workers of the World, was one of a few Blacks who belonged to the steel union. Despite the presence of Hardin and perhaps a few other Blacks, Amalgamated lodges in Western Pennsylvania consisted mainly of Whites.[5]

The steel strike of 1919, which the Amalgamated Association precipitated, grew out of circumstances related to World War I. The need for uninterrupted wartime production compelled both the federal government and major defense industries to make important concessions to organized labor. The most significant agreement concerned management recognition of shop committees and labor unions as legitimate bargaining agents for plant employees, but not as vehicles to destroy non-union shops. The direct result of this action was a nearly two million member increase within the constituent unions of the American Federation of Labor, the major spokesman for organized workers. Moreover, important agencies of the federal government, such as the Advisory Commission of the Council of National Defense and the National War Labor Board, gave unions a role in formulating vital economic policies pertaining to wartime production. In return for this elevation in status and power, the unions agreed to actively discourage strikes.[6] Wartime inflation did not allow the achievement of this goal. The wages earned by most American workers made it difficult for them to adjust to soaring living costs. A growing realization of this unpleasant truth prompted a flurry of strike activity throughout most of the country. This discontent over wage levels, coupled with labor's growing awareness of its new numerical strength and importance, induced workers from the lumber mills and camps of the Pacific Northwest to the munitions factories of New England to violate the wartime taboo on strikes. Throughout the United States in 1919 there occurred a total of 3,374 strikes and lockouts in which more than 4,112,507 workers were involved.[7]

After the war ended in 1918, and government regulation of industrial relations was terminated, industrialists ended their wartime indulgence of their employees. They became increasingly impervious to labor demands and unsympathetic to union efforts to further organize workers. Furthermore, the return to peacetime production resulted in the layoff of large numbers of wartime laborers. Employers also refused to grant their employees an increase in wages to meet the continuing rise in the cost of living. Another rash of strike activity therefore occurred during 1919. In January, 35,000 shipyard workers in Seattle went on strike. Textile workers in New England followed. In New York City, cigarmakers, shirtmakers, carpenters, bakers, teamsters, and even barbers were making their own efforts to improve working conditions.[8] And finally, in September 1919, the Amalgamated Association of Iron and Steel Workers, anxious to receive increases in pay, an eight-hour day, as well as union recognition, called its own strike against the steel industry.[9]

Because of its traditional disregard for Black steelworkers, the Amalgamated Association won few supporters among this important group of laborers during the 1919 strike. Even a plea to a large gathering of Black steelworkers in Pittsburgh by William Z. Foster of the National Organizing Committee failed to compensate for the previous years of union neglect.[10] Moreover, many of these workers had recently migrated into the area from the agrarian South and had little if any acquaintance with labor organizations. Consequently, the majority of Black steelworkers in Western Pennsylvania were either uninformed or unconcerned about the forthcoming strike. William Henry Harrison, a North Carolinian working in the Homestead steel mills, knew nothing about the shutdown until it actually occurred. Like Harrison, Edward Lipscomb, a migrant from Virginia and an employee in the Duquesne steel works, was uninformed about the Amalgamated Association, and simply ignored the strike.[11] Black steelworkers throughout the area were likewise unresponsive to the September strike call. Of the 1,737 Black employees at the Homestead steel works, only eight joined the union, and only one went on strike. Just six out of 300 Black steelworkers at the Carnegie steel plant in Clairton struck against the company. None of the 344 Black employees of the Duquesne steel works joined the walkout.[12]

Black Southerners were easily recruited into the steel mills of Western Pennsylvania during the 1919 strike because they were plentiful, available, and anxious to migrate northward to secure more lucrative employment. According to one official of the Pittsburgh Urban League, word had spread that "good jobs" could be gotten in the steel industry during the strike, and many Black Southerners responded. At one point during the labor unrest, a group of 300 Blacks from Alabama, along with a contingent of 65 Kentucky and Tennessee Blacks, were imported into Western Pennsylvania.[13] A labor agent from Carnegie Steel secured Black workers in Virginia for the company's Duquesne mills, its Carrie Furnaces in Rankin, and its other area facilities.[14] The Pittsburgh Steel Company in Monessen used Black recruiters from Monessen and Charleroi to go South to lure Blacks to Western Pennsylvania to replace striking workers.[15] Since few Black Southerners could earn 64 cents an hour, a prevailing rate in the Northern steel industry, a job in Pittsburgh area mill, even during a strike, was a definite opportunity and a sure way to escape depressed living conditions in the South.[16]

Steel companies in Pittsburgh and throughout most of the outlying mill towns brought in Black Southerners to replace their striking workers. Carnegie Steel, according to one black Virginian, usually dispatched its imported laborers to its various area plants from a designated point in Pittsburgh. These workers quickly filled vacant posts in Homestead, Rankin, Braddock, and Duquesne steel works.[17] At the Carnegie plant in Homestead, Blacks secured such previously racially exclusive positions as shearman and shearman helper.[18] Some even temporarily filled skilled positions. At one plant, the Edgar Thomson Steel Works in Braddock, they, along with the mill's regular Black employees, maintained production and comprised "the majority of the workers."[19] In Monessen, the Pittsburgh Steel Company shuffled them across several departments to satisfy shifting labor demands in its many mills. In both the Braddock and Monessen mills, Black steelworkers "worked, slept, and ate" inside or near the plant facilities. Armed guards protected them and commissary workers fed them. Newly imported Blacks, together with Black and White steelworkers who remained loyal to the steel companies and who drifted back to work during the strike, helped to maintain production in several key steel plants throughout Western Pennsylvania.[20]

The use of Black workers to defeat the demands of White unionists in Northern areas during and just after the war usually sparked violent interracial clashes. The riots in East St. Louis in 1917 and in Chicago in 1919 stand out as the most extreme examples.[21] Similar encounters occurred in Western Pennsylvania during the 1919 steel strike. The use of Blacks both as production workers and as temporary law enforcement officers in area mill towns ignited tremendous ill feeling among striking White steelworkers. In Rankin, White pickets at the Carrie Furnaces frequently barred the mill entrance to Black strikebreakers on their way to work. A Black steelworker in Duquesne who stayed on in spite of the strike earned extra money as a garbage truck driver. On one occasion, as he was attending his duties, a group of White unionists accosted him and turned over his vehicle.[22] In a more serious incident, several White men in Monessen ambushed and wounded two Black steelworkers returning from work in late October 1919.[23]

The importance of steel manufacturing to local town economies in Western Pennsylvania gave the industry great influence upon municipal governments throughout the region. Consequently, during the strike, local police were directed to guard Black strikebreakers, protect plant properties, and arrest recalcitrant White strikers. This evidence of company power and dominance caused deep resentment among Amalgamated Association members. Moreover, the hiring of Black deputies to help keep the peace in these mill communities generated even more hostility toward the steel companies and greater enmity toward Black steelworkers. The recruitment of Blacks to discharge these special responsibilities was more of an attempt by town and company authorities to degrade White strikers than to enhance the status of Blacks in these temporary positions. Moreover, steel officials knew that the union's failure to bring migrants into the Amalgamated Association made Black steelworkers unsympathetic with the strikers. In Duquesne, as in other milltowns affected by the strike, municipal authorities established a safety committee to maintain law and order. C. H. Giles, a Black barber in Duquesne, belonged to the committee. Black deputies, many of them steelworkers, received their badges and instructions from him. Afterwards they went to stand guard on the premises of the Carnegie Steel Company.[24] As in Duquesne, the presence of Black deputies in Monessen enraged steel unionists and their many sympathizers. They accused these Black law enforcement officers of incompetence, and blamed them for promoting lawlessness and violence. A member of the Amalgamated local in Monessen denounced town officials for being U.S. Steel [sic] bosses, and castigated them for hiring deputies of such questionable character.

> . . . about three weeks ago [late September 1919]the burgess swore in as deputies all the men he could find, mostly negroes . . . Sometimes they (the deputies) would search a fellow for weapons, and if he happened to have some money they would take it from him and (even) threaten to shoot him . . . That's an example of law and order in Monessen.[25]

His testimony was corroborated by a local organizer for the United Mine Workers who described Black deputies as "professional gamblers" and "the riff raff of Monessen"

> . . . they started a reign of terror in the town . . . Men were jostled along the street at the points of pistols, and men were struck down and shot down . . . ?[26]

Near the Lawrenceville mills in Pittsburgh scores of Amalgamated members attempted to harass a non-striker on his way home from work. An altercation occurred between the police and the strikers. During the clashes a Black emergency policeman suffered a fractured skull after White strikers beat him on the face and head.[27]

White unionists, however, reported several reputed incidents in Monessen involving Black deputies and their seemingly innocent and unassuming victims. In one incident, John Komer, an immigrant from Europe, heard gunshots near his home. Komer, a striking steelworker, and his neighbor met outside to inquire about the trouble. After standing for only a few minutes, "two negro deputies came to the steps of his home . . . struck Komer with a gun, hitting his face and eye." When his wife tried to retrieve him into their home, a White city policeman, who had come onto the scene, "with the aid of negro deputies . . ." pried Komer away from her. Komer was asked why he was not working. In answer to this question, he told a judge after his arrest that his sympathies lay with the steel strike. He was therefore fined ten dollars. The Black deputy who allegedly beat him was also fined ten dollars, but his partner was released without penalty. Both of Black deputies had their guns returned.[28] Animosities stemming from such incidents only heightened racial tensions between Black workers and White unionists. Moreover, the memory of these confrontations gave Amalgamated Association members cause to blame Black mill laborers, especially those imported from the South, and Black deputies for breaking the strike and retarding the growth of trade unionism.

When the strike finally ended in November 1919, widespread denunciation of Black workers occurred. Union supporters, bitter over their strike defeat, constantly muttered, the "niggers did it." William Z. Foster, an Amalgamated Association official, joined in by criticizing Black workers for trying to solve their (economic) problems by "breaking down the White working man."[29] However, the union's consistent refusal to recruit Black workers into its ranks, especially during the recent wartime migration, encouraged these Black Southerners to do precisely what Foster deplored, that is, to seek selfish economic gains in total disregard of the larger issue of labor solidarity.

Steel companies in the important industrial states of Illinois, Indiana, and Pennsylvania recruited approximately 30,000 Blacks to break the 1919 strike.[30] Although the number specifically involved in the Pittsburgh area is unknown, it was certainly true that a solid core of regular Black employees, as well as imported Black Southerners, enabled key steel mills in Western Pennsylvania to continue operation. Steel plants in Pittsburgh, Homestead, Rankin, Duquesne, Braddock, Clairton, Monessen, and Donora had been important destinations for migrating Black Southerners during the war. Consequently, when the strike came in 1919, these same plants lured additional Black laborers into the area to replace their striking White employees. For many of these workers, the steel strike, like the wartime labor shortage, represented another chance for them to secure employment in the steel industry of Western Pennsylvania and leave behind all the social and economic encumbrances of a Jim Crow existence in the American South.

Because the 1919 strike coincided with the migration of Black Southerners into Northern areas, these workers became an important weapon of steel owners and managers in their conflict with striking steelworkers. It was certain that few of the mills' regular Black employees or imported strikebreakers would consider supporting the union and lose precisely what the steel companies had allowed them to obtain — gainful employment in Northern industry. Of course, Black steelworkers had good reason to individually pursue their own economic interests. The Amalgamated Association did not welcome their membership, nor did they make a major effort to alert them about the reasons for the upcoming strike.

Throughout the 1920s the steel companies exploited this racial division among their workers and maintained a mutually beneficial employment arrangement with Black Southerners. When the mills needed labor, Black workers willingly migrated out of the South into Western Pennsylvania to satisfy these manpower demands. This unofficial arrangement benefited the owners of the steel industry; it did not always benefit the Black workers. When production cutbacks occurred, Black migrants, not company officials, bore the brunt of unemployment. Although Southern Blacks were still anxious to come North, job opportunities, once so plentiful during the war, were no longer so readily available during industry contraction. The persistence of Black migration into Western Pennsylvania during the early 1920s, in spite of sharply reduced job opportunities, disclosed continued Black discontent with conditions in Southern agriculture rather than assured employment opportunities in Northern industry.

Immediately after the war, shifts to peacetime production put Black laborers out of work throughout the steel region. In May 1919, a special agent from the Division of Negro Economics in the United States Department of Labor visited New Castle, and reported "large numbers of colored men . . . unemployed due to the reduction of forces in the plants."[31] He also saw "a great many unemployed Negroes in Braddock and McKeesport" who were furloughed because of mill "shutdowns."[32] In the summer of 1920, another downturn in the steel industry caused additional layoffs of Black workers.

When such layoffs occurred, Blacks normally experienced greater attrition than any other group of laborers. During the recession of 1920–1921 the number of Black laborers in Allegheny county fell from 16,726 to 10,010, a decrease of 40.2 percent. The reduction of immigrant workmen from 82,515 to 54,477 yielded a decrease of only 34 percent. In the key steel milltowns, the reduction of Black employees was even more dramatic. In Braddock, the force of Black workers dropped from 1,548 to 702, a 54.7 percent reduction. The force of immigrant workmen fell from 4,961 to 3,634, a decrease of only 26.7 percent. Similarly, in Duquesne, the number of Black workers fell from 569 to 252, a 50.7 percent decrease. The force of immigrant workmen dropped from 3,021 to 2,668, a reduction of 23.9 percent.[33] During January 1921, within the space of twelve days, 2,100 Black men, many of them steelworkers, poured into the Provident Rescue Mission in Pittsburgh in search of employment referrals and material relief. In one week, the Pittsburgh Urban League received 1,027 applications for only eight available jobs.[34] However, these adverse employment conditions caused only a temporary reduction in the Black migration to Western Pennsylvania, and by the fall of 1922, when the latest recession in the Pittsburgh steel district ended, the influx of Black Southerners into the area recommenced.

Many Blacks returned South during these postwar cutbacks in mill production.[35] When steelmaking resumed, an insufficient number of Black steelworkers were available for recall or rehiring. Therefore, another effort was made to revive a large-scale Black migration from the South. As in World War I, employment ads were placed in Black newspapers and labor agents began traveling and speaking once again about the higher wages and better social conditions for Black workers in Western Pennsylvania.[36] Because the boll weevil was still ravaging Southern agriculture, and Jim Crow continued unabated, rural Blacks who had not participated in the wartime migration finally decided to leave the South in the fall of 1922 and early 1923. A small but important group of newcomers were Black Southerners who had been wartime migrants. Many had been laid off or had become disenchanted with living conditions in Western Pennsylvania. Some had been drafted into the Army. For these and other reasons, they returned South, and later returned to the Pittsburgh vicinity because jobs and better wages were there. A migrant from Chattanooga, Tennessee wanted to return to Pittsburgh in January 1923. He had lived in the city and worked at Carnegie Steel until:

. . . the army draft took me from there in the fall [of] 1917 and I haven't been able to get back since . . . I would like . . . to come back up there because there's (no work) down here.[37]

Still another former Black steelworker from Kinston, North Carolina, expressed an interest in returning to the Pittsburgh area. He had worked in Monessen at the Pittsburgh Steel Company for 15 months during 1920 and 1921. Apparently he had become angry with his superiors at the plant's nail mill because of work assignments outside, especially during the winter. He was receptive to working at any area mill as long as he was offered "an inside job."[38] Another migrant had labored at the Homestead steel mills in 1916, but he eventually left because he disliked working at night. After a few years back in Lowryville, South Carolina, he regretted his decision to leave Homestead. Postwar recovery in the Pittsburgh area enticed him northward again. This time he decided to settle in Western Pennsylvania permanently, in the vain hope that he could get "a daytime job."[39] Those Black steelworkers remaining in Pittsburgh, Duquesne, Braddock, and other mill communities in spite of postwar unemployment were soon joined by these new and veteran migrants from the South, and together they reconstituted a substantial force of Black laborers in the steel industry of Western Pennsylvania. As a result of this second wave of migration, the number of Black steelworkers increased from about 7,000 or 13 percent of the work force in 1918 to at least 16,900 or 21 percent of the work force in 1923.[40]

Nonetheless, another in a series of "business depression(s)" hit the steel industry late in the summer of 1923. Between August 1923 and November 1924, Black employment in the major steel plants in the area declined dramatically. The number of Black steelworkers at the Carnegie mills, for example, dropped from 6,759 to 2,300. Similarly, at Jones and Laughlin, the Black employment rate plunged from 2,900 to 1,200, and at Pressed Steel Car it decreased from 1,700 to 500.[41] (See Table 7.)

An economic upswing in several steel mills throughout the Pittsburgh area was evident again by August 1925 (See Table 7.) At that time the *Pittsburgh Courier* announced the reopening of the Aliquippa Works of Jones and Laughlin Steel and local mills of the Carnegie Steel Company.

All in all the industrial situation in this vicinity shows a more healthy outlook than has been presented for the past 18

**TABLE 7. Black Workers in Selected Steel Mills in the Pittsburgh Vicinity 1923–1925**

| Plant | August 1923 | November 1924 | March 1925 |
|---|---|---|---|
| Carnegie Steel | | | |
|   City Mills | | | 680 |
|   Homestead | | | 1,500 |
|   Duquesne | 6,758 | 2,300 | 720 |
|   Clairton | | | 600 |
|   Braddock | | | 1,150 |
| Jones and Laughlin (4 plants) | 2,900 | 1,200 | 2,000 |
| National Tube | 800 | 500 | 706 |
| Pressed Steel Car Co. | 1,700 | 500 | 832 |
| Pittsburgh Iron and Forge | 150 | 70 | 123 |
| American Steel and Wire | 880 | 400 | 450 |
| Oliver Iron and Steel | 150 | 70 | 123 |
| Crucible Steel | 650 | 125 | 270 |
| A. M. Byers | 350 | 240 | 260 |
| Lockhart Iron and Steel | 350 | 270 | 300 |
| Mesta Machine Company | 30 | 25 | 25 |
| Fort Pitt Malleable Iron Co. | 250 | 100 | 125 |
| Pgh. Steel, Monessen | 200 | 118 | 157 |
| Standard Steel Car, Butler | 475 | 250 | 250 |
| Reliance Steel Casting Co. | — | 35 | 51 |
| Totals | 15,643 | 6,213 | 10,322 |

Source: Ira De Augustine Reid, "The Negro in Major Industries and Building Trades of Pittsburgh" (M.A. thesis, University of Pittsburgh, 1925), p. 10a.

months . . . with the coming of good times on the eve of Fall, a period of unusual prosperity seems 'just beyond the hill' [for] . . . colored workmen . . .[42]

However, for the first time since the effort had begun during the war, the companies made no attempt to revive Black migration into Western Pennsylvania. During the interludes of slackened industrial production, general cutbacks in employment occurred in steel plants thoughout the region and were not fully rescinded during the intervening periods of recovery. Between 1920 and 1930 the total number of plant employees in Pittsburgh declined from 38,628 to 28,244. Layoffs and the federal immigration restriction law of 1924 reduced the number of foreign-born laborers from 18,163 or 47 percent of the work force, to 10,389 or 37 percent of the work force. Since the retention rate for native White steelworkers was significantly higher than for other groups of laborers, they clearly suffered the least from the recession periods. Although their total numbers decreased slightly, from 15,216 to 14,923 between 1920 and 1930, their percentage in the work force rose from 39 percent to 52 percent. More sharply restricted job opportunities for incoming Black Southerners therefore resulted. Thus, the number of Black steelworkers in Pittsburgh dropped from 5,249 or 13 percent of the work force to 2,932 or 10 percent of the work force. (See Table 8.) This pattern was repeated in other milltowns throughout Western Pennsylvania.[43] Consequently, in the spring of 1926, the executive director of the local Urban League, John T. Clark, began to discourage any further migration into the Pittsburgh area because of these more limited employment opportunities:

> Negro workmen from the South and other places who are planning to make a change should be very certain that they are going to a definite job at an adequate wage before making a move. Conditions this Spring while gradually improving are likely to work a serious hardship upon persons finding themselves in this industrial center with no acquaintances and with few resources . . .[44]

Several steel firms, in answering a questionnaire submitted to them by the League, stated that "there (will not be) a great demand for additional labor in our mills this Spring." The League advised the following to prospective migrants:

> Don't come to Pittsburgh looking for work unless you have friends here who have written you to come or that you have sufficient money to float you for at least a couple of weeks.[45]

**TABLE 8. Iron and Steelworkers in Pittsburgh 1910–1930**

| Racial or Ethnic Group | 1910 | | 1920 | | 1930 | |
|---|---|---|---|---|---|---|
| | Number | Percentage | Number | Percentage | Number | Percentage |
| Native White | 8,630 | 29 | 15,216 | 39 | 14,923 | 52 |
| Foreign-Born White | 20,574 | 68 | 18,163 | 47 | 10,389 | 37 |
| Black | 789 | 3 | 5,249 | 13 | 2,932 | 10 |
| Totals | 29,993 | 100% | 38,628 | 100% | 28,244 | 100% |

Source: U.S. Department of Commerce, Bureau of the Census, *Thirteenth Census of the United States, 1910: Population (Occupations)*, 4:590–591; U.S. Department of Commerce, Bureau of the Census, *Fourteenth Census of the United States, 1920: Population (Occupations)*, 4:1197–1198; U.S. Department of Commerce, Bureau of the Census, *Fifteenth Census of the United States, 1930: Population (Occupation by States)*, 4:1416.

Slowdowns in the steel industry occurred in late 1927. Overproduction of such items as pig iron and fluctuations in the demand for such products as rails, pipes, agricultural implements and materials for auto manufacturing caused "seasonal slackening[s]" in the steel industry throughout the 1920s.[46] The new executive director of the Pittsburgh Urban League, Alonzo Thayer, observed:

> A serious readjustment is going on in this Pittsburgh district now. Industry is working on a three-to-four day basis, with about 6 percent of its force of two years ago, so that in addition to many men who are out of work, [there are] those men who do not make full time . . .[47]

A few months later, a prospective migrant from St. Louis wrote the Pittsburgh Urban League to inquire about a job. A League official quickly replied:

> You did a very wise thing to write before coming to this city for employment. Hard as it may seem there, we would not advise you to come here, as work is extremely dull in this district.[48]

Such conditions precluded any further migration into Western Pennsylvania. For the executive director of the National Urban League, this situation posed a serious dilemma, and he sought advice from an official of the Pittsburgh affiliate:

> . . . I sent a release out to the colored newspapers which told of crowded and unemployment conditions in the North generally and advised against coming at this time unless provisions had been made for a job in advance. One newspaper did not publish this because it felt that we were discouraging migration . . . It seems to me we must choose between presenting actual conditions, knowing that we will be misunderstood and misquoted [or] remaining silent when people want advice . . .[49]

This contraction of employment opportunity in the steel industry of Western Pennsylvania in the late 1920s diminished the constant stream of Black migrants coming into the area. The acquisition of a stable and permanent force of Black steel-workers, the defeat of unionism in the industry, and limited plant expansion made any further Black migration to the Pittsburgh vicinity unnecessary. The steel companies, however, discovered that the mere offer of a job was not enough to retain the migrants who had come and stayed. Blacks had left the South to look for better employment opportunities and improved social conditions. Poor working and housing conditions in Pittsburgh and the surrounding milltowns were sources of potential discontent and could conceivably disturb employment arrangements within steel plants. The steel strike of 1919, though defeated, had frightened employers. In order to maintain steady and orderly production processes, the steel companies became particularly concerned with the settlement and adjustment of Black steelworkers to the work regimen of the mills and to life in the milltowns. It was necessary to keep this group of nonunion laborer loyal to them. The generally favorable experience with Blacks during the strike of 1919 — an experience which helped the steel companies to deny the demands of militant White workers — contributed to the creation of welfare programs which became characteristic of the paternal relationship between steel managers and their Black employees during the 1920s.

# 5
# Welfare Capitalism and Black Steelworkers, 1916–1930

The work performance of Black Southerners in the mills and foundries of Western Pennsylvania generally satisfied area steel owners and managers. During the wartime labor shortage, sizeable groups of unskilled laborers were especially needed in the mills' power houses, cupola, open hearth, and blast furnace departments, where "hot jobs" predominated and where turnover among White and foreign-born steelworkers was particularly high. Company officials assigned Black migrants to these departments in large numbers, and by the end of the war, they had demonstrated their suitability to industrial labor. In 1924 the Pittsburgh Committee on the National Association of Corporation Training gave Black steelworkers its highest rating in "hot and wet work, as helpers to skilled workers," and especially in "work requiring speed."[1] Once the mills' experiment with Black workers had proven successful, industry officials committed themselves to the continued use of this large available pool of unskilled laborers. Many had already concluded that "the Negro in industry is here to stay."[2]

Steel managers in Western Pennsylvania had compelling reasons for wanting to retain Blacks as a permanent part of their labor force. First, the continuing new supply of European immigrants, a group upon whom the steel industry had relied for unskilled laborers since the 1890s and early 1900s, had been all but eliminated by the exigencies of World War I and by restrictive federal immigration legislation enacted in 1924. Second, when large numbers of Black Southerners entered the mills both during and after the war, they apparently demonstrated their work superiority over foreign-born laborers. A Central Tube Company official believed that Blacks were "400 percent more efficient than foreign-born men."[3] An executive at Carnegie Steel added that the inability of many foreign-born laborers to understand instructions given to them in English made Blacks much more desirable as workers.[4] Third, most steel officials were convinced or preferred to believe that foreign-born workers inspired by the recent Russian revolution had been responsible for the steel strike of 1919. Blacks, on the other hand, did not support the strike and did not join the union. One foundry manager knew from his own experience that Black workers had not been "influenced by radical or anarchistic propaganda."[5] Finally, poor economic conditions for Blacks in the agricultural South persisted into the postwar period, and industry officials could still profitably tap this vast source of domestic workers for their mills and foundries in Western Pennsylvania.

Newly hired Blacks were not, however, wholly satisfied with their place in the steel mills. Many complained about "the hard, dirty, disagreeable, low-paying jobs" that most of them held. Others had grievances about "the lack of advancement" for Blacks in several area plants.[6] Black laborers in Pittsburgh, Homestead, Clairton, Braddock, and other mill communities expressed discontent about poor and unsanitary housing. In Erie, a special government agent from the Division of Negro Economics identified overcrowded bunkhouses and "hastily erected camps" as the primary causes for unrest among Black steelworkers there.[7] The phenomenally high turnover rates among Blacks in area steel mills were primarily attributable to these and other complaints. During the war, the average length of employment for Blacks was one month. By 1924, it had risen to only three and one half months.[8] In 1919, poor housing conditions caused Herman Boston to quit his job at A. M. Byers after two weeks at work. After twelve days on the job, another Byers employee quit because of a reduction in wages. A migrant from Mississippi endured the galvanizing fumes at Byers for a little less than a month until he quit in February 1923.[8] Turnover among Black employees signified dissatisfaction with mill labor and with the general environment of Western Pennsylvania. The steel companies decided to ameliorate these conditions and remove the sources of discontent through a variety of programs which was known as welfare capitalism.

Mill and factory officials and other businessmen throughout industrial American sponsored welfare work among their employees long before the World War I Black migration to Western Pennsylvania. During the late nineteenth and early twentieth centuries, manufacturers established a wide range of programs to encourage loyalty, cooperation, and contentment in their workers. George M. Pullman, owner of the Pullman Palace Car Company, developed an elaborate model community for his employees near Chicago in the 1880s. William Filene Sons Company in Boston operated a cooperative association which administered a variety of groups and services for its workers. The welfare secretary could also intercede and settle questions of pay and hours for an aggrieved employee. The National Cash Register Company in Dayton, Ohio provided a library and reading room for its laborers. It also sponsored a Sunday School, several choral and musical groups, and an educational program. H. J. Heinz in Pittsburgh employed a welfare secretary who hired and fired workers, and who provided the employees with counseling. To augment these efforts, the company started a recreation room, a relief association, and special facilities for female employees.[10]

By designing and supporting programs for acclimatizing Black Southerners to the social and industrial environment of the Pittsburgh vicinity, steel companies were following well-established precedents. In 1906, the Midland Steel Company founded the town of Midland, Pennsylvania. In 1911, when ownership of the mills passed to Crucible Steel, it formed the Midland Improvement Company, which assumed control of 600 acres of land on which model homes were constructed for employees. Crucible Steel also donated a public park, a band stand, and a playground for steelworkers and their families. At the Carnegie steel works in Duquesne, the company made special efforts to devise elaborate recreational programs for mill-town residents. There were film showings three times a week on the premises of company-built playgrounds and swimming pools and summer classes in sewing, wood carving, and folk dancing. Because of its large number of immigrant workmen during this prewar period, local company officials hired teachers to instruct them in English. In August 1913, the Carnegie plant in Duquesne hired a visiting nurse, who offered advice and secured medical care for all milltown residents. She dispensed charity to the town's poor and found jobs for unemployed youth. She initiated a Little Mothers Club in which milltown women learned sewing, baby care, and other domestic skills. Andrew Carnegie, the best known of the steel magnates, was already famous for his company-initiated and his own personal philanthropies. In practically every milltown in Western Pennsylvania where a Carnegie facility was located, there was a free public library donated by the company. In 1914 in Braddock, the site of the Edgar Thomson Works, Carnegie's first steelmaking venture, New Hope Baptist Church, a Black congregation, received a pipe organ from this now well-known philanthropist.[11]

Steel managers initiated welfare work and supported agencies and institutions within Black communities throughout Western Pennsylvania in order to improve morale and substantially reduce turnover among newly hired Black employees. By creating more favorable living circumstances and providing personnel to supervise the leisure time of Black steelworkers, company officials believed that migrants would be more inclined to stay in the Pittsburgh vicinity, lessen the incidence of turnover, and reduce the need for recruiting a new supply of laborers from the South. Like Americanization programs for immigrant workers in preceding years, welfare work among Black migrants was aimed primarily at making them dependable, efficient, and compliant laborers for the steel companies. Moreover, welfare programs made it unnecessary for plant officials to organize Blacks into company unions. They believed that loyalty to company interests, aims ordinarily pursued through management-initiated organizations, could be more easily accomplished by encouraging welfare work among Black steel employees.

The impetus for hiring Black welfare workers to function as liaisons between steel managers and Black workers came from officials of the Pittsburgh Urban League, an organization which originally started in 1915 as the Pittsburgh Council of Social Ser-

vices Among Negroes. When it became an affiliate of the
National Urban League in 1918, the group began efforts to help
Black newcomers find jobs and housing in the Pittsburgh area.
Problems confronting Black laborers in the mills, however, drew
their immediate attention. Black steelworkers did not accept the
assignment of foreign-born straw bosses or gang leaders to
oversee their labor. These deputy foremen coaxed work out of
the newly hired Blacks and drove them with "rough handling."
Since this treatment offended scores of migrants, many of them
quit their jobs and sought employment in other plants and
foundries. To remedy the problem of turnover, leaders of the
Pittsburgh Urban League in 1918 persuaded steel managers to
hire Black welfare workers.[12]

Several steel firms immediately responded to the League's
suggestion. The Pittsburgh Steel Company in Monessen, Lockhart Iron and Steel in McKees Rocks, and Carnegie steel plants
in Homestead and Duquesne quickly hired Black social service
workers. The Pittsburgh Forge and Iron Company and the Braddock and Clairton Works of Carnegie Steel eventually followed
by attracting their own Black welfare officials.[13] These firms
carefully selected these social service officers because of the
importance they attached to reducing turnover and retaining
Blacks as permanent, nonunion employees. Officials at the
Homestead Steel Works hired Grover Nelson, an employee at
Belfield Dwellings, a residential hotel in Pittsburgh. Nelson, a
native of Columbus, Ohio, was born in 1890 and was an alumnus of Wilberforce University. A friendly White physician who
lived at Belfield suggested that he seek the personnel position
at the Homestead mills.[14] William P. Young of East Orange, New
Jersey, became the welfare officer at Lockhart Iron and Steel in
McKees Rocks in 1918. Young earned the bachelor of arts and
master of arts degrees at Lincoln University in Pennsylvania,
and once taught English, German, and Forensics at his alma
mater. Robert Earl Johnson who was born in Harrisonburg, Virginia had an athletic background when he became the welfare
worker at the Edgar Thomson steel works in Braddock in 1920.
He was a graduate of Morgan State College in Baltimore, Maryland, and was well known as a cross-country runner. He established in Braddock the Edgar Thomson Community Club for
Men and Boys.[15]

Unlike most other industrial plants in the area, the Carnegie Steel Works in Duquesne had a motley succession of several Black welfare officials during World War I and the 1920s. Paul G. Prayer, before coming to Duquesne, worked as a labor representative for businessmen in both Connecticut and Virginia. He recruited 1,500 Southern students to work for the Connecticut Leaf Tobacco Growers Association in Hartford between 1915 and 1917. He then took a similar position at the Newport News Shipbuilding and Dry Dock Company in Virginia, a firm with 4,500 Black employees. From there, he came to the Duquesne steel works. Prayer was succeeded in the early 1920s by Macon D. Lennon, a native of Lumberton, North Carolina and an alumnus of Shaw University in Raleigh, where he was probably trained as a teacher. In 1924, Lennon hired an assistant, Ira J. K. Wells, a writer at the influential *Pittsburgh Courier*. Wells, who worked with Lennon for about a year and a half, was born in Arkansas and was a recent graduate of Lincoln University in Pennsylvania. Another Black welfare official, Charles Marshall, began work in Duquesne during the 1920s, but eventually relinquished his responsibiities to Charles Broadfield, a native of Hampton, Virginia. Broadfield was born in 1897 and attended Hampton Institute to learn the blacksmith trade. He served in the army during World War I in France, and in 1921 he came to Duquesne to become a Black steelworker.[16]

A major part of the official responsibilities of Black welfare workers initially involved the recruitment of Black laborers during World War I and the 1920s. Grover Nelson, the welfare official at the Homestead steel works, traveled widely in Virginia and North Carolina, but he paid particular attention to the Old Dominion city of Lynchburg. He went to the South with a specific idea of how many men his employers needed. After he carefully chose the prospective employees, he used company funds to pay their fares to Homestead. Similarly, Macon Lennon, the welfare officer at the Duquesne steel works, did most of his recruiting in North Carolina, his native state, where he personally selected men for jobs in the Duquesne mills. George E. Jessup of Jones and Laughlin Steel in Pittsburgh traveled as far South as Georgia, where he impressed one particular Black migrant with his plain talk about employment in the Pittsburgh steel district.[17]

In some instances Black labor recruiters, though they were not formally called Negro welfare officers, performed a few of the same duties. John "Jack" Johnson, a native of Winchester, Virginia, for example, migrated to Johnstown in 1903 to work as a hostler for Charles S. Price, the general manager of the Cambria Steel Company. During World War I, Johnson recruited Black workers in Alabama, Mississippi, and other Southern states for the Johnstown mills. Once these migrants settled in Rosedale, the predominantly Black section of town, White physicians refused to visit them when they became sick. Because of this neglect, Black patients frequently died of pneumonia and other serious disorders. To remedy the problem, Johnson went to the Howard University Medical School in Washington, D.C. in 1917 to find a Black doctor willing to move to Johnstown to serve its burgeoning Black community. Dr. Moses Clayborne, a young physician born in Virginia in 1887, responded to Johnson's appeal, and permanently settled in Johnstown.[18]

Besides labor recruitment, Black welfare officials discharged a variety of other responsibilities. Initially, officers in the Pittsburgh Urban League held a weekly conference with them in which they discussed numerous issues related to increased Black employment. They recommended, for example, that plant supervisors choose strawbosses more carefully, that foremen "make the personal acquaintance of each man on the job," and that plant officials participate in "noon hour talks" with their Black employees. Although Black strawbosses were designated to supervise predominantly Black labor gangs in a few mills and foundries, they were still answerable to White superiors who remained unsympathetic to difficulties confronted by Black workers. Consequently, the task of assisting Black mill employees to adjust to industrial labor in Western Pennsylvania became the duty of Black welfare officials.[19]

The housing of newly hired Blacks was the first challenge that these social service workers encountered. The welfare officer usually assigned incoming migrants to company-run boarding houses. In Duquesne, Macon Lennon, the welfare official, inhabited one of the boarding houses, and exercised general supervision over it. He also directed newcomers to other facilities run both by the company and by individual Blacks. William Jennings, for example, migrated to Duquesne from Virginia in the 1890s to work in the steel mill. At the start of the wartime migration, however, he and his wife opened a boarding house for Black newcomers from the South. By 1918, the Carnegie steel works in Duquesne placed them in charge of company-owned housing. Even after her husband's death, Mrs. Jennings worked with Macon Lennon, and continued to run the mill's boarding house into the 1920s.[20]

In many instances, the housing that the steel companies provided for their newly hired Black employees was grossly inadequate. William P. Young, the welfare worker at Lockhart Iron and Steel in McKees Rocks, believed that such conditions caused the high turnover rates among the plant's Black workers. Lockhart initially imported a group of 100 Black Southerners in the fall of 1916. To accommodate these workers, the company "hastily" erected two tenement buildings. Sixteen two-room apartments housed a total of twenty-four familes. Seventy-five men crowded into a bunkhouse with space for only 45 to 50 people. The structures were also "poorly lighted" and "poorly ventilated." Another arrival of Black migrants in 1917 required the construction of two additional tenements, where similar substandard conditions prevailed. Another twenty families crowded into sixteen apartments, while the bunkhouses, enlarged only a bit, had to accommodate fifty more men "in these already overcrowded quarters." According to Young, these conditions contributed to a turnover rate of 25 percent per month for Black employees at Lockhart during 1918 and 1919.[21]

When Young commenced his duties as a welfare worker in 1918, he and concerned members of this worker's village made their grievances known to the Lockhart Company. By linking poor housing to worker instability, Young was able to persuade mill officials to disburse special funds for bunkhouse improvements. Before the end of 1923, more living space had been added to the existing structures. Seven buildings containing forty-eight apartments replaced four shabby tenements. Each family now had three rooms instead of two. The single-mattressed and vermin-ridden wooden cots in the bunkhouses were replaced with double-mattressed iron beds. A steam heating system took the place of three coal stoves. Inside toilets were installed, a janitor was hired, and a weekly change of bedding was instituted. Every year the exteriors of the bunkhouses were repainted and needed renovations were made to the buildings.[22] Young declared that:

> We have finally made our bunk-house a place where men can get proper rest after a long day's grind in the mill. They can keep clean and be refreshed by having adequate bathing facilities at their disposal. They are made comfortable so far as heat and ventilation are concerned . . . . In short, the men are made to feel as much at home as is possible under the circumstances, and they are at least temporarily contented. And since it is the contented man who is usually the steady, reliable worker, this means an increased production that most certainly can be measured in dollars and cents.[23]

Besides, the turnover rate among Black workers at Lockhart Iron and Steel had been reduced to 8 percent per month by January 1924, and Young fervently believed that "no factor has had so great a bearing on this condition as providing the men with a comfortable place in which to live."[24]

These efforts were supplemented by community centers which provided a wide range of educational and recreational activities for Black workers and their families. Black welfare officers supervised all such center progress which included athletics, music and adult education. Early in 1918, the Homestead steel works became the first firm in the area to establish a community center for Black workers. When it first opened, the clientele was so large that by the end of the year, the company had to purchase larger quarters. The new building contained a large reading room, a card and billiard room, a domestic science section, as well as kitchen and bathroom facilities. A ladies department was housed in a separate part of the structure, and a dormitory for incoming Black migrants was located upstairs on the third floor. Concerning Grover Nelson, the Black welfare official, the *Homestead Messenger* reported that the "colored people have said that he has a great deal of influence for good over the men," and because of his efforts at the community center, Black laborers have become "more steady in their [work] habits."[25] Macon Lennon acquired a staff of two nurses for the community center at the Duquesne steel works. They were on hand to dispense health care to needy Black steelworkers and their families.[26] Moreover, he and his assistant, I. J. K. Wells, taught adult education classes, especially to poorly educated Black migrants. In December 1920, Lennon reported that over fifty people enrolled in the classes.[27] Wells gradually took over many of Lennon's classes, and he taught English, arithmetic, civics, and even Negro history.[28]

Lockhart Iron and Steel in McKees Rocks opened a recreational center adjoining the company bunkhouse in early 1920. Black employees, like those at the Homestead and Duquesne steel works, used the facility for checkers, pool, card playing and music listening. William P. Young, the welfare officer, also sponsored dances and birthday parties on a regular basis. In the camp was a chapel where church services were frequently held. Young used the edifice for several secular purposes as well. All legal holidays observed by the company, including Christmas, Thanksgiving, Labor Day, and the Fourth of July, were celebrated in the chapel "with appropriate programs." Young usually invited prominent civic leaders, clergymen, and professionals to speak on subjects with a "desirable educational value" for the workers and their families.[29] In December 1920, the *Clairton Tattler* announced the opening of a community room for Black employees at the Clairton steel works. Plans were made initially for a reading room and a choir. George Foster Jones, the welfare official, organized the "colored community chorus" in January 1921, which was devoted primarily to singing "the Negro folk song." On April 21, 1921, the group sang its first concert with Philadelphian Marian Anderson, the developing young contralto, appearing on the program with them. Jones also managed the mill's Black baseball team.[30]

Black welfare workers also developed close ties with Black pastors and their congregations. Because of these intimate relationships with Black preachers and Black churches, industrialists were certain to have a positive public image within this important segment of the Black population. Macon Lennon of the Duquesne steel works encouraged the Workingmen's Bible class in 1920 by allowing the pastor of a Baptist church in Rankin to preach at a company-run boarding house.[31] One of his successors, Charles Broadfield, belonged to Payne Chapel African Methodist Episcopal Church, where in later years he served as a trustee and choir director. When the congregation outgrew its building in the late 1920s, Broadfield offered the mill's community center to the pastor, Reverend P. A. Rose. Like Broadfield, George Foster Jones of the Clairton steel works served the First African Methodist Episcopal Church as its choir director. When he organized a "colored community chorus" in 1921, it benefitted from the support of First AME Church and Mt. Olive Baptist Church. Jones also brought Black preachers to the mill's community room to speak to Black workers each Sunday. At least twice he invited Reverend C. Y. Trigg, the pastor of Warren Methodist Episcopal Church in Pittsburgh, who in 1920 participated in a conference on Blacks in Northern industry.[32]

Grover Nelson of the Homestead steel works was similarly involved in Black religious affairs. He became acquainted with Reverend J. A. Terry, Sr., the pastor of Homestead's newly founded Blackwell African Methodist Episcopal Zion Church. In 1925 when the denomination's Allegheny Annual Conference convened at Terry's Church, Nelson came to the gathering to represent his employers. During the 1920s, Nelson, who belonged to Rodman Street Baptist Church in Pittsburgh, decided to enter the ministry. Homestead steel officials adjusted his schedule to allow him to attend Western Theological Seminary in Pittsburgh. He briefly served a church established for Black workers by the Pittsburgh Plate Glass Company in Ford City. When Black residents founded another congregation in 1930, Nelson agreed to become its pastor. In subsequent years while still employed at the Homestead steel works, Nelson pastored Mt. Olive Baptist Church in Rankin and Victory Baptist Church in Pittsburgh. In 1937, he served as supervisor of the Western District of the Pennsylvania Baptist Convention.[33]

On other occasions the welfare workers acted in the capacity of Black spokesmen. In 1925, John A. Batch, who replaced the deceased George Foster Jones at the Clairton mills, personally persuaded 260 Blacks to register as voters. One immediate result of this activity was the appointment of two Black men as election officials in Clairton.[34] Similarly, Macon Lennon of the Duquesne steel works was involved in a political group established by Allegheny County Blacks. In 1924, he used his influence to help win an appointment for George Wallington, a fellow Black North Carolinian, to the Duquesne police force.[35]

In 1927, the false arrest of a Black woman caused her pastor and Charles Marshall, Lennon's immediate successor, to lead a Black protest delegation to a city council meeting. There they denounced the disrespectful treatment meted out generally to Blacks in Duquesne and indicated that the arrest of this innocent Black women was "as much as they could bear." This action caused the prosecutor to immediately drop the charges.[36]

Black welfare officials also tried to promote thrift among Black employees, and curb wayward behavior. George Foster Jones succeeded in dissuading Blacks at the Clairton Steel Works from drawing on their wages between paydays.[37] William P. Young convinced most of the Black family men at Lockhart Iron and Steel in McKees Rocks to become bank depositors by 1924. This represented a substantial increase in such bank accounts since 1919.[38] Even the high incidence of intraracial crime was in some way ameliorated by company recreational programs. It had not been uncommon for Black steelworkers, primarily because of congested living conditions, lack of leisure time activities, and accessibility to alcohol, to get drunk and to cut and shoot each other over card games, "crap" tables, and in contests for female affection.[39] When prohibition became the law of the land, Black steelworkers surreptitiously secured liquor. Like other welfare workers, William P. Young conducted his own special crusade to increase the involvement of the men in other kinds of recreation in order to avert such occurrences. When he first came to Lockhart Iron and Steel in 1918, Black workers gambled in the bunkhouses on a regular basis. Fights broke out, stabbings took place, and deaths sometimes resulted. Young proceeded to convert the "bad men" of the bunkhouse, and gain their support for his new recreational programs. By 1924, even a local hospital worker noted the decrease of patients coming from Lockhart for salves and bandages "following some cutting or shooting affray."[40]

Steel managers expressed satisfaction over the success of their social service programs among Black workers. Writing in 1923, J. W. Knapp, personnel director of the Bethlehem Steel Plant in Duquesne, observed:

> One of the many successful efforts has been the investigating of our men off duty, through the Welfare Worker. By this

means we are able to catch up (to) the loafer . . . as well as
. . . render aid . . . to our workmen who are detained home
on account of sickness of self or family.[41]

James Hemphill, the employment director of the Carnegie steel
works in Duquesne, "was the pioneer in arranging dinners in
which the colored Welfare men meet with White officials throughout the district" to effect "a better understanding" with Black
employees. Hemphill was credited also with discharging "foreign bosses . . . who showed any signs of hostility" to Black
workers. Despite his general support of Black welfare officers,
Hemphill opposed the efforts of I. J. K. Wells, the unmanageable
assistant of Macon Lennon. Wells, a recent college graduate,
eagerly organized a group of young Black steelworkers to pool
their money to start a business. These and perhaps other activities angered Hemphill and Lennon who believed that Wells
should have used his talents exclusively in the night school that
the Duquesne steel works established for Black employees. As
a result of starting a "youth movement," Wells lost his job after
a year and a half in the mills' welfare department.[42]

These social service workers acting as spokesmen, trouble-
shooters, and recreational leaders were the main instruments for
implementing welfare programs among Black steelworkers in
Western Pennsylvania. Plant managers also depended upon Black
churches and other community agencies to assist them in their
welfare work among Black migrants. Mill officials gave strong
support to Black churches in order to augment the efforts of
Black welfare officers who were already active participants in religious affairs. They also believed that Black churches would help
in developing a dependable and efficient force of Black laborers
by espousing the work ethic and by preaching thrift and sobri-
ety. A cornerstone was laid in 1919 for the new edifice of Jerusalem Baptist Church in Duquesne. Samuel G. Worton, the
assistant superintendent of the Duquesne steel works, attended
the ceremony, and expressed his pleasure in discovering that
many of the mill's newly imported laborers belonged to Jerusalem
Church and were present to help Reverend John M. Clay in this
major undertaking.[43] In the early 1920s, Clark Memorial Baptist
Church in Homestead erected a new building at a cost exceed-
ing $100,000. In two and one half years, the congregation raised

about $90,000 to pay for the new edifice. In 1924, during a mortage liquidation drive, Clark Memorial was offered a $5,000 contribution from the Carnegie Steel Company, if the congregation agreed to give a comparable sum to match it. The church accomplished the task.[44] The Carnegie contribution seemed all the more worthwhile since most of the Clark Memorial members were Black steelworkers and their families. Moreover, the Church was already sponsoring some basketball teams and operating a community center, which paralleled the mill's own efforts to carry on welfare work among Homestead Blacks. Several churches, though without industry funding, instituted programs which paralleled the efforts of mill welfare departments. For example, John Wesley AME Zion Church in Pittsburgh, took pride in its interest in "the Southern immigrant" and his adjustment to "the complicated social fabric of the modern crowded metropolis." Consequently, in 1926, when plans were formulated for a new edifice, space was alloted for a day nursery, a boy scout troop, and other community needs.[45]

Other Black churches received direct grants from steel companies. In the late 1920s at the Aliquippa Works of Jones and Laughlin Steel gave an annual gift of $150 to the town's Black congregations including Bethel Baptist Church, Tried Stone Baptist Church, Jones Chapel Methodist Episcopal Church, Emmanuel African Methodist Episcopal Zion Church, and the Church of God in Christ.[46] On other occasions industry managers preferred to help Black churches by allowing them to worship on company-owned property. In 1917, in Johnstown, Reverend J. H. Flagg organized Bethel African Methodist Episcopal Church, and another preacher started Mt. Sinai Baptist Church. Since the Cambria Steel Company owned an edifice previously occupied by a White congregation, local mill officials permitted the two Black groups to share the building. The same year Black migrants from Clayton, Alabama organized Shiloh Baptist Church. Cambria Steel responded by donating another company-owned structure for Shiloh to use. In the early 1920s, the Lockhart Iron and Steel Company in McKees Rocks sponsored a Baptist Church for Black employees, and allowed them to use a chapel located in a company-owned recreation center.[47]

The pastors of many of these Black congregations indirectly helped mill managers by espousing the work ethic and encouraging Blacks to value their jobs and obey their employers. In 1923, Reverend Henry P. Jones of Euclid Avenue African Methodist Episcopal Church in Pittsburgh eulogized W. A. Clay, a molder and boss rougher at the Carnegie steel mills. When "a high company official" came to pay his respects to his deceased employee, Jones praised Clay and other Black workers who valued "their positions of trust." Also in 1923, the Pennsylvania Baptist Convention met in Pittsburgh and discussed the issue of "shiftlessness" among Black industrial workers. Before the meeting ended, the clergymen decided to appoint "special representatives" to speak with local employers about ways to improve the attitudes of their Black employees.[48]

The Pittsburgh Urban League also provided a variety of social, recreational, and educational programs for Black workers and their families. In McKees Rocks, for example, the Pittsburgh affiliate organized the wives of Lockhart Iron and Steel employees into sewing clubs and circles.[49] John T. Clark, the executive director of the local League, pointed with special pride to the Community Uplift Club, an organization of thirty-five wives of Black steelworkers in the city's Lawrenceville section. Through its cooperation with the League's Home Economics worker, the club exerted a salutary influence upon their otherwise slum community through bazaars, its sponsorship of League Baby Shows, and its work in caring for the sick.[50]

Because of these and other efforts in behalf of newly hired Black laborers and their families, the Pittsburgh Urban League received financial support from several industrial firms in Western Pennsylvania. In 1923, for example, the two largest steel companies in the region, Carnegie and Jones and Laughlin, each donated $1,000 to the League. The National Tube Company and Standard Sanitary Manufacturing, respectively, contributed $500. Westinghouse Electric and Manufacturing and Westinghouse Airbrake each gave $200. One hundred dollar contributions came respectively from United Engineering and Foundry and Central Tube in Ambridge. The Pittsburgh Meter Company in East Pittsburgh gave $25.[51]

Officials of the Pittsburgh Urban League cooperated with area employers in several important endeavors. In 1920, along with the Employer's Association of Pittsburgh, the League convened an industrial conference to discuss the massive entry of

Black workers into Northern industry. Black welfare officers from area steel plants were among the conference participants. Grover Nelson of the Homestead steel works spoke on the "Effect of Broken Family Ties on Workers' Efficiency;" Paul G. Prayer of the Duquesne steel works addressed the meeting on "Community Programs for Negro Workers in Industrial Towns;" and William P. Young of Lockhart Iron and Steel in McKees Rocks discussed "Married Men Away from Family and With Family."[52]

The League also assisted George E. Jessup, the Black labor agent at Jones and Laughlin's Pittsburgh steel plant. In 1922 and 1923, J and L, like other firms in Western Pennsylvania, resumed their recruitment of Black laborers. Prospective Black steelworkers wrote to John T. Clark of the Pittsburgh affiliate who then referred them to Jessup. A migrant from Maxeys, Georgia, wrote to Clark early in 1923 to announce his intention to migrate to Pittsburgh. He said that "I am depending upon you and Mr. George E. Jessup to make the arrangements and have [a] job for me." Another migrant from Palmyra, Virginia informed Jessup that the Pittsburgh Urban League recommended that he write him to ask for employment at the J and L facilities.[53] In these and other instances, the Pittsburgh Urban League effectively functioned as a liaison between Black mill personnel and prospective Black employees.

Since the Black migration diminished during the late 1920s, some Black welfare officers worried that their usefulness would end. In 1928, Cyrus T. Greene, a graduate of Lincoln University in Pennsylvania and a former YMCA worker, expressed concern about his position at the Westinghouse Electric and Manufacturing Company in East Pittsburgh. He wrote to T. Arnold Hill the executive director of the National Urban League, and told him that "the strict plan of economy" at the Westinghouse plant will "make re-adjustments in the employment department of which I am a member." Although his superiors assured him that he would not be dismissed, Greene thought that retrenchments would occur in Black welfare efforts. Moreover, he was sufficiently apprehensive about his position to ask Hill about possible employment in the Urban League. In 1929, Greene became the executive director of the Tampa Urban League in Florida.[54]

Black welfare officials at Lockhart Iron and Steel in McKees Rocks and the Homestead and Duquesne plants of Carnegie Steel, however, retained their jobs and continued to meet the special needs of Black workers well beyond the 1920s. William P. Young remained with Lockhart until 1963 when Governor William W. Scranton appointed him Secretary of Labor and Industry in Pennsylvania. In the intervening years Young served on the board of directors of the Pittsburgh Urban League, as a GOP precinct committeeman, and as chairman of the Republican Committee of Allegheny County.[55] Grover Nelson stayed at the Homestead Steel Works until the early 1950s when he retired to pursue the ministry full time. While he pastored Victory Baptist Church in Pittsburgh, he devoted himself to raising funds for the Virginia Theological Seminary and College in Lynchburg. In 1954 the institution conferred an honorary Doctor of Divinity degree upon him. Nelson was also an active participant in the Allegheny Union Baptist Association.[56] Charles Broadfield of the Duquesne Steel Works became active with the Monongahela Valley Boy Scouts Council and with the Duquesne Colored Republican Club.[57]

By the end of the 1920s, Black workers had entrenched themselves in the steel mills of Western Pennsylvania. In 1929, they comprised at least one fifth of all shop employees in area mills and foundries. Yet in spite of their sizeable representation in the ranks of steel labor, racial discrimination continued to keep the majority of them in hot, dirty, low-paying jobs. Company welfare programs had not been designed to solve the problem of racial discrimination in the mills or to alter work patterns or wage scales. Their major thrust was to integrate Black workers into many of the unskilled laboring positions once held by immigrants, and to ameliorate some of the unpleasant social and environmental conditions in the mill communities in which Blacks lived. In this endeavor, the companies had attained a good measure of success.

The depression of the 1930s, which affected Blacks most acutely, undercut these efforts, however, and at the same time created severe economic and social distress among Blacks living in Western Pennsylvania. The crisis also generated renewed worker militancy of which Blacks were a part.

# 6

# The Depression, The New Deal and Black Steelworkers in Western Pennsylvania

The Great Depression plunged the nation into the worst economic crisis in American history. Factory gates were closed. Production ceased. Twelve million workers were left unemployed. Hunger and destitution were widespread, both in city and country. Blacks, who had always faced racial discrimination as a bar to their economic progress, now had to fight a losing battle with White workers for rapidly decreasing numbers of jobs in mills and factories throughout the country.

On the eve of the Great Depression, racial bias in work assignments and promotion continued to limit the occupational advancement of Black steelworkers in Western Pennsylvania. Steel managers had permanently assigned the vast majority of Blacks to hard, hot, and dirty work in the blast furnaces, open hearths, and bar mill departments. When the Depression came, Black steelworkers were usually the first to be laid off and last to be recalled when production resumed. Job scarcity made race an asset of tremendous importance to White workers seeking reemployment and promotion in area steel plants during the 1930s. Moreover, the Depression discredited company welfare programs carried on among Black steelworkers. Blacks discovered that these philanthropic practices neither protected them from discrimination nor shielded them from unemployment.

Because of the preferential treatment given to Whites in the steel mills and other industries in the Pittsburgh vicinity, the unemployment rate among Blacks became disproportionately high. In 1931, Blacks comprised 7 percent of the male population of Allegheny County, in which Pittsburgh is located; yet they made up 22 percent of all employment seekers at the County's Emergency Association.[1] By February 1934, 31.9 percent of all Whites and 28.4 percent of all foreign-born workers were without jobs, and represented nearly 60 percent of all unemployed persons in the area. Blacks alone constituted 40.1 percent of the remainder.[2] Conditions were no better for them in Pittsburgh, where 8 percent of the population was Black.[3] In November 1937, for example, 13,384 Blacks made up almost 19 percent of Pittsburgh's 70,717 unemployed workers.[4] Even toward the end of the 1930s, Blacks still had the worst unemployment rate among area laborers. In 1940, there was a total of 30,020 steelworkers in Pittsburgh. Of this number, 5,500 or 18 percent, were without work. Among 2,643 Black steelworkers, 905, or 37 percent, were unemployed. Although young adults between the ages of 18 and 44 populated the ranks of both groups of unemployed steelworkers in Pittsburgh, a slightly higher percentage of these men were Black. Approximately 64 percent of Pittsburgh's jobless steelworkers were between 18 and 44 years old. For Black steelworkers in this age category, however, the rate of unemployment was 71 percent.[5]

During the Depression, several firms in the Pittsburgh vicinity which had jobs available refused to hire any unemployed Blacks. These firms which clearly discriminated against Blacks used anything from a lack of confidence in their ability as workers to fear of negative reactions from White employees as justification for their racially biased employment practices. The Pittsburgh Urban League, in an effort to discover why Blacks appeared on area relief rolls in such disproportionate numbers, surveyed employers in 1934 to determine their attitudes towards hiring Blacks. The manager of a rolling mill which employed 1,100 laborers implied that its work was too specialized for Blacks, so none had applied. Another steel official who had no Blacks among his 500 steelworkers thought that "White labor (was) better," and the "Negroes (were) lazy." A manufacturer of steel pipes with 1,010 laborers on the payroll discharged Black workers when the mill abandoned its puddling department.[6]

Other steel firms in Western Pennsylvania made deliberate efforts to exclude or reduce their force of Black steelworkers. The Superior Steel Company in Carnegie did not ''care for Negro labor'' and held ''out 'little' hope to unemployed Negro steelworkers.'' The employment manager at Firth Sterling Steel in McKeesport, which had an overwhelmingly White labor force, indicated that the sons of mill employees received preferential treatment in job placement, and this ''system would permanently exclude Negroes.'' Officials at the Allegheny Steel Company in Breckenridge replaced their unemployed Black workers with Whites. The alleged gambling, bootlegging, and other kinds of disturbances indulged in by Black steelworkers rationalized the company's elimination of these laborers during the 1930s.[7] Until 1931, the coke department at the Clairton Steel Works was completely staffed by Blacks. When the Depression came, the company began replacing these veteran workers with Whites. By 1934, Blacks comprised only 20 percent of the pushers, "the most desireable jobs," and 90 percent of the door machine attendants, "the least desirable jobs." One Black steelworker in Clairton noted that the company would

> . . . take a White man right out of the street and make you teach him and after you teach him they give him your job or make him your foreman.[8]

The few Blacks who retained their jobs in the steel mills during the Depression continued to endure similar forms of racial discrimination in hiring, promotions and work assignments. In 1935, 5,235 Blacks held positions in the Pittsburgh area steel industry, but the vast majority of them labored in the mill's lowest occupational ranks.[9] Forty-six percent of these steelworkers were unskilled laborers,[10] and in several large plants, lower echelon employees came close to comprising the entire Black work force. The Duquesne steel works, for example, employed 302 Blacks in 1934, but almost 70 percent or 211 men, worked as common laborers. The Edgar Thomson steel works in Braddock employed 316 Blacks, and 284 of them, or 89.9 percent were unskilled workers.[11] Overall a comparable percentage of Black steel laborers (44 percent) worked in semi-skilled positions. In many cases, however, their working conditions were no better than that of common laborers. Many were in the lower semi-skilled categories, where exposure to excessive heat and fumes from the furnaces and to general hazards in the mills gave them almost no edge over their unskilled colleagues. Moreover, some semi-skilled Blacks, especially those working in puddling departments as acid picklers, ash men, cindermen, and sandmen, earned wages similar to those in the unskilled categories. Promotions for Black workers occurred rarely. Those holding semi-skilled jobs in the blast furnace and open hearth departments had little prospect of advancing beyond the rank of first or second helper. The fact that only 10 percent of all Black steelworkers attained a skilled position testified to the low incidence of promotion among this stratum of the industry's work force.[12] Moreover, these skilled Negro workmen were concentrated in small specialty shops where steel managers both hired and promoted Black employees. Some of them, like Lockhart Iron and Steel in McKees Rocks, had a tradition of employing skilled Blacks which began before World War I. This practice, however, was the exception, not the rule. In many of the large plants where most Blacks were employed, few if any held a skilled position.[13] The personnel manager at a Carnegie steel plant reflected the general attitude of most employers. He indicated in 1932 that "it is impossible to hire Blacks in important and skilled positions." His reasoning was that "it just is not done."[14]

Furthermore, racial discrimination, more than a lack of educational background or occupational experience, barred the employment advancement of Black steelworkers. Although few Blacks had had experience working in Southern steel mills, more than 95 percent of all Black males in Pittsburgh in 1930 were at least capable of reading and writing.[15] Promotions, however, were based more upon accessibility to on-the-job manual training than upon literacy skills. Racial discrimination made it difficult for Blacks to learn how to operate mill machinery and to become rollers, millwrights, and heaters. Because Whites generally received these better-paying jobs, they usually earned higher wages than Black steelworkers. In 1935, for example, the average wage earned by a White steelworker was 69.8 cents per hour. The average Black steelworker received 57.7 cents per hour.[16]

Management policy in the steel mills, as in other industries in Western Pennsylvania, was primarily responsible for these discriminatory employment practices during the Depression. Foremen, who had the closest contact with workers, often exercised preferences in determining which employees were promoted and which were retained or recalled during alternating periods of production and slowdown. During the Depression they decided how long particular employees stayed on the job and how long their layoffs would last. In such situations, White steelworkers usually fared better than Blacks. In 1940, for example, 5,495 steelworkers in Pittsburgh were unemployed. Of this number, 4,590 were White and 905 were Black. Approximately 2,160 Whites or 47 percent of all steelworkers within this racial group had been without work from one to five years. The 611 Blacks or 67 percent of all steel laborers within this racial category, however, had been unemployed from one to five years.[17]

The relative inexperience of Blacks who had but recently arrived in Western Pennsylvania played a smaller role in checking their occupational advancement than did racial discrimination. Blacks without work experience competed unsuccessfully with Whites who were also inexperienced. In 1940 there were 6,868 unemployed men in Pittsburgh who were new to the local labor market. Of this number 6,169 were White and 699 were Black. Approximately 31.5 percent of all Whites or 1,945 persons had been jobless for from 1 to 5 years while 62 percent of all Blacks or 440 persons had been searching for employment for the same length of time.[18]

Blacks were extremely conscious of the unfair treatment they encountered in the mills. Because most of them were concentrated in unskilled and semi-skilled positions, they were generally aware of the wage differentials that existed between them and White employees, and also expressed dismay over working conditions, lack of advancement, and other manifestations of race prejudice. A Black steelworker in Clairton said that "white fellows can work up to general foreman," while Blacks had practically "no chance for promotion."[19] A Black steelworker in Duquesne who had "never been promoted" echoed the same sentiments by observing that "I am the oldest on my job and have never been advanced and have no chance."[20] Another Black laborer at the Duquesne steel works complained about racial unfairness in assigning jobs in the blast furnace department:

> the colored has a hard way to go. They are given hot and dirty work . . . they [rush] you. They . . . bawl you out and make you work fast.[21]

Their jobs became particularly grueling when they had to crawl in the blast furnace checkers to clean out the dust and soot and tear out the furnaces:

> First you get a headache and the stomach bothers you and then you have to come out. You . . . put boards down and bags around your knees and . . . still [you] feel the heat . . . colored are given this type of work mostly . . . especially on hot days.[22]

Soon after the stock market crash in 1929 local steel companies began cutting wages for all mill employees. In Glassport, Duquesne, and McKeesport Unemployed Councils came into being, and in some cases planned marches and demonstrations demanding relief for furloughed workers. In those instances when local steel officials distributed food baskets to their employees, the recipients signed statements promising to repay the companies for these emergency benevolences.[23] Moreover, to stem the tide of any major unrest among workers in the Pittsburgh vicinity, steel managers revived Employee Representative Plans (ERPs). In 1933, Section 7a of the National Industrial Recovery Act (NIRA) allowed laborers to bargain collectively with their employers through representatives of their own choosing. Steel managers used ERPs to maintain an open shop under the guise of company unionism. Black steelworkers affiliated with these organizations and in some cases were elected to union offices.[24] Blacks, like other mill employees, joined company unions because NIRA had also encouraged their employers to continue the practice of shortening working hours, a practice already used by the steel companies in order to divide jobs among as many laborers as possible. This practice allowed several groups of steelworkers to put in some time at work. Ashton Allen, a veteran Black employee at the Homestead steel works, started working two or three days a week beginning in 1931.[25] Merril Lynch got a job at Jones and Laughlin Steel in Pittsburgh early in 1929 as a bricklayer helper. His department "worked well" until 1932, when he started working one or two days a week.[26] The McKeesport Tin Plate Company included 229 Blacks among its 2,972 employees, and they were concentrated in the cold roll department.[27] One Black, who labored in that department, sometimes put in an entire week during the 1930s. When tin orders slackened, officials parcelled work among the Black employees, so that none would be permanently furloughed.[28] Yet, in spite of these efforts to enlist Black steelworkers in company unions and to implement work-sharing practices among them, their unemployment rate remained disproportionately high.

Mill layoffs and underemployment made it difficult for most Black steelworkers to maintain themselves and their families adequately. One Black who worked as a sandblaster in a local pipe mill, supported his family of five by selling apples on the streets of Pittsburgh. Another Black steelworker in Pittsburgh, married and with six children, held a steady job in a local steel plant at good wages for four to five years. Then the Depression came, his mill closed, and he was laid off. He walked the streets every day in search of a job, but none was to be found. According to his wife, "He just got discouraged and one day he went out and he didn't come back," hoping that "the welfare people would help me and the kids . . . if he wasn't living at home."[29] An irregularly employed Black steelworker in Homestead allowed one of his sons to sell newspapers and two of his daughters to work in hospitals in order to supplement the family income. Moreover, they maintained a garden and gleaned fruit and vegetables from nearby farms for food. They also used coal from abandoned area mines as their fuel.[30] The Depression had so demoralized some Black steelworkers that employment managers, especially at the Carnegie steel works in Homestead and Clairton, were unfairly hesitant about recalling many of them back to work. According to one contemporary observer, mill officials feared that some of their former Black employees, most of whom had been without jobs for long stretches of time, were becoming "embittered floaters, bums, and panhandlers," and were no longer efficient and dependable workmen.[31]

In any case, most Black steelworkers, whether employed or not, had to rely either on company relief or on the private efforts of several church and community agencies to feed them and provide other kinds of relief assistance in order to survive. None of the company programs were elaborate, and few of them attended to all the needs of their recipients. However, most such programs were helpful in some important, specific ways. Several Carnegie steel plants, for example, instituted a "box system" in which needy employees obtained food supplies and medical attention. Similarly, the A. M. Byers Company in Pittsburgh and Allegheny Steel in Breckenridge financed worker-administered efforts in which food was distributed among furloughed company employees. The Penn Iron and Steel Company in Creighton and the American Sheet and Tin Plate Company in Vandergrift allowed their Black employees to live in company housing without paying rent during the Depression.[32] Steel managers and other businessmen in Pittsburgh donated a five-story building to house and feed many of their unemployed workers, 40 percent of whom were homeless Black men.[33] Frequently steel officials gave lists of their furloughed employees to the Allegheny County Emergency Association and to other agencies dispensing relief to the unemployed.[34] In some instances, Black workers who were only partially employed received endorsements from company officials in their search for relief. In 1930, a Black chainman working at the A. M. Byers Company for only three or four days a week, discovered that his earnings were not enough to maintain his family. When he sought assistance from the Family Welfare Association of Allegheny County, the employment supervisor at A. M. Byers wrote a letter supporting his application for relief.[35]

Other agencies actively offered assistance to Black steelworkers and their families. Those in the Hill District, the North Side, the East End, and other sections of Pittsburgh relied heavily upon the Red Cross and the Association for the Improvement of the Poor.[36] Twice between 1930 and 1931, the City Council of Pittsburgh appropriated a total $200,000 for the relief fund in the Public Welfare Department. Blacks flocked to the city-county building en masse to get their share of relief allocations. Others crowded into the Pittsburgh Urban League office looking for work.[37] Black churches were especially involved in

Figure 9. Hill District of Pittsburgh during the 1930s, the home of many Black steelworkers. (From Stefan Lorant's *Pittsburgh: The Story of an American City*; photo by Arthur Rothstein.)

feeding the hungry. During the early 1930s, Grace Memorial Presbyterian Church in the Hill District offered free meals to the unemployed on specified weekdays. On one particular occasion, as many as 400 people squeezed into its miniature dining hall to stand in line for food. The minister, Reverend Harold R. Tolliver, received donations from local produce yards, from a special women's group in the Pittsburgh Presbytery, and from members of his own congregation, many of whom were severely affected by the Depression themselves.[38]

Most of these local programs were administered sporadically and brought only temporary and inadequate relief to the thousands of unemployed Blacks in Western Pennsylvania. The Roosevelt Administration, on the other hand, believed that only the federal government could provide widespread and substantial relief and also reduce unemployment. Within the first "One Hundred Days" of the new Administration, numerous pieces of legislation designed to rehabilitate agriculture and industry passed quickly through Congress. Other programs including the Civil Works Administration (CWA), the Public Works Administration (PWA), and the Federal Emergency Relief Administration aimed at providing work relief for millions of the unemployed. In 1935, Congress passed the five billion dollar Emergency Relief Appropriation Act which established the Works Progress Administration (WPA). Like other agencies, the WPA sponsored work relief projects in which the unemployed and the partially employed were hired to build roads, schools, hospitals, and government buildings.[39]

New Deal emergency relief programs extended into the mill communities of Western Pennsylvania, and enabled unemployed Black steelworkers to work and earn money to support themselves and their families. After his layoff from the rolling mill of National Tube in McKeesport, one Black mill laborer secured work with the WPA.[40] Similarly, another Black steel worker, who had worked at the tin mill of the McKeesport Tin Plate Company in Port Vue, obtained WPA employment.[41] Production cutbacks compelled Jones and Laughlin Steel in Pittsburgh to temporarily release Jerome Goodman in 1931. He subsequently settled at a Civilian Conservation Corps camp in Kingston, Pennsylvania, where workers pulled trees and constructed new roads. After one year, he secured employment from the

WPA and helped to repair streets in Pittsburgh. He stayed on this project until 1936, when J and L recalled him to his former job.[42] In other instances, mill employees who could work only a certain minimum of days became eligible for work relief on WPA. In 1935, a Black laborer at a New Castle tin plate company was allowed to work a maximum of 150 days during the year. For the remaining 215 days he qualified for federal emergency employment.[43]

Because Blacks were more severly affected by unemployment, they constituted a larger proportion of their race on New Deal emergency projects than did Whites. Although 43,408 Blacks comprised but 6 percent of the male population in Allegheny county in 1937, they constituted 20 percent of the emergency workers. Similarly, in Pittsburgh 27,962 Blacks composed 9.1 percent of the male population, while comprising 23 percent of all local emergency workers. The same pattern prevailed in the region's major steel milltowns. In Braddock, 1,196 Blacks represented 11 percent of the male population, but they totaled 26 percent of all emergency workers. In Clairton, 1,206 Blacks made up 14.7 percent of the male population and constituted 30 percent of all emergency workers. Likewise, in Homestead, where Blacks were 17 percent of the male population, they made up 38 percent of all emergency workers. Although a disproportionately high percentage of Black males worked on New Deal relief projects, an equally high proportion remained among the jobless and the underemployed. Black males in Pittsburgh, for example, composed 14 percent of the jobless and 12 percent of the partially employed. In Clairton, they totalled 26.6 percent of the jobless and 29 percent of the partially employed. Generally, in Allegheny County, Black males made up 11 percent of the unemployed and 9.4 percent of the partially employed.[44]

In many instances, Blacks encountered racial discrimination on federal work relief projects. In 1934, in Johnstown, for example, Dr. Burrell K. Johnson, a dentist who headed the local NAACP, reported color discrimination on a CWA project in Ferndale Borough. The foreman refused to hire "a colored man." The case was resolved, however, when an investigation revealed that the foreman illegally held two jobs. He was relieved of his CWA position.[45] By providing employment to Blacks on CWA, WPA, and other federal projects, the New Deal helped to ameliorate temporarily their condition of joblessness, but did not address the fundamental problem of job discrimination.

The situation was indirectly improved by New Deal legislation designed to improve working conditions and to facilitate union development within several mass production industries like steel. Section 7a of the National Industrial Recovery Act of 1933 gave the President the authority to establish minimum wages and maximum hours per week for labor. While the recommended forty-hour work week was largely responsible for work-sharing programs among mill employees during the worst production cutbacks, the wage differentials existing between Black steelworkers who were concentrated in the lower ranks of semi-skilled and unskilled labor were maintained by NIRA steel codes and drew complaints from Black organizations such as the National Association for the Advancement of Colored People.[46] Those steel employees in ranks above these lower echelon positions were to receive a wage increase of more than 15 percent. This excluded the vast majority of Black steelworkers. Nonetheless, the NIRA guaranteed to labor the right to organize and bargain collectively with employers. Soon after the Supreme Court declared the law unconstitutional in 1935, Congress quickly drafted a National Labor Relations Act (popularly known as the Wagner Act), which reaffirmed the right of workers to organize and bargain collectively "through representation of their own choosing." and established the National Labor Relations Board to protect these privileges.[47]

The passage of Section 7a in 1933 and the Wagner Act in 1935 stimulated efforts to organize Blacks into a revived labor movement. Black leaders feared that the American Federation of Labor would use Section 7a to make itself the primary spokesman for American workers while maintaining its traditional patterns of racial discrimination against Blacks. Most AFL affiliates already banned Blacks either by local rules, initiatory rites, or informal exclusion practices. The few Blacks who did belong to labor organizations held membership in ten unions which kept them segregated in separate locals. The Brotherhood of Sleeping Car Porters, an all-Black union started in 1925 by A. Philip Randolph, was not admitted to the AFL until 1929. Moreover, the craft orientation of the AFL virtually excluded the majority of Black workers who labored mostly in transportation, steel, auto, rubber, and other mass production industries which the AFL had declined to organize. Furthermore, after NIRA went into effect, several AFL affiliates actually prompted the dismissal of Black workers from these newly unionized shops. The Brotherhood of Electrical Workers organized laborers in several supply installations. However, the union denied membership to Blacks, and persuaded shop officials to discharge dozens of non-White employees. A strike of AFL members on the building site of a Black hospital in St. Louis occurred when the General Tile Company hired a Black tile setter. Consequently, the city's Board of Education refused to use Black workers to repair local "colored schools" for fear of antagonizing White workmen.[48]

In 1934 and 1935 Black activists attempted to move the AFL toward support of Black workers. At the 1934 national convention in San Francisco, Black laborers, especially longshoremen, picketed the meeting with signs reading, "Labor Cannot Be Free While Black Labor Is Enslaved." A resolution was presented which called upon AFL affiliates to end racial discrimination. The subgroup to which it was referred recommended the establishment of the Committee of Five that tried to prod various AFL unions towards dropping constitutional bans on Black membership and to practice racial equality. When the 1935 convention rejected their efforts, Randolph, a member of the Five, and others gave support and encouragement to John L. Lewis and his Committee on Industrial Organization.[49]

Lewis, the president of the United Mine Workers (UMW), and other like-minded labor leaders grew increasingly dismayed with the American Federation of Labor for its reluctance to aggressively organize the masses of steel, rubber, and automobile workers and for its disregard of Black employees who made up a large percentage of the major production industries. Lewis and his sympathizers eventually formed the Committee for Industrial Organization (later renamed Congress of Industrial Organizations) to unionize these workers on an industrial basis within the AFL. An angered AFL union hierarchy tried to disband the CIO, and finally succeeded in forcing Lewis and his organization out of the AFL. In 1936, the CIO, now an independent group already consisting of older constituent unions of coal miners, clothing workers, and others, established the Steelworkers Organizing Committee (SWOC) with Philip Murray, a vice president of the United Mine Workers, as its head.[50]

Blacks and industrial unionists before the split with the AFL had grown dismayed with the federation because of its position on Robert F. Wagner's National Labor Relations bill. In 1935, Wagner, a senator from New York, introduced legislation which would retard the growth of company unionism and create a federal agency, the National Labor Relations Board, to oversee fair elections in which workers would freely designate their own representatives for collective bargaining. Before the Supreme Court in 1935 declared NIRA unconstitutional, employers used its Section 7a to start company unions which frustrated the development of independent labor organizations. When Wagner introduced his bill to revive and strengthen the spirit of Section 7a the NAACP, the National Urban League, and other Black groups argued for a clause banning racial discrimination. Black spokesmen warned that the unfair racial practices in organized labor would result in closed shops that would effectively exclude Black workers from employment. They wanted Congress to exempt all unions with a history of racial discrimination from the provisions of the Wagner Bill. The AFL countered by threatening to withdraw its support from the labor proposal if it included the nondiscrimination clause. The clause was therefore dropped from consideration, and the Wagner Act became law without the provision.[51]

Section 7a of the National Industrial Recovery Act revitalized several defunct Pittsburgh area lodges of the Amalgamated Association of Iron and Steelworkers (AAIS). A number of firms established Employee Representative Plans (ERPs) to compete with the steel union. Ultimately employees in most steel plants sidestepped the ERPs and joined the Amalgamated Association. In Duquesne in 1933, William Spang asked Reverend Fletcher Williamson, a Black minister who worked as a steelworker, to assist him in organizing an AAIS lodge. After encouraging company employees to attend a series of meetings in Williamson's storefront church, Spang and a few others traveled to the Amalgamated union headquarters in Pittsburgh, and returned with a charter for Duquesne Lodge No. 187. Soon thereafter a group of steelworkers at the McKeesport Tin Plate Company, including Joseph Barron, the son of a 1919 striker, and Willie Brown, "a Black worker with a sharp wit and [a] keen sense of social concern," secured a charter for McKee Lodge No. 161. At the Clairton Steel Works, Roy Hallas, already a leader of the unemployed, and Nathan Sally, a Black laborer at the mill's coke plant, organized an AAIS lodge in their area. Other locals were soon formed in Pittsburgh, Braddock, Rankin and Versailles.[52]

White leaders of the CIO believed that any hope for success for this organization lay in organizing all workers regardless of race. Fresh in some of their memories was the 1919 steel strike, in which Blacks "scabbed" against the racially exclusive Amalgamated Association. Since that time the union movement had been dormant and there was little need for a racial reconciliation. Circumstances had changed since 1933, however, and a strong steel union now depended on the inclusion of all workers, both skilled and unskilled, and Black as well as White. An official of the Versailles Lodge held that by involving Blacks in the union, "we win the confidence of the race this way and nip race issues in the bud." Black steelworkers who suffered most from discrimination and unfair treatment in the mills believed that joining a union would help to redress their conditions.[53] A Black laborer at the Clairton steel works boldly declared that:

> The reason I joined the union is that they said the Negro will get the same job as the White man if they are qualified to do the work.[54]

A fellow Black steelworker at the Clairton mills hoped that the union movement would give him protection from the arbitrary and capricious behavior of his supervisors:

> The foremen are very hard to get along with; they overwork you and if you say anything about it they are ready to fire you.[55]

Other Blacks supported the Amalgamated organizing drive because it promised to secure "more money" for all steel employees.[56]

The Amalgamated Association had more success than failure in its organizing efforts among Black steelworkers. In 1928, Blacks were a little more than 3 percent of all AAIS members.[57] By the end of 1934, local Amalgamated lodges began including larger percentages of Black employees. At the Park Works of Crucible Steel in Pittsburgh, one-fourth of the plant's 100 Black workers affiliated with Registal Lodge. Approximately 219 of the

288 Blacks at the McKeesport Tin Plate Company were Amalgamated members. At the Homestead steel works, the union claimed 350 of the plant's 700 Black steelworkers, and they totalled 10 percent of the lodge membership. Nearly all of the 63 Blacks within the jurisdiction of McKee Lodge in McKeesport were union members.[58] The majority of Black steelworkers had not, however, been reached by the Amalgamated Association. But, in 1936, when the Steelworkers Organizing Committee began its own massive recruiting campaign, it was able to benefit from these earlier AAIS efforts by absorbing Amalgamated lodges and members into a new steel union with a larger Black membership.

Between 1933 and 1936, the period which marked the transition from NIRA to the era of CIO, the attitudes of Black steelworkers changed significantly. Steel managers tried to maintain an open shop by keeping "a certain percentage of Negro workers employed." They believed that the traditional anti-unionism of Black laborers would thwart efforts to organize the steel industry. They also thought that the possibility of losing their jobs would reinforce Black skepticism about noncompany unionism.[59] But the various employee representatives plans established by several steel firms failed to satisfy most Black laborers. One Black laborer, at the McKeesport Tin Plate plant in Port Vue, became disappointed when the ERP did nothing to break down racial exclusiveness in departmental assignments. Blacks were clustered in the cold roll Section, where they earned the lowest wages in the mills. He therefore concluded that the "company union was no good."[60] A Black steelworker in Clairton also expressed his discontent with company unionism. Laborers in a predominantly Black department elected a representative to take their grievances to company officials. His mill superiors "cut him from four days to one or two days a week" for acting in such an audacious manner. As a result, "he was afraid to go to anyone with a complaint for fear he (would) lose his job altogether."[61] In the meantime, the growing receptivity of the Amalgamated Association to Black steelworkers gave them an alternative to company unionism. Most steel firms were quick to see the potential danger in the successful growth of any kind of independent unionism, and many of them made a major effort to disrupt its development. At the Jones and Laughlin steel plant in Aliquippa, for example, Italian employees made the first efforts to organize an autonomous union. The company tried to keep Blacks from joining by paying "Negro stool pigeons" to pick fights with Italian workers.[62] Such activities, however, had minimal effect. Blacks increasingly identified with the Amalgamated Association because of its potential to advance their interests. Moreover, this initial exposure to biracial unionism prepared Blacks for receptivity to CIO organizing drives in 1936.

The Steelworkers Organizing Committee (SWOC), like the CIO, its parent organization, sought to promote the interests of all steel employees regardless of craft and degree of skill, and to destroy discrimination based on color, both in the mills and within its own rank and file. SWOC pronouncements about racial equality won it immediate support from a cross section of Black leaders and organizations, both national and local. For example, the *Union News Service*, a publication of the Committee of Industrial Organizations, welcomed the support of the *Baltimore Afro-American*, which declared that "the best interests of colored workers . . . would lie in aligning themselves wholeheartedly with the . . . CIO."[63] The National Urban League also lent its endorsement to the industrial union movement. In 1934, the League had established Workers' Councils in several major cities, which were designed to teach Black workers about the purposes and goals of labor unions and public issues related to wage earners.[64] The Workers' Council in Pittsburgh functioned "as an educational movement" and supported the Amalgamated Association because of its policy of "no discrimination toward Negroes."[65] Since the CIO vowed to continue this practice, Lester B. Granger, director of the League's Workers' Bureau, and other national officials tried to assist the group in its organizing drives in 1936 and 1937. Therefore, the League invited Ernest Rice McKinney, a Black organizer at SWOC's Pittsburgh headquarters, to attend its 1936 national convention to speak about the CIO and Black workers.[66] Moreover, Granger promised to aid the CIO by allowing the organization to use the League's Workers' Councils to reach "the masses of Negroes."[67] Speaking at a CIO meeting in 1936, Philip Murray, a Lewis protege, acknowledged that "our policy of absolute racial equality in union membership has served to win the support of the most progressive and intelligent of Negro leaders . . . and a generally favorable attitude on the part of the Negro press and organizations."[65]

The National Negro Congress (NNC), a Black leadership coalition consisting of various civic and religious groups headed by A. Philip Randolph, president of the Brotherhood of Sleeping Car Porters, cooperated with SWOC in several ways. The NNC originally grew out of a 1935 conference at Howard University in Washington, D.C., which focused on the New Deal and its impact upon the economic condition of Blacks. The Social Science Division at Howard and the Joint Committee on National Recovery, an association of several racial groups advocating equal treatment for Blacks under New Deal programs, sponsored the conference. After the meeting, John P. Davis, the executive secretary of the Joint Committee, and Ralph J. Bunche, a Howard political scientist, decided to launch a permanent coalition of Black organizations. Encouraging Blacks to become members of labor unions became a major objective of the newly established National Negro Congress. Consequently, when the CIO inaugurated its organizing campaign, John P. Davis, the coordinator of the NNC, viewed it as an opportunity to "write a Magna Carta for Black labor."[69] Davis personally traveled into various steel communities, particularly to Cleveland and Pittsburgh where he had conferences with SWOC officials and "leading Negro steelworkers" on how to organize Blacks. He contacted John L. Lewis, Philip Murray, John Brophy, and other CIO officials and recommended the use of Black organizers in the steel campaign. He also proposed that the NNC print and distribute leaflets to Black steelworkers explaining the purpose of union organization, the way the campaign could be conducted, and describing the deplorable condition of Blacks in the steel industry. Davis also suggested that representatives of the NNC deal personally and secretly with Black steelworkers, and introduce them to "bonafide" SWOC organizers under circumstances which would shield them from suspicious steel managers. Furthermore, no Black steelworkers would know who else had joined the union until the majority of workers in a local plant had signed up with SWOC. Davis hoped that such a procedure would prevent company attempts to individually intimidate workers. He also planned to build local sentiment for the steel campaign by initiating widespread discussion of the union drives in Black newspapers, churches, and in other racial organizations. He wanted White organizers to speak before Black groups in order to demonstrate the authenticity of SWOC's proposed new biracial unionism, and he suggested that Black organizers do the same before White audiences.[70]

The CIO applauded NNC stands for the "organization of Negro workers with their White fellow workers into democratically controlled trade unions."[71] In order to help Davis implement his plans for organizing Black steelworkers, the CIO made several generous financial contributions to the NNC between 1937 and 1940. At one point during the steel campaign John L. Lewis authorized the donation of $1,000 to the National Negro Congress.[72] Davis, who had argued that such a gift was "vital to the successful operation of the (NNC) as an effective aid to the CIO," used the money for defraying the cost of printing leaflets, hiring Black organizers, and paying other organizational expenses.[73]

The NNC played an important role in the organization of Black steelworkers in Western Pennsylvania. Two members of its affiliate in Pittsburgh became organizers. The local council in Pittsburgh also distributed twenty to thirty leaflets urging Blacks throughout Allegheny County to sign up with SWOC.[74] The NNC and the CIO sponsored a conference of Black leaders in Pittsburgh to discuss strategies for recruiting Black laborers into the steel union. The Black conferees included A. Philip Randolph, T. Arnold Hill of the National Urban League, R. Maurice Moss and other officers in the Pittsburgh Urban League, and Robert L. Vann, the influential editor of the *Pittsburgh Courier*. Also present was Bishop William J. Walls of the Allegheny Annual Conference of the AME Zion Church, a jurisdiction which embraced Western Pennsylvania and West Virginia, and Reverend T. J. King, pastor of Ebenezer Baptist Church, a leading congregation in Pittsburgh. They all agreed to extensive use of church pulpits, the radio, and the press as the best ways to bring Blacks to an awareness of SWOC. In cooperative Black churches in Pittsburgh, specific Sundays were designated to encourage support for the steel organizing drive. *The Amalgamated Journal* wisely recognized the importance of NNC assistance in reaching Black steelworkers and in gaining endorsements from Black leaders and their groups.[75]

The steel campaign also received important support from Black spokesmen in Western Pennsylvania, including some Black clergymen. At a Clairton SWOC gathering a local Black minister, Reverend L. D. Watson, speaking to a crowd of 600 people, announced his support of the organizing drive and leveled "shafts at the steel bosses."[76] According to a Black SWOC official, another Pittsburgh area preacher, Reverend L. E. Dukes opened his church for steelworkers' meetings. Reverend Fletcher Williamson, a Duquesne preacher and chipper at the local steel works, had been a member of the Amalgamated Association in 1933. During the SWOC organizing drives, he testified in Pittsburgh before the National Steel Labor Relations Board, and announced his steadfast support of the CIO.[77]

Robert L. Vann of the *Pittsburgh Courier* lent the weight of his editorial pen to the CIO. He even threatened to expose and verbally castigate any Black steelworkers paid by their employers to hamper the organizing campaign in the Pittsburgh vicinity. He declared that the CIO's practice of racial equality made it an "outstanding labor organization" which offered to Black steelworkers an unprecedented chance to secure "better working conditions."[78] Writing in 1937, Vann said that "to advise [that] Negro labor avoid the responsibility and opportunity which is now in its grasp is little short of criminal."[79] His support of Black unionization stemmed in part from his new allegiance to the Democratic Party which the influential head of the CIO and the UMW, John L. Lewis, forcefully backed. Vann, once a supporter of the Brotherhood of Sleeping Car Porters, generally eschewed labor unions, but his encouragement of SWOC won his plaudits from the party's growing CIO constituency.[80]

Homer S. Brown, a Pittsburgh lawyer, also became an important backer of Black unionization. The son of a prominent Baptist preacher, and a graduate of the University of Pittsburgh Law School, Brown, as president of the Pittsburgh NAACP, involved the affiliate more extensively in Black labor issues. In 1933, he expressed concern about the impact of NIRA upon Black laborers, and he investigated charges that fifty Black dam construction workers in Beaver County, Pennsylvania had been jailed illegally so "White men could get their jobs." Like Vann, and thousands of other Pittsburgh Blacks, Brown joined the Democratic Party. In a 1934 election sweep, Pennsylvania gained a

Democratic governor and senator, and five Black state legislators, including Brown. As an ally of Governor George Earle, a fervent supporter of Franklin Delano Roosevelt and a proponent of a Little New Deal for Pennsylvania, Brown authored legislation to advance the interests of Black workers.[81] Earle backed the McGinnis Labor Relations bill which endorsed the right of Pennsylvania workers to form independent unions and which was modeled after the National Labor Relations Act. Brown successfully introduced an amendment to the bill which withheld protection from labor groups which barred potential Black members. Despite the opposition of the Pennsylvania AFL, Brown's amendment, with support from John L. Lewis, and the CIO, won approval in May 1937. Cumberland Posey, Jr., an owner of the Homestead Grays, a Black baseball team some of whom were steelworkers, also aided union efforts in Western Pennsylvania. When Paul Normile and other SWOC organizers from the J and L plant in Aliquippa needed a meeting place, Posey offered his tavern in Pittsburgh.[82]

In Detroit, the pervasive influence and anti-unionism of Henry Ford and other auto executives hindered the development of the CIO among Black autoworkers. Moreover, the Detroit NAACP and Urban League which received funds from Ford knew that most Black laborers in that city depended upon the firm for employment.[83] The Pittsburgh NAACP did not benefit from industrial philanthropy. Moreover, Homer S. Brown, the local president, believed that his political aspirations could be best served in the Democratic Party. With impetus from the Roosevelt Administration, the party became identified with organized labor. These political realities probably stimulated Brown's interest in the burgeoning union movement. Officials of the National Urban League urged their affiliates in 1934 to support labor unions which eschewed racial discrimination. Since the Pittsburgh Urban League during the 1930s did not rely heavily upon corporation contributions, R. Maurice Moss, the executive director, endorsed the Amalgamated Association and attended the National Negro Congress meeting in Pittsburgh which devised strategies to promote SWOC among Black steelworkers.

Socialist and Communist spokesmen had long believed that the success of any proletarian revolution in the United States depended upon the growth of an organized labor movement. Therefore, on the eve of the CIO campaign in 1936, Socialist and Communist organizers offered to the union leaders their experience and expertise. Since they promised to keep their "politics" out of their CIO activities, Philip Murray, chairman of SWOC, brought them into the steel organizing drive.[84] Most of them came to SWOC from existing organizations. The Communists, for example, had already founded the Steel and Metal Workers Industrial Union in 1932 and the Socialists had launched the National Unemployed League, an association designed to assist the victims of housing evictions and hunger. Murray therefore had an opportunity to recruit personnel from the Pittsburgh affiliates of both organizations.[85] Among those who became SWOC organizers were two Blacks who had been involved in both Socialist and Communist organizations beginning in the 1920s. One was Ben Careathers, who was born near Chattanooga, Tennessee, and had migrated to Pittsburgh shortly before World War I. Careathers worked successively as a janitor and then a "helper" for the Pittsburgh Railway Company. He eventually saved enough money to open his own upholstery shop. He joined the Socialist Party but later became a Communist. During the Depression he was active in the party's Unemployed Council and led demonstrations in Pittsburgh for the hungry and jobless. After his involvement with the Steel and Metal Workers Industrial Union, Careathers joined SWOC as an organizer. Philip Murray and Clinton Golden, coordinator of the steel campaign in Western Pennsylvania, dispatched Careathers to organize Black steelworkers at the Jones and Laughlin steel facilities both in Aliquippa and on Pittsburgh's South Side.[86] The other radical activist was Ernest Rice McKinney, the grandson of a West Virginia coal nimer who had been active in the UMW. McKinney joined the Conference for Progressive Labor Action in 1929. Out of this organization, which had split from the Communist Party (CP), came the Unemployed Leagues. Like the CP's Unemployed Council, the League organized eviction demonstrations and conducted relief stations for the poor in Pittsburgh during the early 1930s. McKinney, who had been involved in League drives to distribute shoes and clothing to needy children, became a SWOC organizer in 1936. He too was sent along with eight to ten other organizers to unionize steelworkers at the J and L plant in Aliquippa.[87]

Communist organizers had modest success in attracting Black workers to the CP. Hosea Hudson, a Black steelworker in Ensley, Alabama, became a Communist in 1931. Al Murphy, a Black mill laborer recruited Hudson and other Blacks in the Birmingham area. In the late 1930s, Hudson became a CIO organizer, and eventually a leader in SWOC and its successor, the United Steelworkers of America. The CP made similar efforts in the Pittsburgh vicinity. A White Communist regularly sold *The Daily Worker* to Black workers at J and L Steel in Aliquippa. Some Black laborers joined the Party. J and L accused one Black employee of Communist membership, and compelled him to appear in a Beaver County court to answer the charge.[88]

The influence of a few unions already established in Western Pennsylvania also helped to bring Black workers into SWOC. Black union membership in the Pittsburgh area, however, reflected the dismal national realities, especially within the AFL. In Pittsburgh, the plumbers, plasterers, sheet metal workers, hoisting engineers and other AFL groups largely excluded Blacks. A few unions including the bricklayers and carpenters allowed only a few Blacks to join. The Pittsburgh local of the Brotherhood of Sleeping Car Porters, a racially separate group, was alone among AFL-affiliated organizations with a large Black membership. Between 1935 and 1937 their numbers grew modestly from 142 to 153.[89]

The United Mine Workers traditionally practiced biracial unionism in Western Pennsylvania and elsewhere in the nation. Since its founding in the late nineteenth century, Black miners especially in Alabama, Kentucky, West Virginia, Ohio, and Pennsylvania participated in national union affairs as organizers and as officers in numerous locals. Black miners played an important role in the UMW in the Pittsburgh area. For a time in the 1920s, Blacks in Local No. 2057 in Whitsett served as vice president, financial secretary, and check-weighman. The National Miner's Union, a splinter group, made a special appeal to Black workers. Isaiah Hawkins of Fredericktown became head of its Negro department, and he organized several groups of Black miners in Pennsylvania and West Virginia.[90]

John L. Lewis, national president of the UMW, provided leadership and financial resources to the CIO, and he brought numerous organizers into the group to unionize the mass production industries. His vice president, Philip Murray, hired an effective Black organizer, Milford Peter Jackson, to work in the CIO. Pete Jackson, a native Pennsylvanian, took his first job in a local coal mine at the age of twelve. Eventually, he became a staunch member of the UMW and later went to organize miners in notorious Harlan County, Kentucky. Jackson returned to the Pittsburgh area to bring Black steelworkers in Clairton, Duquesne, and Homestead into SWOC. Furthermore, Black and White miners from various UMW lodges in Western Pennsylvania also attracted Blacks to the steelworker's union. Luther Cormoldy and Joel Parker, both employees of the Pittsburgh Steel Company in Monessen, recruited fellow Blacks into SWOC. UMW activists from nearby coal mining areas assisted them.[91]

Rank and file steelworkers who became organizers proved most effective in persuading Blacks to join SWOC. Many of these steel employees had already joined the union, and were now distributing SWOC leaflets, brochures, and membership cards among fellow workers, both inside and outside the mills. Local organizers included Blacks, as well as Whites. John Dutchmen, the White CIO director in the Lawrenceville section of Pittsburgh, spoke with small groups of Black steelworkers in their homes at night and sometimes at their churches and community organizations.[92] At the McKeesport Tin Plate Company, a Black pickler in the tin plate mill, actively recruited fellow Black workmen into SWOC.[93] Four Black men, the Taylor brothers — John, Francis, Fred and Tom — staged their own SWOC campaign among Black workers at Lockhart Iron and Steel in McKees Rocks.[94] Likewise, Reverend Fletcher Williamson, a veteran of the recent Amalgamated drive, "Father" Cox, another Black preacher, and John McLaurin actively promoted SWOC among their fellow Black employees at the Duquesne steel works.[95] In 1936, SWOC headquarters dispatched from Pittsburgh a Black organizer, John Thornton, to spread the union in the Beaver Valley. Several Black J and L employees in Aliquippa, including Jim Downing, Jeff Phelps, Frank Sesson, Sam Jackson and Bartow Tipper, also convinced fellow Black workers in the Beaver area to follow them into SWOC.[96]

Union organizers encountered substantial company opposition. At the Duquesne steel works, picketing unionists met with violence from mill police.[97] At the J and L plant in Aliquippa, the company hired "goons," armed them with clubs, and dispatched them to beat up organizers.[98] Such awesome demonstrations of company militancy frightened some Black steelworkers. Moreover, various steel officials threatened to fire any employees who signed up with SWOC.[99] In Homestead and Clairton emissaries from Carnegie Steel visited the homes of Black steelworkers and explicitly told their wives "to keep their husbands out of the union if they wanted them to remain employed."[100] J and L in Pittsburgh made contributions to some Black preachers to enlist their aid in discouraging their parishioners from joining SWOC.[101] Some Blacks, heeding these warnings, made no effort to offend their employers, "the hand that's feeding us," for fear of losing their jobs.[102]

Some Black steelworkers remained skeptical of SWOC and its promises of racial equality. A Black J and L employee in Pittsburgh claimed that "I've never seen a union mean anything to a Negro yet." Paul L. "Red" Payne and John W. Brooks, Black employees at the Clairton Steel Works made similar observations. Payne, a former member of the UMW in West Virginia, asserted that the CIO "want we colored employees" to join "an organization where we would be compelled to pay monthly dues and get absolutely nothing in return." Brooks forcefully declared that "as far as my race" is concerned, the CIO "doesn't mean us any good." He believed that once the union reached its goals, the organization "will kick us out the back door." He added "that the Steel Mills . . . are the only places were our race has free access to work." The closed shop for which the CIO "is clamoring" would harm Blacks. "A closed shop means our race closed out," he asserted.[103]

These anxieties deprived SWOC of some Black support in Western Pennsylvania . A Black unionist in Sharon, William Houston, testified that the majority of the 700 local steel employees voting against SWOC were Black. Similarly, in Johnstown, only 6 out of the 400 Black steelworkers at the local Bethlehem plant wanted SWOC as their bargaining agent. Moreover, Johnstown, unlike most steel communities, had an unusually tense racial atmosphere. Only a decade or so before, the Ku Klux Klan and other elements of the Johnstown working class tried to oust Black steelworkers from the city. Slavic steel employees, who made up the majority of local SWOC supporters, did very little either during the 1920s or during the

1930s to align themselves with Black steelworkers. Because Blacks believed that Slavs held racial views similar to most Whites in Johnstown, they kept away from the Slavic-dominated union. In fact, several incidents of violence between the two groups of steel employees occurred during the organizing drive. Therefore, Blacks, instead of joining SWOC, sided with Bethlehem Steel.[104]

Elsewhere in Western Pennsylvania, however, especially at Carnegie and J and L plants in Pittsburgh, Homestead, Braddock, Duquesne, and Clairton, the SWOC organizing drives met with their greatest success among Black steelworkers. Despite some skepticism, many Blacks had simply become disillusioned with company unionism and responded favorably to the Amalgamated Association. The development of rank-and-file leadership among local Black steelworkers accounted in large measure for SWOC's substantial showing among Blacks. At the beginning of AAIS organizing activity in 1934, its White members, recognizing the importance of labor solidarity and remembering the union's 1919 fiasco, made a major effort to involve Black steelworkers in the organizing drive. Several prospective Black unionists were impressed by the new attitudes of the Amalgamated Association. Throughout the Monongahela region, they joined the organization and remained with it until SWOC eventually absorbed most AAIS lodges in Western Pennsylvania.

These Black Amalgamated members became SWOC's staunchest supporters in the 1936 and 1937 organizing campaigns. In Pittsburgh and the Monongahela milltowns, where Black steelworkers were most numerous, these SWOC recruiters, like their fellow Black laborers, worked in segregated mill departments. This gave them direct contact with their Black clientele and enabled them to personally persuade them to join the union. The Black triumvirate of Williamson, Cox, and McLaurin lobbied for SWOC among Black steelworkers in Duquesne. Another Black did the same at the McKeesport Tin Plate Company. Nathan Sally and Albert McPherson promoted SWOC among Blacks at the Clairton steel works. They, along with White rank-and-file leaders, by recruiting within specific racial and ethnic groups, insured SWOC success in the major steel plants of Western Pennsylvania.[105]

Where such leadership was absent, the SWOC campaign

won few Black members. In Johnstown, for example, Houston Underwood, an employee at Bethlehem Steel, worked actively as SWOC's sole Black organizer. Although most Black steelworkers labored in segregated departments, Underwood did not. Like Williamson in Duquesne and Sally in Clairton, he

Figure 10. A Black steelworker in Western Pennsylvania during the 1930s. (From Stefan Lorant's *Pittsburgh: The Story of an American City*; photo by Arthur Rothstein.)

made common cause with White unionists. And unlike his counterparts in the Monongahela milltowns, Underwood had minimal contact with fellow Black steelworkers. He worked at Bethlehem's wheel plant, where only 6 out of 300 laborers were Black. Prior to working there, he had labored at the mill's Franklin Open Hearth, where only 13 out of 897 employees were Black. Enmity between Blacks and Whites at the Johnstown steel facilities already existed. With the absence of a Black liaison with White unionists, there was limited potential for any racial cooperation in the current steel campaign. Underwood's identification with Whites and his lack of credibility with Black steelworkers damaged his effectiveness. Therefore, few Johnstown Blacks were attracted to SWOC.[106]

According to one estimate, a total of 5,235 Black steelworkers were employed in Western Pennsylvania on the eve of the SWOC organizing drives. Most of them, approximately 81 percent, or 4,248 Black workmen, labored at various Carnegie and J and L steel plants in Pittsburgh, Aliquippa and the Monongahela milltowns of Homestead, Braddock, Duquesne, and Clairton.[107] Extensive campaigning by Black organizers, both from SWOC's Pittsburgh headquarters and from the rank and file of Black steelworkers, proved most effective in recruiting the vast majority of these men into the organization. Although the precise number of Black steelworkers in the Pittsburgh area who joined SWOC is unknown, most contemporary observers agree that their numbers were large. Robert L. Vann of the *Pittsburgh Courier* reported that "thousands of Negro steelworkers from Birmingham to Pittsburgh" had become union members. Local Black organizers declared that Blacks joined SWOC in even "greater proportion(s) than" Whites.[108]

Hopes for better pay, job advancement, job protection through seniority, and general faith in SWOC propaganda about racial fairness convinced the majority of the areas's Black mill employees to sign union cards. Like many who had joined the Amalgamated Association a few years before, J. L. Simmons, a Black coalman at Lockhart Iron and Steel, joined SWOC because he believed that it could curb the "arbitrary will of the bosses."[109] Similarly, Roy McChester, a Black employee at J and L in Pittsburgh, wanted to make more money and have the union stop bosses from "riding" the workers.[110] These and other goals were accomplished when SWOC signed an agreement with Carnegie-Illinois Steel on March 17, 1937. Jones and Laughlin and Crucible Steel, the other two major employers of Black steelworkers, soon followed suit. These companies extended wage increases, permanently established the eight-hour day and the forty-hour week, and gave a seven-day paid vacation to all steelworkers, Black and White, with at least five years of service. Those steelworkers, regardless of color, with seniority had preference in promotions and protection when layoffs came. Also, any steelworker, Black or White, believing that he had been unjustly discharged, could file a grievance with an appropriate committee consisting of labor and management representatives. If the discharge was found unfair, the employee received full back pay for the days missed from work.[111]

Moreover, in almost every SWOC local with a sizeable Black membership, a Black officer was elected as its representative. In Monessen, a Black became the first vice president of Local No. 1229 at the Pittsburgh Steel Company.[112] Another Black was elected vice president of the newly organized Local 1237 at the McKeesport Tin Plate Company.[113] The Penn Iron and Steel company in Tarentum employed 350 men, of whom 250 were Black. After both Black and White employees voted to affiliate with SWOC in 1937, they elected Hunter Howell, a Black puddler, as president.[114] In the early 1940s Jim Downing became vice president of Local No. 1211 at J and L's Aliquippa Steel Works.[115]

An important by-product of Black unionization was the development of Black working-class leadership. Black laborers had relied upon welfare officers to advance their interests and articulate their grievances. When Black steelworkers helped in the revival of the Amalgamated Association and in the establishment of SWOC and later the United Steelworkers of America, they gained valuable organization and oratorical skills and they became union officials. Working-class Blacks now had their own spokesmen to intercede with corporate executives. Some even became community spokesmen who participated in race betterment groups while others entered local politics.

As welfare officers, Charles Broadfield of the Duquesne steel works, Grover Nelson at the Homestead steel works, and William P. Young at Lockhart Iron and Steel in McKees Rocks, could not encourage Black unionization or they would lose their own jobs. Nonetheless, Broadfield and Nelson continued to manage social and recreational activities for Black steelworkers, while Young took care of the housing needs of McKees Rocks Blacks long after steel executives recognized SWOC. In any case, the union replaced Black welfare officers as the official representative of Black workers and Black SWOC officials succeeded them as spokesmen for Black laborers.[116]

Bartow Tipper and Jacques Moragne typified this important group of Black working-class leaders. Born in Americus, Georgia in 1907, Tipper came to Aliquippa in 1922 to join his father, William Tipper, an employee at J and L Steel. In 1923, young Bartow began work in J and L's tube mill. In 1931, he became a member of the company union which consisted mainly of Blacks afraid of losing their jobs. Bartow served as a committeeman in the union, and his brother, Oliver, was secretary. Two important events shaped Tipper into an independent unionist. First, J and L officials angered him when they tried to determine the officers of the company union. Second, J and L fired his friend, Sam Jackson, when he joined the Amalgamated Association. Furious and disenchanted, Tipper followed Jackson into the AAIS in 1935. Tipper, Jackson, and a few other Black steelworkers subsequently joined SWOC, and encouraged other Black J and L employees to sign membership cards. During World War II, Tipper headed the Negro Civic League of Beaver County which fought racial discrimination, especially in the hiring of Black women at J and L. In later years he served as president of the Aliquippa NAACP.[117]

Jacques Moragne, born in Greenwood, South Carolina, studied at Tuskegee Institute before he became an employee at the Clairton Steel Works during the 1920s. He was an organizer of Local No. 1557 of the United Steelworkers of America, and later served on the safety and housing committee. Moragne also entered local politics, and in the 1960s he was elected Clairton's first Black councilman.[118] Numerous other Black unionists became effective spokesmen within the region's mill communities.

Despite these developments, the general condition of Black steelworkers in Western Pennsylvania remained unchanged. Although WPA and other work-relief projects ameliorated their economic conditions, Blacks continued to be unemployed in disproportionate numbers. Section 7a of the National Industrial Recovery Act failed to protect them either from company unionism or discrimination in the American Federation of Labor. The CIO, through the SWOC, offered what appeared to be a real alternative to Black steelworkers. Yet in spite of structural and procedural safeguards, Blacks remained locked in "Negro jobs" and in segregated mill departments. Even under seniority rules, the steel companies had the freedom to pass judgment on a worker's "ability, skill and efficiency." This allowed discrimination in favor of Whites to continue. Furthermore, other kinds of prejudicial treatment against Blacks persisted in area steel mills despite the presence of SWOC. In January 1938, shortly after Crucible Steel signed a union agreement, Alvin Nunley, a furloughed Black employee at the company's Pittsburgh plant, wrote President Roosevelt about the prevalence of race discrimination within the mill:

> They put me in hot places all summer, where not many men will stay; when it gets cool, they layed me off; White men get my job . . . I have went to see the employment manager of the mill [and] all he says is their is no call for colored men. He has sent me to places in the mill where I have worked as good as any other man, but I can't get the job steady, on account of I am not White man . . . I don't think it fair . . . I have a right to a living as well as anyone else, no matter what color I am . . ."[119]

Although World War II restored employment opportunities to Black steelworkers in Western Pennsylvania, their social and economic conditions remained very much the same. In spite of the New Deal, SWOC, and wartime prosperity, Blacks continued to suffer from discriminatory hiring practices, lack of promotion, and poor living conditions. In some cases, SWOC came forward to protect and advance their interests, but on other occasions, Black steelworkers were compelled to resort to wildcat strikes and appeals to the Fair Employment Practices Committee for solutions to their problems.

# 7
# Black Steelworkers in Western Pennsylvania: World War II and its Aftermath

The revival of employment opportunities in the steel industry during World War II eased Black unemployment in Western Pennsylvania and stimulated another wave of Black migration from the agrarian South to the Pittsburgh steel district. Migrants flocked into racially segregated residential areas, overcrowding already limited and substandard housing facilities and expanding the ranks of unskilled and semi-skilled Black laborers in the mills. Despite the greater availability of jobs in the steel industry after a decade of depression, discrimination in hiring, promotion and work assignments persisted.

Inspired by the activism of the NAACP, the National Urban League and the National Negro Congress during the 1930s and Black involvement in the newly formed CIO and SWOC, Black workers learned how to articulate their grievances and how to organize. They recognized their importance both to the labor movement and to the success of national defense efforts during the war. When confronted with continued discrimination in the workplace, Black steelworkers took matters into their own hands and staged work stoppages to protest racial unfairness in employment practices. They also turned to the FEPC (the Fair Employment Practices Commitee) of the federal government.

151

The urgency of securing the cooperation of Black workers during World War II made the FEPC particularly responsive to complaints of discrimination, especially when steel firms and the union, the United Steelworkers of America (formerly SWOC), failed to act on such grievances. The involvement of the FEPC in Black worker affairs helped to stimulate militancy among these rank and file laborers.[1]

As in World War I, manpower deficiencies during the Second World War required steel managers to search beyond their immediate environs for additional mill employees to assist them in meeting expanded production demands. Local mill officials followed previous practices and sent recruiters to the South to attract Black workers to the Pittsburgh steel district. The Homestead Steel Works, for example, again sent Grover Nelson, its welfare official, to recruit Black Southerners to work in its mills.[2] Like their World War I predecessors, Blacks came from areas throughout the South, but particularly from Tennessee, Alabama, and Georgia, and some as far away as Texas.[3] Most were like Calvin Ingram, whose disenchantment with farm labor caused him to leave his native Camden, South Carolina in 1943. He and other Black Southerners flocked into Washington, D.C., where wartime government jobs were especially plentiful. Ingram secured a job building and maintaining army camps in and around the District of Columbia. After three months in the capital area, however, he and Henry Truesdale were recruited into Western Pennsylvania by a fellow hometown acquaintance, Johnnie Johnson. All three became steelworkers at the Carnegie-Illinois facilities in Duquesne.[4] They, like other Black migrants, were lured to the Pittsburgh vicinity because of the "higher wage scales" in local mills and foundries.[5]

Several government agencies, including the United States Employment Service, the War Manpower Commission, and the War Production Board, assisted local managers in securing Black workers for the Pittsburgh steel district. During the war, two open hearth furnaces at the Farrell Works of Carnegie-Illinois Steel were reopened for production. Plant officials quickly notified the War Manpower Commission of their need for 95 men to refurbish these dormant facilities, and for another 141 laborers to fill other unskilled positions. The inadequate supply of local laborers in Farrell made the search for "in migrants" to work in the mills an absolute necessity.[6] The Wyckoff Drawn Steel Company in Ambridge, which reported the "bottleneck" in its shipping department in 1943, asked the War Production Board whether "any available negro laborers . . . could be hired . . . to alleviate their manpower shortages."[7] Labor deficiencies at the Carnegie-Illinois facility in Clairton in about 1945 proved an impediment to steel production. A local mill official wrote the War Manpower Commission, urgently requesting Black workers from "interregional recruitment . . . in [the] Southern states." He noted that such efforts had "brought good results in [the] past."[8]

Consequently, Black Southerners by the "hundreds" migrated to Western Pennsylvania.[9] During the war, approximately 10,595 Black newcomers settled in Pittsburgh and the surrounding milltowns.[10] By 1944, the rehiring of furloughed Black employees, together with these newly arrived Black laborers, brought the number of Black steelworkers to at least 11,500 workmen, 14 percent of the total work force. At most area mills, the percentage of Blacks usually exceeded 10 percent. In some cases, they made up more than 25 percent of all plant employees (see Table 9).

As Black migrants settled in Western Pennsylvania during World War II, several signs of racial progress were evident. Blacks had earlier become policemen in Duquesne, Johnstown, Clairton and some other milltowns.[11] Also, more blatant forms of racial segregation had been abolished. In 1935, the Pennsylvania Legislature passed and the Governor signed equal rights legislation outlawing racial segregation. In Johnstown, for example, twenty eating places, which had since the 1920s refused to serve Blacks, had by 1940 abandoned such discriminatory practices.[12] Other public facilities throughout the region were also available to Black patrons on a nondiscriminatory basis. Yet, in spite of these advances, racial prejudice and discrimination continued in the Pittsburgh area. Shortly before the war, a municipal swimming pool had been constructed in Clairton which excluded Blacks. Dr. Joseph Randall, a local Black physician, and Paul L. (Red) Payne, a Black employee at the Clairton steel works, made public protests against this restriction. Because of Randall's vehement stand, a group of prosegregationists twice burned a cross at his home. After the first cross burning, Clair-

**TABLE 9. Black Workers at Selected Steel Plants in Western Pennsylvania, 1944**

| Plant | Total Work Force | Number of Blacks | Percentage Black |
|---|---|---|---|
| Carnegie-Illinois, Munhall | 12,662 | 2,104 | 16 |
| Carnegie-Illinois, Dravosburg | 3,464 | 1,203 | 35 |
| Bethlehem Steel, Johnstown | 12,903 | 530 | 4 |
| Jones and Laughlin, Pittsburgh | 10,139 | 1,178 | 11 |
| American Radiator, Pittsburgh | 646 | 173 | 26 |
| American Steel Foundries, Vrna | 849 | 155 | 17 |
| Continental Foundry and Machine, Coraopolis | 1,218 | 353 | 28 |
| Fort Pitt Steel, McKeesport | 780 | 170 | 21 |
| National Malleable and Steel Castings, Sharon | 1,986 | 280 | 14 |
| Pittsburgh Steel, Glassport | 1,511 | 230 | 15 |
| Union Steel Castings, Pittsburgh | 1,993 | 560 | 27 |
| Pittsburgh Forging, McKees Rocks | 1,598 | 14 | .07 |
| Fort Pitt Malleable Iron, McKees Rocks | 583 | 215 | 37 |
| Carnegie-Illinois, Clairton | 1,100 | 700 | 63 |
| Crucible Steel, Midland | 7,500 | 1,200 | 16 |

**TABLE 9. Black Workers at Selected Steel Plants in Western Pennsylvania, 1944** *(Continued)*

| Plant | | Total Work Force | Number of Blacks | Percentage Black |
|---|---|---|---|---|
| Carnegie-Illinois, Braddock | | 5,316 | 817 | 15 |
| Duquesne Smelting, Pittsburgh | | 449 | 240 | 53 |
| C. G. Hussey Steel, Pittsburgh | | 922 | 248 | 27 |
| Jessop Steel, Washington | (1943) | 1,600 | 35 | 2 |
| Jones and Laughlin, Aliquippa | | 9,958 | 1,095 | 11 |
| Totals | | 77,177 | 11,500 | 14% |

Source: *War Manpower Commission Records, Bureau of Placement, Industrial Allocation Division, and Fair Employment Practices Commission Records,* Regional Files, Region III, National Archives, Washington, D.C.; *Harold Ruttenberg Collection, War Production Board Correspondence,* Labor Archives, Pennsylvania State University, University Park, Pennsylvania.

ton's police department denied protection to Dr. Randall and the mayor refused him a gun permit. Although the local judge issued an order directing municipal authorities to admit Blacks to the pool, a vigilance club was organized "to aid the mayor" in upholding the original ban on Blacks.[13]

Segregation also persisted in housing. In 1940, 50 percent of all Pittsburgh Blacks lived in the Hill District, primarily in the third and fifth wards. Although most Black migrants settling in the city during the Second World War crowded into the Southside-Beltzhoover area, housing accommodations were generally poor for all. In 1946, nearly 30 percent of all housing for Blacks was substandard. For Whites the proportion was 12.3 percent. Fifty-six percent of all Black homes needed major repairs, and had no private bath. For Whites the rate 43.5 percent. Similarly in Braddock 84 percent of all Blacks occupied substandard dwellings, while 45 percent of all Whites resided in poor housing facilities. In North Braddock and Rankin, the percentages of Blacks living in inferior residences were 65 percent and 80 percent, respectively, while for Whites they were 31 percent and 52 percent, respectively.[14]

Furthermore, the percentage of Black renters during the decade of the 1940s, though declining, nonetheless remained higher than that for Whites. In 1940 in Pittsburgh, the proportion of Black renters was 87 percent, and for Whites it was 65 percent. In 1950, the percentage of Black renters was 76 percent and for Whites it was 55 percent. In Braddock in 1940, the proportion for Blacks was 95 percent but among Whites it was 76 percent. Ten years later, 89 percent of all Black dwellings were rented. A much lower rate, 68 percent, prevailed for Braddock Whites. Similarly, in Clairton, the percentage of Black renters was 94 percent, but the rate for Whites was 50 percent. In 1950, 77 percent of all Blacks were renter, while only 42 percent of Clairton Whites fitted into this category.

Housing was inadequate for Blacks at the beginning of World War II. Wartime plant expansion aggravated this problem. In many mill communities, the construction of additional steel-making facilities required the complete demolition of entire Black neighborhoods. In Homestead, where tank and naval armor were produced, most Blacks lived "below the tracks" in an area close to the local steel works.[16] Shortly after the war began, leveling of these residential areas commenced. Several open hearth furnaces, a forge and machine shop, a plate mill, and other facilities were to take their place.[17] By late January 1942, over 60 percent of these 1,200 homes had been destroyed, and only 10 percent of the 10,000 inhabitants still remained. Indeed, the "population was thinning rapidly," and by early February, "the wrecking of lower Homestead approached its final stages."[18] Similarly, in Duquesne, plans had been made to build three electric furnaces, a conditioning plant, and a heat treating facility.[19] As in Homestead, this meant that more than 2,500 people living in Castle Garden, an area bordering the Duquesne Steel Works, had to vacate their homes to make way for these new facilities.[20]

Shortages resulting from mill expansion and renewed Black migration to Western Pennsylvania were partially allayed by government-sponsored housing. Ironically, plans for these housing units had been formulated only a few years before the war began as a Great Depression measure. Consequently, many of these dwellings were nearing completion when demand for them became heavy. Seven projects were constructed in Pittsburgh, and among them were Aliquippa Terrace, Bedford Dwellings, and Wadsworth Terrace. Several others were built in Duquesne, Clairton, Aliquippa, McKeesport, and some other mill communities.[21] Blacks already residing in the area, as well as incoming migrants, rushed to occupy these new projects. Black Homestead residents displaced from their homes by the local mill expansion moved to the "low rent" Hawkins Village in North Braddock, the Glen Hazel defense housing projects in Pittsburgh, or the Munhall Homesteads, a nearby development.[22] James Wilson, a Black steelworker who had migrated to Duquesne from South Carolina in 1923, lived in Castle Garden. When demolition began for the construction of additional mill facilities, he moved to the newly built Riverview Homes in West Mifflin. Other residents of Castle Garden secured apartments in the Cochrandale Projects in Duquesne.[23] Calvin Ingram, another South Carolinian laboring at the Duquesne Steel Works, had migrated to the area from Washington, D.C., in 1943. Shortly after his arrival, he too settled in the recently completed Cochrandale settlement.[24]

In spite of these efforts, however, housing for Blacks remained in short supply. Much of what was available was segregated and substandard. Because the planners of government-sponsored housing located them in or near racially exclusive neighborhoods, these projects took on a character similar to their surroundings. Griffith Heights and Mount Vernon in Aliquippa, Harrison Village in McKeesport, and Blair Heights in Clairton all lay close to Black neighborhoods, and each mirrored its racial environment.[25] The Allegheny County Housing Authority deliberately made the Cochrandale Project a "Negro settlement in . . . Duquesne." Whites, on the other hand, moved into the Crawford Hill development and the Duquesne Annex defense housing project, which were both situated in White residential areas.[26] Bedford Dwellings in the Hill District in Pittsburgh began as a racially integrated project, but Whites gradually left and it "proved impossible to persuade other White families to take their places." Even at Addison Terrace in Pittsurgh, where few Whites resided, they lived separately from Blacks. This pattern of separation prevailed at other "integrated" housing developments as well. Successful attempts to integrate housing did occur, but not enough to reverse the more general pattern of segregated living in Western Pennsylvania.[27]

At no time during the war were housing accommodations sufficient for Blacks in the Pittsburgh area. Only one housing project, Steel City Terrace, was built in the Farrell-Sharon vicinity. Blacks occupied one-third of the 150 units.[28] Even these were inadequate. Local residents filled them so quickly that none were "available for in-migrants." Instead, Farrell's Black newcomers had to reside in buildings which had been converted into living quarters, but these were also in short supply. Although "40 trailers" were likewise made available to "in-migrants and their families," no single workers were "permitted to rent" these dwellings.[29] The Cochrandale project in Duquesne included 83 units, and the Blair Heights development in Clairton had 148 units, all of which were occupied by Black tenants.[30] Yet, housing among Blacks in both towns remained limited, and in many cases, overcrowded. Consequently, Blacks imported by Carnegie-Illinois Steel to its Clairton works were provided with rooms in Pittsburgh, over twenty miles from their place of employment. Other Blacks working at the Clairton coke facility lived at the Quanset Barracks in Duquesne, seven miles away. Black migrants in Duquesne had similar difficulties in arranging lodging. In addition to the vacancies at the local mill dormitory, officials at the Duquesne Steel Works found "35 rooms in 'nice homes' for Black newcomers." An investigation by the Pittsburgh Urban League, however, revealed "that after a period of a month or two, the men who had been placed in rooms by the plant were expected to have found other accommodations and were forced to move for more incoming men."[31] Housing shortages existed also in Pittsburgh. Shortly after the war, the Pittsburgh Housing Association reported that Blacks needed over 9,000 additional dwelling units "to meet then present deficiencies."[32] Throughout Western Pennsylvania in spite of governmental efforts, housing remained sharply limited for both Blacks and Whites. Because of traditional patterns of racial discrimination, however, Blacks fared worse than Whites in their attempts to find adequate housing.

Black workers also confronted rampant racial unfairness in the workplace. In 1942, the Pennsylvania Temporary Commission on the Urban Conditions among Negroes, a special investigatory group established by the state legislature, revealed that half of all industrial firms in Philadelphia and Pittsburgh either denied employment to Blacks or kept them in menial positions.[33] At the end of World War II, two-fifths of all manufacturing concerns in Allegheny County still refused to hire Blacks.[34] Discriminatory employment practices continued unabated in the steel industry. The Pittsburgh Urban League in 1942 hired a young Black to apply at several mills in the Carnegie and East Pittsburgh vicinities for a job as a common laborer. Officials at Superior Steel and Columbia Steel rebuffed him by simply saying "we're not hiring." Bethlehem Steel and American Steel Band both emphatically stated that "no colored labor" was used in their mills. Shortly thereafter, a local League official concluded in a letter to Robert C. Weaver of the Fair Employment Practices Committee "that there are still plants in this area which refuse to hire Negroes even at common labor."[35] Discrimination also kept Black workers in Allegheny County primarily in the ranks of the unskilled. Although the proportion of Blacks in semi-skilled positions began to equal that of Whites (41.4 percent and 46.5 percent, respectively), Whites continued to outstrip Blacks in the skilled categories. Approximately 41.9 percent of all Whites worked as skilled laborers, while 16.7 percent of all Blacks held such positions. On the other hand, 42 percent of all Blacks worked in unskilled positions, while only 11.6 percent of all Whites fitted within this category.[36] The experiences of Percy Foster and Theodore Spencer, who both sought skilled positions in local steel firms, was common for most Blacks. Foster tried to get hired as a chipper at the Blaw Knox Steel Company in Pittsburgh. Despite his four years' experience in that trade, he was offered a laborer's job "on the grounds that [the] company did not hire Negroes as chippers."[37] Spencer had extensive training as a machinist. After suffering an injury while on active duty in the Marines, he spent an eight-month convalescence in a hospital. Soon thereafter, the United States Employment Service referred him for a job at the Mackintosh and Hemphill Company in Midland. A telephone interview with a company official revealed that Spencer qualified for a vacant position which was consistent with his skills. When he appeared at the plant, however, his race was noted and he was informed that the job had just been taken. Nonetheless, a position "sweeping" was immediately offered to the young Black veteran.[38]

Blacks already employed in area steel facilities frequently encountered discriminatory practices not only from plant officials but also from fellow White workmen. J. Burrell Reid, a migrant from Virginia, had become a chauffeur to a Jones and Laughlin Steel Company official in 1927. When his employer died in 1936, Reid secured a job as a janitor in the all-White metallurgy department at J and L's South Side plant in Pittsburgh. Later on, the wartime draft caused a high turnover of young men in the department, and consequently a friendly mill official persuaded Reid, now in his forties, to inquire about one of the vacant positions. To Reid's great dismay, the foreman in that department flatly refused to consider him for such an advancement because of White worker opposition.[39] Howard Lee, another Black employee at the South Side Mills, tried to get a better job, either as a "rigger, sheeter, strip mill worker, or pipefitter helper," but he met with no success. Lee, a former employee at the Pittsburgh Coal Company mine in Library, Pennsylvania, stated that:

> . . . White men who formerly worked with him and with the same experience were transferred to these jobs while he was told by his foreman . . . [that] there was no point in referring Negroes to those departments as they would not be acceptable because of race.[40]

Louis Causby, a Black steelworker at J and L's Aliquippa Works, had the same trouble securing a promotion. He was a ten-year veteran in the 14-inch mill, working as a straightener helper. In 1943, Causby tried to become a straightener himself, but opposition from the foremen blocked this attempt. Soon thereafter, two Whites, both of whom lacked Causby's experience, were able to gain promotions.[41] The Cohocksink Division of the Combustion Engineering Company in Monongahela, Pennsylvania employed only Whites prior to 1944. When management finally hired Blacks, White employees staged an unsuccessful strike protesting this company action. Plant officials held firm since they feared violation of Executive Orders 8802 and 9346 which mandated withdrawal of federal contracts in cases of racial discrimination.[42]

When Black women became steelworkers in Western Pennsylvania, they encountered the same discrimination which had checked the progress of their husbands and fathers. Because area mills experienced periodic personnel shortages during the war, company officials hired women to replace steelworkers drafted into the armed services. As in World War I, the prospect of earning money, either to supplement family income or to totally support their households, strongly appealed to females, Black and White.

In 1940, Pittsburgh had a Black population of 58,562 men and 56,468 women.[43] Only 4,385 Black women worked outside of their homes. The largest group consisted of 2,613 domestic servants and another group of 1,094 labored in other service fields including work as beauticians, waitresses, and janitors. Approximately 345 worked in professional and semi-professional categories, as proprietors and managers and in clerical pursuits. Another 242 Black women worked as operators in laundries, as dressmakers, and clothing factories. Only two worked in the steel industry.[44]

When World War II created for Black women unprecedented employment opportunities, numerous wives, daughters, and occasionally mothers of Black steelworkers either joined them or replaced them in the mills. Once they entered the steel industry, however, Black women suffered from the familiar patterns of race discrimination which already victimized Black males. An investigator from the Women's Bureau of the United States Labor Department surveyed several steel districts during the war and found that both Black and White women worked chiefly as laborers. Yet even within this category, Black women performed the more difficult tasks. The survey revealed that work around sintering plants was assigned mostly exclusively to female Blacks, and "they . . . were reported as moving as much dirt and material as men."[45] The general condition of Black women in the steel industry of Western Pennsylvania accurately fitted this description.

Unlike White women, female Blacks had initial difficulties just in getting hired. In 1943, nineteen-year-old Frances Stanton needed to support herself and her infant daughter while her husband served in the armed forces. She complained that the Clairton steel works was hiring White women "everyday in the week," while totally ignoring her employment inquiry.[46] Another Black woman who had a son "booked for the Navy," expressed her dismay about job discrimination in a letter to President Franklin D. Roosevelt:

> They don't seem to be hiring colored women in Washington County at all. There are two plants close by, one in Washington, that is, Jessop Steel, and the one in Bridgeville, but they will hire the White girls but when the colored girls go there they always refuse them.[47]

Several women applied for jobs at the Homestead Steel Works and a few other defense plants in the Pittsburgh area, and found that White women received preference in hiring. One of these Black women believed it ridiculous to get relief "when there is so much defense work in demand." She wondered "how is it I cannot have a chance to work. . . .?"[48] The vice president of Sharon Steel Corporation in Sharon openly admitted that the absence of Black females in his plant was due to "women employees (who) will not work with non-Whites."[49] President Roosevelt usually referred such petitions to the FEPC for investigation. The FEPC which Roosevelt established under Executive Order 8802 in 1941 was further strengthened under a second presidential directive, Executive Order 9336 in 1943.[53]

Area steel firms therefore began to hire Black women, but in relatively small numbers.[51] The Carnegie steel plants in Braddock and Homestead, as well as the Pittsburgh and Aliquippa facilities of J and L Steel, employed them within their mills. Others worked as draftswomen at Blaw Knox Steel in Pittsburgh and in the open hearth and blast furnace departments at the Duquesne steel works.[52] Black women worked in the nail mill at American Steel and Wire in Donora. They also labored in the plants rod mill, steel works, and in the labor gang.[53]

Like Black men, however, Black women frequently encountered unfair treatment, particularly in rough and unpleasant job assignments. Ethel M. Cotton worked as a grinder at the Crucible steel plant in Midland. This physically exacting position had "no regulated rest periods," and eventually caused her to injure her wrist. When she saw that White women were being assigned to "lighter work" as paint girls, she too requested a transfer to that department. However, her superior bluntly told her to accept either "grinding" or no job at all.[54] Bessie Simmons had a similar position in the ordnance department at the Carnegie-Illinois steel facility in Farrell. She also wanted to leave her job as a grinder in the burr gang. When she asked her foreman, "if colored girls could get better jobs," he told her that they were simply not "wanted" in other departments.[55] In 1943, the Carnegie-Illinois plant in Clairton hired three Black females as jamb cutters in the mill batteries. Their boss promised them that they would perform these duties for only four of the eight hours on their shift. They would spend the remaining time "on less arduous toil away from the batteries." After working there for six days, their boss approached them again to inquire whether they would work the full eight hours as jamb cutters. When they replied negatively, he fired them. Likewise, when they asked for transfers, he told them "unless you cut jambs, there is no other place here for you." Although plant officials

customarily transferred White women to other departments
after three days in this section of the mill, they refused to inau-
gurate the same practice for Black women.[56]

The discrimination faced by Black women in the steel mills
of Western Pennsylvania elicited sympathetic responses from
their Black male colleagues. John Johnson, an employee at
Carnegie-Illinois Steel in Farrell, protested to plant officials
about the treatment of "colored girls" by white foreman.[57] The
failure of Jones and Laughlin Steel in Aliquippa to initially hire
Black women prompted Bartow Tipper of the Beaver County
Civic League to telegraph President Roosevelt, reminding him
that "we are all Americans . . . fighting for our democracy."[58] A
Black woman who worked at the Crucible steel plant in Midland met with unfair treatment while seeking a transfer to a less
demanding job. William Fountain, a fellow Black employee and
President of the NAACP in nearby East Liverpool, Ohio,
assisted her by writing out her grievances for submission to
their local union.[59] Eventually, FEPC intervention stopped such
discriminatory practices.

These defiant attitudes characterized a general sentiment
held by Black Americans during the 1940s. Throughout the

Figure 11. Bartow Tipper was a Black steel worker-activist at the Jones
& Laughlin Steel Works in Aliquippa. Born in Georgia, Tipper became
an early member of the Steelworkers Organizing Committee, C.I.O. in
the 1930s. He also led protests to end discriminatory hiring practices
against Black men and Black women at J & L during World War II.
(Courtesy of Bartow Tipper, Aliquippa, PA.)

nation, the war inspired unprecedented militancy among Blacks. The reaction of Black workers to their inferior status in the workplace, the attempts of the March on Washington Movement to secure fair treatment for Blacks in the nation's defense industries, the aggressive push for racial equality by the Black press, and the reaction to the abuse of Black soldiers by military and civilian personnel were examples of such militancy and further encouraged Blacks to resist segregation and discriminatory treatment. This defiant mood found expression in racial rioting in Detroit and New York's Harlem, where Black newcomers, discontented over crowded housing and other racial grievances, clashed with Whites in neighboring residential areas and with police charged with the task of quelling the unrest. Black soldiers in camps throughout the country also grew tired of mistreatment and retaliated against those heaping abuse upon them.

Blacks also reacted in Pittsburgh. In July 1943, several hundred Blacks "threatened to storm" a Hill District police station in order to release two Black men held for loitering. The recent riots in Detroit's Paradise Valley were fresh in the minds of the angry protestors. As they gathered around the police station, they loudly chanted, "Do you want another Detroit?" Police reserves arrived, broke up the crowd "without bloodshed," and averted a riot. The next day a battalion of 600 military police stationed several miles outside of the city "paraded" through the Hill District with light tanks and jeeps to quell any further unrest.[61]

After this show of force, nervous municipal and county officials, fearing the influence of the Detroit race riot, behaved in a conciliatory manner toward Pittsburgh Blacks. In August 1943, the annual Grand Lodge convention of the Improved, Benevolent and Protective Order of Elks of the World met at Central Baptist Church in Pittsburgh's Hill District. Since the organization included lodges in nearly every industrial community in Western Pennsylvania, numerous Black workers attended the meeting as delegates. Mayor Cornelius B. Scully attended the convention. Perry W. Howard, the Legal Adviser of the Elks, was cheered by his presence and noted that the mayor did not send a Negro substitute to represent him. Also present were the city's chief law enforcement officer who acknowledged that poor housing generated Black unrest, and a commissioner of Allegheny County who admitted that economic fear poisoned race relations. Dr. William J. Thompkins, chairman of the Elks Health Commission, was so impressed with the oratory of these political leaders that he wrongly concluded that "there is no semblance of social unrest or race riots in Pittsburgh."[62]

Racial militancy also affected Black workers. Especially between July 1943 and December 1944, Blacks in various parts of the country initiated twenty-two strikes to protect limited promotion opportunities, wage differentials based on race, and sorts of unfair treatment.[63] In Western Pennsylvania, Black steelworkers acted swiftly whenever racial discrimination jeopardized their occupational interests. A veteran Black steelworker, Samuel Whitfield, charged his employer, Mackintosh and Hemphill in Midland, with racial discrimination. Whitfield, who labored as a chipper, contended that his assignment to work on a hot casting was unfair, "since none of the White workers" were given this task. He argued that "the only time any chipper was assigned to a hot casting was on emergency jobs or when no other work was available, and such [an] assignment affected everyone alike." In protest of his apparent mistreatment, Whitfield "persuaded" thirty other Black chippers to join him in staging a sitdown strike.[64]

Since 1933, Blacks had completely staffed the coke division of the Carnegie-Illinois by-products plant in Clairton. Company officials required these veteran employees to teach newer White workers how the division operated. When this task had been accomplished, Whites replaced their Black instructors, who were thereafter "transferred to other departments and jobs of a lower classification." These and similar experiences continued on into the war period and prompted a series of work stoppages among Black Clairton steelworkers between December 1943 and February 1944. The stoppages lasted from one to four hours. Finally, on February 25, at midnight, over 600 Black workmen, "claiming that they were being denied promotions and actually being passed over by White men with far less seniority," went on a much longer strike. Since the coke and gas made at the Clairton by-products plant were piped to several Carnegie-Illinois mills which lined the banks of the Monongahela River, this walkout threatened to idle close to 30,000 steel employees. Responsibility for manufacturing these fuels rested with these striking Black workers. Consequently, their swift return to these coke and gas-making operations became a matter of crucial importance. Thereafter, at the instigation of the Fair Employment Practices Committee, the local steelworkers' union formulated a compromise which equally divided twenty "top machine jobs" between Black and White steelworkers. The acceptance of this formula allowed Carnegie-Illinois Steel to resume normal production in all of its nearby mill facilities.[65] Later that year, White rollers in the 18-inch mill at the Clairton Steel Plant went on strike because their daily schedule no longer permitted them to earn overtime pay. This stoppage left Black pilers and chippers in this section of the plant without work. Once they discovered "that immediate consideration was being given to the demands of the rollers," while their own complaints "had been dragging for months," they "became incensed," and thirty of them staged a walkout of their own. During conversations with mediators, these striking Blacks testified that limited housing, exorbitant rents, and the lack of local receptivity toward recent Black migrants further aggravated their lives in Clairton. Promises from representatives of the Office of Price Administration to investigate high rents and an assurance from Carnegie-Illinois Steel to construct another housing project brought Black strikers back to work.[66]

Similar incidents of racial unrest also appeared among Black J and L employees. In 1943, 450 Blacks in the 14-inch bar mill at J and L's Aliquippa plant went on strike to protest the company's refusal to promote two Blacks to the positions of inspector and straightener.[67] In 1944, 30 Black cleaners "shut down operations in the Rod and Wire Mill," idling 2,800 J and L workers. Dissatisfaction with their wages and working conditions caused these Aliquippa Blacks to walk off their jobs.[68] As elsewhere, Black steelworkers at J and L's Pittsburgh plant relied on strikes whenever they encountered discrimination. In 1943, Black firemen at the South Side Works discovered that their White counterparts at the Eliza plant received 93 cents per hour in wages, while they earned only 82 cents per hour. Finally, in 1945, after repeated failures by the union and the FEPC to eliminate this differential with company officials, 28 Black firemen walked off their jobs. As a result, the entire power plant at the South Side Works shut down and 11,000 workmen were idled.[69] The grant of a 5-cent increase in wages finally ended the strike.

On May 5, 1945, 200 Blacks at J and L's by-products plant in Hazelwood stopped work. Because of the heat and general discomfort of this section of the mill, the company had customarily provided tomato juice to these Black employees. On May 1, however, the practice was discontinued. At the same time, mill officials opened "a canteen with iced drinks . . . in a section of the plant manned wholly by Whites." Black workers therefore felt "discriminated against," and immediately went on strike. The FEPC intervened and persuaded J and L to resume its former practice of furnishing tomato juice to this predominantly Black department. This action brought the 200 Black strikers back to work.[70]

Since the CIO and its constituent unions realized that the problems of discrimination acutely affected Black workers, they issued several public pronouncements which condemned race prejudice and advocated fairness to minority workmen. At its 1942 convention, the CIO reiterated "its firm opposition to any form of racial and religious discrimination" and "renewed" its pledge to carry on the fight for protection in law and in fact of the rights of every racial and religious group to participate fully in our social, political and industrial life.[71] At that convention, Philip Murray, the president of the CIO, appointed "a committee to investigate and study the entire problem of equality of opportunity for Negro workers in American industry." CIO Secretary, James B. Carey, and Willard S. Townsend, the president of the predominately Black United Transport Service Employees union, composed the committee. Carey and Townsend, who believed that "passing resolutions in conventions [was] not enough," took on the task of exposing industry's unfair racial practices towards Blacks.[72] After reporting to the federation's executive board several weeks later, Murray directed James J. Leary of the Mine, Mill and Smelter Workers Union and Boyd L. Wilson, a former Black steelworker, to join Carey and Townsend on the CIO Committee for the Elimination of Racial Discrimination.[73] Unlike the AFL, the CIO appeared more serious about discussing racial discrimination within its ranks.

This CIO assignment was only one of several duties that Wilson performed for Black laborers. Philip Murray, who also headed the United Steelworkers of America, designated Wilson as his "personal representative to look into, survey and assist us in the solution of any problem" affecting the union's "colored members."[74] A group of Black steelworkers attending the 1942 steelworkers' convention approached Murray about the absence of Blacks among the union's thirty-three district directors. Because these officers sat on the union's executive board, they thought it important that Blacks be a part of this important policy-making council. Although Murray recognized that Blacks were not numerous enough in any one steel district to elect a Black director, he saw merit in the delegates' request. To end any further discontent, Murray appointed Wilson to serve the dual role as a nonvoting member of the union's executive board as well as his troubleshooter for Black affairs within the steelworkers' organization.[75]

Boyd L. Wilson was born in Linn, Missouri in 1896. After settling in St. Louis, he became a labor organizer among local Black barbers in 1929. This activity, which led him to attend an AFL convention in Indianapolis, cemented his interest in trade unionism. In 1938, SWOC hired him as an organizer and assigned him to the Scullin Steel Company, a St. Louis firm with a predominantly Black labor force. After signing on as a Scullin employee, Wilson met with remarkable success in recruiting Black workmen into SWOC. He remained there until 1942, when Murray placed him in the union hierarchy and moved him to the steelworkers' Pittsburgh headquarters. In this new position, Wilson acted as an advocate for Black steelworkers whenever confrontations occurred between them and their employers. During the mediation of a work stoppage among Black pilers and chippers at the Carnegie-Illinois Steel plant in Clairton in October 1944, Wilson aided in the adjudication of their grievances.[76] Again, in November 1944, when housing problems and poor working conditions created discontent among Black steelworkers in Duquesne and Clairton, Boyd Wilson helped in drafting recommendations to solve these difficulties. Wilson along with others secured a promise from Carnegie-Illinois Steel to build additional housing and to improve working conditions. These efforts helped to solve many of the difficulties.[77]

The presence of Black unionists in Western Pennsylvania and a well articulated national policy against racial discrimination prompted local unions to pay special attention to the plight of Black steelworkers. At the Duquesne steel works, Thomas McIver, Edward Campbell, John Campbell, Carl Dickerson, Roger Payne, Jim Grinage, and other Black unionists were conspicuous in their support of Local No. 1256 in its many disputes with plant officials. Similarly, "Bus" Taylor played an active role in union affairs at the Carnegie-Illinois plant in Homestead.[78] In recognition of Black participation in the Clairton steel union, Local No. 1557 began to contribute to the local NAACP.[79] At J and L's Aliquippa Works, the president of Local No. 1211 gave vigorous support to eight Black laborers denied promotions in the plant's 14-inch mill. Moreover, he vehemently denounced J and L to the War Manpower Commission when it refused to employ 150 Black female applicants "except as dishwashers in the (plant) restaurant."[80] Midland workers, both Black and White, supported a Black steelworker in his encounter with Mackintosh and Hemphill because they believed he suffered discrimination "because of his union activities."[81] James McCoy, a Black employee at the Continental Roll and Steel Foundry in Coraopolis, served in several offices before becoming president of his steelworkers' local. Consequently, when Black employees met "with subtle and flagrant forms of segregation," White unionists threatened to walk off their jobs to protest company discrimination.[82] In addition to union action, appeals were usually made to the FEPC.

It became increasingly evident that Blacks could not rely completely on the United Steelworkers of America to eliminate discrimination. In some cases, local unions were ineffective in presenting Black grievances to employers. In other instances, the union itself held the same racial prejudices as the steel companies. Writing in 1943, Harold Ruttenberg, an official in the Steel Division of the War Production Board and a former member of the CIO hierarchy, warned that "a big unfinished job facing the industrial union movement is giving the meaning of union membership to Negro workers."[83] In this particular endeavor, the steelworkers' union apparently defaulted. Boyd Wilson discovered that Black steelworkers filing grievances pressing "for alteration of discriminatory employment patterns" frequently encountered "unsympathetic union officials" hostile to their concerns. He proposed in a resolution to the International Executive Board in 1945 that district directors be required to notify his office whenever a steelworker filed a charge alleging racial discrimination. Although the proposal won board approval, Wilson received no cooperation in implementing the program. He also tried to educate the union about discriminatory attitudes among its own rank and file. He suggested "regular annual or semi-annual meetings of the Executive Board for the purpose of planning union action and policy in regard to the Negro membership." He wanted to establish a central repository in which "all cases of racial discrimination in the union" would be filed. Wilson also argued for "a program of membership education" to completely rid the United Steelworkers of racial prejudice. Again, his proposals were endorsed, but nothing was done to assist him in bringing these ideas to fruition.[84]

William Fountain, a Black employee at Crucible Steel in Midland, shared Wilson's frustration with the United Steelworkers of America. He attended the organization's convention in Cleveland in 1942, and came away impressed with its outspoken stand "against Hitlerism, both at home and abroad."[85] His optimism changed, however, once he returned to Midland. Plant officials at Crucible Steel hired Blacks almost exclusively in the coke works and in labor gangs. They did not allow them to enter any skilled occupations or to work in the shell factory, except when extra men were needed "to get out production." Fountain complained that "repeated requests to . . . union officials . . . to look into upgrading for Negro workers have been ignored." He accused the president of Local No. 1212 and the district director for the Beaver Valley of having a "do-nothing attitude" which was causing "growing resentment" among Black laborers toward the United Steelworkers.[86] At the Clairton steel plant, Blacks in the coke works had gone on strike because management completed a process of replacing Black machine operators with Whites. In December 1943, the local union concluded an agreement with Carnegie-Illinois Steel which established a line of promotion "from laborer straight . . . to the top machine job." Blacks felt that this new contract provided displaced Black machine operators with no opportunity to regain their jobs, and represented the union's tacit approval of the company's discriminatory practices. Although the matter was adjudicated to the satisfaction of all parties, Local No. 1557 had clearly failed to conduct an "educational program" about the new agreement which was sensitive to the concerns of its Black members.[87]

Local No. 1049 at the American Steel Band Company in Pittsburgh raised no protest when a Black applied for a position in the production department and was told by the personnel officer that "Negroes . . . were used solely as janitors and window washers." The acting district director responded by saying that the issue of whether to hire Blacks "was a matter for the Company to decide." The president of the local union, dismissed the episode by declaring that ". . . we have never had any negroes in our plant and when that negro came for a job we didn't have any kind of opening for him or anyone else." He went on to indicate that his local would take a stand on Black employment at American Steel Band when "our union is confronted with such a situation."[88] Racism among White unionists also revealed itself at Pittsburgh Steel in Monessen. Benjamin Thomas Frezzell, a Black employee, remembered when the firm established a coke plant near the mills in the early 1940s. Only Whites worked in the new facility, and they eschewed membership in the integrated Local No. 1229 at Pittsburgh Steel. Instead they started their own separate White United Steelworkers affiliate.[89]

At times, Black steelworkers relied upon the NAACP to articulate their racial grievances. In 1934, for example, Harry A. Thompson, a mill laborer in McKeesport, started the Monongahela Valley NAACP, principally among his fellow Black workers. In 1939, Matthew L. Dempsey, whom J and L fired in the 1920s for UNIA activity, headed the Aliquippa NAACP which included numerous Black steelworkers. These and other NAACP chapters in milltowns throughout the region continued to function into the 1940s.[90] Without the United Steelworkers of America as a reliable advocate, Black laborers in Western Pennsylvania also looked to the Fair Employment Practices Committee to solve the specific problem of employment discrimination.

President Franklin D. Roosevelt created the FEPC out of Executive Order 8802 in 1941 which assured "full participation in the national defense program by all citizens . . . regardless of race, creed, color, or national origin . . ." Black leaders, especially A. Philip Randolph, president of the Brotherhood of Sleeping Car Porters, feared that Black workers, already hard hit by several years of depression, would not receive their fair share of jobs in expanding defense industries. Consequently, Randolph threatened to mobilize thousands of Blacks into a massive march on Washington to force "the elimination of discrimination in the armed services, government, war industries, and labor unions." This imminent display of Black discontent convinced Roosevelt to issue the executive order. The effect of this presidential directive, however, was weakened by ambivalent Whites who formed a majority on the committee. Labor unions, which were sometimes subject to FEPC scrutiny, did not favor its existence. Southern legislators on Capitol Hill tried to undermine the agency. Furthermore, the chairman of the War Manpower Commission, under whose supervision the FEPC came, did not support it. Not until May 1943, with prodding from Randolph's March on Washington Movement did President Roosevelt issue Executive Order 9346 to strengthen the FEPC. He placed the committee in the Executive Office of the President with an increased budget and authority to investigate defense-related employers and organized labor. Hearings were allowed to determine the validity of charges of discrimination on the basis of race, sex, color and religion in industries holding defense contracts. More money meant that field investigators, many of whom were Black, could pursue complaints of bias by employers and unions against Blacks, women, and religious and ethnic minorities.[91]

Responsibility for receiving complaints and settling disputes rested with the Division of Field Operations of the FEPC. The agency had twelve regional offices located in key cities throughout the nation. Pittsburgh and its environs were included in Region Three, and Black steelworkers in the area made their charges of discrimination to the Philadelphia office. In each case, a field investigator, who was usually Black, went to the plant in question, and tried to secure voluntary compliance from all parties on an agreed settlement.[92] One of them was G. James Fleming. Born in the Virgin Islands in 1904, Fleming was graduated from the University of the West Indies in 1931, and earned the master of arts and doctorate degrees from the University of Pennsylvania in 1944 and 1948, respectively. Between 1935 and 1941, he worked as an editor at two important Black newspapers, the New York *Amsterdam News* and then the *Philadelphia Tribune*. From 1941 to 1945 he investigated complaints for the FEPC.[93]

Fleming and other FEPC examiners spent much time in Western Pennsylvania settling disputes and resolving complaints from Black steelworkers. In November 1944, a Black employee at J and L in Pittsburgh, was placed in charge of a small group of track laborers. He received no raise in pay for performing this extra duty. However, the White man who succeeded him received a bonus in pay for doing the same job. The FEPC intervened after receiving a complaint from this aggrieved Black steelworker. After conferring with plant officials, the field investigator announced that the Black employee would be restored to his job as gang leader and receive a retroactive increase in pay.[94] John Anderson, a Black soldier, was released from duty along with four Whites to work at the Union Steel Castings Company in Pittsburgh. Eventually each of the four Whites was given a chance to do skilled work, while Anderson remained a soldier's helper earning 78 cents per hour. The FEPC, along with an army ordnance official, stepped in, and secured a better job for Anderson, that of making cores at $1.19 per hour.[95]

FEPC investigators also arranged conferences and made inquiries about the employment policies of other mills and foundries in Western Pennsylvania holding defense contracts. When the C. G. Hussey Steel Company had allegedly discriminated against Black women, two field operators went to Pittsburgh to inquire about the charge. After talking with plant officials and to union representatives, the FEPC learned that both had become advocates of "hiring Negro women."[96] Black steelworkers at Local No. 1592 in Pittsburgh told the FEPC that they were "paid less than White workers," Consequently, a field examiner came "to discuss the future plans of the union in regard to seniority rights and pay rates" of these Black workmen.[97] An FEPC representative also traveled to Sharon to confer with a United Citizens Committee about "the employment problems of the Negroes in [that] community . . ." During his stay in the area, the examiner visited the Farrell, Pennsylvania Carnegie-Illinois Steel plant, which had been charged with discrimination against Black women. Since "Negro girls" had been recently assigned in the disputed department, the FEPC official declared it "a correction of [the] original complaint" and closed the case.[98]

Because Blacks unhesitatingly wrote the agency's regional office outlining their grievances, FEPC examiners Milo A. Manly and G. James Fleming became familiar personalities in steel plants throughout the Pittsburgh vicinity. In February 1944, they investigated seven defense plants which denied employment to Blacks while increasing their White personnel.[99] In March 1944 Manly attended a monthly meeting of the Clairton Branch of the NAACP to check on the progress being made by Carnegie-Illinois Steel in the upgrading of Black workers.[100] In December 1944, G. James Fleming filed a compliance report on J and L Steel in Pittsburgh, reporting that plant officials no longer denied employment to Black women.[101]

The volume of work for FEPC examiners had increased so much in Western Pennsylvania that it inspired plans to establish a subregional office in Pittsburgh in February 1945. Hill District Blacks applauded this development when the Centre Avenue YMCA held a special meeting to celebrate the opening of the bureau.[102] The agency's effectiveness clearly helped to stem the tide of racial discrimination in area mills and foundries. With this in mind, the "colored citizens" of Blairsville wrote the agency in 1945, inviting its cooperation in seeing that . . . negro men and women "be hired at a local defense plant." After asking FEPC officials to "make adequate means in helping us," they received a rather dismal reply. Since the status of the FEPC was uncertain in Congress, all "regional and subregional offices (were compelled) to curtail their field trips."[103] In 1946, Congressional appropriations for FEPC ended. Despite its brief existence, the agency attempted to reverse the pattern of discrimination which kept Blacks in lower echelon jobs and denied them pay equal to most Whites. Although it made a substantial effort in the field of equal employment, FEPC did not survive long enough to have a sustained impact.[104]

Since President Harry Truman did not support vigorously a permanent FEPC in 1946, he failed to get congressional endorsement and adequate funding for the agency.[105] Nonetheless, ten states between 1945 and 1950 established their own commissions to bar employment discrimination. Fourteen others had FEPC bills pending in their legislatures. Four major cities, Chicago, Milwaukee, Minneapolis, and Philadelphia, had tough laws against job bias.[106] The federal FEPC had become such an important instrument for Black occupational advancement that Pittsburgh, with encouragement from the local Urban League, set up its own Committee for Fair Employment. In 1947, with wide support "from Protestants, Catholics, Jews, and foreign-born citizens," the commission convinced five department stores to abandon discriminatory treatment of "colored workers." The Pittsburgh Urban League cooperated by generating telegrams, telephone calls, and letters from these groups to help persuade store executives to act.[107]

Homer S. Brown, a Black state representative from Pittsburgh, introduced a bill in the legislature to create a state FEPC in 1945. The Brown bill would set up a permanent commission with five salaried men appointed by the governor and approved by the state senate. The committee would enforce laws against discrimination "on account of race, creed, or national origin," and levy penalties. The bill had support from the state CIO and the United Steelworkers of America. Philip Murray, the president of the USWA, sent a personal message to Governor Edward Martin urging his endorsement of the Brown bill. A competing bill was also introduced in the state senate by two GOP assemblymen. Their measure would put the commission under the supervision of the Pennsylvania Labor Relations Board. Although the proposal was withdrawn, Governor Martin, a Republican, disliked the Brown bill. The GOP, which had a majority in the house, bottled up the Brown measure in the Labor Committee, where it died. A state FEPC, without stiff enforcement powers, did not pass until the early 1950s.[108] Although legislation in Pittsburgh discouraged job bias through exhortation and public pressure, Black steelworkers in other mill communities were deprived of state and federal protection from employment discrimination.

Robert C. Weaver, a veteran member of Roosevelt's Black Cabinet and the former Director of the Negro Employment Service of the War Manpower Commission,[109] had been aware of racial discrimination in the steel region of Western Pennsylvania and knew of specific plants in the area which systematically excluded Blacks from employment.[110] Yet, Weaver remained optimistic about the future of Blacks in the steel industry. The

Harvard-trained economist believed that Whites had greater opportunities to abandon steel labor and obtain better jobs in other industries which were generally inhospitable to Blacks. He argued that White steelworkers drafted into the armed services would also shun their former employers after the war, and look for jobs in other more attractive fields. Weaver concluded that such circumstances would allow Black workers and returning Black servicemen to keep their jobs in the steel industry, and secure new positions left vacant by Whites.[111]

The modest reduction in the number of Black steelworkers in Western Pennsylvania after the war confirmed Weaver's hopeful predictions. When hostilities ended in 1945, the *Pittsburgh Courier* feared that "the pendulum of employment" which had favored Blacks since 1940 would again "touch or drop off the Negro worker."[112] On September 1, 1945, less than a month after the Japanese surrender in the Pacific, 12,500 workers in the Pittsburgh area were released from their jobs. By the fall of the year, however, reconversion to peacetime production enabled area steel mills to create 16,000 jobs, primarily for their recently furloughed employees. For this reason, the *Courier* reported "no marked hysteria on the part of workers and officials" about future employment in the area.[114] Although layoffs and the exit of Black migrants working in wartime Pittsburgh on occupational deferments reduced the number of Blacks in area mills and foundries, the number of Black steelworkers in Western Pennsylvania, which had reached a high of 11,500 or 14 percent of all mill employees in 1944 (See Table 9) stabilized at 9,239 or 6.5 percent of the total work force by 1950.[115]

Weaver and other Black spokesmen also believed that a bright future awaited Blacks in the steel industry because they had "firmly entrenched" themselves in the United Steelworkers of America. Weaver held that through its seniority rules the USWA would preserve occupational gains made by Blacks during the war and insure Black job security in the postwar years. Although progress for Blacks in iron and steel had been slow, he credited the union with cooperating with the federal government in overcoming management and local labor opposition to the upgrading of Black steelworkers.[116]

Public displays of labor solidarity between Black and White steelworkers in 1946 in the steel strike and at the USWA convention seemed to confirm the optimism of Black leaders in the postwar period. At the start of the war the federal government had secured the cooperation of the USWA in discouraging any new demands for a wage increases. In 1945, however, several recent rises in the cost of living caused steelworkers to abandon the wartime agreement. Also, the war was coming to an end, steel production was decreasing, and the industry was reverting from a forty-eight hour work week back to a forty hour work week. An average loss of $52 a month in earnings for each steelworker resulted. Industry officials, however, resisted union demands for wage increase, prompting the USWA to secure a strike petition from the National Labor Relations Board. Shortly after the petition was granted, rank and file steelworkers endorsed a walkout and demanded a two-dollar-a-day increase in pay. Although steel officials initially held firm, a compromise solution from President Truman ended the month-long strike.[117]

Shortly after the walkout began, the *Pittsburgh Courier* reported that six out of the ten pickets "parading" in front of the Carnegie-Illinois Steel Building in Pittsburgh were Black. Black steelworkers in Homestead also planned to picket outside the local Carnegie-Illinois plant gates for one full day.[118] A *Courier* editorial applauded the presence of Blacks "on the picket lines and . . . [in] every news photograph of massed workers." It hoped that Black participation in the strike revealed a permanent identity of interest between Negro and White steelworkers "which the most extreme anti-Negro propaganda will be unable to erase."[119] Horace Cayton, a Black sociologist and a self-proclaimed pessimist, was greatly impressed "with the 100,000 Negro steelworkers striking with their union brothers." He compared the current labor unrest with the steel strike of 1919 when "White workers failed to welcome" Blacks into the Amalgamated Association of Iron and Steelworkers, thereby encouraging Black strikebreaking activities. But in 1946 the new steelworkers' union included Blacks within its ranks, and this prompted Cayton to believe that "some little progress has been made."[120]

Black participation in the steel strike and Black involvement in the 1946 USWA convention in Atlantic City, New Jersey gave the appearance of interracial solidarity in steel union affairs. Sixty Black delegates attended, and some represented locals in

Pittsburgh. James Brantley, vice president of Local No. 1465, and Charles Wilson, president of Local No. 1814, came from integrated lodges in the Smoky City. Other delegates included Harry Johnson and Carl Davis from Pittsburgh, and Hubert Hall of Johnstown.[121]

Postwar cutbacks generally spared veteran steelworkers in the Pittsburgh vicinity and wage increases resulting from the 1946 strike benefited all USWA members, but problems of racial discrimination persisted after 1945. An Allegheny County race relations survey in 1946 revealed that the majority of Black workers remained disproportionately concentrated within unskilled and semi-skilled occupations. Furthermore, over half of all firms in the county continued to segregate Blacks into special job categories that usually paid less than assignments given to Whites.[122] Moreover, Blacks still had fewer opportunities to enter skilled positions than Whites. In 1950, for example, there were 1,431 blacksmiths, forgemen, and hammermen at various Pittsburgh mills and foundries. Of this number only 21 were Black. A total of 3,266 millwrights also worked in the city's mills and foundries. This number included 12 Blacks.[123]

After World War II particular plants in Western Pennsylvania were known offenders in the field of employment discrimination. In 1946, and again 1947, Blacks at J and L Steel in Pittsburgh staged work stoppages to protest their mistreatment by company officials. One Black striker remarked:

> The men knew that they were risking their jobs in this walk-out . . . but they had got worked up to the point where this didn't seem so important . . . they were tired of never getting promoted, and they were tired of being treated like dogs by . . . White . . . foremen . . .[124]

John Hughey, who in 1947 began work at the Carrie Furnaces in Rankin, witnessed a more subtle form of racial discrimination. Originally, Black steelworkers predominated in the sintering plant, the open hearth, and furnace departments. Between 1947 and 1950, Carnegie-Illinois Steel began updating its equipment and machinery. Although these technological advances eased the work of most plant employees, they required a reduction in the number of Carrie furnaces from six to four. Few men were displaced, but new jobs became scarce. Consequently, when veteran employees in these "solid Black" departments began dying and retiring, they were almost always replaced by Whites.[125]

The same discriminatory patterns also continued in the United Steelworkers of America. Philip Murray, president of the USWA, gave public support to issues important to Blacks. At the 1946 convention he denounced Southern poll taxes which hindered Black voting, and he advocated the creation of a permanent FEPC by President Truman and the Congress. In 1949 he endorsed the candidacy of Homer S. Brown for a judgeship in Allegheny County which embraced Pittsburgh and numerous steel communities. Most Pittsburgh area locals made a major effort to elect Blacks to union offices to give at least the appearance of racial concern. In Rankin, for example, the local at the Sterling Steel foundry included a Black among its slate of officers. The union at the American Steel and Wire Company similarly had two Black officers and two Black committeemen. Each steelworkers' local in Rankin supported a NAACP membership drive and even the United Negro College Fund. Nonetheless, Blacks were usually elected to ceremonial posts, and rarely did these local unions or President Murray fight effectively against discrimination within the mills themselves.[126]

Within the USWA Murray and other White union leaders did very little to support Boyd Wilson, the sole national officer monitoring the progress of Blacks in the steel industry. He and other Black unionists, some from Western Pennsylvania, believed that "a one man team . . . with limited or restricted authority" could not effectively upgrade the status of Black steelworkers. Consequently, Wilson and Black delegates attending the union's 1948 convention proposed a resolution "to establish a civil rights department." Unfortunately, the convention committee appointed to deal with this matter had foreknowledge of the proposed resolution and decided to smother it with a "bewildering number of [other] resolutions on the subject . . . 108 in all." When the committee merged all these resolutions into one, it "completely emasculated the purpose and intent of of the [proposal] presented by the Negro group." President Philip Murray referred this watered down resolution to the union's executive board, which authorized the creation of a civil rights department.

Boyd Wilson, who "conducted such civil rights programs as the Union had for eight years" was, however, kept off the committee. In fact, not "a single Negro" served in the newly established department. Tom Shane, a district director in Detroit, and his brother Frank, who served respectively as chairman and executive director of the civil rights committee, assumed many of Wilson's duties. Little was done for Black steelworkers. Wilson testified that Frank Shane "knew absolutely nothing about the Negro problem and had no interest in it."[127]

Despite Black militancy, government pressure, and occasional assistance from the United Steelworkers of America, racial discrimination continued to characterize the steel industry of Western Pennsylvania. As a result Blacks failed to attain economic parity with Whites in the mills or to win an equal voice with them in union affairs. Such barriers limited the gains Blacks had achieved since coming to the region in large numbers some three and a half decades earlier.

During the 1950s, the lingering problems of employment discrimination and union ambivalence continued to hinder the occupational advancement of Black steelworkers. Even the assistance of the Pittsburgh Urban League and Black USWA officials failed to correct the inequities encountered by Black mill employees.

# 8

# The Illusion of Advancement: Black Steelworkers During the 1950s

Employers in the Pittsburgh vicinity made minimal attempts during the 1950s to erase the blot of racial discrimination from the steel industry. With only lukewarm support from the United Steelworkers of America, the absence of a federal FEPC, and a weak state fair employment practices agency, Black steelworkers in Western Pennsylvania experienced little occupational advancement. The Pittsburgh Urban League and Black officials in the United Steelworkers, however, promoted programs to expand job opportunities for Black mill employees. At times, their efforts proved ineffective. The Pittsburgh Urban League, for example, became increasingly concerned with placing Blacks in clerical and professional positions in the steel industry. Hence, better jobs for rank and file Black laborers received less attention. Black USWA officials found that White unionists, while willing to endorse such groups as the NAACP and the National Urban League, opposed vigorous efforts to rid the mills of employment discrimination and to offer Blacks a greater voice in union affairs. Not until the 1960s, when the civil rights movement produced national legislation against unfair employment practices did the condition of Black steelworkers have a chance to improve.

Civil Rights had become an important national issue during the Truman Administration. In 1948, the Democrats adopted a strong civil rights plank in their national platform. The party's growing concern for Black Americans and such injustices as legalized racial segregation, poll taxes, lynchings, and employment discrimination provoked J. Strom Thurmond of South Carolina and other Dixiecrats to bolt the Democratic Party, and run their own presidential and vice presidential candidates.[1] Truman actively sought Black votes and personally went to New York's Harlem to solicit them. His Executive Order 9981 which desegregated the armed forces earlier in 1948 produced a heavy turnout of Black voters, which helped Truman to win a narrow victory over a liberal Republican, Thomas E. Dewey. Moreover, civil rights lawyers won a series of stunning judicial victories during the late 1940s which culminated in 1954 with the landmark Brown decision, which outlawed legalized public school segregation.

Since the existence of the FEPC during World War II and similar agencies in various states and municipalities, employers became more cognizant of racial discrimination in hiring and promotions. Some firms made vigorous efforts to upgrade Black workers' positions while others made an attempt to portray themselves publicly as opponents of unfair employment practices. Truman prodded industrialists in 1951 with Executive Order 10210 which instructed the Department of Defense to insert a nondiscrimination clause in all contracts with private employers. Although the order lacked enforcement power, industry officials clearly knew that racial bias in employment violated federal public policy.[2] Civil rights advocates hoped that such exhortations would help to improve the condition of Black laborers.

In 1954 the United States Steel Corporation announced in the Black press and in letters to the NAACP, the National Urban League, and other groups that the company pursued a policy of nondiscrimination. U.S. Steel executives permitted affiliates of the National Urban League to invite Black applicants to seek jobs at "the new $450,000,000 Fairless Works" in Morrisville, Pennsylvania near Philadelphia. Blacks could get employment in both production and in management and supervisory positions. Company officials failed to mention, however, that housing for workers at the new facility barred Black occupants. Additionally, the firm did not consider seriously Black applicants with technical training in engineering, metallurgy, and chemistry. Although discriminatory treatment of Blacks in the steel industry continued unabated, U.S. Steel and other firms in Western Pennsylvania, principally through the *Pittsburgh Courier*, tried to develop favorable public perceptions of their employment practices and their commitment to racial justice.[3]

Industry executives recognized that the Black press played a crucial role in conveying to Blacks in the Pittsburgh area a positive public image of steel companies. During Brotherhood Week in 1954, U.S. Steel placed a full page ad in the *Pittsburgh Courier* which stressed that "this spirit of brotherhood . . . will help make a better steel industry and an even greater America." Republic Steel saluted "Negro Progress" in another ad in the Black weekly. "Greater safety and better working conditions mean increased security for Republic's 68,000 employees, thousands of whom are Negroes," the advertisement stated. Moreover, "We salute 16 million Negro Americans — and the progress they have made. At the same time we pledge our continued support in helping you continue to progress." Later on in 1954, U.S. Steel paid the *Courier* for another announcement. A picture appeared with a Black gang leader at the Edgar Thomson Steel Works in Braddock, consulting with the plant's assistant superintendent. The following statement accompanied the photograph: "On the production line, in our mills, or in offices, or in transportation, quality people, for a quality product, are our first consideration. Numbered among these people are more than 32,000 Negroes willing and able to perform vital functions as members of a great team dedicated to the service of the nation."[4]

Readers of the *Pittsburgh Courier* learned in 1952 of U.S. Steel's benevolence toward a Black shearman in the 100-inch plate mill in Homestead. Since the man's daughter planned to make her Broadway debut, in "My Darling Aida," Homestead mill officials sent their employee and his wife to New York City to witness the opening performance. "The next time someone tells you these big corporations are cold, impersonal, and don't have heart, take it with a grain of salt," wrote a *Courier* reporter. U.S. Steel and Jones and Laughlin Steel also tried to solidify their relationships with the Black press in 1956 when they helped the *Pittsburgh Courier* host the annual convention of the all-Black National Newspaper Publishers Association.[5]

These efforts to portray the steel industry favorably contradicted Black employment realities. During the 1950s a total of 121,785 laborers worked in Pittsburgh steel mills, and their median earnings amounted to $4,997 annually. Approximately 8,411 or 7 percent received over $10,000 each year. Pittsburgh's 9,269 Black steelworkers earned a yearly average of $4,078. Of this number only 30 persons or less than 1 percent received over $10,000 annually. In most skilled positions, their scarcity fitted the usual pattern of Black underrepresentation in higher paying jobs. As blacksmiths, forgemen, and hammermen, for example, they amounted to a miniscule 21 out of 926. In Johnstown, where Bethlehem Steel was the principal employer, Black laborers numbered 455 out of 14,595. No Blacks, however, were numbered among Bethlehem's 181 millwrights and its 104 metal molders.[6]

A few area steel firms made some progress in the promotion of Blacks to supervisory positions, but restricted them, in most instances, to segregated mill departments. Bartow Tipper, a Black J and L employee and community activist, for example, recalled that officials at the Aliquippa Works in the late 1940s and early 1950s appointed only three Black foremen. Two went to the predominantly Black nail mill while the other supervised the janitorial department.[7]

Like the small number of Black foremen, Black laborers were confined to racially separate sections where they worked in hot, hard, and dirty jobs. Even the better positions within these departments were denied to Black employees. At Jones and Laughlin Steel's South Side facility, a few Whites held the best jobs in the largely Black by-products section. Throughout the 1950s positions in the strip mill, 19-inch mill, and the cold strip remained closed to Black employees. Even into the 1970s J and L prevented Blacks from working as bricklayers and carpenters. Consequently, Black steelworkers experienced mobility within predominantly Black mill departments. Daniel Brooks, who migrated to Pittsburgh in 1950 from Fairfield, Alabama. Although he had two years of college, he began work as a laborer in the open hearth department at the J and L South Side

Figure 12. Aerial view of the Clairton Steel Works, United States Steel, Clairton, PA in 1949. (Courtesy of the Carnegie Library of Pittsburgh, PA.)

facility. After two years he advanced to the open hearth furnace as a stockman and then brakeman, but, like most Black employees, he made only modest occupational progress in the 1950s within separate Black departments.[8]

Like Brooks, Milton Croom migrated from Alabama in 1950, but he settled in Clairton. His father had worked for U.S. Steel in Birmingham, Alabama while an uncle had been an employee at the Clairton, Pennsylvania plant of U.S. Steel since 1932. Croom started at the Clairton coke works, a nearly all-Black department, except for a few Whites who held choice positions as foremen, gang leaders, and motor inspectors. During the 1950s plant officials refused to hire or promote Blacks to work as heaters. Felix Guilford, born in Florida in 1923, migrated to Philadelphia in 1936. Work on a railroad and service in the armed forces preceded his move to Beaver Falls in 1945. He and two other Blacks secured jobs at Babcock and Wilcox, but they soon left because of discriminatory promotion policies. He joined his brother who had been working at the By-Products Coke division of J and L's Aliquippa Works. The four batteries of the coke ovens had about 200 employees, all but six of whom were Black. The wire mill was similarly segregated. Like other area plants, J and L in Aliquippa barred Blacks from becoming heaters and from seeking employment in the seamless tube department.[9]

At times, the United Steelworkers of America proved to be an unreliable advocate for Black steelworkers. National union leaders supported the NAACP, the National Urban League, and other civil rights organizations. Philip Murray and his successor, David J. McDonald, publicly espoused the cause of Black advancement. As leaders of labor, an important group within the liberal/Democratic coalition which included Blacks, they could do no less. Only rarely did their advocacy of Black interests extend to the specific grievances of Black mill workers. In most instances they endorsed Black causes unrelated to the steel industry. Moreover, support for Black occupational progress ranged from indifference to hostility within steelworker's locals. Where local officials proved sympathetic to Black aspirations, non-White employees surmounted company obstacles and gained better jobs. In most cases, such support was rare and Black workers encountered great difficulty in successfully pressing their grievances and achieving favorable results.

Philip Murray who headed both the CIO and the United Steelworkers of America realized that numerically Black workers played an important role in union affairs. He remembered Black solidarity with White Unionists during the 1946 steel strike, and their presence as delegates to national union conventions. Murray and other CIO leaders also had gained prestige during the Roosevelt and Truman Administration as influential labor spokesmen. Both the CIO and Blacks became key constituents of the Democratic Party. As members of the same political coalition, each group promoted the interests of the other. Hence Murray and the national CIO and USWA spoke out for Black civil rights and supported the effort financially.

While president of the CIO, Philip Murray wrote an antidiscrimination clause in the group's constitution. After his death in 1952, the CIO established the Philip Murray Memorial Foundation with a one million dollar fund. In 1954, the NAACP Legal, Defense and Educational Fund received $75,000 from the foundation. Walter White, executive director of the NAACP, made a posthumous award to the deceased CIO leader to commemorate his attempts to improve race relations. As president of the United Steelworkers of America, in 1950 Murray authorized $2,500 to a coalition of civil rights groups led by the NAACP. One Pittsburgh Urban League official was so encouraged that he asked the associate executive director in the national office, "Why can't we get some of that money for the N.U.L.?" In addition to making financial contributions to civil rights organizations, the steelworker's union sent a representative, along with other labor groups, to the 1953 NAACP convention.[10]

When President David J. McDonald received the posthumous award for his USWA predecessor, Walter White, according to the *Pittsburgh Courier*, admonished him "to carry on the fight for human dignity which Murray started." McDonald, like Murray, recognized the numerical strength of Black steelworkers. When the steel strike of 1956 occurred, McDonald must have been pleased that the union had the cooperation of 5,000 Black members in the Pittsburgh vicinity who comprised one-fourth of area steel employees. Apparently, he tried to heed White's admonition. In 1954 he and two other officers prohibited district directors, staff officials, and local representatives from signing contracts which discriminated on the basis of race, color, or creed. At the 1956 United Steelworkers convention, McDonald denounced racial bigotry, and said that the denial of civil liberties constituted "the greatest barriers to real democracy in America since the civil war." He also invited Julius Thomas, director of industrial relations of the National Urban League to speak to the delegates about Black and White wage disparities.[11]

Despite their support of civil rights causes, the United Steelworkers did not escape criticism from Black leaders. David McDonald and other national officers were accused of weakness in dealing with issues of racial discrimination against Black steelworkers in Birmingham, Alabama. The *Pittsburgh Courier* quoted one critic who said that "from the safe bastion" of union headquarters in Pittsburgh "thousands of pieces of high sounding literature have been mailed out, but not a single soldier has appeared to our knowledge on the Southern battlefield where the battle is raging." These comments referred to a cancelled meeting in Birmingham between local White leaders and national union officials to discuss race relations. The *Courier* hinted that McDonald and other union leaders allowed White supremacists in the Birmingham USWA local to disrupt plans for the gathering. In a speech in 1958, Roy Wilkins, who succeeded Walter White as executive director of the NAACP, blamed the United Steelworkers for tolerating locals "guilty of jim crowism" despite resolutions and conferences on the national level which advocated civil rights. A. Philip Randolph also expressed disappointment in the USWA and other unions for having too few Blacks in national policy-making positions in spite of large Black memberships.[12]

In 1948, President Philip Murray, in response to protests from Black members, including Lucious Love and Rayfield Mooty, a black president and secretary-treasurer of a Chicago local, endorsed the creation of a civil rights department in the national office. Thomas Shane and Francis Shane became chairman and executive director, respectively. Their role was mainly educational. Additionally, they supported external efforts to achieve racial equality, but showed great reluctance to pursue similar objectives within the union. Since they were not empowered to intervene directly in local union affairs, they tried to educate and exhort White officers to abandon racial prejudice and treat Black members fairly. In 1953, for example, Francis Shane spoke at a Brotherhood gathering in Monessen. He also served on the State Council for a Pennsylvania FEPC. He assisted the Allegheny County Committee on Fair Employment in its efforts to persuade the state legislature to establish an agency to fight employment discrimination. He wrote to union officials to solicit support for this endeavor. Additionally, Shane informed USWA officers about the "Open Occupancy" policy of the Pittsburgh and Allegheny County Housing Authority. For instance, he told the director of District 19 in the Tarentum area to urge "all local unions . . . to endorse open occupancy" in housing. Shane convinced the United Steelworkers to co-sponsor with the Pittsburgh Regional Conference of Christians and Jews and the Carnegie Museum a meeting to wipe out racial, religious, and ethnic prejudice. Shane regretted the lack of progress in this field while John F. Murray, director of District 16 in Pittsburgh, admitted that White steelworkers "don't want to work with colored people. So we have a big job of education to do." Unfortunately, the task of education, which was Shane's primary responsibility, did little to ameliorate racial discrimination against Black steelworkers. Furthermore, the committee's executive board remained lily-White until Black protests in 1952 resulted in the appointment of Joseph Neal, a Black union official from Baltimore.[13]

The principal problem which Black employees encountered occurred within local steelworkers unions. Hostility to Black promotions and reluctance to submit Black grievances to company managers did more to retard their occupational advancement than inaction and ineffectiveness from national officers. Some locals established civil rights committees to promote fairness for Black workers and to educate members about racial, ethnic, and religious prejudices. In 1954, Richard S. Dowdy, industrial relations secretary of the Pittsburgh Urban League, came to Local No. 1272 at J and L Steel in Pittsburgh, at the request of its civil rights committee, to address 150 unionists. He reviewed how closely the League and labor unions had cooperated in "pursuing fair employment objectives." He noted that the civil rights committee and the League planned to effect a "meaningful implementation of the union's non-discrimination policy."[14]

The national civil rights department of the USWA, which the Shane brothers headed, conducted an extensive survey of local unions in Western Pennsylvania in 1950 to determine their racial practices. They asked two questions. First, they queried, "What range of jobs" were available to "minority groups as compared with jobs open to them before your particular plant was organized." The second question concerned what steps the local union took when "confronted with a racial discrimination problem."[15]

Numerous officials admitted that racial difficulties occurred before the United Steelworkers of America existed at their plants. Several made the questionable claim that Blacks suffered little, if any, discrimination in hiring and promotion since the USWA constitutionally safeguarded their occupational interests. At times, local unions claimed some officers protected Black workers in spite of company opposition. An official of Local No. 1391 in Monessen conceded that before the USWA came to his mill, a few departments and jobs were closed to "colored people." Blacks could not become weightmasters or heaters. Apparently, plant managers catered to White employees when they preferred not to work with Blacks. "White workers," he wrote, "froze out the colored aspirants to . . . jobs by various means . . . you are well acquainted with." Since the formation of the USWA local, "there is no union job closed to colored people." He held that Local No. 1391 enforced provisions of its contract with management which stipulated ability to perform work, physical fitness, and seniority as the only criterion for promotion.[16] An officer of Local No. 1229, also in Monessen, reported incredible racial harmony at his mill. He knew of only one racial incident at the plant between 1937 and 1950. In this case, the union was forthright in its defense of the aggrieved Black steelworker. He said that "a colored employee" sought a transfer from the open hearth pit to a ladleman position. White workers objected. Because the union "insisted that management live up to the seniority clause in the contract," the Black worker obtained the job.[17]

Local union presidents in Johnstown and Midland, to varying degrees, discounted racial discrimination as the principal factor which held back Black workers. The president of Local No. 2633 in Johnstown, reported that before theCIO, "the negro race" was "confined to the job of wheel rolling." Since that time, "discriminatory practices against minority groups [are] a thing of the past." He also made the dubious assertion that Black workers have "never requested advancement, possibly due to the ability clause in the contract." Similarly, the president of Local No. 1274, partially faulted Blacks for their exclusion from the Midland fabrication plant. He said that the mill had not experienced "any troubles." If any problems ever arose, "we will be on the side of the Civil Rights Committee." The official recalled that "about [fifteen] colored girls and women" along with White females worked at the plant during World War II, but all were eventually dismissed when the conflict ended. Although two Black men had once been janitors, the 200 employee facility attracted only skilled workers and apprentices. The lack of a "general labor department," he argued, "probably would account for the absence of colored men applying for employment here." He did not consider why no attempt was made to accept Black apprentices to learn the jobs of craneman, chipper, welder, machinist, and other skilled positions at the plant.[18]

In ostrich-like fashion, other union officials refused to acknowlege the possibility of racial bias at their plants and in their locals. The president of Local No. 1268 at A. M. Byers in Ambridge, wrongly claimed, "that our . . . union . . . has never been confronted with a racial discrimination problem in as much as there have never been Negroes employed" at the mill. The recording secretary of Local No. 1592 at H. K. Porter in Pittsburgh, also believed that the union had no blemishes on its racial record: Blacks first became Porter employees during World War II; neither the company nor the union treated them unfairly.[19]

The president of Local No. 1557 at U.S. Steel in Clairton, blamed the company for the perpetuation of racial discrimination against Blacks. He held that ninety percent of the jobs at the Clairton mill "are open to all groups." Although Black employees had different recollections, the Clairton unionist declared that "discriminatory practices are on the downgrade, since the inception of the union." The "grievance machinery" minimized unfair treatment of Black workers. He suggested, however, that "the Company's right to hire and fire" played a greater role in job placement for Blacks than union efforts.[20]

While some local union officials either denied the existence of racial discrimination or absolved the union of responsibility for it, others candidly admitted that White workers, local unions and management, to differing degrees, frustrated Black occupational advancement. The president of Local No. 1506 in Braddock, frankly declared that "the negro minority is the only group which does not participate in the full range of jobs. This is equally true — both before and after the plant was organized." The government unemployment service required the company to make previously all-White positions available to Black steel-workers. Although management and "some" White workers resisted, "the union officers sided with the unemployment service."[21] The head of Local No. 1736 in Pittsburgh asserted that Blacks had access to all jobs in the plant. He acknowledged, however, that company officials and White workers opposed ambitious Black laborers. Management tried to prevent "a colored lad" from gaining a promotion, but the union inter-vened for the aggrieved employee. During World War II, a com-pany manager assigned "a colored girl" to a tool grinding job. He recalled that her presence "caused a tremendous amount of resentment and unrest with threats of a shutdown from our members." Union officers tried unsuccessfully to allay racial discontent. The company finally transferred the Black woman to another job.[22]

The president of Local No. 1194 in Jeannette, revealed that his plant refused "to hire colored workers" prior to World War II. "The [company] invited discrimination," wrote the Jeannette official, "But we treated the colored workers just the same as our White workers." He stated that "the company still tries to keep certain jobs open only to certain people" with Negroes and probably some Italians "on the company's nonpreferred list." Nonetheless, he contended that Jeannette's USWA "has been quite successful in forcing the placement of workers on any job regardless of race . . ."[23] The recording secretary of Local No. 1758 at Donora Steel and Wire, candidly stated that "I wish to express with regret that the range of jobs now open to minor-ity groups has not changed one bit since our plant organized. In fact, the negroes are worse off now, in some respects, than they were before the plant was organized." He faulted members and officers in both the Donora local union and in District 13 for their disinterest in the race issue. He noted that there were "four or five departments in our plant where White workers will not work with negro employees." He said that "a year or two ago a grievance committeeman tried to "correct some of these evils, but he was cited for starting a racial disturbance, and he gave up."[24]

Company indifference, union inaction, and White worker hostility retarded Black occupational advancement in Pittsburgh area mills. The intervention and advocacy of Black officials in the national and regional offices of the United Steelworkers of America, however, ameliorated these unfavorable conditions. During the 1940s, and 1950s, several CIO affiliates, anxious to appease disenchanted Black members and to adhere to the civil rights rhetoric of the Democratic Party, hired Black staff to allay racial tension and articulate the concerns of Black steelworkers. Black officials played an important role in the CIO hierarchy with Philip Weightman as a field representative of the Political Action Committee, and George L. P. Weaver as an assistant to the secretary-treasurer of the federation. John Dial served as a national representative of the Amalgamated Clothing Workers on the West Coast while Richard Carter of Bridgeport, Connecticut promoted Black interests in the electrical workers union. William H. Oliver headed the Fair Practices Committee of the United Auto Workers, and James E. Turner of Akron, Ohio fought for Black members in the United Rubber Workers.[25]

Boyd L. Wilson occupied an ambiguous position in the United Steelworkers of America. As a special assistant for racial affairs to Philip Murray and later for David J. McDonald, Wilson investigated the grievances of Black union members. To his great dismay, Murray and McDonald sharply limited his authority on racial matters. They forbade him to examine major complaints from Black unionists without their permission. Moreover, they did not appoint him until 1958 to serve with the White Shane brothers in the union's Civil Rights Department. Wilson principally represented the United Steelworkers in external racial affairs. His presence on the board of the National Urban League and in Ghana to celebrate its newly won independence enhanced the union's reputation for promoting Black causes, but did little affect occupational improvements for Black steelworkers. One sociologist, has observed that "caught between a Negro membership to which he generally owes primary allegiance and a White leadership to which he probably owes his position . . . with both making . . . conflicting demands on him, the Negro union official will tend to see his role as "ambassador" of the Negro members, winning as much as possible for the group while at the same time keeping the goodwill of the White leadership."[26] This observation explained the principal paradox in Wilson's role as a United Steelworkers official. As an international representative of United Steelworkers of America, Wilson participated in numerous organizations and activities to help the general Black population and improve race relations. Like other Black leaders and trade unionists, Wilson strongly supported the Democratic Party. He was especially impressed with party leaders in Allegheny County when they agreed to back Homer S. Brown, a Black state legislator in a successful bid to become a county judge. Wilson joined Philip Murray and other CIO officials on a visit to Pittsburgh Mayor David L. Lawrence and Allegheny County Commissioner John Kane, to secure their support of Brown's candidacy. In 1952, he criticized a *Pittsburgh Courier* editorial which doubted Democratic sincerity in pushing for national FEPC legislation and the abolition of poll taxes. Although the party platform failed to mention these issues specifically, Wilson believed that the "symbolic language" in the document gave Black people reasons to trust the party's good intentions. He challenged the GOP to match the record of the Democrats in support of "progressive Federal legislation."[27]

Wilson, during the late 1940s and 1950s, worked with the National Urban League and the Pittsburgh Urban League, and eventually served on their respective boards of directors. He tried in 1946 and 1947 to implement an educational program, probably on race relations, for steelworkers in the Ohio Valley in cooperation with the National Urban League's Department of Industrial Relations. He advised the director, Julius Thomas, on strategies to end unfair employment practices against Black workers. He suggested clauses in union contracts which affirmed the prerogative of management to hire and fire, but added that "this right shall not be exercised so as to discriminate against any person because of race, creed, or national origin. When problems arose among White workers at the St. Louis Car Company about the "upgrading of Negroes," Thomas offered to intercede for Wilson. Ed Meissner, the president of the firm, knew the League official and "really wants to crack through some of the prejudice that engulfs your . . . hometown," Thomas wrote to Wilson. Wilson, in turn, supplied information to Thomas about racial troubles at Carnegie-Illinois Steel in Youngstown, Ohio and Bethlehem Steel in Houston, Texas.[28]

The authority to inquire, however, was different from the power to intervene. Without Murray's permission, Wilson could do little more than monitor racial conditions in union and management affairs. Even his involvement with the National Urban League and other Black organizations was tightly reined. In 1950, for example, Murray authorized $2,500 from the United Steelworkers to help a special NAACP project. "This was a surprise to all including Boyd L. Wilson," observed Louis Mason of the Pittsburgh Urban League to another organizational officer. Apparently, Murray desired no input from Wilson on this important matter.[29]

Even before Murray died in 1952, Wilson probably believed that David J. McDonald, the secretary-treasurer, would succeed him as president. Hence, Wilson wanted to involve McDonald with the National Urban League. As a member of the League's National Conference Planning Committee in 1952, he invited McDonald to speak on Labor and Industry Day. In 1957, the National Urban League wanted "to formalize 'plans of cooperation' " with several important unions within the newly merged AFL–CIO. Boyd Wilson, now a McDonald subordinate, met with the executive director and the industrial relations secretary of the Pittsburgh Urban League "to give thought to a possible USW–NUL agreement." If implemented, the plan would foster cooperation between the civil rights efforts of the steelworkers union and the industrial relations division of the National Urban League and its local affiliates to advance "equal opportunity." It is unclear whether anything came of this proposed agreement.[30]

Wilson also played an advisory role as a board member of the Pittsburgh Urban League. He assisted Richard S. Dowdy, the industrial relations secretary, in 1954 to gain labor support for the annual conference of the National Urban League, and in 1959 he advised him "on several matters having to do with Negro employment in the steel industry." When Dowdy became concerned about Black employment in breweries, Wilson directed him to a knowledgeable United Auto Workers official in Detroit for information. In 1956 Dowdy learned from a Black steelworker about the failure of his local union to administer seniority rules properly. "This matter . . . having possible racial overtones, was referred" by Dowdy to Boyd L. Wilson.[31]

Wilson also went abroad to represent the United Steelworkers of America. He attended the International Labor Organization Conference in Geneva, Switzerland, the International Conference of Free Trade Labor Unions in Milan, Italy, and the International Metalworkers Conference. He traveled to Ghana in 1957 to witness its Independence Celebration. Wilson declared at a meeting of the Trade Union Committee of the National Urban League that "America's so-called race problem is no longer our private affair. The whole world is watching democracy in action in the United States, and many millions of non-White people are not too impressed with what they see."[32] Extensive involvement with civil rights organizations and foreign travel helped Wilson place Jim Crow in America in a broadened perspective. Unfortunately, he could do little to convince White steel managers and unionists to share his understanding of employment discrimination and the larger race problem of which it was a part.

Although Wilson carefully cultivated the goodwill of his White superiors, he did not ignore the persistence of racial discrimination in union and managment affairs. In 1957, for example, a Black member of the United Rubber Workers in Philadelphia and a former representative of the Mine, Mill, and Smelter Workers, accused the CIO of discriminatory practices, especially in the hiring of "Negro clericals and typists." In a lengthy letter to Philip Murray, the CIO president, he conceded that George L. P. Weaver, Boyd Wilson and others on the Committee to Abolish Racial Discrimination "are doubtless doing all they can . . . but it is at best a fatuous, self-righteous organization." "Have you ever wondered how many colored CIO members would like to have their daughters working in CIO offices typing [and], clerking," Hill asked Murray. "Are Negroes supposed to be satisfied with membership, paying their dues dollars for predominantly White clerical help — in most cases all White help?" According to this dissatisfied Black unionist, Boyd Wilson and other important Black unionists "heartily" endorsed his charges against the federation. In later years, Wilson made similar observations about the personnel practices of the Civil Rights Department of the United Steelworkers. He criticized Francis and Thomas Shane of never hiring a single Black to work in their civil rights department.[33]

Since Murray and McDonald restricted his power to intervene and adjudicate troublesome racial issues, Wilson's effectiveness was compromised. Moreover, confrontations with hostile district directors, recalcitrant White steelworkers and indifferent industry officials encumbered his efforts. At times, these hindrances caused Wilson to behave with unwarranted caution. An inquiry from Benjamin C. Cashaw, chairman of the Labor and Industry Committee of the Johnstown NAACP and a Black Bethlehem Steel employee, embarrassed Wilson and made him appear ineffective. In 1950 and 1955 Cashaw wrote detailed articles in the *Johnstown Democrat* which discussed the pervasiveness of racial discrimination at the local Bethlehem plant.[34]

Cashaw witnessed a steady deterioration in the condition of Black laborers during his nearly thirty years with the company. Bethlehem officials usually assigned Blacks to the most undesirable positions, but "when drudgery and danger" disappeared "from a job," observed Cashaw, "the few remaining Negroes are allowed to stay until they die or quit." Seldom were younger Blacks hired to replace them. In 1950, Cashaw, in reference to Blacks in the Bethlehem wire mill reflected that "we are probably the last Negroes who will ever work in this division of the Johnstown plant. There are only 49 Negroes working in all departments of the wire mill . . . More than 40 of these are past the age of 40. There have not been 10 Negroes assigned to jobs in the wire mill in the last 10 years." He deplored the declining number of Black wire drawers, and noted that "only one Negro . . . has been trained" in this occupation "in the last 10 years." He also said that "the wire mill has expanded," but "the number of Negro employees continues to shrink each year."[35]

In 1955, Cashaw observed that 65 Blacks originally worked at the Bethlehem steel plant, principally as chippers and wheel rollers. Although mechanization eliminated these positions, the improved machinery created additional jobs for Whites. Since "there has not been a Negro hired since 1944," Black retirements and deaths helped to produce an increasingly White department. Similarly, in the Lower Cambria Division of the Bethlehem plant, numerous Blacks worked as chippers, but when scarfing rendered this job obsolete, management assigned only Whites to "the newest machines." Cashaw made similar observations about the blast furnaces and coke plant in Bethlehem's Franklin Division. In both cases "the number of White workers [is] increasing where Negroes formerly predominated."[36]

Cashaw blamed Bethlehem officials for the systematic attempt to reduce Black employment in the Johnstown mills. He cited the rod mill as an example. Rod dockman "was classified as an almost exclusively Negro job." Nonetheless, Cashaw was convinced that Blacks would no longer work in this occupation. "Not long ago," he wrote in 1950, "there was an urgent need for additional men on the rod dock . . . a Negro who had been laid off from another part of the Johnstown Plant contacted the foreman and applied . . . so far as the foreman and superintendent were concerned he was in line for the job. But when he went to the employment office a personnel representative flatly refused to assign him." Cashaw grimly added that "since that time almost a score of young White men have been assigned to the rod dock."[37]

Cashaw sent an open letter to Boyd Wilson through the labor correspondent of the *Pittsburgh Courier*. Cashaw was "interested in finding whether these conditions are widespread throughout the Bethlehem Steel Company or do they just exist in Johnstown." He also asked, "are these conditions industry-wide relative to the Negro in all other steel corporations?" Although this public inquiry probably embarrassed Wilson, he unfairly chose to circumvent the principal issue of racial discrimination in the steel industry. In an open letter to the *Courier's* labor reporter, Wilson noted that he had spoken to Cashaw about the Johnstown plant "during the last State CIO convention." Wilson "asked . . . that more detailed information on the subject be submitted," and he promised, if the evidence required, he would "refer the matter to the proper authorities in our union." In spite of Cashaw's exhaustive explanation about racial conditions at the Bethlehem plant, a cautious Boyd Wilson avoided his legitimate questions. Without union support, especially from the Shane's civil rights department, Wilson wanted no one-man showdown with the Bethlehem Steel Corporation.[38]

Blacks also held a few other positions on the national and district levels of the United Steelworkers of America. At least three unionists, besides Boyd Wilson, worked on the national staff. In 1955 Charles R. Lockett of Detroit served on the United Steelworkers wage negotiating committee for employees of the Aluminum Company of America. Roland Sawyer, former director of the Pittsburgh Housing Authority, became a housing consultant at national union headquarters. John Thornton, who served as a SWOC organizer in the 1930s in the Beaver Valley of Western Pennsylvania, worked with the Steelworkers National Political Action Committee. During the 1950s, the union assigned him to northeast Ohio as a district PAC director. Later, he went to the union's Washington, D.C. office to work in public relations.[39] Additionally, Blacks became staffmen in several regional offices of the United Steelworkers. They included George Kimbley in Gary, James Hart and Everette Brown in Cleveland, Lucious Love in Chicago, Sam Stokes in Columbus, Ellison Jeffries in Cincinnati, and James Jones in Philadelphia.[40]

The need to cooperate with Whites and to voice the grievances of Blacks placed competing demands upon Black union officials. Like Boyd Wilson, Milford Peter "Pete" Jackson, the Black staffman in District 15, had trouble satisfying both groups. Born in Finleyville, Pennsylvania on February 19, 1904, Jackson worked as a check-weighman in Library, Pennsylvania at a Pittsburgh Coal Company mine. As a staunch member of the United Mine Workers, Philip Murray himself a veteran UMW official, invited Jackson to become a CIO organizer among autoworkers, rubber workers, railroad workers, and steelworkers. In 1949 he joined the staff of District 15, a jurisdiction which embraced United States Steel plants in Homestead, Braddock, Duquesne, McKeesport, and Clairton.[41]

Jackson investigated the grievances of Black steelworkers in District 15. In 1954, for example, the superintendent of the Munhall Works of U.S. Steel allowed employees in the mostly White Central Maintenance department to displace workers in the predominately Black General Maintenance division. When Richard S. Dowdy, the industrial relations secretary of the Pittsburgh Urban League, learned about the matter, he referred it to Boyd Wilson. Wilson apparently asked Pete Jackson to intervene. Jackson helped "the aggrieved workers" to process their complaint through the union's grievance machinery. At times, Jackson's efforts did not satisfy Black steelworkers. In 1957, over 100 Black employees at the Homestead Steel Works "packed into the union hall of . . . Local No. 1397" to declare their disillusionment with both the United Steelworkers and the company for their failure to end discriminatory hiring and promotion practices. Albert Everett, a former assistant grievance committeeman and a fired employee, contended that "the Negro in Homestead either works as a general laborer for the rest of his life or else moves over to the track department" where promotions eluded Black employees. Another Black employee accused U.S. Steel of hiring inexperienced White inspectors and cranemen. "Although we have been in the mill a long time," he asserted, "we can't even get these jobs." As Pete Jackson and John Duchy, a White grievance committeeman, sat through the meeting, Everett harshly criticized them for providing weak explanations for why he was fired from his job and why the grievances of Black workers "have not been processed." "We are not getting representation for our men," Everett said, "and we want to know why." Hence, Pete Jackson in District 15, like Boyd Wilson in the national steelworkers union, encountered difficulty in advancing the interests of Black workers in an atmosphere of stubborn resistance from White unionists and company officials.[42]

The presence of Boyd Wilson as an international representative and Pete Jackson as a staffman in District 15 signified Black progress in the United Steelworkers of America. Moreover, Blacks also held offices in numerous locals throughout the Pittsburgh area and in steel centers elsewhere in the nation. For example, Robert Woods headed Local No. 1843 at the Hays J and L plant in Pittsburgh, and Roy Battles was president of a predominantly White local in Coraopolis. Although the United Steelworkers, either through election or appointment, put Blacks in visible positions within the union, they did not support vigorously Black advancement within the mills.[43]

Officials in the Pittsburgh Urban League, particularly the executive director, Alexander J. Allen, Jr., and the industrial relations secretary, Richard S. Dowdy, also pressed the steel companies to treat Blacks more equitably. They referred the grievances of Black laborers to board members William P. Young, the Black welfare worker at Lockhart Iron and Steel in McKees Rocks and

Boyd Wilson of the steelworkers union. At times, League officers intervened directly to assist steel companies and Black employees to settle disputes amiably. Since the Pittsburgh Urban League received its primary financial support from the Community Chest, it could not solicit corporate contributions.[44] Nonetheless, Alexander Allen involved corporate executives in League affairs and urged them to improve employment opportunities for Blacks in both office and mill occupations.

Alexander Joseph Allen, Jr. became executive director of the Pittsburgh Urban League in 1950. His father, a bishop in the African Methodist Episcopal Church, supervised between 1948 and 1956 a jurisdiction which included AME congregations throughout the Pittsburgh area. His uncle, Nimrod B. Allen, organized the Columbus, Ohio Urban League and served as its executive director since 1921. Born in 1916, Allen earned his bachelor of science degree from Wilberforce University, a divinity degree from Yale, and a master's degree in social work from Columbia University. In 1942, he became the industrial relations secretary and later executive director of the Baltimore Urban League. Eight years later, at the age of 34, he came to Western Pennsylvania to head the Pittsburgh affiliate.[45]

Allen seemed optimistic about favorable changes in the racial attitudes of Pittsburgh's major employer. "Since the second world war, there has been a discernible trend in the Pittsburgh area toward equal economic opportunity for Negro workers," wrote Allen in the *Pittsburgh Courier* in 1954. He noted several firms "which have opened new opportunities in skilled work," and they included department stores, cab companies, RCA, Bell Telephone, and Jones and Laughlin Steel. He congratulated U.S. Steel for its commitment to accept qualified youth, regardless of race, into apprenticeship programs. Allen also tried to solidify a relationship with the steel industry in several different ways. In 1953, when a vacancy occurred in the industrial relations office of the Pittsburgh Urban League, a board member, W. Everett McLaine, a public relations official in U.S. Steel, suggested a corporate replacement. "McLaine thinks it may be possible," wrote Allen to his boss, "to find a man in the Industrial Relations Department of U.S. Steel . . . who could be made available on a temporary basis." Allen added that "McLaine thinks it would be a valuable experience for a member of the steel company staff and I am inclined to believe that it could have some real benefits for us." Allen and McLaine spoke to U.S. Steel vice president, Earl Moore, about the idea. Although Moore "expressed interest," he apparently did little or nothing to push the proposal.[46]

Allen, however, developed another strategy to broaden the participation of the steel companies in League affairs. U.S. Steel, J and L, Allegheny Ludlum, and Blaw Knox regularly supported the League's annual luncheon meetings where Allen delivered his annual report. In 1957, for example, T. S. Fitch, the mayor of Washington, Pennsylvania and president of the Washington Steel Corporation, delivered the keynote address at the League gathering. Nonetheless, W. Everett McLaine remained one of few steel executives on the board of the Pittsburgh affiliate. Though pleased with his active role, Allen believed that McLaine, as a public relations officer, was not high enough in the U.S. Steel hierarchy to effect meaningful gains for Blacks. Allen sought other ways to draw steel executives into Urban League activity. In 1951, he established the Defense Manpower Project to place Blacks especially "in positions in which Negro workers are used for the first time." Officials from H. J. Heinz, Harbison–Walker, and Earl Moore, vice president of U.S. Steel, made up the committee. In 1953, Alvin Snyder, an industrial management counselor affiliated with both Levinson Steel and Reliance Steel, became chairman of the League's Industrial Committee. To elicit greater corporate involvement in League affairs, Allen formed a Management Council to advise the industrial relations secretary and "assist in interpreting [the] Urban League program and procedures" to other Pittsburgh businessmen. In 1958, twenty-four executives, including four from the iron and steel industry, belonged to the group. Allen drew to the council Buckley M. Byers, president of A. M. Byers, S. A. McCaskey, vice president of Allegheny Ludlum Steel, Earl Moore, vice president of U.S. Steel, and Aaron Levinson, president of Levinson Steel. Since the group met only a few times each year, its impact was probably negligible.[47]

Board member, William P. Young, functioned as another link to the steel industry for Alexander Allen. In 1950, Young, a Black welfare officer at Lockhart Iron and Steel in McKees Rocks, convinced his employer to support financially the fortieth anniversary yearbook of the National Urban League. Young, who supervised the apartments Lockhart maintained for Black employees, headed in 1952 a special housing committee for the Pittsburgh Urban League. He persuaded the Housing Authorities of Pittsburgh and Allegheny County to bar racial segregation in public housing. Not only did Allen depend upon William P. Young, but he did not discount the potential influence of union officials. Emery Bacon, the education director of the United Steelworkers, and Boyd Wilson both belonged to the Pittsburgh Urban League board. Bacon, whom Allen described as a man of principle, and Wilson, another well-intentioned official, exercised little power within the United Steelworkers. Like William P. Young, Bacon and Wilson exerted greater influence in external racial affairs than within their respective organizations.[48]

When Alexander Allen assumed his duties at the Pittsburgh Urban League, he found Louis Mason, Jr. as the industrial relations secretary. Mason, who remained for less than two years, was followed by two interim successors. One served until Allen replaced him with Richard S. Dowdy in November 1952. The industrial relations department between 1950 and 1952 cultivated cooperative relations with steel officials and convinced some of them to provide better employment opportunities for Blacks. In 1950 Mason put on a radio broadcast about the Urban League. Alexander Allen and Theodore Smith, president of Oliver Iron and Steel, served as panelists. In 1952, the industrial relations department, with cooperation from the McKeesport office of the Pennsylvania State Employment Service, brought Blacks into an all-White McKeesport steel fabricating mill.[49]

Richard S. Dowdy, Jr. served as industrial relations secretary of the Pittsburgh Urban League from November 1952 until November 1959. He spent a year at Morehouse College in Atlanta, Georgia in hopes of becoming a Baptist minister. He later earned his bachelor's and master's degrees in Economics at Duquesne University in Pittsburgh in 1949 and 1952, respectively. Marshall Field and Company in Chicago wanted to hire this well-educated Pittsburgher. When store officials discovered that Dowdy was Black, they did not make a job offer. He then complained to the Chicago Commission on Human Relations. Although Dowdy did not join the firm, Marshall Field hired six other Blacks in previously all-White office jobs. In addition to his impressive credentials, Dowdy came to the Pittsburgh Urban League with some experience in the steel industry. While he attended Duquesne University, he worked at various Pittsburgh area steel mills, sometimes in hot and dangerous open hearth furnace departments.[50]

Dowdy sought a cooperative relationship with steel officials. To demonstrate the usefulness of the Pittsburgh Urban League, Dowdy gave advice to companies on such important matters as government contracts compliance reviews. In 1951, President Harry Truman's Executive Order 10308 established the Committee on Government Contract Compliance, which forbade racial discrimination by any firm doing business with the federal government. Dowdy reported in 1957, for example, that "the League provided consultative assistance" to Blaw Knox Steel in Pittsburgh during "its Compliance Review by the Atomic Energy Commission." He hoped that steel officials would reciprocate and provide broadened employment opportunities to Blacks.[51] Dowdy also helped Jones and Laughlin's Southside Blast Furnaces in 1955 when he served as an intermediary between mill supervisors and a Black steelworker. A jailed Black employee failed to get a leave of absence and lost his job. Although his personal difficulties elicited sympathy from his superiors, his blast furnace superintendent refused to rehire him seemingly due to his unsatisfactory job performance. Dowdy, who investigated the matter, concluded that "the company had been entirely within its prerogative in discharging the worker."[52]

Dowdy also made some attempts to improve promotion prospects for Black mill laborers. In 1954, he met with the Director of Education and Training for U.S. Steel, to learn about admission requirements to the firm's apprenticeship training programs. Dowdy and Alexander Allen learned from a Black union official that the program met with success in 1956 at the Duquesne Steel Works where efforts "had begun to integrate Negro employees as apprentices." In a meeting with U.S. Steel's Director of Employment and Placement, Dowdy discussed, with dismay, the presence of only two Black foreman in the company's Pittsburgh area mills. One of the foremen headed a sanitation department. He secured no commitment on plans to increase the number of Black foremen. Dowdy also tried to upgrade Black employment at J and L's Southside Blast Furnaces in Pittsburgh.[53]

The policy of the National Urban League, however, compelled Dowdy to devote greater attention to the development of employment opportunities for Blacks in clerical, professional, and technical occupations in the steel industry. In 1948, the League established a Pilot Placement Project to help Black college graduates to find professional and technical positions in major firms. Despite the persistence of racial discrimination, continued prodding by the National Urban League and the NAACP aided trained Blacks to get jobs as chemists, mathematicians, retail clerks, television servicemen, and stenographers. By 1955, the Radio Corporation of America, North American Aviation, International Harvester, Lockheed Aircraft, and Detroit Edison responded favorably to efforts to improve Black employment prospects. Dowdy's predecessor, Louis Mason, reported in 1950 that he planned "to obtain technical and professional employment for qualified Negro workers." He wanted to begin at Carnegie-Illinois Steel, Jones and Laughlin Steel, Westinghouse Electric, and Allis-Chalmers. In a letter to a national League official, Mason noted that the industrial relations department of the Pittsburgh affiliate deserved credit for the hiring of a Black engineer at Westinghouse Electric.[54]

Dowdy scheduled numerous meetings and made frequent telephone calls to steel industry officials to urge cooperation with the Pittsburgh Urban League and with the Minority Groups Representative of the Pennsylvania State Employment Service in the recruitment of educated and technically trained Blacks. In 1956, Dowdy and Alexander Allen met with the new vice president of the Industrial Engineering division of U.S. Steel. Since he had been active in the Gary, Indiana Urban League, the two officers wanted him to continue his League participation in Pittsburgh. Perhaps they also concluded that industrial engineering was a field that Blacks could possibly enter at U.S. Steel.[55]

Dowdy pursued any possibility to place a Black scientist or secretary in the steel industry. In 1954, he learned that J and L planned to hire Blacks to fill two vacancies. One position as a physicist required the applicant to have a Ph.D. or a master's degree working toward the doctorate. The other job in the teletype division would start the prospective employee as a messenger. When J and L abruptly decided not to seek a Black physicist, Dowdy persisted and secured an interview for a qualified Black candidate with the firm's Coordinator of Training and Recruitment.[56]

Support from the Pennsylvania State Employment Service and Dowdy's tenacity yielded some positive results. He reported in 1954 that J and L had a young Black man at work in the shipping department at the main office in Pittsburgh. In 1956, J and L promoted a Black at the downtown headquarters to clerk in the traffic department. Additionally, a Black engineer close to completing his master's degree in industrial administration at Carnegie Institute of Technology, was hired at J and L's Pittsburgh Works Engineering Laboratory. U.S. Steel in 1955 brought in a Black research assistant in chemistry to work at its Research Center in Monroeville.[57]

Aside from Dowdy's continued prodding, some Pittsburgh area employers believed that racial discrimination was counterproductive and deprived them of the broadest range of talent available in the marketplace. Several companies elsewhere in the nation set important precedents. Griffith Laboratories in Chicago employed a Black as technical director while CBS television hired another Black as head of graphic arts. Percy Julian, a gifted chemist, worked for the Glidden Company as research director before opening his own laboratory in Chicago. In Pittsburgh, M. H. Jacob, the personnel director at Jones and Laughlin Steel, contended that leadership from large businesses "with merit employment policies and practices" would cause other firms to "follow the good examples." Aaron Levinson, president of Levinson Steel, a fabricating firm on Pittsburgh's Southside, proudly showed a delegation of League officials touring the plant "tangible evidence" of the company's "fair, equitable and humanistic employment policy." The firm regularly hired Blacks for well-paying positions. Moreover, "the various manuals" used in Levinson's personnel office contained "positive and definitive non-discrimination statements."[58]

In 1957, however, Dowdy investigated the employment practices of five area steel firms including Blaw Knox, Allegheny Ludlum, Crucible, J and L, and U.S. Steel. Most of his ratings for plant, office, and technical positions ranged from poor to fair. He gave Blaw Knox the best evaluation. Although he described job opportunities for Blacks at the Blaw Knox plant and office as fair, he applauded the company's record in the technical area. He noted that the firm hired a Black engineer during the early 1950s. The employee began as a draftsman, but was elevated to senior design engineer and department supervisor. Dowdy seemed unimpressed with racial progress at the other four firms. Despite few contacts with Allegheny Ludlum in Breckenridge, Dowdy rated its record in plant and office employment for Blacks from poor to fair. He concluded that Crucible Steel had a good record at its plant, but "much remains to be done . . . as regards office personnel." Jones and Laughlin Steel drew "fair" ratings in plant and office employment. He was encouraged, however, by attempts to upgrade Black employment through transfers, promotions, and new hiring, especially at the headquarters office. "Conservative beginnings have been made in both office and plant toward widened use of Negro personnel," Dowdy wrote a National Urban League official. He hoped that this trend meant an "acceleration" of J and L's fair employment efforts.[59]

Dowdy judged U.S. Steel's record as the worst among the five steel companies. He deemed prospects for improved Black employment in both plant and technical positions as "fair" while he assessed office opportunities as "poor." Perhaps his extensive discussions in 1954 with E. C. Meyers, Assistant Vice President of Industrial Relations Administration, and C. D. Feight, the Director of Employment and Placement, help to explain the firm's dismal performance. Myers conceded that the racial views of "many men highly placed in industry . . . have not kept pace with changing times." Of course, he did not place himself into that category. Nevertheless, he asserted that the elevation of a Negro to the post of interviewer in the personnel department "represented a very definite step in the right direction." He argued that Black applicants preferred "to be interviewed by one of their own kind." Dowdy disagreed. Most Blacks, he contended, viewed this action as "a very definite affront." They believed that the employer wished to set them apart "as Negroes . . . rather than Americans."[60]

Furthermore, Feight, a member of the vocational advisory committee of the Pittsburgh Urban League, interjected that jealousy among Negroes hampered integration efforts. Whenever a Black employee attained a promotion "his Negro fellow workers begin to grumble," and question the individual's "character and fitness for the new position." Again, Dowdy responded. He held that in some cases "the grumbling might be justified." Generally, Blacks were cynical about promotions "since Negroes have risen in positions . . . in the past because of some extra friendly kind of relationship between them and their White superiors." Dowdy believed that "when more Negroes of immediately recognizable fitness and ability are holding better jobs in industry," such skepticism "will disappear or be greatly diminished." When Feight said that he had been led "to believe that Negroes prefer to keep to themselves — that is, to live and to work together in groups," Dowdy tried to enlighten him.[61]

Feight also noted that he employed a Black secretary and that three additional Black women, whose qualifications he praised, would be considered when a vacancy occurred. Moreover, thirty-two Black floor receptionists worked at the downtown office building. Unimpressed, Dowdy observed that receptionists performed duties similar to "an advanced messenger." Feight admitted that U.S. Steel hired too few Blacks in clerical, professional, management, and supervisory positions. Consequently, in 1957, Dowdy wrote that the employment practices of U.S. Steel "leave much to be desired." Although he thought that the size of the corporation made it difficult to communicate policy initiatives to improve Black job opportunities, Dowdy knew that naive and uninformed executives misunderstood the perspectives and aspirations of Black employees.[62]

Despite only modest success, Black steelworkers depended mainly upon the United Steelworkers of America and the Pittsburgh Urban League to help broaden employment opportunities for them. The establishment of the Pennsylvania Fair Employment Practice Commission also provided some assistance to aggrieved Black workers. Additionally, Pittsburgh, Johnstown, and Clairton created municipal FEPCs to improve Black employment. Homer S. Brown, a Black state legislator from Pittsburgh, led an unsuccessful attempt in 1945 to create a Pennsylvania FEPC. Governor John S. Fine, a Democrat, revived the idea in 1952 when he appointed a Voluntary Industrial Race Relations Committee. He selected Brown, who had become an Allegheny

County judge, as one of his fourteen appointees. The committee conducted a study which revealed "wide-spread job discrimination" against Blacks, Jews, and other minorities in the state. The group surveyed 1,229 companies and discovered that 90 percent were unfair to Blacks, especially in skilled occupations, supervisory jobs, and professional positions. Even in unskilled labor 38 percent of the employers treated Blacks inequitably.[63]

In 1955 with strong backing from Fine's Democratic successor, Governor George M. Leader, the state legislature enacted the Fair Employment Practice Act. Although the agency it established lacked enforcement power, it was authorized to set up conferences between aggrieved persons and employers, unions, or the local or state government unit charged with discrimination. Moreover, conciliation, persuasion, the right to subpoena documents, and to hold either informal or public hearings were alternatives available to the Pennsylvania FEPC. In 1957 out of 144 cases the Commission found discrimination in 31, and the members dismissed 37 cases. Another 76 cases remained under investigation. Also, in 1957, 41 cases or over one-fourth of all complaints, emanated from the Pittsburgh area office. Moreover, the agency proved helpful to Black steelworkers. In 1959, one laborer complained that his employer kept him in the same job while Whites consistently received promotions. Despite the steel company's reputation for fairness to Blacks, the state FEPC discovered that a foreman refused to advance Blacks to better jobs "for fear of 'causing trouble.'" Company officials settled the dispute amiably with the commission, and the aggrieved employee and eleven other Blacks secured promotions.[64]

A few municipalities in Pennsylvania also established FEPCs to expand Black employment opportunities. The Pittsburgh FEPC predated the state agency by a decade. Renamed the Commission on Human Relations during the early 1950s, the committee made a major attempt to improve the status of Black steelworkers. In 1954 its annual report criticized labor unions for their racial bias. In 1956 Louis Mason, deputy director of the commission and a former Urban League official, dealt with Jones and Laughlin Steel and alleged racial discrimination in the firm's apprenticeship program. The president of Local No. 1272 at J and L claimed that the union had no jurisdiction in the matter. Mason decided to investigate company practices and secure equitable treatment for a Black J and L employee who wished full participation in the apprenticeship program. Alexander Allen of the Pittsburgh Urban League credited the agency with accelerating "the trend toward equal job opportunities" in the Smoky City.[65]

Clairton and Johnstown followed Pittsburgh's lead. In 1953, the Clairton city council created a FEPC to hear and investigate complaints of racial discrimination. In 1954, Johnstown councilmen also established a fair employment practices committee. Benjamin C. Cashaw, a Black steelworker and a Johnstown NAACP officer, endorsed the ordinance. He asserted that persistent racism against Blacks in the Bethlehem Steel Mills warranted FEPC legislation. Although these state and municipal agencies frequently lacked effective enforcement power and inadequate funding, various FEPCs gave occasional, but important assistance to Black steelworkers.[66]

Some historians contend that Blacks between 1940 and 1960 experienced greater occupational stability than downward mobility in major industries like steel in the Pittsburgh industrial area. While generally true for veteran Black steelworkers protected by enforced seniority rules, these historians ignore numerous firms which refused to hire Blacks, promote them, or admit them to apprenticeship training programs. Both steel companies and the United Steelworkers of America adopted the rhetoric of racial fairness and equal employment opportunity; they pointed to a handful of Blacks who held responsible positions in the mills and in company and union offices. Black steelworkers in the rank and file knew a different reality. The existence of a few Black foremen, skilled workers, and important Black union officers like Boyd Wilson and Milford "Pete" Jackson, revealed an illusion of advancement, not substantive progress for the vast majority of Black steel employees. Because they recognized these realities, they occasionally took matters into their own hands. At the Clairton steel works during the early 1950s, a Black steelworker with sufficient seniority was denied the job of pusher. He and fellow Blacks staged a successful strike which was belatedly supported by the union. In 1957, more than one hundred Black workers at the Homestead Steel Mills met to denounce both Black and White staffmen in the United Steelworkers for their failures to articulate their desire for improved Black employment opportunities.[67] During the 1960s, buoyed by the national civil rights movement, Black steelworkers resorted more frequently to protest and picketing to press their demands for equitable treatment both by steel managers and national union officials.

# 9
# Pyrrhic Victories:
# Black Steelworkers During the
# Civil Rights Era, 1960–1980

The national civil rights movement during the 1960s made major improvements in the condition of Black Americans.[1] For Southern Blacks, the nightmare of Jim Crow which mandated racial discrimination and segregation in education, employment, public accommodations, and voting lost its legitimacy when the Civil Rights Act of 1964 and the Voting Rights Act of 1965 passed Congress and gained the signature of President Lyndon B. Johnson. For urban Blacks, mostly in the industrial North and West, Title VII of the 1964 Civil Rights Act established the Equal Employment Opportunity Commission which compelled numerous companies with a history of racial discrimination to hire and upgrade the status of Black workers. Moreover, the tactics of nonviolent direct action, especially picketing, marches, and boycotts, were used successfully by several civil rights groups to win important victories in the Greensboro sit-ins, the Birmingham demonstrations, and the Selma marches. Influenced by the activism of the Southern Christian Leadership Conference (SCLC), the Student Nonviolent Coordinating Committee (SNCC), the Congress of Racial Equality (CORE), the NAACP and other groups, Black steelworkers and their allies in the Pittsburgh area borrowed their tactics to press their own employment demands upon the steel industries and the United

Steelworkers of America. With unprecedented support from newly enacted federal laws and judicial decisions, Black steel employees moved to important jobs previously reserved for Whites. These advancements, however, proved to be Pyrrhic victories since they occurred as the steel industry in Western Pennsylvania encountered serious financial and technological decline.

After a period of employment expansion, Pittsburgh area steel officials decreased the work force from 141,536 in 1950 to 123,651 in 1960. Although the number of Blacks during this period fell from 9,239 to 8,231, their percentage rose slightly from 6.5 percent to 6.7 percent. Seniority agreements, despite their shortcomings, probably protected enough Blacks to prevent even greater decreases within their ranks. Significant job expansion occurred during the early 1960s in the Pittsburgh vicinity, and Blacks shared modestly in these employment opportunities. In 1963, 10,975 Blacks or 7 percent worked for Pittsburgh area steel employers. In 1964, their numbers grew to 11,762, and they made up 7.2 percent of all employees. As the total number of employees decreased between 1965 and 1968, the number of Black employees also dropped. In 1968, the industry employed 10,380 Blacks or 6.9 percent. Despite the reduction more than 2,000 more Blacks worked in the steel industry of Western Pennsylvania in 1968 than in 1960.[2] (See Table 10.)

Racial discrimination, a perennial problem in the steel industry, continued to restrict Black hiring and occupational advancement. According to Benjamin Cashaw, a Black steelworker in Johnstown, the industry did not want "to employ Negroes in any capacity where they cannot overwork them and underpay them." In 1963, when Blacks comprised 7 percent of all Pittsburgh district steel employees, only 3.1 percent held skilled positions. In 1968, Blacks constituted 6.9 percent of the work force, but they made up only 3.4 percent of all craftsmen. In 1968, in a hard-hitting speech to the American Iron and Steel Institute, Whitney M. Young, Jr., the influential executive director of the National Urban League, criticized employers in the Pittsburgh vicinity for the presence of only 735 Blacks among 23,000 skilled workers. At the Clairton steel works in 1965, U.S. Steel officials circumvented seniority rules to prevent the promotion of qualified Black steelworkers. Moreover, numerous departments at the Clairton plant included no Blacks. At Amer-

**TABLE 10. Black Employees in the Steel Industry in the Pittsburgh Area, 1960–1968**

| Year | Total Number of Employees | Number of Black Employees | Percentage of Black Employees |
|------|---------------------------|---------------------------|-------------------------------|
| 1960 | 123,651 | 8,231 | 6.5 |
| 1963 | 155,681 | 10,975 | 7.0 |
| 1964 | 163,063 | 11,762 | 7.2 |
| 1965 | 153,974 | 10,515 | 6.8 |
| 1966 | 151,626 | 10,314 | 6.8 |
| 1968 | 150,518 | 10,380 | 6.9 |

Compiled from: Richard L. Rowan, "The Negro in the Steel Industry," in Herbert R. Northrup, et. al. *Negro Employment in Basic Industry: A Study of Racial Policies in Six Industries*, Volume I, (Philadelphia, Industrial Research Unit, Wharton School of Finance and Commerce, University of Pennsylvania, 1970), pp. 279, 338–339.

ican Bridge in Ambridge, a division of U.S. Steel, the company employed less than 120 Blacks out of 620 employees, and most of them worked in menial positions. The West Leechburg plant of Allegheny Ludlum Steel employed only 28 Blacks out of 3,100 workers.[3]

The racial unrest of the 1960s made some employers defensive about their Black employment policies. U.S. Steel responded to critics in 1966 with a special article in *U.S. Steel News*, its corporate magazine. In Western Pennsylvania, for example, U.S. Steel showed in the magazine pictures of a Black clerk in the company's medical department in Pittsburgh and of a Black design engineer also in the Smoky City. Readers were reminded that U.S. Steel voluntarily became a participant in the President's Committee on Equal Employment Opportunity and its Plans for Progress which promoted nondiscrimination in employment. As a result, U.S. Steel officials held meetings with church and community leaders to inform them about job opportunities in the company and to reaffirm its commitment to the Plans for Progress. A photograph also appeared of a Black furnaceman at the basic oxygen furnace of the Duquesne steel works. Despite the importance of his position, the article did not discuss the vast majority of Black steelworkers who remained locked in unpleasant, low-paying jobs in numerous U.S. Steel plants throughout the Pittsburgh vicinity.

Steel employers seldom promoted fair employment practices for Black steelworkers without prodding either from the federal government or militant Black employees. Although the United Steelworkers of America frequently responded to racial grievances with reluctance, Black members expected some support from union officials. David J. McDonald, the president of the steelworker's union in 1961, instructed all international, district, and local officers to endorse full equality in jobs, housing, education, and voting for excluded groups. In cooperation with the union's civil rights committee McDonald called for an "end" to "discrimination in all its open and hidden forms." In 1962, he successfully proposed the insertion of a nondiscrimination clause in upcoming contracts with U.S. Steel, Jones and Laughlin, Bethlehem and other firms. The agreement insured that all workers, regardless of race, would be promoted or would enter apprenticeship programs with qualifications and seniority as the only criteria. McDonald claimed that the clause excluded hiring because a presidential executive order already compelled companies to file compliance reports on nondiscrimination.[5]

Francis Shane, executive director of the USWA Civil Rights Committee from 1948 to 1965, sponsored conferences for union members and delivered speeches to promote civil rights. In 1960, Shane spoke before the Republican Party platform committee to urge the members to insert a strong statement on civil rights. He also criticized the U.S. House of Representatives for sending to the Senate a weak civil rights bill which would do little to protect Black voting rights. In 1962, he wrote to Vice President Lyndon B. Johnson, chairman of President John F. Kennedy's Committee on Equal Employment Opportunity, to tell him of steel union efforts to support civil rights.[6] Shane's civil rights committee also regularly sponsored conferences and symposia. In 1961, for example, in cooperation with the union's education department and the division of labor education at Pennsylvania State University in University Park, Shane convened a conference on equal employment opportunity. More than seventy United Steelworkers officials attended. Shane informed the participants about President Kennedy's Executive Order 10925 which strengthened prohibitions against racial discrimination in federal government agencies and in companies with federal contracts. He also discussed the Pennsylvania Human Relations Act. Thomas Murray, a White member of the civil rights committee, boasted that Shane and his fellow committeemen had been effective in the promotion of fair employment practices. These gatherings, however, did not impress some of Shane's Black critics. In reference to a similar conference at Indiana University in Bloomington, Indiana in 1960, the *Pittsburgh Courier* noted that these sessions were designed to make the civil rights committee "look good." The *Courier* also criticized Shane and his committee for their neglect of Black perspectives. Perhaps, in response to this allegation, Boyd L. Wilson and Roland Sawyer, two Black USWA international representatives, appeared on the program of the 1961 Penn State meeting.[7]

Despite the public posturing of the civil rights committee, Black steelworkers faulted the union for inaction on important racial grievances. President David J. McDonald responded to critics of Shane's committee between 1958 and 1962 by the appointment of Blacks. Joseph Neal, a Black staffman in Baltimore, had been a member of the committee since 1952. McDonald chose Boyd L. Wilson, the international representative for racial affairs, Roland Sawyer, the union's housing consultant, and James Jones, a Black staffman in Philadelphia. Additionally, in 1962, McDonald appointed Ernest L. Clifford, as a staff representative to work with the civil rights committee. Clifford, born in Clairton, Pennsylvania in 1927 began work at the Clairton plant of U.S. Steel in 1943. Also, in 1965, McDonald assigned him to prepare a report on labor contracts and minority group problems. Despite the presence of Blacks on the committee, Shane remained in charge and the committee continued to stress issues related to the general condition of the Black population rather than the difficulties which confronted Black steel-workers.[8]

Moreover, Roland Sawyer and Boyd Wilson, who both had additional union responsibilities, responded to Black concerns as ineffectively as did Shane's committee. Sawyer, a housing expert who served from 1958 to 1965, mainly wrote booklets on public housing, appeared before state legislative committees to argue for better homes for Blacks, and belonged to the AFL–CIO Housing Committee. Black steelworkers benefited indirectly from Sawyer's efforts, but his presence in the union hierarchy did little to improve their occupational condition. Until his retirement in 1966, Boyd Wilson remained caught between a rock and a hard place. As an international representative and a member of the civil rights committee, Wilson had little authority beyond what McDonald and Shane relinquished to him. Consequently, Wilson, as a visible advocate for Black unionists, had few opportunities to satisfy those whom he represented.[9]

Boyd Wilson deplored the absence of Black speakers at the union's annual Steelworkers Education Conference. With the cooperation of the Pittsburgh Urban League, he successfully suggested Whitney M. Young, Jr., Dean of the School of Social Work at Atlanta University, as a speaker at the Indiana University meeting. A veteran League official in St. Paul, Minnesota and Omaha, Nebraska, and the future executive director of the National Urban League, Young spoke on "Integration: The Role of Labor Education." Wilson told Young that "in the past I have been the only man of color" at the education gatherings. The 1960 conference, however, would have "some six or eight Negroes . . . including three or four University professors and five or six Negro steelworkers." "Even you as a speaker" wrote Wilson to Whitney Young, "is within itself a departure from past gatherings." An officer in the Pittsburgh Urban League advised Young to mention in his speech that "Boyd Wilson . . . feels that in 1960 labor education needs to take bold steps in the field of race relations, and that the Urban League knows about steelworkers problems through Boyd."[10]

As a board member for both the National Urban League and its Pittsburgh affiliate, Wilson developed cordial relations with numerous League officials. His interaction with Black unionists, however, frequently proved less amiable. Wilson's inability to act independently limited his effectiveness in settling Black employment disputes. The Atlantic Steel Company in Atlanta, Georgia, for example, employed 1,600 workers of whom 37 percent or 592 were Black. Nonetheless, Black workers, despite seniority rules, remained concentrated in low-paying positions. Moreover, Local No. 2401, an integrated steelworkers local, had no high-ranking Black officers. In 1960, Black members accused local union officials of failure to negotiate in their behalf. During contract talks the union pressed for the maintenance of classifications of Black workers which kept them in menial categories. Consequently, no Black Atlantic employees worked in skilled and semi-skilled positions. Nathaniel Brown, a veteran Black worker at Atlantic and a member of the union's bargaining committee, contended that the company wanted to eliminate the discriminatory job differentials between Black and White employees, but Local No. 2401 officials opposed any changes. When Black members sent Brown to Pittsburgh to discuss these complaints with Boyd Wilson, he alleged that Wilson gave him little cooperation. Moreover, Brown was barred from a meeting devoted to the Atlantic situation. Wilson and James Jones, a Black staffman from Philadelphia, were present with several White officials including Francis Shane and the union's Atlantic district director. The *Pittsburgh Courier* reported that Wilson preferred to settle the dispute through the union's regular grievance machinery. Although Blacks in Local No. 2401 expressed reservations about Boyd Wilson, the veteran unionist responded that his stand for equal employment opportunity during his twenty years in the labor movement spoke for itself. Black Atlanta steelworkers expected swift and decisive action from Wilson, but the involvement of high-ranking union officers circumscribed his independence.[11]

Wilson's participation in the Negro American Labor Council (NALC) eroded his credibility even further. Black unionists led by A. Philip Randolph, president of the Brotherhood of Sleeping Car Porters, established the organization in 1959. Randolph wanted the group to agitate and prod the AFL–CIO to take stronger action to rid racial discrimination from such areas as skilled worker apprenticeships, Jim Crow locals, and the exclusion of Blacks from various unions. Blacks from the teamsters, hod carriers, laundry workers, electrical workers, housewreckers, and building and common laborers joined the NALC chapter in Pittsburgh. Additionally, Blacks from six United Steelworkers' locals in Western Pennsylvania joined the group. With a vague explanation, John Thornton, a ranking Black United Steelworkers official and an officer in the NALC, labeled Wilson as a saboteur of both the Pittsburgh chapter and the national organization.

When another Black steelworkers' official allegedly wrote an uncomplimentary letter to David J. McDonald about John Thornton, Wilson, one of NALC officers who investigated the matter, believed that the issue should be dropped. Disappointed and angered, Thornton resigned from the Negro American Labor Council. Wilson's ineffectiveness among White union leaders and his limited credibility among Black USWA members crippled his efforts to improve their occupational status.[12]

The efforts of Francis Shane and the steelworkers civil rights committee, and of Boyd Wilson, while important, did not improve the condition of Black steelworkers as much as did the civil rights movement of the 1960s. The crusade for racial equality and increasing federal involvement in Black workers' affairs helped to broaden opportunities for Blacks in steel employment and in union participation. President John F. Kennedy's Committee on Equal Employment Opportunity convinced employers to cooperate with the Plans for Progress, a voluntary program to encourage the upgrading of Black workers. Moreover, the Equal Employment Commission, which grew out of Title VII of the 1964 Civil Rights Act, possessed enforcement authority to prevent racial discrimination both by companies and unions. Additionally, activism associated with Southern civil rights marches, voter registration drives, sit-ins, and freedom rides strongly influenced Black steelworkers in Western Pennsylvania. They staged their own marches against discriminatory employers, they pressed for a greater voice in United Steelworkers' affairs and more representation in the union hierarchy.[13]

James McCoy, Jr., a former Black steelworker who held important positions in the United Steelworkers of America, used demonstrations and protests to convince steel firms and other employers to improve the hiring and upgrading of Black workers. Born in Houston, Texas, McCoy migrated to Pittsburgh, and later found a job at Continental Rolling Steel in Coraopolis. He rose to shop steward and eventually president of Local No. 1904 of the steelworker's union. During the 1960s he served as a staffman in District 16, a jurisdiction which embraced Pittsburgh's Southside and vicinity. He was liaison officer for the District's civil rights committee. An active member of the NAACP, McCoy became an organizer of the group's state Labor and Industry Committee during the 1950s.

Influenced by the national civil rights movement, McCoy in 1963 founded the United Negro Protest Committee (UNPC).[14]

In 1966 the UNPC criticized the Mesta Machine company, a steel casting firm in West Homestead, for its dismal record in Black employment. In a joint effort with Reverend Churchill Carter of Park Place AME Church in Homestead and local Black residents, the Committee learned that Mesta employed only 50 Blacks out of a work force of 2,700. Negotiations with a top company executive yielded a promise to hire more Blacks. A few months later, McCoy sought statistics on Black employment at U.S. Steel plants along the Monongahela River. He was particularly interested in the number of Blacks who held positions as apprentices, foremen, and clerical workers. A confidential memo to a United Steelworkers official revealed that "McCoy is reported to have inquired of a Homestead colored employee whether [the] Homestead Works would be an appropriate plant where such a demonstration should be conducted." The United Negro Protest Committee also uncovered additional information about employment practices at U.S. Steel, Allegheny Ludlum, and Jones and Laughlin. In Monroeville, at U.S. Steel's research laboratory, only 15 Blacks worked among 1,500 employees. At company headquarters in Pittsburgh, the industrial coordinator for the UNPC, while applauding the placement of 115 Blacks in clerical positions, stated that "more can be done" to gain a better Black representation in the 4,500 work force.[15]

Despite McCoy's involvement in the United Negro Protest Committee, he continued active participation in the Pennsylvania NAACP. The organization targeted U.S. Steel in 1966 for demonstrations to protest racial discrimination in plant and office employment. The NAACP criticized U.S. Steel's hiring and promotion policy toward Blacks at its Birmingham, Alabama area facilities and "tokenism" in the employment of Blacks at the main offices in Pittsburgh. At times, McCoy's affiliation with both the Pennsylvania NAACP and the Pittsburgh branch stirred opposition within the United Steelworkers of America. In 1963, McCoy participated in a NAACP demonstration to achieve Black employment on a federal building project in Pittsburgh. The Pittsburgh Police Department notified union authorities that McCoy, a staffman on the District 16 civil rights committee used a steelworker's union car for NAACP business. Francis Shane,

executive director of the USWA's Civil Rights Committee, called
in McCoy and charged that he violated organization policy when
he tried to expand job opportunities "for Negroes alone." The
USWA, contended Shane, was concerned about "equal opportunity for all people," not just Blacks. Although Shane demanded
that McCoy quit the NAACP, the veteran unionist steadfastly
refused. In 1966, McCoy and the NAACP sought the union's
cooperation in forthcoming talks with various steel companies
about Black employment. Shane's successors on the civil rights
committee shunned McCoy and the NAACP, and expressed a
preference for working with the less combative state civil rights
commission to upgrade Black workers in the steel industry.[16]

McCoy frequently encountered in the United Steelworkers
of America reticence toward Black activism. This stirred him
and other Blacks to protest and to organize for change in the
union. Buoyed by earlier battles for racial equality in union
affairs and by civil rights activism in the South, Black steelworkers attempted during the 1960s to gain more representation and greater influence within the USWA. Numerous Black
members grew disenchanted with David J. McDonald, president of the steelworkers union. They blamed him for the ineffectiveness of the Civil Rights Committee and the paucity of
Black staffmen. Despite the presence of 225,000 Blacks in the
1,000,000 member union, non-Whites held a little more than
twenty positions out of 800 in the early 1960s. In 1957, Black
steelworkers in Homestead organized the Fair Share Group of
Steelworkers. They wrote to McDonald and George Meaney,
president of the AFL–CIO to protest "the neglect of Negro problems" by the unions. In 1960, twenty-seven Blacks in District 15
formed a "permanent organization for action." They came from
Jones and Laughlin, Southwest Steel, National Tube, Atcheson
Foundry, and U.S. Steel plants in Homestead, Duquesne, Braddock, and Rankin. A spokesmen told a *Pittsburgh Courier*
reporter that "Negroes in our district are sick and tired of getting promises which are never filled." The group also discussed
the possibility of running Blacks for both local and international
union offices.[127]

Carl Dickerson, one of the disenchanted steelworkers, was
no stranger to such activism. An employee at the Duquesne
Steel Works since 1936, Dickerson became an active member of

Local No. 1256. In the 1940s and 1950s he held a succession of local and district offices, which included member of the By-Law Committee, and in later years, recording secretary of Local No. 1256, member of the District 15 wage policy committee, delegate to the international wage policy meeting, and delegate to the 1956 USWA convention in Los Angeles. Despite his loyalty to the union, he grew disappointed with the commitment of union leaders to racial equality. When a steelworker's convention met in Atlantic City in 1948, Dickerson and another eight or nine Blacks threatened to picket the hotel where Philip Murray and David McDonald were lodged. The establishment bore a sign which read "No Negroes, No Jews, and No Dogs"! The Black delegation which included Dickerson convinced their union leaders, particularly the reluctant McDonald, to move elsewhere. These and other examples of racial insensitivity accumulated during the 1950s and stirred Dickerson and other Black unionists in the early 1960s to challenge McDonald to improve his advocacy for Black concerns. Hence, Dickerson joined with other Blacks in District 15 who planned to protest the union's sluggish support for its Black members when the 1960 convention opened in Atlantic City. As a delegate to the 1964 convention, the Duquesne steelworker took to the convention floor to castigate the ineffectiveness of the union's Civil Rights Committee. He later served as an officer in the Ad Hoc Committee of Black steelworkers which in 1968 sought greater representation for Blacks in the union hierarchy.[18]

White opponents of McDonald made overtures to Blacks hoping to benefit from their discontent with the union president. The Organization for Membership Rights (OMR), a group which consisted mainly of Whites, became angered with McDonald about increased dues obligations. Originally called the Dues Protest movement, unionists, especially in Western Pennsylvania, grew furious when a 1956 wage agreement with the steel companies failed to benefit laborers in fabricating mills, while increasing the salaries of McDonald and other international officers by $10,000. McDonald's compensation would rise from $40,000 to $50,000 annually. In 1959 steel negotiations, after a strike which lasted 116 days, McDonald disappointed his rank and file with a wage increase of 34 cents per hour, instead of the expected 39 to 41 cents.[19]

In 1960, Nichola Mamula, president of Local No. 1211 at the Aliquippa plant of Jones and Laughlin Steel and an OMR leader, made appeals to Black steelworkers. He supported changes in supplemental agreements at the Aliquippa mill "which had hamstrung the advancement of Negroes." He pointed out that "prior to 1958 no Negro had ever operated a locomotive diesel engine." He indicated that Blacks now worked on diesel locomotives and in the previously all-White seamless tube mill. Mamula cited these cases as evidence of what the OMR had done to promote the occupational interests of Black Aliquippa laborers. "We welcome the Negro because he is a steelworker," declared the OMR leader. Other members of the group considered running a Black for district director in District 15 and a Black on the international ticket against the McDonald slate. David Rarick, the OMR opponent to McDonald, unlike his rival, vowed "to make civil rights a No. 1 issue, not merely the subject for fine speeches." The McKeesport unionist added that "we want a union where Negro steelworkers can represent White steelworkers and White steelworkers can represent Negro steelworkers." He also desired the elimination of "the twin evils of outright discrimination and tokenism."[20]

Iorwith Wilbur Abel, secretary-treasurer of the United Steelworkers of America since 1952, became in 1963 McDonald's most formidable opponent. Born in 1908 in Magnolia, Ohio, I. W. Abel worked in Canton at the Timkin Bearing Division of U.S. Steel. Although Abel had not been a vocal crusader for Black members, he had a respectable record in securing Black appointments to union offices. When he became the district director in the Canton, Ohio area in 1942, he hired two Blacks as staff representatives. He convinced the district director in the Cincinnati region to appoint a Black unionist to his staff. Moreover, in 1960, when David McDonald declined to attend the first convention of the Negro American Labor Council, Abel and Walter Reuther went and endorsed efforts by A. Philip Randolph to organize Black union members.[21]

Disgruntled, like many other unionists, in McDonald's leadership, Abel decided by 1964 to challenge his boss for the top office in the United Steelworkers. Since Abel's record on racial quality was generally unknown among Blacks, he responded enthusiastically to assistance offered to him by Alex Fuller.

Fuller, an active unionist in Detroit's District 29 and a vice president of the Wayne County AFL–CIO, knew first-hand about McDonald's racial insensitivity. When Fuller and other Black steelworkers organized the Ad Hoc Committee, they asked McDonald to convene a meeting of the Civil Rights Committee. Fuller and his group wanted to present the grievances of Black unionists to Francis Shane and his fellow Civil Rights Committee members. After McDonald refused to honor their request, Fuller called a meeting of the Ad Hoc Committee. The fifty-eight Black unionists advocated a reorganization of the Civil Rights Committee and greater integration of Blacks into district positions. Since McDonald shunned their demands and Abel fully embraced them, the latter received their endorsement for the presidency of the United Steelworkers of America. Not to be outdistanced by Abel in trying to win Black voters, McDonald called upon his Black loyalists to battle the campaign workers of his recalcitrant colleague for Negro support. Fuller, who became second-in-command in the Abel organization, placed huge ads in the *Pittsburgh Courier* extolling the virtues of his candidate. He contended that while McDonald was "too busy" to support the concerns of Black unionists, Abel met with Black steelworkers at an Indianapolis gathering to go "over their problems in detail" and find "ways in which the union could help solve them." McDonald, on the other hand, with the power of incumbency, made hurried appointments of Black unionists, and tried to eliminate or neutralize opposition to him, especially among Black steelworkers in the populous Pittsburgh steel region. Although Abel narrowly defeated McDonald with 306,801 votes to 298,949 votes, it is unclear whether Blacks supplied the former with his margin of victory. What is certain was the high visibility of Alex Fuller in Abel's winning campaign and Fuller's argument that Blacks would receive better from the Abel administration.[22]

At the time that Abel took office, civil rights activism in the Birmingham demonstrations, the Selma to Montgomery march, and other similar events helped to persuade Congress to enact the Civil Rights Act of 1964 and the Voting Rights Act of 1965. Although the AFL–CIO executive council refused to endorse the historic 1963 March on Washington, the organization lobbied for the 1964 civil rights bill. The hopes of Black workers were buoyed by the inclusion of Title VII in the 1964 law, which established the Equal Employment Opportunity Commission (EEOC), an agency empowered to seek legal remedies for racial discrimination practiced both by companies and unions. Moreover, in 1965, President Lyndon B. Johnson issued Executive Order 11246 to prevent racial discrimination by unions, especially in the construction industry. Contractors with the federal government were also required to hire and promote Blacks and the Office of Federal Contract Compliance in the Department of Labor had authority to persuade companies to fulfill their duty to include Blacks in the work force. When Alex Fuller organized the Ad Hoc Committee of Black steelworkers in 1964, he and other unionists brought the militant demands of the civil rights movement to the United Steelworkers of America. Blacks generally sought equal treatment in employment education, politics and housing. Similarly, within the steelworkers union they wanted greater Black representation in the union hierarchy and vigorous efforts to fight company discrimination against Black steel employees. I. W. Abel, influenced by the civil rights movement and the Black support which Fuller helped to mobilize for his successful presidential candidacy, attempted to move the United Steelworkers to respond more effectively to Black grievances.[23]

Not long after the election, Abel spoke to the Negro Trade Union Leadership meeting in Philadelphia, where he promised to insert nondiscrimination clauses in all steel contracts. He also backed efforts to enact civil rights legislation in Pennsylvania. The bill would strengthen the Pennsylvania Human Relations Commission, giving it subpoena power in hearings and authority to stop both housing discrimination and de facto school segregation. Joseph Molony, Abel's running mate and vice president, in an address to steel unionists in Midland, urged support for NAACP picketers at the U.S. Steel headquarters in Pittsburgh. He endorsed their efforts to move the corporation to establish racial equity in the Birmingham, Alabama facilities and to desegregate sales and clerical occupations at the Pittsburgh headquarters. "There is enough merit to these charges," said Molony, "to cause" great distress among United Steelworkers.[24]

Abel tried hard to restore the confidence of Black steelworkers in the union's commitment to expanding Black participation in organizational affairs and to the vigorous promotion of civil rights. He brought William Fletcher, a member of Local No. 1397 at the Homestead Steel Works, to the International Education Department as a staff representative. An alumnus of both Duquesne University and the University of Pittsburgh, Fletcher had been a manager of the Bedford Dwellings, a public housing development in the Smoky City and an employee of the Pittsburgh Housing Authority. The forty-year-old Fletcher served the United Steelworkers for only fifteen months, however, since he died in 1967. To the Civil Rights Committee, Abel named his vice president, Joseph Molony, as presiding officer, and he appointed Alex Fuller as the executive director. Francis C. Shane, Fuller's predecessor, remained as a member of the group. Other Black appointees included Samuel Stokes of Canton, Ohio, Curtis Strong of Gary, Indiana, and James Jones of Philadelphia.[25]

Largely because of the renewed commitment to civil rights by I. W. Abel and his chief lieutenants, Joseph Molony and Alex Fuller, international, district, and local committees on civil rights were encouraged toward greater activism. In 1960, for example, in District 15, an area with several hundred Black unionists at U.S. Steel plants in Homestead, Braddock, Duquesne, and Clairton, a planned civil rights conference "fell flat." Both the International Civil Rights Committee and the Education Department in cooperation with District 15 invited Arthur J. Edmonds of the Pittsburgh Urban League, Elwood Keppley of the Pennsylvania AFL–CIO, and others to appear as speakers. Although district officials expected 110 participants in the civil rights meeting, only 25 unionists intended to come. "You can't hold a conference on that basis," remarked a district officer to the *Pittsburgh Courier.* Some local unions claimed that a lack of money undermined their support of the District 15 gathering. One official said that a union civil rights program was "too much for our locals" since they already backed legislative efforts in government, community service and other activities. These unconvincing excuses evaporated by the mid-1960s, when the Abel Administration, the Ad Hoc organization of Black steel unionists, and external civil rights activities both locally and nationally caused United Steelworkers in District 15 to pay greater attention to the grievances of Black workers. In early August, 1967, District 15, held two civil rights conferences. Paul

Hilbert, the district director, met with 45 local union presidents "to review civil rights efforts on the local level" and to draft a "positive action" program. Two weeks later in McKeesport a one day civil rights conference attracted "two hundred delegates and guests." Milford Peter "Pete" Jackson, a veteran Black official in District 15, served as temporary chairman. His boss, Paul Hilbert, in remarks "likened the drive, for Civil Rights to the union's earlier drive for industrial and economic equality." In an address to the conferees, Joseph Molony, said that the United Steelworkers have "nothing to be ashamed of in the area of civil rights . . . but we must work a little harder because the job is far from finished." Alex Fuller followed his colleague with a discussion about the new Civil Rights Manual which the international committee had recently published. Molony stressed that "it is not worth the paper it is written on, if it isn't read and studied. If it isn't lived up to, it is a meaningless scrap of paper."[26]

Paul Normile, the director of District 16 which embraced Pittsburgh's Hazelwood, South Side, and West End sections, convened a civil rights conference in 1966. According to Normile "the purpose of the conference was to acquaint the district's local union officers and members of civil rights committees of their rights and obligations under recent federal and state civil rights legislation." He admitted that "there is still quite a bit of tokenism in the plants and we must help Negroes obtain equal opportunity in employment." James McCoy, the NAACP activist who chaired the District 16 Civil Rights Committee, added that "the goals of the civil rights movement are synonymous with the goals of the labor movement." Molony, who attended the meeting, told unionists that the United Steelworkers had an obligation "to combat bigotry and discrimination wherever it exists." Alex Fuller, who also came, noted that some people wondered "whether Negroes weren't moving too fast." To Fuller, "it seemed that these people were worrying because Negroes were moving too close." He added that the USWA Committee on Civil Rights wanted to stimulate "a positive discussion of civil rights in local union halls."[27]

During the Abel presidency, international, district and local civil rights committees attempted to match rhetoric with performance. In 1965, at U.S. Steel in Clairton, the chairman of the Civil Rights Committee at Local No. 1557, "discovered an underlying system of discrimination . . . on the basis of our present Local Seniority Agreement." Whenever layoffs occurred in particular departments, older employees entered a plant-wide labor pool. Other areas of the mill without excess workers drew from the pool according to employee seniority. He found that seniority rules and pool set-ups at the Clairton plants worked to the detriment of Black steelworkers. In a letter to the recording secretary of Local No. 1557, the civil rights committee chairman noted that "longer service employees are being denied their seniority rights" under various "pool arrangements . . . and it appears they were set up . . . to enable the Company to legally prevent Negroes and other minority groups from progressing [to] top jobs." He further observed that "there are a number of Units and Departments which employ no Negroes . . . and this Agreement would prevent a qualified Negro from moving into these Units and Departments." According to the chairman, "the language used in this Local Seniority Agreement is too discriminating and too detrimental, specifically to Negro employees." He urged officials in Local No. 1557 to notify the National Labor Relations Board, the union's International Civil Rights Committee, and District 15 of these accusations. Furthermore, he informed the recording secretary that a group of Clairton employees believed "that their Union [Representative] also practices discriminating tactics" in presenting their views.[28]

Alex Fuller responded by sending Ernest L. Clifford to help resolve these racial grievances. Clifford, a staff man at the union's Pittsburgh headquarters, was a former Black steelworker in Clairton. He met with the civil rights committee chairman, a staff representative from District 15, grievance men from the Clairton mills, and other union officials. All agreed that "the language of our local seniority agreements was discriminatory" and that changes were needed to "desegregate" departments in the Clairton mills which were off limits to Black laborers. The chairman of the grievance committee of Local No. 1557 promised "to iron out the discriminatory language." Clifford was relieved that the Clairton unionists would solve "the problems within the framework of our [local] Union." The civil rights committee chairman noted "that if reasonable action is undertaken and sincere effort upon the part of Local No. 1557 is exerted, he will withhold from going to any outside agency for the good of the Union."[29]

Similar militancy characterized union civil rights efforts at the Pittsburgh Works of Jones and Laughlin. An official in the United Steelworkers arbitration department, the general counsel of the union, and Alex Fuller of the Civil Rights Committee investigated complaints in 1966 about J and L seniority practices. They met with Paul Normile, director of District 16, others on his staff, and with the officers and members of Local No. 1272 and No. 1843. They informed I. W. Abel and his vice president, Joseph Molony, that they would look into the issues and "develop recommendations for union proposals to rectify the situation" if the complaints were valid. Despite the hostility of "some of the local union people" toward any investigation, Fuller and his colleague made clear their intention to proceed.[30]

Several months later, a civil rights committeeman and assistant grievance man at Local No. 1272, filed a specific complaint. One of them observed "that temporary vacancies have been perpetuated for ten and fifteen years." Moreover, "the failure to fill these vacancies on a permanent basis had civil

Figure 13. Veteran Black steelworker at Jones & Laughlin Steel Corporation in Pittsburgh around 1960. (Courtesy of the United States Steelworkers of American, Pittsburgh, PA.)

rights implications." Certain departments at Jones and Laughlin Steel secured their laborers from a plant labor pool. Since the seniority of the workers in the pool, many of them Black, was not applicable beyond the pool, company officials could "pick and choose" which employees they wished to assign to labor deficient departments. Seniority rules within particular departments were only operative in filling temporary vacancies from within the units. Since pool employees were outside of these departments, company officials assigned pool laborers according to preference rather than seniority. The civil rights committeeman observed that J and L's Garage division never had a Black as a Garage attendant, a position company officials had been filling temporarily for two years. He feared that "when permanent vacancies arise in the Garage attendant job, the senior Negro applicant from the labor pool may not" get the position. Despite local union efforts in 1965 contract negotiations to rectify the anomalous status of the plant labor pool, the unfair situation for Blacks remained.[31]

One international officer suggested that "before we do anything . . . we should talk the matter over thoroughly with the officers of Local Union #1272." His colleague, a United Steelworkers attorney, disagreed. The attorney suspected that a violation of Title VII of the 1964 Civil Rights Act "may exist" if the system of assigning employees in the labor pool resulted "in a disproportionate number of qualified Whites being "favored" [while] Negroes with comparable qualifications . . . [were] not selected." He added that "inasmuch" as Scheiding concluded "that the company "apparently does not select Negroes" for temporary vacancies," J and L "is violating the act." The lawyer also noted that "the union's apparent acquiescence in the system, as evidenced by its failure to process grievances to arbitration, may make the union equally responsible, at least in those cases when a grievance is filed by a Negro" with "comparable qualifications." He wanted "immediate action to remedy this problem."[32]

The aggressiveness of the civil rights committeeman at Local No. 1272 drew international officials into efforts to correct inequities suffered by Black J and L employees. Similarly, the chairman of the civil rights committee of Local No. 1843 at J and L, pressed the grievances of Black workers at a five-hour meeting with company executives. Because the encounter yielded only "a few half-hearted promises, none of them in writing," twenty unionists picketed the Pittsburgh offices of Jones and Laughlin "protesting alleged discriminatory practices."[33]

International officers of the United Steelworkers of America expressed pride in their union's record on civil rights. During the Abel presidency more Blacks, especially in U.S. Steel, moved from labor pool jobs to skilled positions than during the McDonald years. In 1968, Abel negotiated a basic steel agreement with changes in seniority and apprenticeship procedures to provide veteran Black steelworkers with "interplant mobility with job security." The agreement also established a joint union-management civil rights committee. At the 1968 convention, Abel's revitalized Civil Rights Committee reported that a majority of local unions had their own civil rights committees and all but two of the more than thirty districts had Civil Rights Coordinators. The Committee also prepared a complaint form to speed up investigation of alleged discrimination.[34]

Nonetheless, Blacks in the steelworkers union, like in other labor organizations, grew increasingly disenchanted with their lack of participation in high level offices within the United Steelworkers of America.[35] The Ad Hoc Committee of Black steelworkers which Fuller helped to found in 1964 continued efforts to increase Black representation in international union positions. Just before the 1968 convention, eighty Black unionists from twelve districts met in Chicago, and agreed on three demands. They included better jobs for Black steelworkers, more Black staffmen, and a Black international vice president. Still affiliated with the caucus, Fuller delivered the demands to I. W. Abel and other international officers. The Ad Hoc Committee noted that out of a thousand international officers, Blacks held less than a hundred positions. In the fourteen international departments, only two employed Blacks. None of the more than thirty steel union districts had a Black district director. Although Blacks comprised a quarter of the union's 1.2 million members, they were not concentrated in enough numbers in any particular district to elect one of their own to high office. Similarly their numbers were too small in the organization at large to elevate a Black to the international vice presidency. Abel, in defence to the union tradition of electing officers, refused to appoint a

Black district director or a Black vice president. An irritated Thomas Johnson, a leader of the Ad Hoc group and a Black steelworker from Fairfield, Alabama, contended that his organization supported Abel's presidential bid in 1965 "on the understanding that he . . . would help Blacks to achieve positions of leadership" in the United Steelworkers. Johnson's fellow caucus members picketed Abel, and noted that "Blacks were in the forefront during the formation of this union 24 years ago. Through the acceptance of crumbs down through the years," Johnson and others believed that the concerns of Black steelworkers were unimportant to the union.[36]

The Ad Hoc Committee offered the 1968 convention delegates another option when the issue reached the floor. The caucus suggested a constitutional amendment to establish the position of Second Vice President to the Executive Board. Abel would appoint a Black to the office. Later, the appointee would face an election. With the advantages of incumbency, the Second Vice President would likely win the office in his own right. Joseph Molony, however, opposed the idea of a Second Vice President. Molony, already the vice president of the United Steelworkers and chairman of the Civil Rights Commitee, said that the position "would be a contradiction in the basic theme of the civil rights movements, that people should be judged, hired, or elected on the basis of their ability."[37]

The secretary of the Constitution Committee also argued against the proposal. He noted that he "would welcome a Negro member to run for . . . a position on our Executive Board." Still, he wanted such a person to be chosen "under our election machinery" otherwise it would be tokenism. A Black delegate, a protege of I. W. Abel, said that "if a Negro gets on this Executive Board by appointment . . . he will be merely a figurehead . . . and you will be one of the first ones along with me to call him an Uncle Tom." I. W. Abel, while not declaring himself on the proposal, observed that the Black delegates "are here because you were elected . . . from your Local Union." He also stated that "I don't think our good Negro brothers . . . want equal but separate privileges in the union."[38]

The majority of Black delegates favored the new position of Second Vice President. An active Black unionist from the Duquesne steel works, Carl Dickerson, appealed to the convention to disregard "the high sounding phrases that come from the Chairman of the Committees because they know it would be impossible for us to elect a Director from any particular [district], unless we had all the Negro citizens in that . . . area." Another delegate who echoed these sentiments, noted that if Abel and other officers had been "placing Negroes in position to work themselves . . . where they could have got elected" then the proposal would have never come about. Still another Black steelworker remarked "that there is only one thing wrong with this resolution, that it didn't come up two conventions ago. It is a shame, an absolute shame, that in all these years, we have had to sit . . . in front of an all White Executive Board . . . [in] a Union that is 22 percent Black."[39]

Although the Ad Hoc Committee of Black steelworkers failed to win convention approval for a Black Second Vice President, I. W. Abel, who faced a re-election bid in 1969, could not afford to have disenchanted Black members switch their loyalties to his opponent, Donald Rarick. In return for the endorsement of the Ad Hoc Committee for his re-election candidacy, Abel entered into "a secret 'confidential' agreement" with the group. This understanding probably pertained to an important district election in the Baltimore area. Two staffmen, Edward E. Plato, a White, and Leander Simms, a Black, battled to succeed retiring District Director, Albert Attallah. Abel made it clear that he supported Simms. Although he made an appearance in the district for Simms, Plato won handily 7,549 votes to 5,669. Apparently, poor voter turnout among Black unionists helped defeat Simms. Nonetheless, Abel retained some credibility among Black members; when Nathaniel Lee, a Black unionist from Youngstown and an international teller since 1965, ran on the same ticket in the 1969 election, he emerged victorious with the rest of the Abel team.[40]

The response of the United Steelworkers of America to the civil rights movement was due mainly to the activism of Black members. Although many had fought for more Black representation in the union in the 1940s and 1950s, the national civil rights movement of the 1960s gave their grievances greater urgency. The formation of the Ad Hoc Committee made Black unionists more effective in articulating their demands. Casting their lot with I. W. Abel in his victorious presidential bid in 1965 and 1969 resulted in unprecedented activism by international, district, and local Civil Rights Committees. In 1968, however, Black unionists learned the limits of Black militancy within predominantly White institutions. Although the union exhibited greater concern for civil rights than ever before, the United Steelworkers failed to develop a concensus on how to equitably empower Blacks to share in the governance of the organization.

Steel companies, like the steel union, were induced by legislative enactments, especially Title VII of the 1964 Civil Rights law, and Black activism, both nationally and locally, to respond more favorably to Black employment demands. Between 1963 and 1966, a modest representation of Blacks worked in white collar occupations in Pittsburgh area steel companies. An equally embarrassing number of Blacks held positions as skilled laborers. Most Blacks, however, found jobs in semi-skilled, unskilled, and service occupations. In 1963, they comprised 7 percent of 10,975 workers out of 155,681 in Pittsburgh district steel firms. Approximately 196 or .6 percent held white collar positions. Another 1,115 or 3.1 percent worked as skilled laborers. The largest number, 6,130 or 10.4 percent were semi-skilled operatives while 3,215 or 13.4 percent were unskilled workers. Black service workers numbered 319 or 11.7 percent. In 1964, slight progress occurred within the ranks of the skilled with the number and percentage of Blacks in other occupational categories remained about the same. Despite a few fluctuations in numbers and percentages, the profile of Blacks in the steel industry of Western Pennsylvania changed little in 1966.[41] (See Table 7).

During this period, Blacks were grossly underrepresented in skilled occupations and disproportionately clustered in lower level unskilled, semi-skilled, and service positions. One observer noted that in 1965 at steel plants in Allegheny, Beaver, Washington, and Westmoreland counties that Blacks made up 3.21 percent of all craftsmen, although they constituted 6.4 percent of all steel employees. Conversely, they comprised 12.27 percent of all unskilled workers, 12.93 percent of all service employees, and 10.86 percent of all semi-skilled laborers. Additionally, the participation of Blacks in training programs for jobs in which their numbers were small remained limited. For example, Black steelworkers in the Pittsburgh vicinity comprised 3.21 percent of all skilled workers, but they made up only 2.5 percent of the enrollees in craft apprenticeships.[42]

**TABLE 11. Occupational Breakdown of Blacks in the Steel Industry in the Pittsburgh Area, 1963–1966**

| Occupational Category | 1963 | | | 1964 | | | 1966 | | |
|---|---|---|---|---|---|---|---|---|---|
| | Total | Blacks | % | Total | Blacks | % | Total | Blacks | % |
| White Collar | 34,450 | 196 | .6 | 38,133 | 225 | .6 | 36,683 | 380 | .8 |
| Skilled Workers | 33,528 | 1,115 | 3.1 | 37,631 | 1,283 | 3.4 | 34,464 | 1,063 | 3.1 |
| Semi-Skilled Workers | 58,973 | 6,130 | 10.4 | 59,428 | 6,462 | 10.9 | 54,810 | 5,292 | 9.7 |
| Unskilled Workers | 24,004 | 3,215 | 13.4 | 25,084 | 3,472 | 13.8 | 23,196 | 3,386 | 14.6 |
| Service Workers | 2,726 | 319 | 11.7 | 2,787 | 320 | 11.5 | 2,473 | 293 | 11.8 |
| Totals | 115,681 | 10,975 | 7.0% | 163,063 | 11,762 | 7.2% | 151,626 | 10,314 | 6.8% |

Compiled from Rowan, "The Negro in the Steel Industry," pp. 350–351, 353.

To remedy these persistent Black employment inequities, the Pittsburgh Commission on Human Relations in 1967 initiated a study to examine the occupational status of Black steelworkers in twenty-five area facilities. The Equal Employment Opportunity Commission funded the research of an investigator from the Wharton School of Finance and Commerce at the University of Pennsylvania to study Blacks in the steel industry. The report predictably observed "an underrepresentation of minority group employees in office and skilled craft positions" in Pittsburgh area steel plants.[43]

Jones and Laughlin Steel and United States Steel believed that the Pittsburgh Commission on Human Relations lacked the authority to impose an affirmative action program to improve the condition of Blacks. The passage of the 1964 Civil Rights Act induced several steel companies, including J and L and U.S. Steel, to initiate their own affirmative action efforts. Additionally, the involvement of the Equal Employment Opportunity Commission and the federal Defense Contract Review agency with the Human Relations group in 1968 probably prompted J and L and U.S. Steel to step up Black hiring and promotions.[44]

While the investigator from the Wharton School studied Blacks in Pittsburgh area steel mills, U.S. Steel reported 8 percent minority hiring and J and L reported 37 percent. Other steel firms claimed increases in Black hiring between 60 percent and 80 percent. Between 1964 and 1969, several steel companies placed a few Blacks in positions traditionally held by Whites. At Pittsburgh Steel in Monessen, Ronald Minnie, became in 1964 a Junior Buyer. His father, Arthur Minnie, was hired in the company's nail mill in 1936 and retired as a custodian in the blast furnace department. The younger Minnie returned to Monessen after he earned a degree in business administration in 1960 from Westminster College in New Wilmington, Pennsylvania. Six months after he joined Pittsburgh Steel, he was promoted to Buyer. In 1965, Bethlehem Steel in Johnstown named Otis Holliday, a veteran steelworker, as its first Black production supervisor. In the late 1960s, William Turner, who had thirty years at the open hearth at Jones and Laughlin's Pittsburgh Works, also became a foreman.[45]

Overall, only modest improvements had occurred for Blacks in the steel industry by the end of the 1960s. In 1968, 10,380 Blacks out of 150,518 employees made up 6.9 percent of the work force in the Pittsburgh vicinity. The percentage of white collar employees rose slightly from 280 or .8 percent in 1966 to 375 or 1 percent two years later. A few more Blacks entered craft occupations. There were 1,063 or 3.1 percent in 1966. In 1968, there were 1,227 or 3.4 percent, an insignificant increase of 164 Blacks. Despite these changes, Blacks in the steel industry of Western Pennsylvania remained overwhelmingly represented in semi-skilled, unskilled and service positions.[46] (See Table 12)

Racial discrimination against Blacks in the steel industry of Western Pennsylvania persisted into the 1970s despite the previous decade of Black protest and legislative enactments to correct employment inequities. In fact, the continued existence of poor housing, unequal education, and discriminatory employment practices, particularly in the steel industry, intensified Black resentment and activism. In 1970 in Aliquippa, for example, clashes between Blacks and Whites occurred. Seven persons, including two policemen, suffered injuries. Fist fights and gunshots required the town's thirty-one policemen to enlist the aid of eighty-five other law enforcement officers from nearby communities. Municipal officials also closed the Aliquippa schools.[47] A concerned Governor Milton J. Shapp in 1971 launched

**TABLE 12. Occupational Breakdown of Blacks in the Steel Industry in the Pittsburgh Area 1968**

| Occupational Category | Total | 1968 Number of Blacks | Percentage |
| --- | --- | --- | --- |
| White Collar | 37,867 | 375 | 1.0 |
| Skilled Workers | 35,892 | 1,227 | 3.4 |
| Semi-Skilled Workers | 54,096 | 5,404 | 10.0 |
| Unskilled Workers | 20,037 | 3,052 | 15.2 |
| Service Workers | 2,626 | 322 | 12.3 |
| Totals | 150,518 | 10,380 | 6.9% |

Compiled from Rowan, "The Negro in the Steel Industry," p. 354.

an interagency task force to cooperate with the Pennsylvania Human Relations Commission to investigate the causes of the racial unrest in Aliquippa. Aside from the Human Relations group, Shapp named representatives from the Pennsylvania Departments of Commerce, Community Affairs, Education, Justice, Labor and Industry, State Police, and Public Welfare to help the borough "discover the basic underlying causes of tension and discrimination and to attempt to resolve these problems.[48]

Investigatory hearings revealed that the lack of employment opportunities at Jones and Laughlin Steel, Aliquippa's largest employer, was a major cause of Black discontent. In 1970, J and L's Aliquippa plant employed 11,982 persons of whom 967 or 8 percent were Black. A pitifully small number of Blacks, however, held white collar and craft positions. The facility employed 982 officials and managers, but only 4 were Black. Out of 154 technicians, only 4 were black. Only 8 Blacks worked among the plant's 812 office and clerical employees. Out of 2,310 skilled workers, only 8 were Black. Merely 24 or 2.4 percent of J and L's 967 Blacks held white collar or craft positions at the Aliquippa facility. In most instances, these 24 Blacks comprised less than 1 percent of all employees within their respective occupational categories.[49]

Instead, the company clustered the vast majority of Black employees in lower level positions. The plant's 564 Black semi-skilled workers constituted 11 percent of the 5,153 laborers within this group. Out of a total of 2,811 unskilled workers, 353 or 12 percent were Black. Service employees numbered 109 and 22 or 20 percent were Black. Moreover, entire departments remained off limits to Black steelworkers. A Black J and L employee in Aliquippa since 1946, recalled that the Heater Department stayed lily-White for most of the 1970s. Additionally, state investigators observed that Blacks who wished to enter apprenticeship programs to qualify for better positions met stiff resistance from White workers.[50]

Since these Black employment patterns existed elsewhere in Western Pennsylvania, protests against racial discrimination in the steel industry continued unabated. Some local union civil rights committees and the Pittsburgh NAACP pressed steel employers to improve their record on Black hiring and promotions. Black employees at the Homestead Works of U.S. Steel appealed to the Civil Rights Committee of Local No. 1397 to take action against the plant's persistent discriminatory hiring and promotional policies. They claimed that while the transportation and general services departments were overwhelmingly Black, mill officials appointed only White foremen. Additionally, Blacks hired for government-sponsored hard-core training programs received minimal instruction from Homestead plant officials and were assigned custodial duties. Similar complaints arose in 1970 at the Clairton facility of U.S. Steel. Two officers in Local No. 1557, the president, and the chairman of the civil rights committee, charged discrimination against maintenance and other workers excluded from incentive pay. They also blamed Clairton plant managers for their failure to hire Blacks in trade and craft positions. They told the Pennsylvania Human Relations Commission that only 2 percent of Clairton maintenance employees were Black.[51]

At the South Side Works of Jones and Laughlin Steel existed the United Black Protest Committee, a group affiliated with the Pittsburgh NAACP. The organization included co-chairmen James Grover and Dock Gandy, and other Black J and L employees. In 1970 they accused J and L and the United Steelworkers local of "collusion" in denying skilled jobs to veteran Black steelworkers and giving preference to "Whites with junior plant seniority." Grover and Gandy contended that the union and the company prevented Blacks from assuming jobs in J and L in the millwright, painting, carpenters', and plumbers' departments. In negotiations with J and L's South Side plant officials, the United Black Protest Committee ended "unwritten agreements" between the company and the union of assigning "furloughed Whites" to skilled jobs, on a temporary basis, "above Blacks with more seniority in the labor pool."[52]

Black steelworkers in Western Pennsylvania who remembered the Fair Employment Practices Committee in the 1940s knew that the intervention of the federal government in Black labor affairs yielded greater gains than the reluctant and belated efforts of either steel management or organized steel labor. The Johnson Administration in the 1960s, like the Roosevelt Administration in the 1940s, was especially sympathetic to the aspirations of Black workers. Strengthened by the Civil Rights Act of 1964 and Executive Order 11246 of 1965 which authorized the

Secretary of Labor to supervise and coordinate nondiscriminatory employment activities of contractors using federal funds, the Johnson Administration prodded steel companies and the steelworkers union to equalize occupational opportunities for Black employees. Federal laws, especially Title VII of the 1964 Civil Rights Act, provided the Justice Department during the Johnson and Nixon presidencies with enough legal ammunition to sue steel firms and local steel unions for their alleged discriminatory treatment of Black laborers.[53]

In 1967 the Office of Federal Contract Compliance accused the Sparrows Point Plant of Bethlehem Steel of discrimination against Black workers. At this facility near Baltimore, Blacks comprised 75 percent of the coke workers and 99 percent of the sinter plant employees. In the coke and sinter divisions of the mill, Blacks held the "dirtiest, lowest paying jobs." Bethlehem responded to these conditions by allowing Blacks to transfer out of these departments, but only if they relinquished their seniority. The union assented to this concept of departmental seniority in which workers accumulated seniority within the unit in which they labored. A federal district court decision in 1973 mandated plant-wide seniority which permitted Black workers to transfer to jobs anywhere within the facilty without the loss of scniority. In 1970 another federal district court, in response to a Justice Department suit, ordered the Lackawanna, New York facility of Bethlehem Steel, to revise seniority rules to allow Black employees to seek better-paying jobs in other departments without losing their seniority. The court noted that the United Steelworkers of America had a role in facilitating discrimination against Black steelworkers because of "discriminatory contract provisions" in their 1962, 1965, and 1968 agreements with Bethlehem Steel. In noting the importance of this decree, Herbert Hill, longtime labor secretary of the NAACP, quoted the federal court which observed that "the Lackawanna plant was a microcosm of classic job discrimiation in the North, making clear why Congress enacted Title VII of the Civil Rights Act of 1964." Also in 1970, the Justice Department sued U.S. Steel, the AFL–CIO and twelve locals of the United Steelworkers of America in the Birmingham, Alabama area for discrimination against Blacks in hiring, job assignments, and compensation. Like the Bethlehem Steel cases, a plant-wide seniority agreement resulted, but Whites as well as Blacks benefited from it.[54]

These court decisions established an important principle for Black steelworkers. Although membership in the steelworker's union brought Blacks the safeguard of seniority, that occupational protection was limited. They had, in most cases, departmental seniority. Since Black steelworkers usually labored in segregated departments, their seniority became useless if they wished transfers to better-paying departments. These court decisions by granting plantwide seniority to Blacks ended several decades of limited mobility for Black steelworkers who transferred to other departments at risk of losing their hard-earned seniority.[55]

In further recognition of the long years of racial discrimination by steel companies and the steelworker's union: in April 1974 the Equal Employment Opportunity Commission, the Department of Labor, and the Department of Justice filed a consent decree with nine steel companies and the United Steelworkers of America in the United States District Court of the Northern District of Alabama. The federal government asserted that Blacks, women, and Hispanics in the steel industry "were systematically assigned to lower-paying jobs with little opportunity for advancement, denied training opportunities, and judged by more stringent qualification criteria than were White males." In their acceptance of the consent decree Allegheny–Ludlum, Armco Steel, Bethlehem, U.S. Steel, Jones and Laughlin, National Steel, Wheeling–Pittsburgh Steel, Republic, Youngstown Sheet and Tube, and the United Steelworkers of America acknowledged their role in employment discrimination against Black steelworkers. After a century of involvement with the steel industry, Black laborers finally witnessed steel employers and the steel union admit what had been evident to Blacks for numerous decades: that racial considerations hindered their occupational advancement.[56]

The steel companies agreed to pay $31 million to 34,449 Black and Hispanic steelworkers and to 5,559 women employees hired before 1968. Moreover, an Audit and Review Committee consisting of five steel company members, five union members, and a government representative implemented the individual settlements and monitored the establishment of similar committees within each company. The consent decree also set up goals and timetables for the hiring and promotion of Blacks, women, and Hispanics especially in supervisory, technical, and clerical jobs, and in management training programs. Additionally, the decree eliminated departmental seniority and replaced it with plant-wide seniority as the basis for promotions, demotions, layoffs, and recalls in the steel industry.[57]

Of the nine steel companies cited in the consent decree, six firms operated plants in Western Pennsylvania. They included Allegheny–Ludlum, Armco, Bethlehem, Wheeling–Pittsburgh, U.S. Steel and Jones and Laughlin. Significant gains developed for Black steelworkers in the Pittsburgh area as a result of the decree. Although the total number of Black steel employees increased modestly from 5,129 to 5,586 between 1974 and 1980, Blacks made discernible progress in improving their occupational position in the steel industry. At Jones and Laughlin, Daniel Brooks, a veteran Black employee, became a foreman. In 1974 the Equal Employment Opportunity Commission surveyed 27 steel employers and discovered 734 Black craft workers or 4.3 percent of the total. In 1978 in a survey of 25 steel firms, EEOC investigators found 907 craft workers or 5.6 percent of the total.[58] (See Table 13.)

Despite evidence of significant occupational gains, Blacks in the steel industry had won a Pyrrhic victory. Progress in entering craft occupations and supervisory positions in production occurred at a time of decline for American steel production. During the 1970s steel producers competed intensely with foreign steelworkers who increased their share of the American market to 20 percent in 1977. Industry analysts predicted that steel imports could rise to 30 percent and eliminate 96,000 steel jobs by the 1980s. Additionally, the failure to reinvest steel profits to update outmoded plants also jeopardized employment and the industry's capacity to compete with more efficient foreign producers. These conditions helped to cause record layoffs and plant closings in steel centers throughout the nation, especially in Western Pennsylvania. In 1977 Bethlehem furloughed employees at its Johnstown plant while U.S. Steel laid off hundreds of workers in the Pittsburgh area. Although Blacks in supervisory and professional positions at Bethlehem in Johnstown rose modestly from 1 percent to 1.4 percent, the percentage of Black skilled workers declined from 2 percent to 1.5 percent and the percentage of Black laborers dropped from 2.6 percent to 2.2 percent. By the early 1980s, U.S. Steel closed numerous plants in the Monongahela River Valley in such towns as Homestead, Duquesne, and McKeesport. Nearly

**TABLE 13. Occupational Breakdown of Blacks in Selected Steel Companies in Western Pennsylvania, 1974, 1978**

| Occupational Category | 1974 Total | 1974 Blacks | 1974 % | 1978 Total | 1978 Blacks | 1978 % |
|---|---|---|---|---|---|---|
| Officials, Managers | 5,850 | 112 | 1.9 | 6,916 | 175 | 2.5 |
| Professionals | 1,243 | 8 | .6 | 3,164 | 44 | 1.4 |
| Technicians | 1,422 | 31 | 2.2 | 2.028 | 71 | 3.5 |
| Sales | 240 | 2 | .8 | 548 | 15 | 2.7 |
| Office and Clerical | 4,727 | 168 | 3.6 | 6.425 | 304 | 4.7 |
| Craft Workers | 15,810 | 734 | 4.6 | 16,190 | 907 | 5.6 |
| Semi-skilled Workers | 27,995 | 2,852 | 10.2 | 26,874 | 2,917 | 10.9 |
| Laborers | 8,670 | 1,067 | 12.3 | 7,252 | 984 | 13.6 |
| Service Workers | 1,143 | 155 | 13.6 | 1,063 | 169 | 15.9 |
| Totals | 67,100 | 5,129 | 7.6% | 70,460 | 5,586 | 7.9% |

Compiled from: *1974 EEO-1 Report Summary by Industry*, SMSA 451 Pittsburgh, Pennsylvania, SIC 331 Blast Furnace and Basic Steel Prod. p. 14,426; *1978 EED-1 Report*, SMSA-6280, Pittsburgh, Pennsylvania; p. 25,663; Equal Employment Opportunity Commission, Washington, D.C.

4,000 steelworkers, Black and White, lost their jobs.[59] Seniority protected few workers from the unhappy results of plant closings. After several decades of protest and struggle, Black steelworkers during the 1960s and 1970s secured the assistance of the federal government in pressing steel employers and the United Steelworkers of America to remove racial barriers which blocked their occupational advancement. This moral victory, however, did not translate into any lasting employment gains for Black steelworkers in Western Pennsylvania.

# Epilogue

Racial discrimination sharply limited the advancement of Blacks in the steel industry of Western Pennsylvania and prevented them from attaining occupation parity with their fellow White workmen between 1875 and 1980. Throughout the period, discriminatory practices and attitudes of plant managers, foremen, and workmen kept Blacks in dirty, dangerous, and low-paying "Negro jobs," and made it difficult for them to acquire better positions which would earn them higher wages and improved working conditions. For a brief period between 1875 and 1916 Blacks in the steel industry made some occupational progress, but their small numbers prevented them from sustaining these gains and allowing subsequent groups of Black workers to benefit from them. During the succeeding decades Blacks, because of institutional barriers deliberately erected by companies and unions, lagged behind White workers in promotions, pay, and working conditions.

Before coming to Western Pennsylvania, Black steelworkers had labored in the South as poor agricultural workers and had lived under the rigid system of legalized segregation. Most believed that migration to the North would allow them to secure better jobs and a life free of the indignities of Jim Crow. Although de facto segregation and poor environmental conditions existed in the Pittsburgh vicinity, Blacks improved themselves economically by entering the steel industry. Still, the same racial prejudices which Blacks had experienced in the South impeded their occupational success in the mills and foundries of Western Pennsylvania.

The gains Blacks made did not measure up to the advantages achieved by employers, White workmen and trade unionists resulting from the presence of Blacks in the steel industry. Millowners used Blacks to solve their manpower deficiencies during World War I, and to defeat the demands of the predominantly White Amalgamated Association of Iron and Steelworkers in various steel strikes between 1875 and 1919. Two decades later White unionists depended on Black participation in the CIO to insure the success of the Steelworkers Organizing Committee. Although Blacks benefited by obtaining jobs from steel mill employers and some employment safeguards from the union, neither effectively protected them from racial discrimination, particularly in hiring, job assignments, and promotions. Seniority rules, for example, seemingly provided Black steelworkers with job security. These safeguards, however, were available to Black unionists only in the segregated mill departments in which they worked. Since a transfer to another department robbed them of seniority protection, Blacks remained locked in Jim Crow sections of the mills where seniority insured only against arbitrary displacement, not significant employment advancement.

Nonetheless, during the 1930s the federal government in its fight against the depression ameliorated the condition of Black steelworkers through such New Deal programs as WPA and PWA. Also, during the 1940s, the federal government exercised considerable pressure through the FEPC to end job discrimination in steel and other defense-related industries in order to guarantee maximum uninterrupted war production. Yet, in spite of these efforts to improve the condition of Blacks in Pittsburgh area mills, Whites continued to hold better jobs, to have better opportunities for occupational advancement and to labor under better working conditions than did the Blacks.

During the 1950s, despite union and company pronouncements about the importance of equal employment opportunity for workers regardless of race, color or creed, Black steelworkers lagged behind their fellow White laborers. Numerous steel companies refused to promote or transfer Blacks out of departments with dead end, dangerous, and dirty jobs. Several local unions refused to process Black complaints, press their grievances, or oppose departmental seniority. The United Steelworkers of

America, moreover, failed to empower Black officials to fight effectively for Black advancement both within the union and the mills.

The civil rights movement of the 1960s brought about important executive, legislative, and judicial action which prodded steel companies and the steel union to respond more favorably to the grievances of Black steelworkers. Title VII of the 1964 Civil Rights Act, federal court cases, and the 1974 consent decree in which several major steel firms and the United Steelworkers of America agreed to make substantive efforts to improve the occupational status of Blacks in the steel industry represented unprecedented progress. Ironically, these advances occurred at a time of decline for the steel industry. Black steelworkers won an important moral victory, but failed once again to make lasting employment gains in the steel industry.

Within the first few years of the 1980s most mill communities along the Three Rivers looked more like ghost towns. Plant closings sharply reduced the area work force. In Duquesne, the Dorothy Blast Furnace, the largest in the Monongahela Valley, was scheduled for demolition. Moreover, the Duquesne–McKeesport National Works of U.S. Steel, of which Dorothy was a part, dropped within a two year period from 3,500 workers to 400. U.S. Steel effected similar reductions at plants in Clairton, Homestead, Braddock and several other facilities throughout the Pittsburgh vicinity.[1]

Numerous milltowns plunged deeply into debt because of shrinking revenues from unemployed steelworkers and shut down facilities. Clairton laid off all fourteen policemen, ten firemen, five clerical workers, and turned off most street lights. Similarly, McKeesport, with a $700,000 budget deficit, furloughed several policemen and other city employees. West Homestead followed suit in laying off all but five of its fourteen public works employees. Braddock curtailed maintenance funds for the Carnegie Public Library.[2]

Plant closings had a levelling effect upon Black and White employees. Despite the declining fortunes of the steel industry, seniority safeguards and affirmative action efforts probably afforded Black workers some temporary protection from initial layoffs. In Pittsburgh, reduction in the work force between 1970 and 1980 brought White male employment in the steel mills downward from 84,727 to 77,208. The number of Black male steelworkers dropped during this same period from 5,946 to 5,454. A sharper decrease occurred at Bethlehem Steel in Johnstown where the number of White male employees plunged downward from 12,132 in 1970 to 8,233 in 1980. Black male steelworkers fared worse than their counterparts in Pittsburgh with a 50 percent reduction from 301 to 141 during the 1970s.[3]

Affirmative action efforts in behalf of women, both Black and White, in Pittsburgh, resulted in employment increases for them between 1970 and 1980. The number of White women working in the steel industry in Pittsburgh grew from 5,850 to 8,190. A noticeable gain occurred also for Black women whose numbers rose from 179 to 1,077. Most of these advancements, however, took place in nonproduction areas, particularly in office jobs at U.S. Steel and J and L headquarters, where layoffs occurred with less frequency than in the mills. In Johnstown, however, women had as little immunity from employment cutbacks as men. The number of White women at Bethlehem Steel dropped from 314 to 272 while the number of Black women between 1970 and 1980 remained at eight employees.[4]

Whatever gains Blacks managed to sustain because of seniority rules and affirmative action efforts proved temporary. As steel companies continued to roll back production even further, Black and White steelworkers faced uncertain futures. Seniority protected veteran workers only long enough to choose early retirement while their younger colleagues awaited with justified anxiety for another round of layoffs. In Pittsburgh in 1980, unemployment caused mainly by the steel industry, produced a rate of 7.3 percent for 41,376 jobless Whites. A more tragic reality existed for Blacks whose unemployment rate was 17.4 percent. Among these 6,105 unemployed Blacks were hundreds laid off from local steel facilities and numerous others, with little hope of ever finding jobs in Pittsburgh's once flourishing mills.[5]

Black Southerners had come to the Pittsburgh steel district to improve their economic condition and to secure better jobs in area mills and foundries. For more than a century, however, Blacks confronted discriminatory treatment from steel management, union officials, and fellow White workmen. Sometimes company benevolence, governmental pressure, and union protection improved their occupational status, but these efforts were usually sporadic and self-serving. The FEPC in the 1940s effectively curbed racial discrimination in the steel industry, but that was a short-lived effort. Similarly, Title VII of the 1964 Civil Rights Act and the 1974 consent decree made similar advances for Black steelworkers, but these endeavors were nullified ultimately by decline in the steel industry. After more than a century as steel employees, Black workers in Pittsburgh, Homestead, Braddock, Clairton, Johnstown, and many other mill communities finally attained equality with Whites as they stepped together into local unemployment lines. To understand the current problems confronting jobless, underemployed, and unskilled Blacks in contemporary American society, one needs only to examine the experiences of Black steelworkers in Western Pennsylvania and others like them in the declining industrial centers of America.

# Notes

---

## Introduction

1.  Compiled from U.S. Congress, Senate, Reports of the Immigration Commission, *Immigrants in Industry, Part 2: Iron and Steel Manufacturing*, Vol. I, 61st Congress, 2nd Session, 1920, p. 234; U.S. Department of Commerce, Bureau of the Census, *Thirteenth Census of the United States: Population: 1910*, Volume IV, Occupation Statistics, pp. 590–591.

2.  Abram Harris, "The New Negro Workers in Pittsburgh," (M.A. thesis, University of Pittsburgh, 1924), pp. 45–46.

3.  John T. Clark, "The Negro in Steel," *Opportunity*, October 1924, p. 300.

4.  William H. Harris, *The Harder We Run: Black Workers Since the Civil War*, (New York: Oxford University Press, 1982).

5.  Gilbert Osofsky, *Harlem: The Making of a Ghetto, 1890–1930*. New York, Harper & Row, 1963.

6.  Herbert G. Gutman, "Introduction" in Sterling Spero and Abram Harris, *The Black Worker* (New York: Atheneum, 1931, reprinted 1968) p. xi.

7.  August Meier and Elliott Rudwick, *Black Detroit and the Rise of the UAW* (New York: Oxford University Press, 1979).

8.  Joe William Trotter,Jr., *Black Milwaukee: The Making of an Industrial Proletariat, 1915–1945* (Urbana: University of Illinois Press, 1985).

## Chapter 1

1. *The Iron Age*, January 21, 1875, March 4, 1875, March 18, 1875, March 25, 1875; *National Labor Tribune*, March 13, 1875.

2. *National Labor Tribune*, October 9, 1875.

3. Charles B. Dew, *Ironmaker to the Confederacy: Joseph R. Anderson and the Tredegar Iron Works*, (New Haven, Yale University Press, 1966), pp. 22–32, 262–264, 314.

4. Robert S. Starobin, *Industrial Slavery in the Old South*, (New York, Oxford University Press, 1980), pp. 14–15.

5. *The Iron Age*, February 16, 1888.

6. *The Iron Age*, May 23, 1889.

7. Margaret Byington, *Homestead: The Households of a Milltown* (New York, The Russell Sage Foundation, 1910), p. 14. Byington indicated that some Blacks entered the Homestead mills during the 1892 strike. An article in *The Iron Age*, November 24, 1892 entitled "The Homestead Strike Broken" did not mention Blacks at all.

8. *Survey*, August 21, 1909; August 28, 1909.

9. *National Labor Tribune*; August 8, 1901.

10. *Solidarity*, August 30, 1913.

11. *National Labor Tribune*, October 9, 1875.

12. *The Iron Age*, February 16, 1888.

13. *National Labor Tribune*, May 9, 1907; June 27, 1907.

14. *National Labor Tribune*, August 19, 1909.

15. Philip S. Foner, *Organized Labor and the Black Worker, 1619–1973* (New York, International Publisher's, 1974), pp. 26, 47–51, 64–81.

16. *New York Age*, February 18, 1909.

17. Richard R. Wright, Jr., "A Study of the Industrial Conditions of the Negro Population of Pennsylvania and Especially of the cities of Philadelphia and Pittsburgh," in *Annual Report of the Secretary of Internal Affairs*, Part 3, Fortieth Report of the Bureau of Industrial Statistics or Volume XL, 1912, (Harrisburg, Pennsylvania, 1914), pp. 78–80.

18. Foner, *Organized Labor and the Black Worker, 1619–1973*, p. 64; *National Labor Tribune*, July 8, 1882.

19. Richard R. Wright, Jr., *The Negro in Pennsylvania: A Study in Economic History,* (Philadelphia, A.M.E. Book Concern, 1912), p. 95.

20. Wright, *The Negro in Pennsylvania: A Study in Economic History,* p. 95; *New York Age,* August 20, 1914; Richard R. Wright, Jr., "The Economic Condition of Negroes in the North: The Negro Skilled Mechanic in the North," *Southern Workman,* March 1909, pp. 165–166; Helen A. Tucker, "The Negroes of Pittsburgh" in *Wage Earning Pittsburgh,* The Pittsburgh Survey, (New York Russell Sage Foundation, 1914), p. 428.

21. Richard R. Wright, Jr., "One Hundred Negro Steelworkers," in *Wage Earning Pittsburgh,* The Pittsburgh Survey, (New York Russell Sage Foundation, 1914), pp. 106–107.

22. *National Labor Tribune,* August 13, 1881.

23. *Proceedings of the Sixth Annual Convention of the National Lodge of the Amalgamated Association of Iron and Steelworkers* (Pittsburgh, 1882), pp. 743, 744; *Proceedings of the Seventh Annual Convention . . .* (Pittsburgh, 1882) pp. 795, 1012, 1026, 1033.

24. *Proceedings of the Seventh Annual Convention . . .* (Pittsburgh, 1882), pp. 796, 953. (I am indebted to Dr. Peter Rachleff for bringing this Richmond information to my attention.) He has written a useful study, *Black Labor in the South* (Philadelphia, Temple University Press, 1984).

25. *National Labor Tribune,* October 1, 1881; February 18, 1882. (The references in this note and the following one were brought to my attention by Dr. Rachleff.)

26. *National Labor Tribune,* March 4, 1882; March 25, 1882.

27. *National Labor Tribune,* July 1, 1882; February 11, 1888; June 20, 1888.

28. *The Iron Age,* May 23, 1889.

29. W. E. Burghardt Du Bois, editor, *The Negro Artisan,* (Atlanta, Atlanta University Press, 1902), p. 174.

30. Du Bois, *The Negro Artisan,* p. 164.

31. Wright, *The Negro in Pennsylvania,* p. 98.

32. Booker T. Washington, "The Negro and the Labor Unions," *Atlantic Monthly,* June 1931, p. 761.

33. David Brody, *Steelworkers in America: The Non-union Era* (Cambridge, Massachusetts, Harvard University Press, 1960), p. 74; *National Labor Tribune*, March 28, 1907.

34. *National Labor Tribune*, September 12, 1907.

35. Wright, "One Hundred Negro Steelworkers," pp. 106–108.

36. *National Labor Tribune*, July 20, 1905.

37. *The Iron Age*, June 13, 1889.

38. Du Bois, *The Negro Artisan*, p. 145.

39. Wright, *The Negro in Pennsylvania*, pp. 226–227.

40. Horace R. Cayton and George S. Mitchell, *Black Workers and the New Unions*, (Chapel Hill, North Carolina, University of North Carolina Press, 1939), p. 8.

41. U.S. Department of Commerce, Bureau of the Census, *Negro Population in the United States, 1790–1915*, p. 68; U.S. Department of Commerce, Bureau of the Census, *Thirteenth Census of the United States, 1910: Population*, Vol. 1, p. 212.

42. Richard R. Wright, Jr., "The Migration of Negroes to the North," *Annals of the American Academy of Political and Social Science*, XXVII, January to June 1906, pp. 104–105.

43. Clyde Vernon Kiser, *Sea Island to City*, (New York, Columbia University Press, 1932), pp. 118, 121, 218–219.

44. Duquesne Observer, March 16, 1906; January 3, 1908; *Duquesne Times* May 17, 1929; September 25, 1931; May 1, 1952; *History of Pittsburgh and Environs*, Volume III, (New York, 1922), p. 722; *Payne Chapel A.M.E. Church, 61st Anniversary*, June 15–23, 1952, Duquesne, PA. (Courtesy of the late Mrs. Lina Whiddon, Duquesne, PA).

45. *History of Pittsburgh and Environs*, pp. 724–726; *Clairton Crucible*, October 10, 1902; February 6, 1903; January 4, 1904; August 24, 1906; *Clairton Progress*, May 26, 1939.

46. Mrs. Catherine Gardiner, interviewed by Dennis C. Dickerson, January 24, 1975 Homestead, Pennsylvania; U.S. Department of Commerce, Bureau of the Census, Microfilm Roll of 1900 Census, Allegheny County, Homestead, Pennsylvania.

47. *Duquesne Observer*, November 3, 1905; *Pittsburgh Courier*, April 1, 1911; April 20, 1912; *New York Age*, January 6, 1916; December 21, 1916.

48. John Stephens Durham, "The Labor Unions and the Negro," *Atlantic Monthly*, February 1898, p. 229; Wright, "One Hundred Negro Steelworkers," pp. 100–101, 105; Byington, *Homestead*, p. 14.

49. U.S. Department of Commerce, Bureau of the Census, *Thirteenth Census of the United States: Population, 1910*, occupations statistics, pp. 590–591; Byington, *Homestead*, p. 214; U.S. Congress, Senate, Reports of the Immigration Commission, *Immigrants in Industry, Part 2: Iron and Steel Manufacturing*, Vol. I, 61st Congress, 2nd Session, 1910, p. 259.

50. U.S. Congress, Senate, Reports of the Immigration Commission, *Immigrants in . . . Iron and Steel*, p. 234. U.S. Department of Commerce and Labor, Bureau of Census, *Twelfth Census of the United States: 1900: Occupations*, pp. 484, 680; U.S. Department of Commerce, Bureau of the Census, *Thirteenth Census . . .: Population: 1910*, pp. 590–591. See 1900 microfilm census of Homestead, McKeesport, Rankin, Braddock, North Braddock, Canonsburg, Connellsville, Johnstown, and New Castle in the Microfilm Room, National Archives, Washington, D.C. The latter four towns had fewer than a dozen Black iron and steel employees in 1900; Byington, *Homestead*, p. 214; Wright, *The Negro in Pennsylvania*, pp. 226–227.

51. Byington, *Homestead*, p. 214; U.S. Department of Commerce, Bureau of the Census, *Thirteenth Census . . . Population: 1910*, pp. 590–591.

52. *Pittsburgh Courier*, January 20, 1923; *New York Age*, February 8, 1917; John Bodnar, Michael Weber, and Roger Simon, "Migration, Kinship, and Urban Adjustment: Blacks and Poles in Pittsburgh, 1900–1930," *Journal of American History*, December 1979, p. 565; Epstein, *The Negro Migrant in Pittsburgh*, p. 31. Also see John Bodnar, Robert Simon and Michael Weber, *Lives of Their Own: Blacks, Italians, and Poles in Pittsburgh, 1900–1960*, (Urbana, Illinois, University of Illinois Press, 1982), pp. 17, 55–71; Brody, *Steelworkers in America*, p. 86.

## Chapter 2

1. *New York Age*, April 27, 1916; February 1, 1917; *Pittsburgh Courier*, August 16, 1924.

2. U. S. Department of Commerce, Bureau of the Census, *Historical Statistics of the United States, Colonial Times to 1957*, p. 56.

3. The Southern states included Virginia, North Carolina, South Carolina, Georgia, Florida, Tennessee, Alabama, Mississippi, Louisiana, Texas, Arkansas and Oklahoma. According to the 1910 census, the South had 99.7% of the nation's total acreage of cotton. The leading states in cotton acreage were Texas, with 9,930,179 acres; Georgia, with 4,883,304 acres; Alabama, with 3,730,482 acres; Mississippi, with 3,400,210 acres; South Carolina, with 2,556,467 acres; Arkansas, with 2,153,222 acres; Oklahoma, with 1,976,935 acres; and North Carolina, with 1,274,404 acres. U.S. Department of Commerce, Bureau of the Census, *Thirteenth Census of the United States, 1910: Agriculture* ,5:680.

4. R. H. Leavell, *et al.*, *Negro Migration in 1916–1917* (Washington, D.C., 1919), pp. 59–61.

5. Ibid.

6. Greene and Woodson, *The Negro Wage Earner*, p. 207.

7. Ibid., p. 205; U.S., Department of Commerce, Bureau of the Census, *Fifteenth Census of the United States, 1930: Agriculture*, 4:151; U.S., Department of Commerce, Bureau of the Census, *Negroes in the United States, 1920–1932*, p. 601.

8. *Negroes in the United States, 1920–932*, p. 15.

9. *Historical Statistics of the United States, Colonial Times to 1957*, p. 301; John W. Fanning, *Negro Migration*, Phelps-Stokes Fellowship Studies, No. 9, *Bulletin of the University of Georgia*, June 1930, p. 16.

10. Murray R. Benedict, *Farm Policies of the United States, 1790–1950* (New York, 1953), p. 159 fn. no. 62.

11. *Historical Statistics in the United States, Colonial Times to 1957*, p. 301.

12. C. Vann Woodward, *The Strange Career of Jim Crow* (New York, 1955, 1974), pp. 83–85.

13. On several occasions since the end of the Civil War, Blacks desiring to improve their plight and escape racial discrimination left the South and migrated to the North and West. See Carter G. Woodson, *A Century of Negro Migration* (New York, 1918, 1969), and R. R. Wright, Jr., "The Migration of Negroes to the North," *Annals*, American Academy 27:543–609, May 1906. An important monographic study on the subject is Nell I. Painter's *Exodusters: Black Migration to Kansas After Reconstruction* (New York, 1977). Some dissatisfied Black Southerners considered settlement in Africa. See Edwin S. Redkey, *Black Exodus* (New Haven, 1969).

14. U.S. Department of Commerce, Bureau of the Census, *Fourteenth Census of the United States, 1920: Agriculture*, 5:203.

15. *Historical Statistics in the United States, Colonial Times to 1957*; p. 45–47.

16. William Rossiter, *Increase of Population in the United States, 1910–1920* (Washington, D.C., 1922), p. 128; *Negroes in the United States, 1920–1932* (Washington, D.C., 1935), p. 32; Allan Spear, *Black Chicago* (Chicago, 1967), p. 12.

17. Kenneth L. Kusmer, *A Ghetto Takes Shape: Black Cleveland, 1870–1930* (Urbana, Ill., 1976), p. 10; the most recent study dealing with the wartime migrations is Florette Henri, *Black Migration* (Garden City, N.Y., 1975); another study which examines the northward migration of Black Southerners during the war is Gilbert Osofsky, *Harlem: The Making of a Ghetto* (New York, 1966).

18. Clyde V. Kiser, *Sea Island to City*, (New York, Columbia University Press, 1981), pp. 158–189; Henri, *Black Migration*, pp. 50–51.

19. Elizabeth Rauh Bethel, *Promiseland*, (Philadelphia, Temple University Press, 1981), pp. 171–186.

20. Emmett J. Scott, *Negro Migration During the War* (New York, 1920), pp. 55, 102.

21. Abraham Epstein, *The Negro Migrant in Pittsburgh* (Pittsburgh, The University of Pittsburgh, 1918), p. 35. No estimate on the total number of Blacks transported North on railroads is available.

22. Scott, *Negro Migration During the War*, pp. 72–76.

23. This matter will be further discussed and documented in Chapter 5, "Welfare Capitalism During the 1920s."

24. Scott, *Negro Migration During the War*, pp. 36–37; *Iron Trade Review*, April 12, 1917.

25. Isaac W. Read to William C. Redfield, May 14, 1917, William B. Wilson Papers 1917, Box 1, Historical Society of Pennsylvania, Philadelphia, PA. The AFL did not welcome Black migration. It believed that Blacks "are being brought North for the purpose of filling the places of union men demanding better conditions." Although resolutions favoring the organization of Black workmen into trade unions were passed at the AFL's 1916, 1917 and 1918 conventions, the federation did little to implement the idea. Philip S. Foner, *Organized Labor and the Black Worker, 1916–1973* (New York, 1974), pp. 136–143.

26. "Minutes of Interdepartmental Advisory Committee VII," May 25, 1917, *Wilson Papers*, 1917, Box 1, Historical Society of Pennsylvania.

27. *Monthly Labor Review*, January, 1918.

28. Scott, *Negro Migration During the War*, pp. 36–37, 72–73.

29. In Scott, *Negro Migration During the War*, p. 7.

30. George E. Haynes, *Negro Newcomers in Detroit* (New York, 1918), p. 14; Greene and Woodson, *The Negro Wage Earner*, pp. 257–258.

31. Spear, *Black Chicago*, pp. 141, 152.

32. Sadie Tanner Mossell, "The Standard of Living Among One Hundred Negro Migrant Families in Philadelphia," *Annals of the American Academy of Political and Social Science* (November 1921), p. 175.

33. Greene and Woodson, *The Negro Wage Earner*, pp. 342, 344.

34. According to the *Monthly Labor Review*, January 1921, p. 206, the total number of laborers in Allegheny County industrial plants increased only a little, from 220,060 in 1916 to 221,621 in 1919. Because of high turnover rates among laborers and postwar layoffs, the work force may have been substantially higher than that which is reflected in the statistics. One contemporary observer in Pittsburgh stated that industrial plants in the city at no time during the war secured a sufficient supply of workers, Black or White. So these totals do not reflect the actual manpower demands for firms in the Smoky City. Epstein, *The Negro Migrant in Pittsburgh*, p. 20. Peter Gottlieb deals extensively with the Black migration in his Ph.D. dissertation, "Making Their Own Way: Southern Blacks' Migration to Pittsburgh, 1916–1930," (Ph.D. dissertation, University of Pittsburgh, 1977).

35. U.S., Department of Commerce, Bureau of the Census, *Thirteenth Census of the United States, 1910: Population*, 1:1358; U.S., Department of Commerce, Bureau of the Census, *Fifteenth Census of the United States, 1930: Population*, 2:77; *Monthly Labor Review*, January 1921, p. 106; Epstein, *The Negro Migrant in Pittsburgh*, p. 31. The relationship of Black and immigrant workers is discussed in John Bodnar, Michael Weber, and Roger Simon, "Migration, Kinship, and Urban Adjustment: Black and Poles in Pittsburgh, 1900–1930," *Journal of American History*, December 1979, 548–565.

36. The 1910 census gives a larger estimate of Black steelworkers than either Cayton and Mitchell or Tucker. U.S., Department of Com-

merce, Bureau of the Census, *Thirteenth Census of the United States, 1910: Population*, 4:590–591. Also see Horace R. Cayton and George S. Mitchell, *Black Workers and the New Unions* (Chapel Hill, N.C., 1939), p. 7: Helen A. Tucker, "The Negroes of Pittsburgh," in *Wage Earning Pittsburgh, The Pittsburgh Survey* (New York, 1914), p. 106. In 1909, 346 Blacks worked in all Carnegie steel plants throughout the Pittsburgh areas. (Tucker, p. 106.)

37. Harris, "The New Negro Workers in Pittsburgh," pp. 45–46.

38. *Duquesne Times–Observer*, May 5, 1916, December 15, 1916.

39. U.S., Congress, Senate, Committee on Education and Labor, *Investigation of Strike in Steel Industries*, 1919, 66th Congress, pp. 529, 531.

40. Cayton and Mitchell, *Black Workers and the New Unions*, p. 8.

41. Sterling D. Spero and Abram L. Harris, *The Black Worker* (New York, 1931), p. 259; Margaret Byington, *Homestead: The Households of a Milltown* (Russell Sage Foundation, New York, 1910), p. 13.

42. *The Iron Age*, June 1917.

43. Epstein, *The Negro Migrant in Pittsburgh*, p. 7.

44. U.S., Department of Commerce, Bureau of the Census, *Negroes in the United States*, 1916, Bulletin 129, p. 113; U.S., Department of Commerce, Bureau of Census, *Negroes in the United States, 1920–1932*, pp. 63–64.

45. Epstein, *The Negro Migrant in Pittsburgh*, p. 27.

46. *New York Age*, February 8, 1917.

47. William Henry Harrison, interviewed by Dennis C. Dickerson, Duquesne, Pennsylvania, April 18, 1975.

48. Edward Lipscomb, interviewed by Dennis C. Dickerson, Duquesne, Pennsylvania, September 8, 1975.

49. Mildred Trent, interviewed by Dennis C. Dickerson, Philadelphia, Pennsylvania, May 28, 1975.

50. Willie Smith, interviewed by Peter Gottlieb, Pittsburgh, Pennsylvania, September 1974; Pittsburgh Oral History Project, Pennsylvania Historical and Museum Commission, Harrisburg, Pennsylvania.

51. Ashton Allen, Jr., interviewed by Dennis C. Dickerson, Homestead, Pennsylvania, September 6, 1975; Ashton Allen, Brod-

nax, Virginia to John T. Clark, December 18, 1922, *John T. Clark Papers, Pittsburgh Urban League (Concerning Migration from the South)*, Container 9, File 125, *Carter G. Woodson Collection*, Manuscript Division, Library of Congress, Washington, D.C.; Ashton Allen to Jones and Laughlin Steel Corporation, n.d., *Clark Papers.*

52. Lucious Corley, interviewed by Dennis C. Dickerson, Monessen, Pennsylvania, September 4, 1975.

53. James Wilson, interviewed by Dennis C. Dickerson, West Mifflin, Pennsylvania, April 23, 1975.

54. John T. Clark, "The Migrant in Pittsburgh," *Opportunity*, October 1923, p. 303.

55. Ibid., pp. 303–304.

56. U.S., Department of Commerce, Bureau of the Census, *Negroes in the United States, 1920–1932*, pp. 63–64.

57. John T. Clark, "The Negro in Steel," *Opportunity*, October 1924, p. 300; Harris, "The New Negro Worker in Pittsburgh," pp. 45–46; U.S., Department of Commerce, Bureau of the Census, *Thirteenth Census of the United States, 1910: Population, Occupational Statistics*, 4:590–591.

58. Ira De Augustine Reid, "The Negro in Major Industries and Building Trades of Pittsburgh" (M.A. thesis, University of Pittsburgh, 1925), p. 10a.

59. Barnie Smith, Thomasville, Georgia to John T. Clark, May 1, 1923, *Clark Papers*, Library of Congress, Container 8, File 119.

60. Rush Gaylord, Savannah, Georgia to John T. Clark, March 6, 1923, *Clark Papers*, Library of Congress, Container 8, File 120.

61. John D. Maxwell, Savannah, Georgia to John T. Clark, March 3, 1923, *Clark Papers*, Library of Congress, Container 8, File 120.

62. W. B. Mitchell, Shreveport, Louisiana to John T. Clark, January 16, 1923, *Clark Papers*, Library of Congress, Container 9, File 122 or 125.

63. Lillie Smith, Mt. Zion, South Carolina to John T. Clark, December 26, 1922, *Clark Papers*, Library of Congress, Container 9, File 124.

64. W. S. Hurt, Maxeys, Georgia to John T. Clark, January 15, 1923, *Clark Papers*, Library of Congress, Container 8, File 119.

65. S. M. Jenkins, Houston, Texas to John T. Clark, December 17, 1923, *Clark Papers*, Library of Congress, Container 9, File 122.

66. G. P. Washington, Savannah, Georgia to John T. Clark, April 27, 1923, *Clark Papers*, Library of Congress, Container 8, File 120.

67. A. Blond, St. Louis, Missouri to John T. Clark, December 3, 1922, *Clark Papers*, Library of Congress, Container 8, File 121.

68. *Obituary* — John McKinley Worthey — 1896–1975 (Courtesy of Mrs. Lillie Wheeler, West Mifflin, Pennsylvania); E. A. Brown, Dante Virginia to John T. Clark, December, 1922, *Clark Papers*, Library of Congress, Container 9, File 123.

69. Peter Gottlieb, "Migration and Jobs: The New Black Worker in Pittsburgh, 1916–1930," *The Western Pennsylvania Historical Magazine*, January 1978, p. 10. My own study of the A. M. Byers Company Personnel Files at the University of Pittsburgh confirm these findings.

70. *A. M. Byers Company, South Side Plant*, Pittsburgh, Pennsylvania, *Employment Records*, Archives of Industrial Society, University of Pittsburgh Libraries, Pittsburgh, Pennsylvania.

71. Alex Brown, Sumter, South Carolina to John T. Clark, December 28, 1922, *Clark Papers*, Library of Congress, Container 9, File 124.

72. Robert Tippins, Savannah, Georgia to John T. Clark, March 3, 1923, *Clark Papers*, Library of Congress, Container 8, File 120.

73. D. W. White, Savannah, Georgia to John T. Clark, March 4, 1923, *Clark Papers*, Library of Congress, Container 8, File 120.

74. *National Labor Journal*, July 20, 1917.

75. *Pittsburgh Courier*, July 28, 1923.

76. Blanche J. Paget, "The Plight of the Pennsylvania Negro," *Opportunity*, October 1936, p. 310.

77. Epstein, *The Negro Migrant in Pittsburgh*, p. 23.

78. *Negro Survey of Pennsylvania*, directed by Forrester B. Washington, Commonwealth of Pennsylvania, Department of Welfare (Harrisburg, Pennsylvania, 1927), p. 21.

79. Ibid.

80. U.S., Department of Commerce, Bureau of the Census, *Fourteenth Census of the United States, 1920: Population (Occupations)*, 4:1197–1198.

81. Reid, "The Negro in Major Industries and Building Trades of Pittsburgh," pp. 9–10. Black frequently filled semi-skilled positions in which the work and pay differed very little from unskilled jobs. It is difficult, however, to determine exactly how high this number goes because laboring categories were sometimes imprecise. It is probably very high since Blanche Paget in "The Plight of the Pennsylvania Negro" found that Black labor in lower echelon jobs in area steel mills was 98% in 1918. Most contemporary commentators confirm this relatively high percentage.

82. *Fourteenth Census of the United States, 1920: Population*, 4:1197–1198; Reid, "The Negro in Major Industries and Building Trades of Pittsburgh," pp. 9–10.

83. Reid, "The Negro in Major Industries and Building Trades of Pittsburgh," pp. 15–16.

84. *Report*: Director of Negro Economics to Secretary of Labor Through the Assistant Secretary, May 1 to 17, 1919, Box 18, File 8/102d, Chief Clerk's Files, Boxes 17–18 RG 174, National Archives, Washington, D.C.

85. Epstein, *The Negro Migrant in Pittsburgh*, p. 31.

86. John Warady, interviewed by Larry Gorski, McKeesport, Pennsylvania, April 20, 1974, Pennsylvania State University, United Steelworkers of America, Oral History Project, Department of Labor Studies, Pattee Library Collections, University Park, Pennsylvania.

87. Reid, "The Negro in Major Industries and Building Trades of Pittsburgh," pp. 26 and 28; Warady interview.

88. "Black Workers at the Aliquippa Works," *Beaver Valley Labor History Journal*, September 1979, p. 5.

89. Reid, "The Negro in Major Industries and Building Trades of Pittsburgh," pp. 9 and 11; Epstein, *The Negro Migrant in Pittsburgh*, p. 32.

90. Bart Richards, interviewed by Joe Uehlein, Pittsburgh, Pennsylvania, February 21, 1971, United Steel Workers of America, Oral History Project.

91. Reid, "The Negro in Major Industries and Building Trades of Pittsburgh," pp. 19–20.

92. "Black Workers at the Aliquippa Works," p. 5.

# Chapter 3

1. Ernest Rice McKinney, interviewed by Dennis C. Dickerson, New York City, November 21, 1974. McKinney, a Black man reared in Ohio and a graduate of Oberlin, was living in Pittsburgh during the Black migration. He served as a recreation worker at the "colored" YMCA and an early member of the Pittsburgh NAACP.

2. Quoted in Lincoln Steffens, *The Shame of the Cities* (New York, Hill and Wang, 1902, 1948), p. 147.

3. H. G., interviewed by Peter Gottleib, Pittsburgh, Pennsylvania, August 28, 1974, Pittsburgh Oral History Project, PHMC.

4. U.S., Congress, Senate, Committee on Education and Labor, *Investigation of Strike in Steel Industries*, Testimony of Elbert H. Gary, 66th Cong., 1st sess., 1919, pp. 264–265.

5. Harris, "The New Negro Worker in Pittsburgh," p. 14.

6. U.S., Department of Commerce, Bureau of the Census, *Fourteenth Census of the United States, 1920: Population*, 3:900–901.

7. U.S., Department of Commerce, Bureau of the Census, *Fifteenth Census of the United States, 1930: Population*, 3:750–751.

8. Harris, "The New Negro Worker in Pittsburgh," pp. 18–19.

9. Reverend Harold R. Tolliver, interviewed by Dennis C. Dickerson, Pittsburgh, Pennsylvania, October 9, 1974.

10. *Pittsburgh Courier*, December 1, 1923.

11. "Black Immigration into Woodlawn, 1905–1925," *Beaver Valley Labor History*, March 1979, p. 3.

12. Pennsylvania, Department of Welfare, (Harrisburg, Pennsylvania, 1927), *Negro Survey of Pennsylvania*, directed by Forrester B. Washington, p. 40. Pennsylvania had no law mandating residential segregation. Racial custom and discriminatory practices in the selling and renting of homes to Blacks often resulted in residential segregation. Washington, pp. 31–32, 39.

13. U.S., Department of Commerce, Bureau of the Census, *Fifteenth Census of the United States, 1930: Population (Families)*, 6:1136, 1146–1148.

14. Ibid., p. 1124.

15. Ira De Augustine Reid, *Social Conditions of the Negro in the Hill District of Pittsburgh*, General Committee on the Hill Survey, 1930, p. 41.

16. *Mortality Statistics, 1918*, Nineteenth Annual Report (Washington, D.C., 1920), p. 230; Washington, *Negro Survey*, p. 52.

17. *Duquesne Times*, January 18, 1918.

18. *Duquesne Times*, May 2, 1919.

19. *Duquesne Times*, February 6, 1920.

20. *Monessen Daily Independent*, December 29, 1919.

21. Clark, "The Negro in Steel," p. 300.

22. H. G. interview, A. C., interviewed by Major Mason, McKeesport, Pennsylvania, July 22, 1974, Pittsburgh Oral History Project, PHMC.

23. A. M. Byers Company, Personnel Files, Archives of Industrial Society, University of Pittsburgh Libraries, Pittsburgh, Pennsylvania.

24. U.S., Department of Commerce, Bureau of the Census, *Fourteenth Census of the United States: 1920: Occupations*, p. 1004. *The Bulletin of the Department of Labor Industry*, "Industrial Accident Reports," Vol. VII (Harrisburg, Pennsylvania, 1920), p. 54.

25. Richard Cobbs, interviewed by Peter Gottleib, Pittsburgh, Pennsylvania, August 8, 1974, Pittsburgh Oral History Project, PHMC.

26. *Duquesne Times*, June 13, 1919.

27. *Duquesne Times*, December 12, 1919.

28. *Pittsburgh Courier*, June 23, 1923.

29. *Pittsburgh Courier*, October 27, 1923.

30. *Pittsburgh Courier*, November 17, 1923.

31. *Pittsburgh Courier*, September 5, 1925.

32. Tolliver interview.

33. *Pittsburgh Courier*, February 19, 1927.

34. David Brody, *Steelworkers in America: The Non-union Era* (Cambridge, Massachusetts, Harvard University Press, 1960), pp. 186–187.

35. *Duquesne Times–Observer*, June 30, 1916; September 1, 1916; September 29, 1916; October 6, 1916.

36. *Duquesne Times–Observer*, October 6, 1916.

37. The phenomenon of police rioting is developed in *The Politics of Protest: A Report* by Jerome H. Skolnick, *National Commission on the Causes of Violence Task Force*, Vol. 3, (Washington, D.C., 1969), pp. 183–217.

38. Richard B. Sherman, "Johnstown v. The Negro: Southern Migrants and the Exodus of 1923," *Pennsylvania History*, October 1963, pp. 456–458.

39. Ibid., pp. 456–458.

40. Ibid.; Florence M. Hornback, *Survey of the Negro Population of Metropolitan Johnstown, Pennsylvania* (Johnstown, Pennsylvania, 1941), p. 17; *New York Times*, September 1, 1923; September 15, 1923.

41. David M. Chalmers, *Hooded Americanism*, New York New Viewpoints, 1965), pp. 8–21; Kenneth T. Jackson, *The Ku Klux Klan in the City, 1915–1930*, (New York, Oxford University Press, 1967), pp. 3–23.

42. Emerson H. Loucks, *The Ku Klux Klan in Pennsylvania*, (New York–Harrisburg, Pennsylvania, The Telegraph Press, 1936), pp. 25–27; Chalmers, *Hooded Americanism*, pp. 236–242.

43. George Kutska, interviewed by Jack Severson, Monessen, Pennsylvania, April 15, 1969, Pennsylvania State University, United Steelworkers of America, Oral History Project, Department of Labor Studies, Pattee Library Collections, University Park, Pennsylvania.

44. *Duquesne Times*, May 1, 1952; *Pittsburgh Courier*, September 18, 1926.

45. Pennsylvania, Department of Welfare, *Negro Survey of Pennsylvania*, Harrisburg, 1927, p. 63; Randall K. Burkett, *Black Redemption*, (Philadelphia, Temple University Press, 1978), p. 114, *The Crisis*, April 1918; *Pittsburgh Courier*, October 9, 1926.

46. *Duquesne Times*, April 25, 1919; *Homestead Messenger*, November 1, 1924; "The Story of Woodlawn, Pa.," Woodlawn *Gazette*, October 24 and 31, 1924, B. F. Jones Library, Aliquippa, Pennsylvania.

47. McKinney interview; Tolliver interview; Mr. and Mrs. Edward Raby, interviewed by Dennis C. Dickerson, Philadelphia, Pennsylvania, April 1, 1976.

48. U.S. Department of Commerce, Bureau of the Census, *Religious Bodies*, 1916, Part I, Summary and Detailed Tables, p. 417; *Religious Bodies*, 1926, Vol. I, Summary and Detailed Tables, p. 481; Florence M. Hornback, *Survey of the Negro Population of Metropolitan Johnstown*,

*Pennsylvania,* pp. 15–17; Edward Maurey, *Where the West Began: A Story of Coraopolis and the Ohio Valley,* (1930), pp. 65–66; *Semi-Centennial Borough of Coraopolis, Golden Jubilee,* 1937, (Archives of Industrial Society, University of Pittsburgh Libraries, Pittsburgh, Pennsylvania), *Churches in Homestead, Pa.* (undated manuscript, circa 1939–1940), Carnegie Public Library, Munhall, PA.

49. *The Christian Index,* July 20, 1916; January 31, 1918; February 28, 1918; May 3, 1923, November 8, 1923; July 14, 1927; June 11, 1931; U.S. Department of Commerce, Bureau of the Census, *Religious Bodies: Summary and Detailed Tables,* Vol, I, 1926, p. 511; *Yearbook of the 21st Session of the Ohio Annual Conference,* CME Church, 1954, pp. 25, 35, 51, CME Publishing House, Memphis, Tennessee.

50. *Pittsburgh Courier,* July 24, 1926; "The Story of Woodlawn, Pa." . . . B.F. Jones Library, Aliquippa, Pennsylvania. *Souvenir Program, Mortgage Burning Celebration,* Monday, July 1 through Tuesday, July 9, 1946, Holliday Memorial AME Zion Church, Braddock, Pennsylvania, (Courtesy of Rev. T. B. Thornhill, Braddock, Pa.).

51. *Duquesne Times,* April 25, 1919; August 8, 1919; *Pittsburgh Courier,* October 16, 1926.

52. *Pittsburgh Courier,* July 27, 1929.

53. *Duquesne Times,* May 26, 1933; May 2, 1941; January 14, 1954.

54. "Heritage, A Black History of Johnstown," *Tribune-Democrat,* February 12, 1980, p. 4; *A.M.E. Christian Recorder,* December 25, 1978; Bartow Tipper, interviewed by Dennis C. Dickerson, Aliquippa, Pennsylvania, March 4, 1980.

55. *47th Anniversary of First Baptist Church, North Vandergrift, Pa.* (1967) Edited by Judith Faire (Courtesy of Mrs. Mildred Trent, Philadelphia , PA): Mrs. Mildred Trent, interviewed by Dennis C. Dickerson, Philadelphia, Pennsylvania, May 28, 1975.

56. Reverend J. L. Simmons, interviewed by Peter Gottlieb, Pittsburgh, Pennsylvania, June 13, 1974, Pittsburgh Oral History Project.

57. Reverend Charles W. Torrey, interviewed by Dennis C. Dickerson, Duquesne, Pennsylvania, March 21, 1975.

58. *Duquesne Times,* September 12, 1941; October 16, 1956; November 1, 1956.

59. *Duquesne Times,* January 10, 1919.

60. *Duquesne Times,* March 21, 1919; April 11, 1919.

61. *Duquesne Times,* May 9, 1919.

62. *Homestead Messenger,* April 9, 1919; April 11, 1919.

63. *Duquesne Times,* May 4, 1928; April 3, 1952; Edward Maurey, *Where the West Began: A Story of Coraopolis and (the) Ohio Valley,* (1930), Archives of Industrial Society, University of Pittsburgh Libraries, Pittsburgh, Pennsylvania.

64. Lerone Bennett, Jr., *Pioneers in Protest* (Chicago, Johnson Publishing Company, 1968), p. 32; Monroe N. Work, *Negro Year Book 1925–1926* (Tuskegee Institute, Alabama, Negro Year Book Publishing Company, 1925), pp. 462–463; Charles H. Wesley, *History of the Improved, Benevolent and Protective Order of Elks of the World* (Washington, D.C., Associated Publishers, 1955), pp. 39–52.

65. *Pittsburgh Courier,* January 20, 1923; April 25, 1925; August 14, 1926.

66. *Duquesne Times,* May 17, 1918; February 25, 1954; "Heritage . . . ," *Tribune-Democrat,* February 12, 1980, p. 11.

67. Allen Griffey, interviewed by Dennis C. Dickerson, Monessen, Pennsylvania, September 5, 1975.

68. *Minutes* (of the) *Twenty-Fourth Annual Meeting of the Grand Lodge, IBPOEW,* Chicago, Ill., August 28–30, 1923 (privately printed in Newark, New Jersey), pp. 141–142; *Minutes of the Forty-Fourth Annual Meeting* (of the) *Grand Lodge IBPOEW,* Pittsburgh, Pa., August 22–27, 1943, pp. 281–282.

69. Paul L. (Red) Payne, interviewed by Dennis C. Dickerson, Clairton, Pennsylvania, March 15, 1975.

70. "28th Anniversary and Testimonial Banquet, J. T. Brandy Lodge No. 1047, I.B.P.O.E. of W." (privately printed, 1968); William Patterson, interviewed by Dennis C. Dickerson, Duquesne, Pa., March 16, 1975. Marvin Ward and Carl O. Dickerson were the president and secretary of the Duquesne "Elks to be Club."

71. *Duquesne Times,* October 6, 1933; June 1, 1945; Patterson interview; *The Daughters of the Improved, Benevolent, Protective Order of the Elks of the World, Golden Jubilee Celebration, 1902–1952* (Norfolk, Va., 1952), pp. 318, 320–324; *Minutes of the . . . Grand Lodge . . . 1943,* pp. 241–242.

72. *Monessen Daily Independent,* October 7, 1919; *Duquesne Times,* March 11, 1948; January 8, 1953; November 20, 1958.

73. Anne M. Barton and Margaret Staudenmaier, "Ethnic and Racial Groups in Rankin, Pennsylvania (A Study of Relationships Between Them as Expressed Through Various Social Forces)" (unpublished M.S.W. thesis, University of Pittsburgh, 1947), p. 57.

74. *Pittsburgh Courier*, January 20, 1923; April 3, 1926. *Homestead Messenger*, June 2, 1919, *Monessen Daily Independent*, August 23, 1919.

75. *Pittsburgh Courier*, June 13, 1925; Robert Peterson, *Only the Ball was White: A History of Legendary Black Players and All Black Professional Teams*, (New York, McGraw-Hill Book Company, 1970, pp. 91–92; 160–162; Payne interview. Donn Rogosin, *Invisible Men: Life in Baseball's Negro Leagues*, (New York, Atheneum, 1983), p. 52.

76. *Homestead Messenger*, February 12, 1919; March 20, 1919; September 16, 1919; *Minutes of the Forty-Third Annual Meeting, Grand Lodge, I.B.P.O.E. of W.*, Philadelphia, Pa., August 23–29, 1942, pp. 160–164.

77. Rogosin, *Invisible Men*, pp. 14–17.

78. *Homestead Messenger*, January 21, 1919; March 20, 1919; June 2, 1919; *Monessen Daily Independent*, August 23, 1919; Peterson, *Only the Ball Was White*, pp. 271–273.

79. Charles Flint Kellogg, *N.A.A.C.P.* (Baltimore, Johns Hopkins Press, 1967), pp. 117, 126–128, 135.

80. Andrew Buni, *Robert L. Vann of the Pittsburgh Courier: Politics and Black Journalism*, (Pittsburgh, University of Pittsburgh Press, 1974), pp. 57–59.

81. J. C. Austin to Mary White Ovington, February 11, 1921, *N.A.A.C.P. Papers*, NAACP Branch Files, Box G–190, Pittsburgh, Pa., 1923–1924 folder, Library of Congress, Manuscript Division, Washington, D.C.

82. Sara B. Writt to James Weldon Johnson, January 14, 1924, *N.A.A.C.P. Papers*, NAACP Branch Files, Box G–190, Pittsburgh, Pa., 1923–1924 folder, Library of Congress, Manuscript Division, Washington, D.C.

83. Jeanne S. Scott to Walter White, June 14, 1934, *N.A.A.C.P. Papers*, NAACP Branch Files, Box G–191, Pittsburgh, Pa., April to June 1934 folder, Library of Congress, Manuscript Division, Washington, D.C.

84. "Application for Charter," Donora, Pa. File, *N.A.A.C.P. Papers*, NAACP Branch Files, Box G–181, Library of Congress, Manuscript Division, Washington, D.C.

85. "Application for Charter," Monessen, Pa. 1926–1938 File, *N.A.A.C.P. Papers*, NAACP Branch Files, Box G–184, Library of Congress, Manuscript Division, Washington, D.C.

86. Dr. Henry F. Owens to Robert Bagnall, November 12, 1929; Dr. Henry F. Owens to William Andrews, November 27, 1931; William Andrews to Dr. Henry F. Owens, December 4, 1931; Sam Spurlock to Walter White, November 17, 1931; Monessen Pa., 1926–1938 File, NAACP Branch Files, Box G–181, Library of Congress, Washington, D.C.

87. E. David Cronon, *Black Moses*, (Madison, Wisconsin, University of Wisconsin Press, 1955), pp. 16–45, 205–207.

88. Tony Martin, *Race First: The Ideological and Organization Struggles of Marcus Garvey and the Universal Negro Improvement Association*, (Westport, Connecticut, Greenwood Press, 1976), pp. 366–367; *The Negro World*, August 22, 1931.

89. "Salesman's Report — Loan," *U.N.I.A. Central Division (New York) files*, microfilm Reel 1, Box 104, Schomberg Collection, New York Public Library, New York City. Amy Jacques Garvey, ed., *Philosophy and Opinions of Marcus Garvey*, Volume 2, (New York, Atheneum, 1969), pp. 382–383.

90. Lionel M. Yard, "George Weston, Organizer of U.N.I.A. Branches, Oral Historian of the Garvey Movement, Black Nationalist," June 1975, p. 16; in *George Weston Papers*, Box 1, File 1, Schomberg Collection; Garvey, ed., *Philosophy and Opinions*, p. 48.

91. Randall K. Burkett, *Garveyism as a Religious Movement* (Metuchen, New Jersey, The Scarecrow Press, Inc., 1978), pp. 114–117, 133. J. G. St. Clair Drake was originally an AME minister. After spending a lengthy interlude in the Baptist church, he returned to the AME church by the 1930s. See "Rev. John Gibbs St. Clair Drake" in Richard R. Wright, Jr., ed., *Encyclopedia of African Methodism* (Philadelphia, A.M.E. Book Concern, 1947), pp. 98–99; *Pittsburgh Courier*, January 20, 1923; *The Negro World*, July 3, 1926; August 22, 1931.

92. "Bureau of Investigation Reports," June 28, 1920, in Robert A. Hill, editor, *The Marcus Garvey and Universal Negro Improvement Association Papers*, Volume II, (Berkeley, California, University of California Press, 1983), pp. 399–401.

93. "Matthew L. Dempsey," *Beaver Valley Labor History Journal*, June 1979, p. 4. During this period, the town of Aliquippa was known as Woodlawn.

94. Ibid.; R. B. Spencer to William J. Burns, August 29, 1922, Marcus Garvey Files, FBI Reading Room, J. Edgar Hoover FBI Building, Washington, D.C.; *Report* — Pittsburgh Pa., R. B. Spencer, Special Agent in Charge, Marcus Garvey case, May 5, 1923, Garvey Files, FBI, Washington, D.C.

95. *Report* — Pittsburgh, Pa., R. B. Spencer, Special Agent in Charge, Marcus Garvey case, May 5, 1923, Garvey Files, FBI, Washington, D.C.: *Report* — Pittsburgh, Pa., R. B. Spencer, Special Agent in Charge, Garvey case, October 5, 1922, Garvey Files, FBI, Washington, D.C.

96. *Report* — Pittsburgh, Pa., R. B. Spencer, Special Agent . . ., October 5, 1922, Garvey Files, FBI, Washington, D.C.: "The Story of Woodlawn, Pa." . . . B. F. Jones Library, Aliquippa, Pennsylvania.

## Chapter 4

1. See Chapter 1, pp. 2–3.

2. Philip S. Foner, *Organized Labor and the Black Worker, 1916–1973* (New York, International Publishers, 1974), pp. 139–141.

3. Abraham Epstein, *The Negro Migrant in Pittsburgh* (Pittsburgh, University of Pittsburgh, 1918), pp. 36–42.

4. Ira De A. Reid, *Negro Membership in American Labor Unions* (New York, The National Urban League Department of Research and Investigations, 1930), pp. 138–139; William H. Harris, *Keeping the Faith: A. Philip Randolph, Milton Webster and the Brotherhood of Sleeping Car Porters, 1925–1937*, (Urbana, Illinois, University of Illinois Press, 1977), p. 227.

5. Bart Richards, interviewed by Joe Uehlein, Pittsburgh, Pennsylvania, February 21, 1974; USWA Oral History Project, Pennsylvania State University; Ernest Branch, interviewed by Dennis C. Dickerson, Monessen, Pennsylvania, March 6, 1980; August Meier and Elliott Rudwick, *Black Detroit and the Rise of the UAW*, (New York, Oxford University Press, 1979), pp. 40–41.

6. Jeremy Brecher, *Strike!* (San Francisco, Straight Arrow Books, 1972), pp. 102–103; David Brody, *Labor in Crisis* (Philadelphia, Lippincott, 1965), pp. 50–53. Because of growing unrest among workers, especially about low wages, some of them paid no heed to this no-

strike agreement among union spokesmen, government officials and industry representatives. In Bridgeport, Connecticut, munitions workers went on strike in spite of union and National (War) Labor Board requests to the contrary. The men returned to war work after President Woodrow Wilson threatened to take away their jobs.

7. Alexander M. Bing, *War Time Strikes and Their Adjustment* (New York, E. P. Dutton & Co., 1921), p. 293.

8. Brecher, *Strike!*, pp. 104–117.

9. Brody, *Labor in Crisis*, p. 101.

10. Spero and Harris, *The Black Worker*, p. 258. William Z. Foster made this speech at the prodding of John T. Clark, the executive director of the Pittsburgh Urban League. No follow-up occurred because of opposition from the hierarchy of the Amalgamated Association. Also see Chapter 1, this volume.

11. William Henry Harrison, interviewed by Dennis C. Dickerson, Duquesne, Pennsylvania, April 18, 1975; Edward Liscomb, interviewed by Dennis C. Dickerson, Duquesne, Pennsylvania, September 8, 1975.

12. Spero and Harris, *The Black Worker*, pp. 259–260.

13. Synopsis of Interview on November 20, 1919 with Mr. K — Official of the Urban League of Pittsburgh, Pennsylvania, from Wayne State University, Archives of Labor History and Urban Affairs — Xerox copy; *Heber Blankenhorn Papers, 1919–1937*, Archives of Industrial Society, University of Pittsburgh Libraries, Pittsburgh, Pennsylvania.

14. B. R., interviewed by John E. Bodnar, February 26, 1973, Pittsburgh Oral History Project, Ethnic Studies Program, PHMC.

15. Allen Griffey, interviewed by Dennis C. Dickerson, Monessen, Pittsburgh, September 4, 1975.

16. Commission of Inquiry, *Blankenhorn Papers*, University of Pittsburgh Libraries, p. 18.

17. B. R. interview.

18. Harrison interview. Most of these positions were semi-skilled jobs requiring work with mill machinery. Normally most Blacks were common laborers who cleaned debris from furnaces, conveyed bricks to mill masons rebuilding the insides of furnaces, and other jobs demanding little manual skill or training in running a machine.

19. Charles W. Torrey, interviewed by Dennis C. Dickerson, Duquesne, Pennsylvania, March 21, 1975; James Thompson, interviewed by Dennis C. Dickerson, Homestead, Pennsylvania, October 7, 1974; S. Adele Shaw, "Closed Towns," *Survey*, November 8, 1919, p. 6.

20. *Amalgamated Journal*, November 27, 1919; Torrey interview.

21. See *Race Riot at East St. Louis, July 2, 1917* (Edwardsville, Illinois, Southern Illinois University Press, 1964); and William M. Tuttle, Jr., *Race Riot: Chicago in the Red Summer of 1919* (New York, Atheneum, 1972), pp. 108–156.

22. B. R. interview.

23. *Monessen Daily Independent*, October 24, 1919.

24. Lipscomb interview; *Duquesne Times*, January 9, 1920. One of these Black deputies, Sergeant Pinckney, was a veteran of World War I.

25. *Amalgamated Journal*, October 16, 1919.

26. U.S., Congress, Senate, Committee on Education and Labor, *Investigation of Strike in Steel Industries*, 66th Cong., 1st sess., 1919, pp. 533–535.

27. *Pittsburgh Post*, September 24, 1919.

28. *Public Opinion and the Steel Strike*, Interchurch World Movement (New York, Reprint 1970), pp. 205–206.

29. Report on the Steel Strike of 1919, Commission of Inquiry, Interchurch World Movement (New York, 1920), p. 177; Commission of Inquiry, *Blankenhorn Papers*, University of Pittsburgh Libraries, Testimony of William Z. Foster, November 17, 1919.

30. Brody, *Labor in Crisis*, pp. 162–163.

31. *Report*: Director of Negro Economics to Secretary of Labor, through the Assistant Secretary, May 1 to 17, 1919; *Chief Clerk's Files*, Record Group 174, Box 18, File 8/102d, National Archives, Washington, D.C.

32. *Report*: Director of Negro Economics to Secretary of Labor, through the Assistant Secretary, May 18 to 31, 1919, Record Group 174, Box 17, File 8/102d, National Archives, Washington, D.C.

33. Reid, "The Negro in Major Industries and Building Trades of Pittsburgh," pp. 8–9. In some of the steel-producing areas, the decrease in immigrant workers exceeded that of Blacks, but overall in

Allegheny County, Black workers were laid off in greater proportions than immigrants. Data concerning native Whites is not available.

34. Philip Klein, *The Burden of Unemployment* (New York, 1923), pp. 943-94; *Survey*, February 26, 1921.

35. An examination of the personnel files of the A. M. Byers Company in Pittsburgh points directly to this trend.

36. These labor agents were, in this instance, primarily Negro welfare officers from Jones and Laughlin and Carnegie Steel Companies.

37. William Polite, Chattanooga, Tennessee to John T. Clark, January 16, 1923, *Clark Papers*, Pittsburgh Urban League (Concerning Migration from the South), Container 9, File 123, Carter G. Woodson Collection, Manuscript Division, Library of Congress, Washington, D.C.

38. Samuel Moore, Kinston, North Carolina to John T. Clark, January 27, 1923, *Clark Papers*, Library of Congress, Washington, D.C.

39. J. W. Mitchell, Lowryville, South Carolina to John T. Clark, December 12, 1922, *Clark Papers*, Library of Congress, Washington, D.C.

40. Clark, "The Negro in Steel," p. 300; Harris, "The New Negro Worker in Pittsburgh," pp. 45-46.

41. Reid, "The Negro in the Major Industries and Building Trades of Pittsburgh," p. 10a.

42. *Pittsburgh Courier*, August 29, 1925.

43. U.S., Department of Commerce, Bureau of the Census, *Fourteenth Census of the United States, 1920: Population (Occupations)*, 4:1197-1198; U.S., Department of Commerce, Bureau of the Census, *Fifteenth Census of the United States, 1930: Population (Occupations)*, 4:1416.

44. *Pittsburgh Courier*, March 27, 1926.

45. *Pittsburgh Courier*, March 27, 1926.

46. *New York Times*, July 8, 1924, August 7, 1927, October 31, 1927.

47. Alonzo C. Thayer to Arnold Hill, September 12, 1927, *Records of the National Urban League, Industrial Relations Department*, Affiliates File, Series 4, Box 34, Manuscript Division, Library of Congress.

48. Virginia M. Woodson, Pittsburgh Urban League to Renand T. Lowry, St. Louis, Missouri, February 27, 1928; *Carter G. Woodson Collection*, Manuscript Division, Library of Congress, *Papers of the Detroit Urban League*, Container 14, File 177.

49. T. Arnold Hill to John T. Clark, April 30, 1926, *Records of the National Urban League*, Affiliates File, Library of Congress, Series 4, Box 34.

## Chapter 5

1. Clark, "The Negro in Steel," p. 300.

2. A. H. Wyman, "The Value and Trend of Welfare Work Among Negroes in Industry," p. 7; *Records of the National Urban League, Industrial Relations Department*, Affiliates File, Series 4, Box 34, Library of Congress, Manuscript Division, Washington, D.C.

3. "Unskilled Labor and Americanization Section," February 2, 1911, p. 2, *Minutes of Meeting*, National Association of Corporation Training, Pittsburgh Chapter; *Records of the National Urban League* . . . Library of Congress, Washington, D.C.

4. Wyman, "The Value and Trend of Welfare Work Among Negroes in Industry," p. 6; *Records of the National Urban League* . . . Library of Congress, Washington, D.C.

5. "Unskilled Labor and Americanization Section," p. 2, *Minutes of Meeting; Records of the National Urban League* . . . Library of Congress, Washington, D.C.

6. Wyman, "The Value and Trend of Welfare Work Among Negroes in Industry," p. 6; *Records of the National Urban League* . . . Library of Congress, Washington, D.C.

7. George E. Haynes, *The Negro at Work During the World War and During Reconstruction* (Washington, D.C., 1921), p. 117.

8. Clark, "The Negro in Steel," p. 301.

9. *A. M. Byers Company, Personnel Files*, Archives of Industrial Society, University of Pittsburgh Libraries, Pittsburgh, Pennsylvania.

10. Stanley Buder, *Pullman* (New York, Oxford University Press, 1967); Daniel Nelson, *Managers and Workers*, (Madison, University of Wisconsin Press, 1975), pp. 101–116.

11. W. C. Rice, "Midland: A Forerunner of Modern Housing Development for Industrial Sections," *The Survey*, December 12, 1914, pp. 296–297. "Features of Welfare Work at Duquesne, Pennsylvania," *The Iron Age*, January 20, 1916, pp. 193–195; *New York Age*, October 8, 1914; *Crisis*, December 1914.

12. Andrew Buni, *Robert L. Vann of the Pittsburgh Courier: Politics and Black Journalism*, (Pittsburgh, University of Pittsburgh Press, 1974), pp. 59–60. Two Whites, Reverend Charles Zahneiser and Dr. Charles Cooper, once director of Kingsley House, a social service settlement, were founders of the Pittsburgh Council of Social Services Among Negroes. They were joined by the Black secretary of the Centre Avenue Branch of the YMCA, Samuel R. Morsell. Morsell held degrees from Oberlin and Yale Divinity School. He served as a supply pastor of Grace Memorial Presbyterian Church in Pittsburgh and also became an ordained minister in the African Methodist Episcopal Church. See Buni, p. 60 and *Who's Who in Colored America, 1928–1929*, p. 272; "Negro Welfare Workers in Pittsburgh," *The Survey*, August 3, 1918, p. 513.

13. "Negro Welfare Workers in Pittsburgh," *The Survey*, p. 513; "Robert Earl Johnson," in *Who's Who in Colored America, 1928–1929* (Brooklyn, New York, 1929), p. 213; Paul L. Payne, interviewed by Dennis C. Dickerson, Clairton, Pennsylvania, March 15, 1975.

14. Mrs. Irma Baskerville, interviewed by Dennis C. Dickerson, Pittsburgh, Pennsylvania, March 4, 1980.

15. "William P. Young," *The Pennsylvania Manual, 1965–1966*, Vol. 97 (Harrisburg, Pennsylvania, 1966), p. 371. On January 15, 1963, Governor William W. Scranton appointed William P. Young as the first Black to serve as Secretary of Labor and Industry in Pennsylvania; W. P. Young, "The First Hundred Negro Workers," *Opportunity*, January 1924, p. 15; "Robert Earl Johnson," *Who's Who in Colored America, 1928–1929*, p. 213.

16. *New York Age*, September 13, 1917; *Duquesne Times*, April 22, 1921; *Pittsburgh Courier*, February 19, 1927; I. J. K. Wells, interviewed by Dennis C. Dickerson, Philadelphia, Pennsylvania, February 11, 1975. Colesta Long, interviewed by Dennis C. Dickerson, Philadelphia, Pennsylvania, March 27, 1979.

17. Baskerville interview; Wells interview; Jewell Simmons, Brunswick, Georgia to John T. Clark, January 28, 1923. *John T. Clark Papers, Pittsburgh Urban League* (Concerning Migration from the South), Container 8, File 120, Carter G. Woodson Collection, Manuscript Division, Library of Congress, Washington, D.C.

18. "Heritage: A Black History of Johnstown," *The Tribune–Democrat*, February 12, 1980, pp. 7, 22.

19. Clark, "The Negro in Steel," p. 300; "Negro Welfare Workers in Pittsburgh," *The Survey*, p. 513.

20. Wells interview; *Duquesne Times*, November 29, 1918. James Wilson, interviewed by Dennis C. Dickerson, West Mifflin, Pennsylvania, April 23, 1975.

21. W. P. Young, "The First Hundred Negro Workers," *Opportunity*, January 1924, pp. 15, 17.

22. Ibid., pp. 16–17.

23. Ibid., pp. 17.

24. Ibid.

25. *Homestead Messenger*, September 30, 1918; October 2, 1918.

26. Wells interview; *Duquesne Times*, March 5, 1920.

27. *Duquesne Times*, December 17, 1920.

28. Wells interview.

29. W. P. Young, "The First Hundred Negro Workers," pp. 17–18.

30. *Clairton Tattler*, December 17, 1920, February 4, 1921; April 22, 1921; Paul L. Payne, interviewed by Dennis C. Dickerson, Clairton, Pennsylvania, March 15, 1975.

31. *Duquesne Times*, July 20, 1920.

32. Mrs. Mattie Christian, interviewed by Dennis C. Dickerson, Duquesne, Pennsylvania, April 22, 1975; Long interview; *Clairton Tattler*, March 18, 1921; April 22, 1921; January 13, 1922; "Industrial Conference Meets," *Competitor*, March 1920, p. 75; Payne interview.

33. Reverend J. A. Terry, Jr., interviewed by Dennis C. Dickerson, Pittsburgh, Pennsylvania, March 3, 1980; Baskerville interview; *Pittsburgh Courier*, August 21, 1937.

34. *Pittsburgh Courier*, October 17, 1925.

35. *Pittsburgh Courier*, January 20, 1923; Wells interview.

36. *Pittsburgh Courier*, February 19, 1927.

37. "Unskilled Labor and Americanization Section," *Minutes of Meeting* . . . Library of Congress, Washington, D.C., p. 3.

38. Young, "The First Hundred Negro Workers," p. 18.

39. *Duquesne Times–Observer*, January 19, 1917; February 16, 1917.

40. Young, "The First Hundred Negro Workers," pp. 15–16, 18.

41. J. W. Knapp, "An Experiment with Negro Labor," *Opportunity*, February 1923, p. 19.

42. Wells interview; Papers of the Urban League of Pittsburgh, (uncatalogued) Pittsburgh Urban League Office, 200 Ross Street, Pittsburgh, Pennsylvania.

43. *Duquesne Times,* August 8, 1919.

44. *Pittsburgh Courier,* August 23, 1924.

45. *Homestead Messenger,* February 7, 1925; *Pittsburgh Courier,* October 9, 1926.

46. Bartow Tipper, interviewed by Dennis C. Dickerson, Aliquippa, Pennsylvania, March 4, 1980.

47. Florence M. Hornback, *Survey of the Negro Population of Metropolitan Johnstown, Pennsylvania* (1941 ), pp. 190–191, University of Pittsburgh Libraries, Pittsburgh, Pennsylvania; "Heritage . . .," *Tribune–Democrat,* February 2, 1980, p. 7; *Golden Anniversary Souvenir Booklet of Shiloh Baptist Church, 1917–1967,* Johnstown, Pennsylvania, Pennsylvania Historical and Museum Commission, Harrisburg, Pennsylvania.

48. *Pittsburgh Courier,* January 20, 1923; October 27, 1923.

49. Young, "The First Hundred Negro Workers," p. 18.

50. John T. Clark, "The Migrant in Pittsburgh," *Opportunity,* October 1923, p. 305.

51. *Papers of the Urban League of Pittsburgh;* (uncatalogued) Pittsburgh Urban League Office, 200 Ross Street, Pittsburgh, Pennsylvania.

52. "Industrial Conference Meets," *Competitor,* March 1920, pp. 74–75.

53. W. S. Hurt, Maxeys, Georgia to John T. Clark, January 24, 1923; Clark Papers, Container 8, File 119, Library of Congress, Washington, D.C.; M. F. Gunnell, Palmyra, Virginia to George E. Jessup, April 19, 1923; Clark Papers, Container 9, File 125, Library of Congress, Washington, D.C.

54. Cyrus T. Greene to T. Arnold Hill, August 7, 1928; *Records of the National Urban League,* Series 4, Box 34, Industrial Relations Department, Affiliates File, Manuscript Division, Library of Congress, Washington, D.C.; *Opportunity,* June 1929, p. 196.

55. *Pittsburgh Courier,* December 14, 1968.

56. Baskerville interview, Letter from Reverend Dr. Donald A. Tunie to Dennis C. Dickerson, September 15, 1980.

57. Long interview; *Duquesne Times*, February 23, 1940.

58. T. Arnold Hill, "Comment on Pittsburgh," *Opportunity*, January 1929, p. 23.

## Chapter 6

1. "Two Groups of the Unemployed in Allegheny County in the Winter of 1930–1931," *Pittsburgh Business Review*, Bureau of Business Research, University of Pittsburgh, October 29, 1931, pp. 12–13.

2. J. P. Watson, *Economic Background of the Relief Problem* (Pittsburgh, 1937), p. 33.

3. H. A. Lett, "Work: Negro Unemployed in Pittsburgh," *Opportunity*, March 1931, p. 80.

4. Census of Partial Unemployment and Occupations: November 1937, United States Employment Service, *Laurence A. Oxley Files*, Record Group 183, Box 1388, Pennsylvania Folder, National Archives, Washington, D.C.

5. U.S., Department of Commerce, Bureau of the Census, *Sixteenth Census of the United States, 1940: Population, The Labor Force*, 3:111–112, 115–116.

6. "Industrial Color Bans in Pittsburgh," Table III, Pittsburgh Urban League Survey Conducted Through the F.E.R.A. 1934, *Reasons for the Disproportionate Number of Negroes on Relief Rolls*, Reel #1, *National Negro Congress Records*, New York Public Library, Schomburg Collection, New York, New York.

7. F. Alden Wilson, "Occupational Status of the Negro in the Iron and Steel Industry (in) Pittsburgh and Environs," March–April–May 1934, pp. 32–33, 35–36; *U.S. Employment Service, Laurence A. Oxley Files*, Record Group 183, Box 1396, National Archives, Washington, D.C.

8. Cayton and Mitchell, *Black Workers and the New Unions*, p. 38.

9. Wilson, "Occupational Status of the Negro . . . Environs," p. 5.

10. Paget, "The Plight of the Pennsylvania Negro," p. 310.

11. Wilson, "Occupational Status of the Negro . . . Environs, p. 52.

12. Ibid., pp. 9–11; Paget, The Plight of the Pennsylvania Negro," p. 310.

13. Wilson, "Occupational Status of the Negro . . . Environs," pp. 51–53; James Thompson, interviewed by Dennis C. Dickerson, Homestead, Pennsylvania, October 7, 1974.

14. John V. Anderson, "Unemployment in Pittsburgh with Reference to the Negro," (M.A. thesis, University of Pittsburgh, 1932), pp. 43–44.

15. U.S., Department of Commerce, Bureau of the Census, *Fifteenth Census of the United States, 1930: Population*, 2:1280.

16. Cayton and Mitchell, *Black Workers and the New Unions*, p. 28.

17. U.S., Department of Commerce, Bureau of the Census, *Sixteenth Census of the United States, 1940: Population*, 3:154, 156.

18. Ibid., p. 146.

19. Cayton and Mitchell, *Black Workers and the New Unions*, p. 34.

20. Ibid.

21. Ibid., p. 33.

22. Ibid.

23. George Powers, *Cradle of Steel Unionism, Monogahela Valley, Pennsylvania*, (East Chicago, Indiana, 1972), pp. 33–38.

24. Ibid., p. 110.

25. Ashton Allen, Jr., interviewed by Dennis C. Dickerson, Homestead, Pennsylvania, September 6, 1975.

26. Merril Lynch, interviewed by Peter Gottleib, Pittsburgh, Pennsylvania, August 22, 1974; Pittsburgh Oral History Project, PHMC.

27. Wilson, "Occupational Status of the Negro . . . Environs," p. 52.

28. K. L., interviewed by Major Mason, McKeesport, Pennsylvania, Summer 1974, Pittsburgh Oral History Project: A. C., interviewed by Major Mason, McKeesport, Pennsylvania, July 22, 1974, Pittsburgh Oral History Project.

29. Lett, "Work: Negro Unemployed in Pittsburgh," p. 81.

30. Wilson, "Occupational Status of the Negro . . . Environs," pp. 25–26.

31. Wilson, "Occupational Status of the Negro . . . Environs," pp. 18–20; Mildred Trent, interviewed by Dennis C. Dickerson, Philadelphia, Pennsylvania, May 28, 1975.

32. Lett, "Negro Unemployed in Pittsburgh," p. 80.

33. Wilson, "Occupational Status of the Negro," pp. 18.

34. Mildred Junginger to J. L. Stanley, November 6, 1930; J. L. Stanley to Mildred Junginger, November 12, 1930; *A. M. Byers Personnel Files*, Archives of Industrial Society, University of Pittsburgh Libraries, Pittsburgh, Pennsylvania.

35. John V. Anderson, "Unemployment in Pittsburgh with Reference to the Negro," (M.A. thesis, University of Pittsburgh, 1932)," pp. 3-4.

36. Lett, "Negro Unemployed in Pittsburgh, pp. 79-80.

37. Reverend Harold R. Tolliver, interviewed by Dennis C. Dickerson, Pittsburgh, Pennsylvania, October 9, 1974.

38. William E. Leuchtenburg, *Franklin D. Roosevelt and the New Deal, 1932-1940* (New York, Harper and Row, 1963), pp. 120-126, 133-134.

39. W. D., interviewed by Gordon Mason, Sr., McKeesport, Pennsylvania, August 1974; Pittsburgh Oral History Project.

40. S. B., interviewed by Gordon Mason, Sr., McKeesport, Pennsylvania, August 1974; Pittsburgh Oral History Project.

41. Jerome Goodman, interviewed by Peter Gottleib, Pittsburgh, Pennsylvania, Summer 1974; Pittsburgh Oral History Project.

42. *Study of Consumer Purchases*, Bureau of Labor Statistics; 1-1-35 to 12-31-35, Expenditure Cards, Pennsylvania (New Castle), Record Group 257, National Archives, Washington, D.C.

43. U.S., Department of Commerce, Bureau of the Census, *Census of Partial Employment, Unemployment, and Occupations, 1937*, 3:209, 238, 243-244.

44. Burrell K. Johnson, D.D.S. to NAACP, January 5, 1934, *N.A.A.C.P. Papers*, NAACP Branch Files, Box G-183, Johnstown, Pa. File 1934; "Monthly Report of Johnstown, Pa." Branch of the NAACP, February 12, 1934; Box G-183, Johnstown, Pa. file 1934, Library of Congress, Manuscript Division, Washington, D.C.

45. Roy Wilkins, Assistant Secretary, NAACP to John Frey, Labor Advisory Board, National Recovery Administration, August 3 and 10, 1933, *John Frey Papers*, Library of Congress, Washington, D.C. (courtesy of Professor Henry W. Berger, Washington University, St. Louis, Missouri.)

46. Irving Bernstein, *Turbulent Years*, (Boston, 1971), p. 30; Cayton and Mitchell, *Black Workers and the New Unions*, pp. 95–98.

47. Raymond Wolters, "Section 7a and the Black Worker," *Labor History*, Summer 1969, pp. 460–461, 464–465, 469; Harris, *Keeping the Faith*, pp. 154–155.

48. Philip S. Foner, *Organized Labor and the Black Worker, 1619–1973*, (New York, International Publishers, 1974), pp. 204–212.

49. Bernstein, *Turbulent Years*, pp. 355–398.

50. Wolters, "Section 7a and the Black Worker," pp. 470–472.

51. Power, *Cradle of Steel Unionism*, pp. 42–44.

52. Cayton and Mitchell, *Black Workers and the New Unions*, pp. 162–163.

53. Ibid. p. 174.

54. Ibid. p. 172.

55. Ibid.

56. Laurence A. Oxley to J. Luther Thomas, July 31, 1934, *L.A. Oxley Files, Record Group 183, Correspondence Folders, Box 1395, U.S. Employment Service*, National Archives, Washington, D.C.

57. Cayton and Mitchell, *Black Workers and the New Unions*, p. 167.

58. John P. Davis to All Local Councils (of the National Negro Congress) July 10, 1936, Memorandum, *Adolph Germer Papers*, Box 3, State Historical Society of Wisconsin, Madison, Wisconsin (courtesy of Professor Henry W. Berger of Washington University, St. Louis, Missouri).

59. A. C., interviewed by Major Mason, McKeesport, Pennsylvania, July 22, 1974, Pittsburgh Oral History Project.

60. Cayton and Mitchell, *Black Workers and the New Unions*, pp. 171–172.

61. John P. Davis, "'Plan Eleven' — Jim Crow in Steel," *Crisis*, September 1936, p. 262.

62. *Union News Service*, May 10, 1937.

63. Nancy Weiss, *The National Urban League, 1910–1940* (New York, 1974), p. 283.

64. R. Maurice Moss to John T. Clark, September 15, 1934, *Papers of the Urban League of St. Louis,* Washington University Libraries, St. Louis, Missouri; John T. Clark files, Workers' Councils folder.

65. *Pittsburgh Courier,* October 10, 1936.

66. Weiss, *The National Urban League, 1910–1940,* p. 290.

67. "Statement by Philip Murray to CIO meeting, November 8, 1936," *Katherine Pollack Ellickson Papers,* microfilm edition, reel no. 1, Pennsylvania State University, University Park, Pennsylvania (courtesy of Professor Henry W. Berger of Washington University, St. Louis, Missouri).

68. Lawrence S. Wittner, "The National Negro Congress: A Reassessment," *American Quarterly,* Winter 1970, pp. 884–885.

69. Davis memorandum, July 10, 1936, *Germer Papers,* State Historical Society of Wisconsin (courtesy of Professor Henry W. Berger).

70. *Union News Service,* September 20, 1937.

71. John P. Davis to Ralph Hetzel, July 20, 1940, Hetzel memo to John P. Davis, July 29, 1940, *C.I.O. Central Office Corespondence, Alpha File,* Box 16, Catholic University, Washington, D.C.; Ralph Hetzel to John P. Davis, August 27, 1937, *C.I.O. Central Office Correspondence* (courtesy of Professor Henry W. Berger).

72. John P. Davis to John L. Lewis, August 13, 1937; John P. Davis to John L. Lewis, Memorandum, *C.I.O. Central Office Correspondence, Alpha File,* Box 16, Catholic University (courtesy of Professor Henry W. Berger).

73. Wittner, "The National Negro Congress: A Reassessment," pp. 891–893.

74. J. Ernest Wright, "The Negro in Pittsburgh," pp. 19–20; Wittner, "The National Negro Congress: A Reassessment," p. 893; William J. Walls, *The African Methodist Episcopal Zion Church: Reality of the Black Church* (Charlotte, AME Zion Publishing House, 1974), p. 262; *The Pittsburgh Courier,* July 31, 1937, *The Amalgamated Journal,* July 23, 1936.

75. *The Daily Worker,* July 21, 1936.

76. *Pittsburgh Courier,* September 4, 1954; June 4, 1960. Also see my article, "The Black Church in Industrializing Western Pennsylvania, 1870–1950," *Western Pennsylvania Historical Magazine,* October 1981, *64* (4), pp. 341–343.

77. Andrew Buni, *Robert L. Vann of the Pittsburgh Courier: Politics and Black Journalism* (Pittsburgh, University of Pittsburgh Press, 1974), p. 282.

78. *Pittsburgh Courier*, August 28, 1937.

79. Buni, *Robert L. Vann*, pp. 279–282; Harris, *Keeping the Faith*, pp. 1331–41. James Brewer discusses Vann's political behavior in "Robert L. Vann, Democrat or Republican: An Exponent of Loose-Leaf Politics," *Negro History Bulletin*, XXI, February 1958, pp. 100–103.

80. "Homer S. Brown" in *Who's Who Among Black Americans, 1975–1976*, (Northbrook, Illinois, Who's Who Among Black Americans, Inc., Publishing Company, 1976), pp. 72–73; *Pittsburgh Courier*, January 28, 1933; Homer S. Brown to Walter White, September 6, 1933, *N.A.A.C.P. Papers*, NAACP Branch files, Pittsburgh, Pa. September 1933, Box G–191; Buni, *Robert L. Vann*, pp. 213–214.

81. *Pittsburgh Sun Telegraph*, April 29, 1937, May 27, 1937; *Pittsburgh Press*, May 12, 1937; *Pittsburgh Post Gazette*, May 12, 1937; newspaper clippings in the *Homer S. Brown Papers*, Volume 2, Archives of Industrial Society, University of Pittsburgh Libraries, Pittsburgh, Pennsylvania. "Paul Normile," in *Beaver Valley Labor History*, December 1980, 2 (3), p. 1; Buni, *Robert L. Vann*, p. 145; *Minutes of the Forty-Third Annual Meeting, Grand Lodge, I.B.P.O.E.W.*, Philadelphia, Pa., August 23, 29, 1942, pp. 160–164.

82. August Meier and Elliott Rudwick, *Black Detroit and the Rise of the U.A.W.*, (New York, Oxford University Press, 1979), pp. 5–6, 18–21.

83. Philip Bonosky, "The Story of Ben Careathers," *Masses and Mainstream*, July 1953, p. 34.

84. Linda Nyden, "The History of the Steel and Metal Workers Industrial Union," (seminar paper, History Department, University of Pittsburgh, December 1973), p. 3; "Ernest Rice McKinney," Columbia University Oral History Collection, Part II, Microfiche No. 123.

85. Bonosky, "The Story of Ben Careathers," pp. 34, 39; Nyden, "The History of the Steel and Metal Workers Industrial Union," p. 6; Allen interview.

86. McKinney interview, Columbia Oral History Collection.

87. Nell Irvin Painter, *The Narrative of Hosea Hudson: His Life as a Negro Communist in the South*, (Cambridge, Harvard University Press, 1979), pp. 13–14, 85. Hosea Hudson, *Black Worker in the Deep South*, (New York, International Publishers, 1972), pp. 65–79, Bartow Tipper,

interviewed by Dennis C. Dickerson, Aliquippa, Pennsylvania, March 4, 1980.

88. Ira De Augustine Reid, *Negro Membership in American Labor Unions*, 1930, National Urban League, Department of Research and Investigations (New York, Negro Universities Press, Reprint 1969), pp. 138–139; Harris, *Keeping the Faith*, p. 227.

89. Reid, *Negro Membership*, p. 70; Foner, *Organized Labor*, pp. 194–195.

90. *Steel Labor*, December 1970; Allen interview, Carl O. Dickerson interviewed by Dennis C. Dickerson, Philadelphia, Pennsylvania, October 5, 1975. Lucious Corley, interviewed by Dennis C. Dickerson, Monessen, Pennsylvania, September 4, 1975.

91. Romare Bearden, "The Negro in 'Little Steel,'" *Opportunity*, December 1937, p. 364.

92. T. H., interviewed by Major Mason, McKeesport, Pennsylvania, August 1974; Pittsburgh Oral History Project.

93. Reverend J. L. Simmons, interviewed by Peter Gottleib, Pittsburgh, Pennsylvania, June 13, 1974; Pittsburgh Oral History Project.

94. Roger Payne, interviewed by Dennis C. Dickerson, Philadelphia, Pennsylvania, April 12, 1976.

95. *Pittsburgh Courier*, June 11, 1960, Tipper interview.

96. Payne interview.

97. McKinney interview, Columbia Oral History Collection.

98. Edward Raby, interviewed by Dennis C. Dickerson, Philadelphia, Pennsylvania, April 1, 1976.

99. Davis Memorandum, July 10, 1936, *Germer Papers*, State Historical Society of Wisconsin (courtesy of Professor Henry W. Berger).

100. *Pittsburgh Courier*, July 31, 1937.

101. *Clairton Progress*, January 11, 1937; H.G., interviewed by Peter Gottlieb, Pittsburgh, Pennsylvania, August 28, 1974, Pittsburgh Oral History Project.

102. *Pittsburgh Courier*, July 31, 1937; *Clairton Progress*, January 11, 1937; January 22, 1937.

103. *Pittsburgh Courier*, July 24, 1937.

104. Powers, *Cradle of Steel Unionism*, pp. 64–65, 96–97.

105. Tipper interview.

106. *1557 Labor Journal*, November 1967.

107. Alvin Nunley to Franklin D. Roosevelt, January 28, 1938, *L.A. Oxley Files, Record Group 183, Box 1388, Pennsylvania folder, U.S. Employment Service*, National Archives, Washington, D.C.

## Chapter 7

1. An important study of Black Americans during World War II is Neil A. Wynn's *The Afro-American and the Second World War* (New York, 1975). Another one is A. Russell Buchanan, *Black Americans in World War II* (Santa Barbara, California, Clio Books, 1977). Other studies on Blacks and the World War II period are Rayford W. Logan, ed., *What the Negro Wants* (Chapel Hill, 1944), Herbert Garfinkel, *When Negroes March* (New York, 1959), and Harvard Sitkoff, "Racial Militancy and Interracial Violence in the Second World War," *Journal of American History*, December 1971, pp. 661–681.

2. William See, interviewed by Dennis C. Dickerson, Glen Hazel, Pennsylvania, April 22, 1975; Ashton Allen, interviewed by Dennis C. Dickerson, Homestead, Pennsylvania, September 6, 1975; Edward Lipscomb, interviewed by Dennis C. Dickerson, Duquesne, Pennsylvania, September 8, 1975.

3. George E. DeMar, "Pittsburgh's Potential Labor Supply," *Opportunity*, January 1942, pp. 18–19; James Wilson, interviewed by Dennis C. Dickerson, West Mifflin, Pennsylvania, April 23, 1975.

4. Calvin Ingram, interviewed by Dennis C. Dickerson, Duquesne, Pennsylvania, September 8, 1975.

5. DeMar, "Pittsburgh's Potential Labor Supply," pp. 18–19.

6. "Additional Information on the Carnegie-Illinois Steel Company, Farrell, Pittsburgh," *War Manpower Commission Records, Bureau of Placement, Division of Industrial Allocation, Carnegie-Illinois File*, Box 1470, National Archives, Washington, D.C., (hereafter N.A.).

7. Bert Hough to Harold Ruttenberg, January 28, 1943, *Harold Ruttenberg Collection, War Production Board Correspondence, Statistics, and Press Releases*, Box 7, Labor Archives, Pennsylvania State University,

University Park, Pennsylvania. Harold Ruttenberg had been an official in the CIO, but became Assistant to the Director of the Steel Division of the War Production Board of the federal government after the outbreak of World War II.

8. Telegram: Patrick J. Fagan to War Manpower Commission, March 2, 1945 (?), Steel Plants File, *War Manpower Commission Records, Bureau of Placement, Industrial Allocation Division*, Box 1471, N.A.

9. DeMar, "Pittsburgh's Potential Labor Supply," pp. 18–19.

10. Charles S. Johnson, Director, *Allegheny County Race Relations Survey, 1946, Archives of Industrial Society*, University of Pittsburgh Libraries, Folder H., p. 1.

11. *Pittsburgh Courier*, July 17, 1926; July 24, 1937; *Clairton Progress*, June 11, 1937.

12. *Pittsburgh Courier*, July 24, 1937. Andrew Buni, *Robert L. Vann of the Pittsburgh Courier: Politics and Black Journalism* (Pittsburgh, 1974), p. 218. This bill was introduced by a Black legislator from Philadelphia, Hobson R. Reynolds. However, the equal rights bill was unevenly observed and rarely enforced. Buni, p. 219.

13. Paul L. (Red) Payne, interviewed by Dennis C. Dickerson, Clairton, Pennsylvania, September 1975; *Clairton Progress*, July 21, 1939; August 4, 1939.

14. *Allegheny County Race Relations Survey*, pp. 1, 32; *The Braddock Steelworker*, United Steelworkers of America (Pittsburgh, 1945), p. 38.

15. U.S., Department of Commerce, Bureau of the Census, *Sixteenth Census of the United States, 1940: Housing, Part 4*, 2:860,899; U.S., Department of Commerce, Bureau of the Census, *Seventeenth Census of the United States, 1950, Part 5*, 1:38–19, 38–20, 38–24.

16. Harold Ruttenberg to H. G. Batcheller, Director of Steel Division, W.P.B., January 25, 1943; *Harold Ruttenberg Collection, War Production Board, Correspondence, Statistics, and Press Releases*, Box 7, Labor Archives, Pennsylvania State University, University Park, Pennsylvania.

17. M. W. Reid to Edwin Brown, January 14, 1943; *Ruttenberg Collection*, Box 7, Pennsylvania State University, University Park, Pennsylvania; *Homestead Messenger*, February 3, 1942.

18. *Homestead Messenger*, January 26, 1942; February 3, 1942.

19. Reid to Brown, January 14, 1943; *Ruttenberg Collection*.

20. *Duquesne Times*, August 15, 1941.

21. Florence Murray, ed., *The Negro Handbook*, 1946–1947 (New York, 1947), pp. 195–196.

22. *Homestead Messenger,* February 5, 1942.

23. James Wilson, interviewed by Dennis C. Dickerson, West Mifflin, Pennsylvania, April 23, 1975.

24. Ingram interview.

25. Murray ed., *The Negro Handbook*, pp. 195–196.

26. *Duquesne Times*, August 15, 1941.

27. Bryn Hovde, "Negro Housing in Pittsburgh," *Opportunity,* October–December 1945, pp. 213–215.

28. Murray, ed., *The Negro Handbook*, p. 196.

29. "Additional Information on the Carnegie–Illinois Steel Company, Farrell, Pennsylvania," Carnegie–Illinois File, *War Manpower Commission Records, Bureau of Placement, Division of Industrial Allocation,* Box 1070, N.A.

30. Murray, ed., *The Negro Handbook*, pp. 195–196.

31. Federal Security Administration, "Minutes of Meeting between the Urban League of Pittsburgh and War Production Board," *Records of the Fair Employment Practices Committee, Regional Files, Region III, Active Cases, Unarranged, Clairton, Pennsylvania, File,* Box 598, N.A.

32. *Allegheny County Race Relations Survey,* p. 31.

33. Untitled Report, p. 3, in the *Homer S. Brown Papers,* Volume 16, Archives of Industrial Society, University of Pittsburgh Libraries, Pittsburgh, Pennsylvania.

34. *Allegheny County Race Relations Survey,* p. 23.

35. George E. DeMar to Robert C. Weaver, September 15, 1942, *F.E.P.C. Records, Regional Files, Region III, Closed Cases,* N.A.

36. *Allegheny County Race Relations Survey,* p. 28.

37. G. James Fleming to Will Maslow, August 24, 1944, *F.E.P.C. Records, Regional Files, Region III,* Box 596, N.A.

38. Mackintosh and Hemphill Company File, *F.E.P.C. Records, Regional Files, Region III,* Box 598, N.A.

39. J. Burrell Reid, interviewed by Dennis C. Dickerson, Pittsburgh, Pennsylvania, September 6, 1975.

40. George M. Johnson to Reginald A. Johnson, March 31, 1945; *Jones & Laughlin Steel Company File, F.E.P.C. Records, Regional Files, Region III*, Box 597, N.A.

41. Joseph Krivan to Reginald A. Johnson, February 22, 1943, *J. & L. File, F.E.P.C. Records*, Box 597, N.A.

42. M. A. Manly to G. James Fleming, March 13, 1944, *F.E.P.C. Records, Region III*, Box 600, N.A.

43. U.S., Department of Commerce; Bureau of the Census, *Sixteenth Census of the United States, 1940: Population, Characteristics of the Population*, Vol. II, Part 6: Pennsylvania-Texas, 2:266.

44. U.S., Department of Commerce; Bureau of the Census, *Sixteenth Census of the United States, 1940: Population, The Labor Force*, Vol. III, Part 5: Pennsylvania-Wyoming, 3:58.

45. "Negro Women War Workers," *Bulletin No. 205, Women's Bureau, U.S. Department of Labor, 1945*, p. 5.

46. Frances Stanton to Franklin D. Roosevelt, April 5, 1943, *Carnegie-Illinois File, F.E.P.C. Records, Regional Files, Region III*, N.A.

47. Mrs. William J. Scott to Franklin D. Roosevelt, April 22, 1944, *F.E.P.C. Records*, Box 610, N.A.

48. Ruth L. Boyd et al., to Franklin D. Roosevelt, July 16, 1943, *F.E.P.C.* Records, Box 610, N.A.

49. *National Malleable and Steel Casting Company File, F.E.P.C. Records, Region III*, Box 612 N.A.

50. Louis C. Kesselman, *The Social Politics of F.E.P.C.*, (Chapel Hill, University of North Carolina Press, 1948), pp. 15, 22.

51. Although government documents give little information on the number of Black women employed in the area steel mills, when they are mentioned, their numbers are small. At the Carnegie-Illinois plant in Farrell, about 30 Black women were employed. *Carnegie#Illinois File, F.E.P.C. Records, Region III*, Box 604. Information of this sort is sparse for other steel plants.

52. George E. DeMar, "Negro Women are American Workers, Too," *Opportunity*, April 1943, p. 77; Nola Lindsay, interviewed by Dennis C. Dickerson, Duquesne, Pennsylvania, September 4, 1975.

53. Simon Baker, interviewed by Dennis C. Dickerson, Donora, Pennsylvania, March 6, 1980.

54. Ethel M. Cotton File, *F.E.P.C. Records, Region III*, Box 599, N.A.

55. *Farrell & Sharon, Pennsylvania File; F.E.P.C. Records, Region III,* Box 599, N.A.

56. George E. DeMar to R. J. Greenly, May 4, 1943, *F.E.P.C. Records, Region III,* Box 604, N.A.

57. *Farrell & Sharon, Pennsylvania File, F.E.P.C. Records, Region III,* Box 599, N.A.

58. L. B. F. Raycoft to Reginald A. Johnson, April 8, 1943, *F.E.P.C. Records, Region III,* Box 597, N.A. A Copy of the telegraph was contained in this correspondence.

59. Ruth Ormes Dickerson File, *F.E.P.C. Records, Region III,* Box 599, N.A.

60. Wynn, *The Afro-American,* pp. 60–78; Sitkoff, "Racial Militancy and Interracial Violence," pp. 661–681; Sitkoff, "The Detroit Race Riot of 1943," *Michigan History,* Fall 1969, pp. 183–206. Also see Dominic Capeci, Jr., *The Harlem Riot of 1943* (Philadelphia, Temple University Press, 1977).

61. *New York Times,* July 18, 1943.

62. *Minutes of the Forty–Fourth Annual Meeting, Grand Lodge, Improved Benevolent and Protective Order of Elks of the World,* convened in Central Baptist Church, Pittsburgh, Pennsylvania, August 22–27, 1943, pp. 139, 147, 280–282.

63. *First Report, Fair Employment Practice Committee, July 1943– December 1944* (Washington, D.C., 1945), p. 80.

64. Milo A. Manly to G. James Fleming, May 20, 1944; *Reports on Pittsburgh Area Field Trips, F.E.P.C. Records, Region III,* Box 600, N.A.

65. *First Report,* pp. 81–82; Milo A. Manly to G. James Fleming, March 7, 1944; *F.E.P.C. Records, Region III, Carnegie–Illinois File,* Box 604, N.A.

66. Milo A. Manly to G. James Fleming, October 13, 1944; Manly to James, October 16, 1944; *F.E.P.C. Records, Region III, Clairton, Pennsylvania File,* Box 598, N.A.

67. *First Report,* p. 82.

68. Milo A. Manly to G. James Fleming, December 28, 1944, "Reports on Pittsburgh Area Field Trips," *F.E.P.C. Records, Region III,* Box 600, N.A.

292 NOTES

69. Milo A. Manly to Will Maslow, April 28, 1945, *J. & L. Boiler Firemen, Water Tenders and Stokers File, F.E.P.C., Region III*, Box 599, N.A.

70. G. James Fleming to Eugene Davidson, May 31, 1945, *J. & L. Ovens Dept. South Side (Hazelwood) Pittsburgh Works File, F.E.P.C. Records, Region III*, Box 599, N.A.

71. *Daily Proceedings of the Fifth Constitutional Convention of the Congress of Industrial Organizations*, November 9–13, 1942, Boston, Massachusetts, p. 172.

72. *C.I.O. News*, August 24, 1942.

73. *Daily Proceedings*, p. 160.

74. Boyd L. Wilson, interviewed by Dennis Brunn and Dennis C. Dickerson, St. Louis, Missouri, March 28, 1974.

75. Boyd L. Wilson, interviewed by John G. Spiese, October 23, 1967, United Steelworkers of America, Oral History Project, Pennsylvania State University, Labor Archives, University Park, Pennsylvania.

76. Milo Manly to G. James Fleming, October 13, 1944 *F.E.P.C. Records, Region III, Pennsylvania, File*, Box 598, N.A.

77. Meeting: Federal Security Agency, Urban League of Pittsburgh, and War Production Board, November 27, 1944; *F.E.P.C. Records, Region III, Pennsylvania File*, Box 598, N.A.

78. Roger Payne, interviewed by Dennis C. Dickerson, Philadelphia, Pennsylvania, April 12, 1976.

79. *1557 Labor Journal*, Clairton, Pennsylvania, December 15, 1962.

80. Joseph Krivan to Reginald A. Johnson, February 22, 1943, *F.E.P.C. Records, Region III, J. & L. File*, Box 597, N.A.

81. Viola Twyman to G. James Fleming, March 11, 1944, *F.E.P.C. Records, Region III, Mackintosh–Hemphill File*, Box 611, N.A.

82. James McCoy, interviewed by Mark B. Lapping, Pittsburgh, Pennsylvania, November 7, 1968; *U.S.W.A. Oral History Project*, Labor Archives, Pennsylvania State University.

83. Harold J. Ruttenberg to John A. Fitch, January 5, 1943, *Ruttenberg Collection*, Box 7, Pennsylvania State University.

84. Thomas Augustine, "The Negro Steelworkers of Pittsburgh and the Unions," (M.A. thesis, University of Pittsburgh, 1948), pp. 36–37.

85. *Pittsburgh Courier*, May 30, 1942.

86. *Crucible Steel Company of America File, F.E.P.C. Records, Region III*, Box 598, N.A.

87. G. James Fleming to Will Maslow, June 22, 1944, *Carnegie-Illinois Steel Corporation File, F.E.P.C. Records, Region III*, Box 604, N.A.

88. George M. Johnson to American Steel Band Company, September 26, 1942; George M. Johston to Joseph Bowman, February 11, 1943; George M. Johnson, to John Brophy, January 8, 1942; American Steel Band File, *F.E.P.C. Records, Region III, Closed Cases*, Boxes 601, 604, 606, 612, N.A.

89. Benjamin Thomas Frezzell, interviewed by Dennis C. Dickerson, Monessen, Pennsylvania, March 6, 1980.

90. Walter White to Daisy Lampkin, September 8, 1934, *N.A.A.C.P. Branch Files*, McKeesport, Pa. file, Box G–183, Series G., *N.A.A.C.P. Papers*, Library of Congress, Manuscript Division, Washington, D.C.; Monongahela (Valley), Pa., 1925–1939 file, Application for Charter, *N.A.A.C.P. Branch Files*, Box G–184; William Pickens to Matthew L. Dempsey, January 3, 1939, *N.A.A.C.P. Branch Files*, Box G–177, Series G, Aliquippa, Pa., 1936–1939 file; Application for Charter, *N.A.A.C.P. Branch Files*, Aliquippa, Pa., 1936–1939 file, Box G–177.

91. Kesselman, *The Social Politics of F.E.P.C.*, pp. 13–15, 22; William H. Harris, *The Harder We Run* (New York, Oxford University Press, 1982), pp. 117–118.

92. *First Report*, pp. 8, 11.

93. "G. James Fleming," *Who's Who Among Black Americans, 1980–1981*, 3rd edition (Northbrook, Illinois, Who's Who Among Black Americans, Inc., Publishing Company, 1981), p. 260.

94. M. A. Manly to Will Maslow, April 28, 1945, *Roger Williams File, F.E.P.C. Records, Region III*, Box 600, N.A.

95. M. A. Manly to Will Maslow, March 29, 1945; *John A. Anderson File, F.E.P.C. Records, Region III*, Box 599, N.A.

96. G. James Fleming to Frank L. McNamee, August 8, 1944, *F.E.P.C. Records, Region III*, Box 610, N.A.

97. M. A. Manly to G. James Fleming, June 8, 1944, *F.E.P.C. Records, Region III*, Box 600, N.A.

98. G. James Fleming to James E. Matthews (1944), *F.E.P.C. Records, Region III*, Box 598, N.A.

99. M. A. Manly to G. James Fleming, February 18, 1944, F.E.P.C. *Records, Region III,* Box 600, N.A.

100. M. A. Manly to G. James Fleming, March 13, 1944, F.E.P.C. *Records, Region III,* Box 600, N.A.

101. G. James Fleming to Will Maslow, December 29, 1944, F.E.P.C. *Records, Region III,* Box 600, N.A.

102. *New Jersey Afro-American,* February 17, 1945; Milo A. Manly to Mrs. Homer Brown, February 19, 1945, *Homer S. Brown Papers,* Vol. 10, University of Pittsburgh Libraries, Archives of Industrial Society, Pittsburgh, PA.

103. John E. Peoples et al., to Director of War Mobilization and Reconversion, February 12, 1945; Mae Patterson to F.E.P.C., May 9, 1945; Karyl Keen Klinger to Mae Patterson, June 16, 1945; F.E.P.C. *Records, Region III,* Box 600, N.A.

104. See Kesselman, *The Social Politics of F.E.P.C.,* pp. 15–24, 166–177, 222–228; also see Louis Ruchames, *Race, Jobs and Politics: The Story of F.E.P.C.,* (New York, 1953). The FEPC also played an important role in improving the economic conditions of Black workers in other parts of the nation. Recent scholarly studies on Black auto workers in Detroit and Black shipyard laborers in some western states illustrate this point. See August Meier and Elliott Rudwick, *Black Detroit and the Rise of the U.A.W.,* (New York, Oxford University Press, 1979), pp. 156–174, and William H. Harris, "Federal Intervention in Union Discrimination: F.E.P.C. and West Coast Shipyards During World War II." *Labor History,* Summer 1981, 22 (3), pp. 325–347.

105. Barton J. Bernstein, "The Ambiguous Legacy: The Truman Administration and Civil Rights" in Barton J. Bernstein, editor, *Politics and Policies of the Truman Administration* (Chicago, Quadrangle Books, 1972), pp. 274–275; William C. Berman, *The Politics of Civil Rights in the Truman Administration* (Ohio State University, 1970), pp. 24–29.

106. "Does State F.E.P.C. Hamper You?" *Business Week,* February 25, 1950, pp. 114–116.

107. *New Jersey Afro-American,* February 15, 1947.

108. Newspaper clippings, *Homer S. Brown Papers,* Volumes 8, 9, & 10.

109. "Robert C. Weaver," Who's Who Among Black Americans, 1975–1976 Vol. I, (Northbrook, Illinois, 1976), p. 655. Weaver held several positions in the Roosevelt Administration including Advisor on Negro Affairs in the Department of Interior and Consultant in the

Housing Division of the Public Works Administration, 1933–1938, Special Assistant to the Administrator of the U.S. Housing Authority, 1938–1940, and Director of the Negro Employment Service of the War Manpower Commission 1942–1944. Also see Alma R. Williams, "In Spite of His Race: Robert C. Weaver, Black Administrator in Turbulent Times," (Ph.D. dissertation, Washington University, 1978).

110. DeMar to Weaver, September 15, 1942, *F.E.P.C. Records, Regional Files Region III, Closed Cases,* N.A.

111. Robert C. Weaver, *Negro Labor: A National Problem* (New York, 1946), p. 300.

112. *Pittsburgh Courier,* August 25, 1945.

113. "Labor Market Conditions in Selected Areas Following Japanese Surrender (as of August 31, 1945)," p. 10, *Labor Market File, War Manpower Commission, Bureau of Placement, Industrial Allocation Division,* Box 1487, N.A.

114. *Pittsburgh Courier,* August 25, 1945.

115. Richard L. Rowan, *The Negro in the Steel Industry* (Philadelphia, University of Pennsylvania, 1970), p. 279.

116. Weaver, *Negro Labor: A National Problem* pp. 268–300.

117. Vincent D. Sweeney, *The United Steelworkers of America: The First Ten Years* (Pittsburgh, 1946), pp. 62–65. Steel producers agreed to a wage increase of 18.5 cents. In return for this concession of the Office of Price Administration authorized price increases of $5 for each ton of steel. Barton J. Bernstein, "The Truman Administration and the Steel Strike of 1946," *Journal of American History,* March 1966, p. 800.

118. *Pittsburgh Courier,* January 26, 1946.

119. Ibid.

120. *Pittsburgh Courier,* February 9, 1946.

121. *New Jersey Afro-American* May 25, 1946.

122. *Allegheny County Race Relations Survey,* p. 28.

123. U.S., Department of Commerce, Bureau of the Census, *Census of Population: 1950, Characteristics of the Population, Part 38, Pennsylvania,* 2:38–370, 38–373.

124. Augustine, "The Negro Steelworkers of Pittsburgh and the Unions," p. 41.

125. John Hughey, interviewed by Dennis C. Dickerson, Rankin, Pennsylvania, September 8, 1975.

126. Newspaper clipping, *Homer S. Brown Papers*, Volume 12, University of Pittsburgh Libraries; Anne M. Barton and Margaret Staudenmaier, "Ethnic and Racial Groups in Rankin, Pennsylvania (A Study of Relationships Between Them as Expressed Through Various Social Forces)," (M. S. W. thesis, University of Pittsburgh, 1947). pp. 68–69, *Allegheny County Race Relations Survey*, p. 27.

127. Wilson interview, USWA Oral History Project, Pennsylvania State University, University Park, Pennsylvania.

## Chapter 8

1. Harvard Sitkoff, "Harry Truman and the Election of 1948: The Coming of Age of Civil Rights in American Politics," *Journal of Southern History*, 37, (4) November 1971, pp. 597–616.

2. Jesse Thomas Moore, Jr., *A Search for Equality, The National Urban League, 1910–1961* (University Park, Pennsylvania State University Press, 1981), pp. 135–136.

3. Moore, *A Search for Equality*, (pp. 169, 172–175; *Balance Sheet: A Newsletter from the Urban League of Pittsburgh*, January–February 1953, p. 1, in the *National Urban League Records*, Series I, Box 120, Administrative Department, Affiliates File, Pittsburgh, Pennsylvania folder, 1951–1953, Library of Congress, Manuscript Division, Washington, D.C.; *Pittsburgh Courier*, January 16, 1954.

4. *Pittsburgh Courier*, February 27, 1954, September 4, 1954.

5. *Pittsburgh Courier*, October 18, 1952, June 16, 1956.

6. U.S. Department of Commerce, Bureau of the Census, 1960, *Census of Population*, Vol. I, *Characteristics of the Population*, Part 40, Pennsylvania: 40-743-744, 752-753, 925, 953, 955.

7. Bartow Tipper, interviewd by Dennis C. Dickerson, Aliquippa, Pennsylvania, March 4, 1980.

8. Daniel Brooks, interviewed by Dennis C. Dickerson, Pittsburgh, Pennsylvania, March 3, 1980.

9. Milton Croom, interviewed by Dennis C. Dickerson, Clairton, Pennsylvania, March 6, 1980; Felix Guilford, interviewed by Dennis C. Dickerson, Beaver Falls, Pennsylvania, March 5, 1980.

10. *Pittsburgh Courier,* January 24, 1953, July 18, 1953, May 22, 1954; Louis Mason to R. Maurice Moss, January 13, 1950, Pittsburgh, Pa. folder #1, Series I, Box 119, Administrative Department, Affiliated File, *National Urban League Records,* Manuscript Division, Library of Congress, Washington, D.C.

11. *Pittsburgh Courier,* January 24, 1953; July 4, 1956; September 29, 1956; Lloyd Ulman, *The Government of the Steel Workers' Union* (New York, John Wiley and Sons, Inc. 1962), p. 178.

12. *Pittsburgh Courier,* April 21, 1956; May 5, 1956; May 26, 1956; June 16, 1956; May 31, 1958, January 9, 1960.

13. Francis Shane to John F. Murray, January 14, 1953, File 4, Box 5, *U.S.W.A., Civil Rights Department,* Labor Archives, Pattee Library, Pennsylvania State University, University Park, Pennsylvania; Francis Shane to William J. Hart, May 19, 1953, File 22, Box 5, *U.S.W.A., Civil Rights Department,* Labor Archives, Penn State; *Sixth Annual Monessen Brotherhood Meeting,* Program, February 22, 1953, File 23, Box 6, Civil Rights Department, Labor Archives, Penn State; *Pittsburgh Courier,* January 24, 1953; June 11, 1960; June 18, 1960.

14. Monthly Activities Report, November 10, 1954; p. 4; Industrial Relations Department, Urban League of Pittsburgh, *Richard S. Dowdy Papers,* Private Collection, Hamden, Connecticut.

15. Letter to Thomas Shane, March 10, 1950, *U.S.W.A., Civil Rights Department,* File 12, U.S.A. Survey, February–April 1950, Box 4, 1951, Labor Archives, Penn State.

16. Ibid.

17. G.K. to Thomas Shane, March 22, 1950; *U.S.W.A., Civil Rights Department,* U.S.A. Survey.

18. H. P. to Thomas Shane, February 27, 1950; H. M. to Thomas Shane, February 27, 1950; *U.S.W.A. Civil Rights Department,* U.S.A. Survey.

19. L. L. to Thomas Shane, March 8, 1950; M. C. to Thomas Shane, March 11, 1950; *U.S.W.A. Civil Rights Department,* U.S.A. Survey.

20. J. V. to Thomas Shane, March 15, 1950; *U.S.W.A. Civil Rights Department,* U.S.A. Survey.

21. W. S. to Thomas Shane, March 10, 1950; *U.S.W.A. Civil Rights Department,* U.S.A. Survey.

22. W. G. to Thomas Shane, March 14, 1950; *U.S.W.A. Civil Rights Department,* U.S.A. Survey.

23. Letter from S. C., February 28, 1950; *U.S.W.A. Civil Rights Department*, U.S.A. Survey.

24. H. D. to Thomas Shane, March 8, 1950; *U.S.W.A. Civil Rights Department*, U.S.A. Survey.

25. *Pittsburgh Courier*, June 27, 1953, February 19, 1955.

26. William Kornhauser, "The Negro Union Official: A Study of Sponsorship and Control," reprinted in John Bracey, Jr., August Meier, and Elliott Rudwick, editors, *Black Workers and Organized Labor* (Belmont, California, Wadsworth Publishing Company, Inc., 1971), p. 195; *Pittsburgh Courier, June 18, 1960*.

27. *Pittsburgh Courier*, July 2, 1949; September 13, 1952.

28. Julius A. Thomas to Boyd Wilson, October 17, 1946; Leroy W. Jeffries to Boyd Wilson, October 16, 1947; Boyd Wilson to Julius A. Thomas, October 25, 1946; Julius A. Thomas to Boyd Wilson, December 2, 1947; *National Urban League Records*, General Department File, Industrial Relations Department, United Steelworkers of America folder, 1943–1948, Series IV, Box 19, Library of Congress.

29. Mason to Moss, January 13, 1950.

30. Montly Activities Report, Urban League of Pittsburgh, June 10, 1952, Industrial Relations, *N.U.L. Records*, Pittsburgh, Pa. folder 1951–53, Series I, Box 120, Administrative Department, Affiliates File, Library of Congress; Bi-Monthly Summary of Activities, Industrial Relations Department, Urban League of Pittsburgh, July–August 1957, p. 3, *Richard S. Dowdy Papers*, private collection, Hamden, Connecticut.

31. Montly Activities Report, June 10, 1954, p. 1; Bi-Monthly Activities Report, January–February 1959, pp. 9–10; Monthly Activities Report, September 1955; p. 1; Monthly Activities Report, September 1956; p. 1; *Dowdy Papers*.

32. *Pittsburgh Courier*, November 14, 1953, *Steel Labor*, September 1966.

33. James H. Hill to Philip Murray, October 21, 1951; James H. Hill to Lester Granger, February 16, 1952; *National Urban League Records*, General Department File, Industrial Relations Department, Series IV, Box 19, USWA 1949–1961 folder, Library of Congress; Boyd L. Wilson, interviewed by John G. Spiese, October 23, 1967, United Steelworkers of America, Oral History Projects, Pennsylvania State University, pp. 12–13.

34. Newspaper clippings concerning Benjamin Cashaw, *N.U.L. Records*, Industrial Relations Department, General Dept. File, Series IV, Box 19, USWA folder, 1943–1948, Library of Congress.

35. Ibid.

36. Ibid.

37. Ibid.

38. Ibid.

39. *Pittsburgh Courier*, September 4, 1954; July 23, 1955, June 18, 1960.

40. *Pittsburgh Courier*, September 4, 1954; June 11, 1960.

41. Mrs. Mabel Jackson, interviewed by Dennis C. Dickerson (telephone), Pittsburgh, Pennsylvania, August 19, 1980; *Steel Labor*, August 1970. Milford Peter "Pete" Jackson died on October 28, 1970.

42. Monthly Activities Report, July 10, 1954, pp. 7–8, *Dowdy Papers*; *Pittsburgh Courier*, January 26, 1957.

43. *Pittsburgh Courier*, June 18, 1960.

44. Alexander J. Allen, Jr., interviewed by Dennis C. Dickerson, New York, New York, April 30, 1980.

45. Allen interview; Richard R. Wright, Jr., ed., *Encyclopedia of African Methodism*, (Philadelphia, Book Concern of the A.M.E. Church, 1947), pp. 27–28; Richard R. Wright, Jr., *The Bishops of the A.M.E. Church*, (Nashville, AME Sunday School Union, 1963), pp. 41–45.

46. *Pittsburgh Courier*, September 4, 1954; Alexander J. Allen to Lester B. Granger, September 30, 1953; Alexander J. Allen to Lester B. Granger, October 8, 1953; Pittsburgh, Pa. folder 1951–1953; Admin. Dept., Affiliates File, 1 Series I, Box 120, *N.U.L. Records*, Library of Congress.

47. 39th Annual Meeting and Luncheon, Urban League of Pittsburgh, October 9, 1957; Pittsburgh Branch, Urban League folder, Admin. Dept., Affiliates File, Series I, Box 121, *N.U.L. Records*, Library of Congress; Allen interview; "To Help a Child" (The Urban League of Pittsburgh), Pgh. Pa. folder 1958, Admin. Dept. Affiliates Files, Series I, Box 121 *N.U.L. Records*; Monthly Activities Report, Urban League of Pittsburgh, June–August 1951; *N.U.L. Records*, Series I, Box 120, Pgh. Pa. folder, 1951–1953; *Balance Sheet, A Newsletter from the Urban League of Pittsburgh*, May–June 1953, p. 1, *N.U.L. Records*, Series I, Box 120, Pgh. Pa. folder, 1951–1953, Library of Congress.

48. Gordon H. Barrie, Ohio Township, Pittsburgh, Pennsylvania to Dennis C. Dickerson, May 28, 1980; Allen interview; Alexander J. Allen to R. Maurice Moss, January 3, 1953, Admin. Dept. Affiliates File, Pgh. Pa. folder, 1951–1953, Series I, Box 120, *N.U.L. Records*; Alexander J. Allen to the Executive Board, Memo, November 17, 1950; Pgh., Pa. folder 1951–1953, *N.U.L. Records*, Series I, Box 119, Library of Congress.

49. Monthly Activities Report, Urban League of Pittsburgh, January 1952; Pgh. Pa. folder, 1951–1953, Series I, Box 120; Louis Mason, Jr. to Lester B. Granger, August 24, 1950; Pgh. Pa. folder 3; Series I, Box 119; Annual Report of the Urban League of Pittsburgh for 1952, Series XIII, Box 22, *N.U.L. Records*, Library of Congress.

50. *Time*, September 14, 1953, p. 25; Resume 1980, Richard S. Dowdy, Jr.

51. Moore, *A Search for Equality*, p. 136; "Bi-Monthly Summary of Activities, May–June 1957; *Dowdy Papers*, p. 7.

52. Monthly Activities Report, July–August 1955, pp. 6–7, *Dowdy Papers*.

53. Monthly Activities Report, April 8, 1954, Richard A. Dowdy, Jr.; Pittsburgh, Pa. folder, 1954; p. 5; Monthly Activities Report, April 1956, p. 5; *Dowdy Papers*; Field Report, Urban League of Pittsburgh, March 4, 1954; Series I, Box 120, *N.U.L. Records*,, Library of Congress; Monthly Activities Report, September 1955; p. 4, *Dowdy Papers*.

54. Moore, *A Search for Equality*, pp. 145–146; *Newsweek*, September 12, 1955, pp. 86–88; Tentative Program Prospectus May–December 1950, Pgh. Pa folder 2, 1950, Series I, Box 119, *N.U.L. Records*; Louis Mason, Jr. to R. Maurice Moss, April 4, 1950; Pgh. Pa folder 2, Series I, Box 119, *N.U.L. Records* Library of Congress.

55. Monthly Activities Report, May 10, 1954, pp 4–5; Monthly Activities Report, January 1956, p. 3; *Dowdy Papers*.

56. Monthly Activities Report, February 10, 1954; p. 4; Monthly Activites Report, March 10, 1954; pp. 3–4; *Dowdy Papers*.

57. Monthly Activities Report, February 10, 1954; p. 4; Monthly Activities Report, June 1956, pp. 4–5; Monthly Activities Report, October 1955; p. 5; *Dowdy Papers*.

58. *Newsweek*, September 12, 1955, p. 85; Summary Report, Pittsburgh Field Assignment, Julius A. Thomas, Director of Industrial Relations, National Urban League, December 1–3, 1954; Pgh. Pa. folder, 1954, *N.U.L. Records*, Series I, Box 120, Library of Congress, pp. 6–7, 9.

59. Memorandum, Richard S. Dowdy, Jr. to Julius A. Thomas, February 7, 1957; Corporate Contacts, pp. 2–5; *Dowdy Papers*.

60. Ibid., p. 2; "Field Report" . . . March 4, 1954, pp. 2–3; *N.U.L. Records*.

61. "Field Report" . . . March 4, 1954, p. 3; *N.U.L. Records*.

62. "Field Report" . . . March 4, 1954, p. 3–4; *N.U.L. Records*; Dowdy Memorandum, February 7, 1957; *Dowdy Papers*.

63. Clipping, *Pittsburgh Press*, June 1, 1952 in the *Homer S. Brown Papers*, Vol. 14, University of Pittsburgh Libraries, Pittsburgh, Pa.; *Pittsburgh Courier*, March 14, 1953.

64. Pennsylvania Fair Employment Practice Commisison, *First Annual Report*, For Period Ending March 1, 1957, pp. 16, 23; *Dowdy Papers*; Press Release; Pennsylvania FEPC, rough draft, July 3, 1958, pp. 1–2; *George M. Leader Papers*, MG207, Subject File, Carton 13; FEPC Correspondence, Folders 1 and 2, Pennsylvania Historical and Museum Commission, Harrisburg, Pennsylvania, Pennsylvania Fair Employment Practice Commission, *Third Annual Report*, March 1, 1959, pp. 4, 6; *Dowdy Papers*.

65. *Business Week*, April 10, 1954, p. 168; Louis Mason, Jr. to Evan Jones, June 19, 1956; Evan Jones to Louis Mason, Jr., June 21, 1956; Boyd L. Wilson to Julius A. Thomas, June 26, 1956; Gen. Dept., Industrial Relations, Series IV, USWA folder, 1949–1961; *N.U.L. Records*, Box 19, Library of Congress; *Pittsburgh Courier*, March 14, 1953; September 5, 1954.

66. *Clairton Progress*, November 24, 1953; Newspaper clippings concerning Benjamin Cashaw, *N.U.L. Records*, Gen. Dept. Series II, Box 19, USWA folder, 1943–1948; Industrial Relations Department, Library of Congress.

67. John Bodnar, Roger Simon, Michael R. Weber, *Lives of Their Own*, (Urbana, University of Illinois Press, 1982), pp. 250–251; Croom interview; *Pittsburgh Courier*, January 26, 1957.

## Chapter 9

1. A useful survey of the civil rights movement is Harvard Sitkoff, *The Struggle for Black Equality, 1954–1980* (New York, Hill and Wang, 1981). Also see August Meier and Elliott Rudwick, *CORE: A Study in the Civil Rights Movement, 1942–1968* (New York, Oxford Uni-

versity Press, 1973); Clayborne Carson, *In Struggle: SNCC and the Black Awakening of the 1960s* (Cambridge, Harvard University Press, 1981); Stephen B. Oates, *Let the Trumpet Sound: The Life of Martin Luther King, Jr.,* (New York, Harper and Row Publishers, 1982); also James Farmer, *Lay Bare the Heart* (New York, Arbor House, 1985).

2. Richard L. Rowan, "The Negro in the Steel Industry," in Herbert R. Northrup, et al., *Negro Employment in Basic Industry: A Study of Racial Policies in Six Industries, Volume I,* (Philadelphia, Industrial Research Unit, Wharton School of Finance and Commerce, University of Pennsylvania, 1970), pp. 279, 338–339.

3. Rowan, "The Negro in the Steel Industry," pp. 350, 354; Address by Whitney M. Young, Jr. at the American Iron and Steel Institute, New York, New York, p. 5; American Iron and Steel Institute File, May 22, 1968, Box 160, *Whitney M. Young, Jr. Collection,* Rare Book and Manuscript Library, Columbia University, New York, New York; *Business Week,* December 10, 1966, p. 156; Robert E. Nelson to Joseph Sabo, Jr., December 10, 1965; File 24, Box 18, *Civil Rights Department, United Steelworkers of America,* Pennsylvania State University, Department of Labor Studies, Pattee Library Collections, University Park, Pennsylvania; *Pittsburgh Courier,* January 5, 1963.

4. "The Negro in U.S. Steel," *U.S. Steel News,* December, 1966, pp. 2–5.

5. *Steel Labor,* August 1961; April 1962.

6. *Steel Labor,* April 1960; August 1960, Francis C. Shane to Lyndon B. Johnson, October 22, 1962; *Pre-Presidential Papers,* Civil Rights Folder, Box 3, Lyndon Baines Johnson Library, Austin, Texas.

7. *Pittsburgh Courier,* May 7, 1960; *Steel Labor,* January 1962.

8. *Steel Labor,* September 1962; February 1965; Shane to L.B.J., 10–22–62, L.B.J. Library; *Pittsburgh Courier,* June 11, 1960, June 18, 1960.

9. *Steel Labor,* July 1965.

10. Boyd L. Wilson to Whitney Young, February 8, 1960; Victoria C. Hargon, February 1, 1960; *Whitney M. Young, Jr. Collection,* Box 32 United Steelworkers of America folder; Rare Book and Manuscript Room, Butler Library, Columbia University, New York, New York.

11. *Pittsburgh Courier,* March 19, 1960; July 23, 1960.

12. Jervis Anderson, *A. Philip Randolph: A Biographical Portrait,* (New York, Harcourt, Brace, Jovanovich, Inc., 1972, 1973), pp. 305–306; *Pittsburgh Courier,* May 12, 1960; May 14, 1960, May 19, 1960, July 23, 1960.

13. See James C. Harvey, *Black Civil Rights During the Johnson Administration*, (Jackson, University and College Press of Mississippi, 1973), pp. 103–154.

14. Jerry Byrd, "From Slaves to Statesmen: A History of Blacks in Pittsburgh," *The Pittsburgh Press Roto*, October 17, 1982, pp. 42–43; *Business Week*, December 10, 1966; *Pittsburgh Courier*, June 22, 1963.

15. *Pittsburgh Courier*, March 26, 1966; Memorandum, B. F. to A. F., July 22, 1966, "Rumored Civil Rights Demonstration," *Civil Rights Department, U.S.W.A.*, Penn State, Pattee Library, Box 18, File 27; *Business Week*, December 10, 1966.

16. *Business Week*, June 11, 1966; December 10, 1966; *Pittsburgh Courier*, June 22, 1963.

17. John Herling, *Right to Challenge: People and Power in the Steelworkers Union* (New York, Harper and Row, Publishers, 1972), p. 220; *Pittsburgh Courier*, July 2, 1960; September 24, 1960; Philip S. Foner, *Organized Labor and the Black Worker, 1619–1973*, (New York International Publishers, 1974), p. 324.

18. Carl O. Dickerson, interviewed by Dennis C. Dickerson, Philadelphia, Pennsylvania, October 5, 1975; *Pittsburgh Courier*, September 24, 1960.

19. Herling, *The Right to Challenge*, pp. 44–45, 69.

20. *Pittsburgh Courier*, July 2, 1960; August 27, 1960; September 3, 1960.

21. Herling, *The Right to Challenge*, pp. 83–84, 220–221.

22. Herling, *The Right to Challenge*, pp. 220, 222, 227–228, 273; *Pittsburgh Courier*, February 6, 1975; Foner, *Organized Labor and the Black Worker*, p. 405.

23. Foner, *Organized Labor and the Black Worker*, pp. 349–350; William H. Harris, *The Harder We Run: Black Workers Since the Civil War*, (New York, Oxford University Press, 1982), p. 163.

24. *Pittsburgh Courier*, October 16, 1965; *Steel Labor*, January 1966; July 1966.

25. *Pittsburgh Courier*, October 30, 1965; *Steel Labor*, April 1966; August 1967.

26. *Pittsburgh Courier*, November 19, 1960; *Steel Labor*, September 1967.

27. *Steel Labor*, December 1966; *Pittsburgh Post Gazette*, November 19, 1966.

28. R. E. N. to J. S., Jr., December 10, 1965; File 24, Box 18, *Civil Rights Department*, Penn State, Labor Studies, Pattee Library, University Park, Pa.

29. R. E. N. to A. F., March 7, 1966; File 24, Box 18, *Civil Rights Department*, Penn State, Labor Studies, Pattee Library, University Park, Pa.

30. Herling, *The Right to Challenge*, p. 183; *Memorandum*: B. F. to I. W. A., and J. M., June 16, 1966; File 9, Jones and Laughlin — Misc. 1967; Box 20, *Civil Rights Department*, Penn State, Labor Studies, Pattee Library, University Park, Pa.

31. *Memorandum*: B. K. to P. S., November 28, 1966; *Civil Rights Department*, Pattee Library, Penn State; *Memorandum*; P. S. to B. K. and W. N., December 22, 1966; *Civil Rights Department*, Penn State; Box 20, File 9 (S & L — Misc. 1967).

32. *Memorandum*: P. S. to B. K. and W. N., December 22, 1966, File 9, Box 20; *Memorandum*: W. N. to P. S., December 27, 1966; File 9, Box 20, *Civil Rights Department*, Pattee Library, Penn State.

33. *Pittsburgh Press*, October 24, 1967.

34. Foner, *Organized Labor and the Black Worker*, pp. 405–406; William V. Deutermann, Jr., "Reports on Four Union Conventions," *Monthly Labor Review*, November 1968, Volume 91, Number 11, p. 16; *Proceedings of the Fourteenth Constitutional Convention of the United Steelworkers of America*, A.F.L.-C.I.O., August 19–23, 1968, Chicago, Illinois, p. 71.

35. In the United Auto Workers, for example, Blacks formed several caucuses to press for a greater voice in union affairs and for equity in the workplace. These groups included the Detroit Black Caucus, the Dodge Revolutionary Union Movement, the League of Revolutionary Black Workers, and the Ad Hoc Committee of Concerned Negro Auto Workers. See Foner, *Organized Labor and the Black Worker*, pp. 413–424; James A. Geschwender, *Class, Race and Worker Insurgency: The League of Revolutionary Black Workers* (Cambridge, Cambridge University Press, 1977).

36. Foner, *Organized Labor and the Black Worker*, p. 406; Deutermann, "Reports . . .", pp. 16–17.

37. Deutermann, "Reports . . .," p. 17.

38. *Proceedings of the Fourteenth Constitutional Convention*, pp. 108, 116, 120–121.

39. Ibid. pp. 109–111.

40. *Pittsburgh Courier*, December 14, 1968; Herling, *The Right to Challenge*, pp. 371–372, 377, 379; *Steel Labor*, June 1965.

41. Rowan, "The Negro in the Steel Industry," pp. 350–351; 353; also see Darold T. Barnum, "A Statistical Analysis of Negro Employment Data in the Pittsburgh Area Basic Steel Industry 1965," Department of Industry, Wharton School of Finance and Commerce, University of Pennsylvania, Philadelphia, Pennsylvania, April 1968, p. 2. Pittsburgh Commission on Human Relations.

42. Barnum, "A Statistical Analysis . . .," pp. 1, 3.

43. Darold T. Barnum, "Pittsburgh Commission on Human Relations, *Final Report*, Steel Affirmative Action Project," pp. 1–6; MS Pittsburgh Commission on Human Relations.

44. Ibid.

45. Ibid., p. 6; "Heritage: A Black History of Johnstown," *The Tribune–Democrat*, February 12, 1980; Ronald Minnie to Dennis C. Dickerson, March 24, 1980. Daniel Brooks, interviewed by Dennis C. Dickerson, Pittsburgh, Pennsylvania, March 3, 1980.

46. Rowan, "The Negro in the Steel Industry," p. 354.

47. *Pittsburgh Courier*, May 30, 1970.

48. "Investigatory Hearing Report," Pennsylvania Human Relations Commission, Aliquippa, May 24 to 26, 1971; pp. 7–8.

49. Ibid., p. 31.

50. Ibid., p. 31. Felix Guilford, interviewed by Dennis C. Dickerson, Beaver Falls, Pennsylvania, April 5, 1980.

51. *Pittsburgh Courier*, September 19, 1970; (Press) Release, March 5, 1970; United Steelworkers of America: Local Union No. 1557, Folder 25, Box 1, *Civil Rights Department*, Pattee Library, Penn State.

52. *Pittsburgh Courier*, February 7, 1970; March 21, 1970.

53. Harvey, *Black Civil Rights During the Johnson Administration*, p. 117.

54. *Business Week*, September 15, 1973, pp. 228–229; *The Iron Age*, May 8, 1970, p. 62; *Pittsburgh Courier*, December 26, 1970. Herbert Hill,

"Race and Ethnicity in Organized Labor: The Historical Sources of Resistance to Affirmative Action," *Journal of Intergroup Relations*, Winter 1984, Volume XII, No. 4, p. 35.

55. See William B. Gould, *Black Workers in White Unions*, (Ithaca, New York, Cornell University Press, 1977), pp. 395-397.

56. *Federal Civil Rights Enforcement Effort — 1974*, Volume V; *A Report of the U.S. Commission on Civil Rights*, July 1975, p. 556.

57. Ibid., pp. 556-558.

58. *United States of America v. Allegheny-Ludlum Industries, et al*, Consent Decree I, (1974), United States District Court, Northern District of Alabama, Southern Division pp. 8-12; Brooks interview; *1974-EEO-1 Report Summary By Industry*, SMSA 451 Pittsburgh, Pennsylvania, SIC 331 Blast Furnace and Basic Steel Prod., p. 14, 426; *1978 EEO-1 Report*, SMSA-6280, Pittsburgh, Pennsylvania; p. 25, 663; Equal Employment Opportunity Commission, Washington, D.C.

59. *U.S. News and World Report*, June 6, 1977, p. 60; October 10, 1977, p. 56; *New York Times*, January 10, 1984; R. D. to Dennis C. Dickerson, April 21, 1980.

## Epilogue

1. *New York Times*, January 10, 1984; January 30, 1985.

2. *New York Times*, October 6, 1985.

3. U. S. Department of Commerce. Bureau of the Census. *Census of Population: 1970, Characteristics of Population*, Part 40, Pennsylvania, Section 2, Vol. 1, pp. 40-1309-1310; 40-1315-1316; U. S. Department of Commerce. Bureau of the Census. *Census of Population: 1980, Characteristics of Population, Chapter D, Detailed Population Characteristics*, Part 40, Pennsylvania, Section 1 of 2, Vol. 1, pp. 40-884; 40-908.

4. Ibid.

5. U. S. Department of Commerce. Bureau of the Census. *Census of Population: 1980, Characteristics of Population, Chapter D, Detailed Population Characteristics*, Part 40, Pennsylvania, Section 1 of 2, Vol. 1, p. 40-242.

# References

---

## Primary Sources

*Manuscript Collections*

Columbia University, Butler Library, Rare Book and Manuscript Room, *Whitney M. Young, Jr. Collection*, Box 32, United Steelworkers of America folder.

Historical Society of Pennsylvania, Philadelphia, Pennsylvania, *William B. Wilson Pepers*, 1917, Box 1.

J. Edgar Hoover F.B.I. Building, Washington, D.C., *Marcus Garvey Files*.

Library of Congress, Manuscript Division, Washington,D.C., *Carter G. Woodson Collection*
*John T. Clark Papers*, Pittsburgh Urban League (Concerning Migration from the South).
*Records of the National Association for the Advancement of Colored People*, Branch Files.
*Records of the National Urban League, Industrial Relations Department*, Affiliates File.

National Archives, Washington, D.C.
Record Group 174, *Chief Clerk's Files*, Box 18.
Record Group 183, *United States Employment Service, Laurence A. Oxley Files*, Boxes 1388, 1395.
Record Group 257, Bureau of Labor Statistics, *Study of Consumer Purchases*, 1-1-35 to 12-31-35, Expenditure Cards, Pennsylvania.
*Records of the Fair Employment Practices Committee, Regional Files, Region III*, Boxes 596-601, 604, 606, 610-612.
*War Manpower Commission Records, Bureau of Placement, Division of Industrial Allocation*, Boxes 1470-1471.

New York Public Library, Schomburg Collection, New York, New York
*George Weston Papers*
*National Negro Congress Records*, Reel 1, microfilm.
*U.N.I.A. Central Division (New York) Files.*

Pennsylvania State University Library, Labor Archives, University Park Pennsylvania.
*Harold Ruttenberg Collection, War Production Board. Correspondence, Statistics, and Press Releases*, Box 7.
*United Steelworkers of America, Civil Rights Department Records.*

Pittsburgh Urban League, Pittsburgh, Pennsylvania. *Papers of the Pittsburgh Urban League* (uncatalogued).

*Richard S. Dowdy Papers*, (Private Collection) Hamden, Connecticut.

University of Pittsburgh Libraries, Archives of Industrial Society, Pittsburgh, Pennsylvania.
A. M. Byers Company, *Personnel Files.*
*Heber Blankenhorn Papers 1919–1937.*
*Homer S. Brown Papers*
*Allegheny County Race Relations Survey*, 1946 Folder H.

Washington University Libraries, Washington University Archives, John M. Olin Library, St. Louis, Missouri.
*Papers of the Urban League of St. Louis, John T. Clark Files, Worker's Council folder.*
*Bulletin of the Urban League of St. Louis*, December 1943.
"Twenty-Sixth Annual Report of the Work of (the) Urban League of St. Louis, 1944."

## Newspapers and Periodicals

*Amalgamated Journal*
*Beaver Valley Labor History Journal*
*C.I.O. News*
*Clairton Progress*
*Clairton Tattler*
*Competitor*
*Crisis*
*Duquesne Times*
*Duquesne Times-Observer*
*1557 Labor Journal*
*Homestead Messenger*
*Iron Trade Review*
*Masses and Mainstream*
*Monessen Daily Independent*

*Monthly Labor Review*
*National Labor Tribune*
*Negro World*
*New York Age*
*New York Times*
*Opportunity*
*Pittsburgh Business Review*
*Pittsburgh Courier*
*Steel Labor*
*The Daily Worker*
*The Iron Age*
*The Survey*
*Union News Service*

## Public Documents

Pennsylvania. *The Bulletin of the Department of Labor and Industry,* "Industrial Accident Reports," Vol. 7, Harrisburg, 1920.

Pennsylvania. Department of Welfare, *Negro Survey of Pennsylvania,* Harrisburg, 1927.

Pennsylvania. Department of Property and Supplies, *The Pennsylvania Manual, 1965–1966,* Vol. 97, Harrisburg, 1966.

U.S. Congress. Senate. *Reports of the Immigration Commission, Immigrants in Industry,* Part 1: Iron and Steel Manufacturing, Vol. I, 61st Congress, 2nd Session: 1910.

U.S. Congress. Senate. Committee on Education and Labor, *Investigation of Strike in Steel Industry,* 66th Congress, 1st Session, 1919.

U.S. Department of Commerce. Bureau of the Census. *Thirteenth Census of the United States, 1910: Population,* Vol. 1

U.S. Department of Commerce. Bureau of the Census. *Thirteenth Census of the United States, 1910: Population,* Vol. 4.

U.S. Department of Commerce. Bureau of the Census. *Thirteenth Census of the United States, 1910: Agriculture,* Vol. 5.

U.S. Department of Commerce. Bureau of the Census. *Fourteenth Census of the United States, 1920: Population,* Vol. 3.

U.S. Department of Commerce. Bureau of the Census. *Fourteenth Census of the United States, 1920: Population (Occupations),* Vol. 4.

U.S. Department of Commerce. Bureau of the Census. *Fourteenth Census of the United States, 1920: Agriculture,* Vol. 5.

U.S. Department of Commerce. Bureau of the Census. *Fifteenth Census of the United States, 1930: Population,* Vol. 2,

U.S. Department of Commerce. Bureau of the Census. *Fifteenth Census of the United States, 1930: Population*, Vol. 3.

U.S. Department of Commerce. Bureau of the Census. *Fifteenth Census of the United States, 1930: Population (Occupations)*, Vol. 4.

U.S. Department of Commerce. Bureau of the Census. *Fifteenth Census of the United States, 1930: Agriculture*, Vol. 4.

U.S. Department of Commerce. Bureau of the Census. *Fifteenth Census of the United States, 1930: Population (Families)*, Vol. 6.

U.S. Department of Commerce. Bureau of the Census. *Sixteenth Census of the United States, 1940: Population, Characteristics of the Population*, Part 6, Pennsylvania–Texas, Vol. 2.

U.S. Department of Commerce. Bureau of the Census. *Sixteenth Census of the United States, 1940: Housing*, Part 4, Vol. 2.

U.S. Department of Commerce. Bureau of the Census. *Sixteenth Census of the United States, 1940: Population, The Labor Force*, Vol. 3.

U.S. Department of Commerce. Bureau of the Census. *Seventeenth Census of the United States, 1950: Housing*, Part 5, Vol. 1.

U.S. Department of Commerce. Bureau of the Census. *Census of Population: 1950: Characteristics of Population*, Part 38, Pennsylvania, Vol. 2.

U.S. Department of Commerce. Bureau of the Census. *Census of Population: 1960, Characteristics of Population*, Part 40, Pennsylvania, Vol. 1.

U.S. Department of Commerce. Bureau of the Census. *Census of Population: 1970, Characteristics of Population*, Part 40, Pennsylvania, Section 2, Vol. 1.

U.S. Department of Commerce. Bureau of the Census. *Census of Population: 1980, Characteristics of Population, Chapter D, Detailed Population Characteristics*, Part 40, Pennsylvania, Section 1 of 2, Vol. 1.

U.S. Department of Commerce. Bureau of the Census. *Historical Statistics of the United States, Colonial Times to 1957*.

U.S. Department of Commerce. Bureau of the Census. *Mortality Statistics*, Nineteenth Annual Report, 1918.

U.S. Department of Commerce. Bureau of the Census. *Negroes in the United States*, Bulletin 113, 1916.

U.S. Department of Commerce. Bureau of the Census. *Negroes in the United States*, 1920–1932.

U.S. Department of Commerce. Bureau of the Census. *Census of Partial Employment, Unemployment, and Occupations*, 1937, Vol. 3.

U.S. Department of Labor. Women's Bureau, "Negro Women War Workers" *Bulletin No. 205*, 1945.

*Interviews*

Pennsylvania Historical and Museum Commission, Ethnic Studies Program, Pittsburgh Oral History Project, Harrisburg, Pennsylvania.

B. R. Interviewed by John E. Bodnar, February 26, 1973.

Cobbs, Peter. Interviewed by Peter Gottlieb, Pittsburgh, Pennsylvania, August 8, 1974.

H. G. Interviewed by Peter Gottlieb, Pittsburgh, Pennsylvania, August 28, 1974.

Goodman, Jerome. Interviewed by Peter Gottlieb, Pittsburgh, Pennsylvania, Summer 1974.

Lynch, Merril. Interviewed by Peter Gottlieb, Pittsburgh, Pennsylvania, August 22, 1974.

McChester, Roy. Interviewed by Peter Gottlieb, Pittsburgh, Pennsylvania, September 9, 1974.

Simmons, J.L. Interviewed by Peter Gottlieb, Pittsburgh, Pennsylvania, June 13, 1974.

Smith, Willie. Interviewed by Peter Gottlieb, Pittsburgh, Pennsylvania, September 1974.

S. B. Interviewed by Gordon Mason, Sr., McKeesport, Pennsylvania, August 1974.

W. D. Interviewed by Gordon Mason, Sr., McKeesport, Pennsylvania, August 1974.

A. C. Interviewed by Major Mason, McKeesport, Pennsylvania, July 22, 1974.

T. H. Interviewed by Major Mason, McKeesport, Pennsylvania, August 1974.

K. L. Interviewed by Major Mason, McKeesport, Pennsylvania, Summer 1974.

Columbia University Oral History Project, New York, New York.

McKinney, Ernest Rice. Part II, Microfiche No. 123.

Pennsylvania State University, Labor Archives, United Steelworkers of America Oral History Project, University Park, Pennsylvania.

Kutska, George. Interviewd by Jack Severson, Monessen, Pennsylvania, April 15, 1969.

Farr, Ruben. Interviewed by Alice Hoffman and Jack Spiece, Birmingham, Alabama, March 27, 1968.

McCoy, James. Interviewed by Mark Lapping, Pittsburgh, Pennsylvania, November 7, 1968.

Richards, Bart. Interviewed by Joe Uehlein, Pittsburgh, Pennsylvania, February 21, 1971.

Warady, J. Interviewed by Larry Gorski, McKeesort, Pennsylvania, April 20, 1974.

Wilson, Boyd L. Interviewed by John G. Spiese, October 23, 1967.

## Personal Interviews

Allen, Alexander J., Jr. Interviewed by Dennis C. Dickerson, New York, New York, April 30, 1980.

Allen, Ashton, Jr. Interviewed by Dennis C. Dickerson, Homestead, Pennsylvania, September 6, 1975.

Baker, Simon. Interviewed by Dennis C. Dickerson, Donora, Pennsylvania, March 6, 1980.

Baskerville, Irma. Interviewed by Dennis C. Dickerson, Pittsburgh, Pennsylvania, March 4, 1980.

Brooks, Daniel. Interviewed by Dennis C. Dickerson, Pittsburgh, Pennsylvania, March 3, 1980.

Christian, Mattie. Interviewed by Dennis C. Dickerson, Duquesne, Pennsylvania, April 22, 1975.

Corley, Lucious. Interviewed by Dennis C. Dickerson, Monessen, Pennsylvania, September 4, 1975.

Croom, Milton. Interviewed by Dennis C. Dickerson, Clairton, Pennsylvania, March 6, 1980.

Dickerson, Carl O. Interviewed by Dennis C. Dickerson, Philadelphia, Pennsylvania, October 5, 1975.

Gardiner, Catherine. Interviewed by Dennis C. Dickerson, Homestead, Pennsylvania, January 24, 1975.

Griffey, Allen. Interviewed by Dennis C. Dickerson, Monessen, Pennsylvania, September 4, 1975.

Guilford, Felix. Interviewed by Dennis C. Dickerson, Beaver Falls, Pennsylvania, March 5, 1980.

Harrison, William H. Interviewed by Dennis C. Dickerson, Duquesne, Pennsylvania, April 18, 1975.

Hughey, John. Interviewed by Dennis C. Dickerson, Rankin, Pennsylvania, September 8, 1975.

Ingram, Calvin. Interviewed by Dennis C. Dickerson, Duquesne, Pennsylvania, September 8, 1975.

Jackson, Mabel. Interviewed by Dennis C. Dickerson (telephone), Pittsburgh, Pennsylvania, August 19, 1980.

Lindsay, Nola. Interviewed by Dennis C. Dickerson, Duquesne, Pennsylvania, September 4, 1975.

Lipscomb, Edward. Interviewed by Dennis C. Dickerson, Duquesne, Pennsylvania, September 8, 1975.

Long, Colesta. Interviewed by Dennis C. Dickerson, Philadelphia, Pennsylvania, March 27, 1979.

McKinney, Ernest Rice. Interviewed by Dennis C. Dickerson, New York, New York, November 21, 1974.

Payne, Paul L. Interviewed by Dennis C. Dickerson, Clairton, Pennsylvania, March 15, 1975.

Payne, Roger. Interviewed by Dennis C. Dickerson, Philadelphia, Pennsylvania, April 12, 1976.

Raby, Edward. Interviewed by Dennis C. Dickerson, Philadelphia, Pennsylvania, April, 7, 1976.

Reid, J. Burrell. Interviewed by Dennis C. Dickerson, Pittsburgh, Pennsylvania, September 6, 1975.

See, William. Interviewed by Dennis C. Dickerson, Glen Hazel, Pennsylvania, April 22, 1975.

Terry, J. A., Reverend. Interviewed by Dennis C. Dickerson, Pittsburgh, Pennsylvania, March 3, 1980.

Thompson, James. Interviewed by Dennis C. Dickerson, Homestead, Pennsylvania, October 7, 1974.

Tipper, Bartow. Interviewed by Dennis C. Dickerson, Aliquippa, Pennsylvania, March 4, 1980.

Tolliver, Harold R., Reverend. Interviewed by Dennis C. Dickerson, Pittsburgh, Pennsylvania, October 9, 1974.

Torrey, Charles W., Reverend. Interviewed by Dennis C. Dickerson, Duquesne, Pennsylvania, March 21, 1975.

Trent, Mildred. Interviewed by Dennis C. Dickerson, Philadelphia, Pennsylvania, May 28, 1975.

Wells, Ira J. K. Interviewed by Dennis C. Dickerson, Philadelphia, Pennsylvania, February 11, 1975.

Wilson, Boyd L. Interviewed by Dennis Brunn and Dennis C. Dickerson, St. Louis, Missouri, March 28, 1974.

Wilson, James. Interviewed by Dennis C. Dickerson, West Mifflin, Pennsylvania, April 23, 1975.

## Secondary Sources

*Unpublished Theses and Seminar Papers.*

Anderson, John V. "Unemployment in Pittsburgh with Reference to the Negro." M. A. thesis, University of Pittsburgh, 1932.

Augustine, Thomas, "The Negro Steelworkers of Pittsburgh and the Unions." M. A. thesis, University of Pittsburgh, 1948.

Barton, Anne M. and Staudenmaier, Margaret. "Ethnic and Racial Groups in Rankin, Pennsylvania (A Study of Relationships Between Them as Expressed Through Various Social Forces)." M.S.W. thesis, University of Pittsburgh, 1947.

Gottlieb, Peter. "Southern Black Migrants in the Pittsburgh Area, 1916–1925." Seminar paper, University of Pittsburgh, Department of History, 1973, Pennsylvania Historical and Museum Commission, Harrisburg, Pennsylvania.

Harris, Abram. "The New Negro Workers in Pittsburgh." M. A. thesis, University of Pittsburgh, 1924.

Nyden, Linda. "The History of the Steel and Metal Workers Industrial Union." Seminar paper, University of Pittsburgh, Department of History, December 1973.

Reid, Ira De Augustine. "The Negro in Major Industries and Building Trades of Pittsburgh." M. A. thesis, University of Pittsburgh, 1925.

*Articles*

Bernstein, Barton J. "The Truman Administration and the Steel Strike of 1946." *Journal of American History* 52 (March 1966): 791–803.

Bodnar, John, Weber, Michael, and Simon, Roger. "Migration, Kinship, and Urban Adjustment: Blacks and Poles in Pittsburgh, 1900–1930," *Journal of American History*, December 1979 66 (3), 548–565.

Dickerson, Dennis C. "The Black Church in Industrializing Western Pennsylvania, 1870–1950," *Western Pennsylvania Historical Magazine*, October 1981 64 (4), 329–344.

Dickerson, Dennis C. "Black Steelworkers in Western Pennsylvania, 1900–1950," *Pennsylvania Heritage* December 1977 4 (1) 52–58.

Hill, Herbert, "Race and Ethnicity in Organized Labor: The Historical Sources of Resistance to Affirmative Action," *Journal of Intergroup Relations*, Winter 1984, *12* (4) 5–49.

Mossell, Sadie Tanner. "The Standards of Living Among One Hundred Negro Migrant Families in Philadelphia." *Annals of the American Academy of Political and Social Science* 98 (November 1921): 169–218.

Sherman, Richard B. "Johnstown v. The Negro: Southern Migrants and the Exodus of 1923." *Pennsylvania History* 30 (October 1963): 454–464.

Sitkoff, Harvard. "Racial Militancy and Interracial Violence in the Second World War." *Journal of American History* 58 (December 1971): 661–681.

Wittner, Lawrence. "The National Negro Congress: A Reassessment." *American Quarterly* 22 (Winter 1970): 883–901.

Wolters, Raymond. "Section 7a and the Black Worker." *Labor History* 10 (Summer 1969): 459–474.

Wright, Richard R., Jr. "One Hundred Negro Steelworkers" in *Wage Earning Pittsburgh*, the Pittsburgh Survey, (New York, Russell Sage Foundation, 1914), 97–110.

*Books and Special Reports*

*Agreement Between Carnegie–Illinois Steel Corporation and the Steelworkers Organizing Committee.* Pittsburgh, 1937. Courtesy of William Menzie, National–Duquesne Works, United States Steel Corporation, McKeesport, Pennsylvania.

Benedict, Murray. *Farm Policies of the Untied States, 1790–1950.* New York: Twentieth Century Fund, 1953.

Bernstein, Irving. *Turbulent Years.* Boston: Houghton Mifflin Company, 1971.

Bing, Alexander. *War-Time Strikes and Their Adjustment.* New York: E. P. Dutton and Company, 1921.

Bodnar, John, Simon, Roger, and Weber, Michael. *Lives of Their Own: Blacks Italians, and Poles in Pittsburgh*, (Urbana, Illinois, University of Illinois Press, 1982).

Brecher, Jeremy. *Strike!* San Francisco: World Publishing Company, 1972.

Brody, David. *Labor in Crisis.* Philadelphia: J. B. Lippincott Company, 1965.

Brody, David. *Steelworkers in America: The Nonunion Era.* Cambridge: Harvard University Press, 1960.

Brooks, Robert R. R. *As Steel Goes.* New Haven: Yale University Press, 1940.

Buni, Andrew. *Robert L. Vann of the Pittsburgh Courier: Politics and Black Journalism.* Pittsburgh: University of Pittsburgh Press, 1974.

Byington, Margaret. *Homestead: The Households of a Milltown.* New York: Russell Sage Foundation 1910.

Cayton, Horace R., and Mitchell, George S. *Black Workers and New Unions.* Chapel Hill: University of North Carolina Press, 1939.

*Daily Proceedings of the Fifth Constitutional Convention of the Congress of Industrial Organizations.* November 9–13, 1942, Boston, Massachusetts.

Epstein, Abraham. *The Negro Migrant in Pittsburgh.* Pittsburgh: University of Pittsburgh, 1918.

Fanning, John. *Negro Migration.* Phelps-Stokes Fellowship Studies, No. 9, *Bulletin of the University of Georgia*, June 1930.

*First Report, Fair Employment Practices Committee, July 1943–December 1944.* Washington, D. C. Government Printing Office, 1945.

Foner, Philip S. *Organized Labor and the Black Worker, 1619–1973.* New York: International Publishers, 1974.

*Proceedings of the Fourteenth Constitutional Convention,* United Steelworkers of America, A.F.L.–C.I.O., August 19 to 23, 1968, International Amphitheatre, Chicago, Illinois.

Gould, William B. *Black Workers in White Unions,* (Ithaca, New York, Cornell University Press, 1977.

Greene, Lorenzo J., and Woodson, Carter G. *The Negro Wage Earner.* Washington, D. C.: Associated Publishers, 1930.

Harvey, James C. *Black Civil Rights During the Johnson Administration.* Jackson, Mississippi: University and College Press, 1973.

Haynes, George E. *Negro Newcomers in Detroit.* New York: Home Missions Council, 1918.

Herling, John. *The Right to Challenge: People and Power in the Steelworkers Union.* New York: Harper and Row, 1972.

Hornback, Florence. *Survey of the Negro Population of Metropolitan Johnstown, Pennsylvania.* Johnstown, 1941.

Kesselman, Louis. *The Social Politics of F.E.P.C.* Chapel Hill: University of North Carolina Press, 1948.

Kiser, Clyde V. *Sea Island to City.* New York: Columbia University Press, 1932.

Klein, Philip. *The Burden of Unemployment.* New York: Russell Sage Foundation, 1923.

Kusmer, Kenneth L. *A Ghetto Takes Shape: Black Cleveland, 1870–1930.* Urbana: University of Illinois Press, 1976.

Leavell, Robert et al. *Negro Migration in 1916–1917.* Washington, D. C.: Government Printing Office, 1919.

Moore, Jesse Thomas, Jr. *A Search for Equality, The National Urban League, 1910–1961.* University Park: Pennsylvania State University Press, 1981.

Murray, Florence, ed. *The Negro Handbook, 1946–1947.* New York: Current Books, 1947.

Powers, George. *Cradle of Steel Unionism, Monongahela Valley, Pennsylvania*, East Chicago, Indiana: Figueroa Printers, Inc. 1972.

*Proceedings of the Sixth Annual Convention of the National Lodge of the Amalgamated Association of Iron and Steelworkers.* Pittsburgh: 1882.

*Proceedings of the Seventh Annual Convention of the National Lodge of the Amalgamated Association of Iron and Steelworkers.* Pittsburgh: 1882.

*Public Opinion and the Steel Strike.* Interchurch World Movement, New York: Harcourt, Brace and Company, 1921.

Reid, Ira De Augustine. *Social Conditions of the Negro in the Hill District of Pittsburgh.* Pittsburgh, General Committee on the Hill Survey, 1930.

Rossiter, William. *Increase of Population in the United States, 1910–1920.* Washington, D. C.: Government Printing Office, 1919.

Rowan, Richard L. *The Negro in the Steel Industry.* Philadelphia: University of Pennsylvania, 1970.

Scott, Emmett. *Negro Migration During the War.* New York: Oxford University Press, 1920.

Spear, Allan. *Black Chicago: The Making of a Negro Ghetto* Chicago: University of Chicago Press, 1967.

Spero, Sterling D., and Harris, Abram L. *The Black Worker.* New York: Columbia University Press, 1931, 1968.

Sweeney, Vincent D. *The United Steelworkers of America: The First Ten Years.* Pittsburgh, 1946.

*The Braddock Steelworkers.* Pittsburgh: United Steelworkers of America, 1945.

*Wage Earning Pittsburgh. The Pittsburgh Survey.* New York: Russell Sage Foundation, 1914.

Watson, J. P. *Economic Background of the Relief Problem.* Pittsburgh: University of Pittsburgh, 1937.

Weaver, Robert C. *Negro Labor: A National Problem.* New York: Harcourt, Brace and Company, 1946.

Weiss, Nancy. *The National Urban League, 1910-1940.* New York: Oxford University Press, 1974.

*Who's Who Among Black Americans, 1975-1976.* Vol. I, Who's Who Among Black Americans, Inc. Publishing Compnay, Northbrook, Illinois, 1976.

*Who's Who Among Colored Americans, 1928-1929.* Brooklyn, New York, Thomas Yenser, 1929.

Woodward, C. Vann. *The Strange Career of Jim Crow.* New York: Oxford University Press, 1955, 1974.

Wright, J. Ernest. *The Negro in Pittsburgh.* W.P.A. Survey, American Guide Series, Ethnic Survey 1940 MS, Pennsylvania Historical and Museum Commission, Harrisburg, Pennsylvania.

Wright, Richard R., Jr.. *The Negro in Pennsylvania: A Study in Economic History.* Philadelphia: A. M. E. Book Concern, 1912.

# Index

Abel, I. W., 226, 227, 228, 229, 230, 234, 235, 236

Ad Hoc Committee of Black Steelworkers, 225, 228, 234, 236

African Methodist Episcopal Church (A.M.E.), 11, 18, 57, 65, 67, 70, 110, 111, 114, 115, 223

African Methodist Episcopal Zion Church (A.M.E.Z.), 65, 68, 72, 80, 111, 114, 137

A. M. Byers Company, Pittsburgh, 48, 60, 61, 102, 126

Allegheny Ludlum Steel Company, Pittsburgh, 204, 217, 223

Allegheny Steel Company, Breckenridge, 121, 126

Allen, Alexander J., Jr., 202, 203, 204, 205, 206, 212

Amalgamated Association of Iron, Steel and Tin Workers, 8, 12, 13, 14, 86, 87, 88, 90, 91, 92, 132, 133, 134, 135, 144

American Bridge Company, Ambridge, 217

American Federation of Labor (A.F.L.), 10, 11, 86, 130, 131

American Sheet and Tin Plate Company, Sharon/Farrell, 40, 51

American Sheet and Tin Plate Company, Vandergrift, 41, 126

Associated Brotherhood of Iron and Steel Heaters, 11

Austin, Junius C., 66, 78, 81

Bethlehem Steel (Cambria Steel), Johnstown, 63, 186, 245, 250

Black Baptists, 11, 65, 67, 68, 69, 70, 104, 111, 113, 114, 115, 137

Black Coal Miners, 11, 141

Black Diamond Steel Workers, Pittsburgh, 8, 12, 20

Black Fraternal Organizations, 72, 73, 74, 75, 165, 166

Black Migration, 17–19, 27–50, 94–100, 151–153, 186–188

Black Steelworkers
  Civil Rights Movement, 215–239
  Housing, 56–59, 156–159
  National Economic Problems, 93–99, 119–130, 176–177, 245–246, 246–251
  Strikes, 8–10, 13–14, 85–93, 166–168, 177–178, 189, 212
  Unions, 10–17, 85–92, 130–147, 168–172, 188–202, 218–237
  Wages, 12, 49–50, 122, 186
  Welfare Capitalism, 103–117

Black Women, 70, 72, 73–74, 163–164

Blaw Knox Steel Company,

319